D0992463

THE VANISHING AMERICAN

Brian W. Dippie

THE VANISHING AMERICAN
White Attitudes and U.S. Indian Policy

WESLEYAN UNIVERSITY PRESS

Middletown, Connecticut

Copyright © 1982 by Brian Dippie
The publishers gratefully acknowledge the support of the University of Victoria
toward the publication of this book.

Library of Congress Cataloging in Publication Data

Dippie, Brian W.
  The vanishing American.
  Includes index.
  1. Indians of North America—Government relations.
  2. Indians of North America—Public opinion—History.
  3. Public opinion—United States—History.
  I. Title.
  E93.D58   973'.0497   82-2804
  ISBN 0-8195-5056-6   AACR2

Manufactured in the United States of America
First edition

For Donna

CONTENTS

x   Contents

PREFACE

In 1938 John Collier, Commissioner of Indian Affairs, reported the "astounding, heartening fact" that "the Indians are no longer a dying race."[1] Anthropologists, census takers, historians, popular writers, government officials, and Indian spokesmen have all attempted to set the record straight. Statistics show, they point out, that, far from declining, the Indian population is on the rise. Since the end of the nineteenth century, when it reached its nadir, it has nearly tripled; the current estimate is that Indian numbers are increasing at an annual rate of 3.3 percent—three times the national average. It is now commonplace to remark, as *Time* magazine did in 1970, that the Indians, "no longer vanishing . . . are now the nation's fastest growing minority."[2]

The fact that *Time*, like Collier thirty-two years before, felt it necessary to mention that the Indians were no longer vanishing, suggests that mundane truth has failed to dislodge a tradition rich in pathos and older than the Republic. The Indians, this tradition holds, are a vanishing race; they have been wasting away since the day the white man arrived, diminishing in vitality and numbers until, in some not too distant future, no red men will be left on the face of the earth. The notion of the Vanishing American provides the central thread in my study of popular attitudes toward the Indian and of the formulation of federal Indian policy from the late eighteenth century through to the middle of the twentieth century.

My concern here is not with the historical reality—the actual number of Indians, the actual causes and extent of population decline—but rather with the Vanishing American as a constant in American thinking. This is not a book about the Indian, then, but about perceptions of the Indian, and the entrenched idea that the Indians are a "bold, but wasting race"[3] strikes me as the most important of them all in terms of both primacy and longevity. It is a concept shot through with ambivalence. Eighteenth-century intellectuals knew that history moved in cycles, and that societies rose and fell with the regularity of the turning wheel of time. But the red man's history was racial, not social: as a *type* of mankind he was destined to vanish, leaving no trace behind. Ruth Miller Elson has written that nineteenth-century school readers, testaments of conventional wisdom, held the Indian's extinction to be "inevitable by mysterious decrees of God and nature."[4] From the 1820s on, the standard school reader included a poem or a prose passage on this theme, inviting the student to mourn for "Lo, the poor Indian" before accepting his fate as the will of God, who had erected the United States of America on the red man's former domain. The Vanishing American, in short, represented a perfect fusion of the nostalgic with the progressive impulse.

The belief in the Vanishing American has had far-reaching ramifications. Based on what was thought to be irrefutable evidence, it became self-perpetuating. It was prophecy, self-fulfilling prophecy, and its underlying assumptions were truisms requiring no justification apart from periodic reiteration. The Vanishing American achieved the status of a cultural myth. The point was no longer whether or not the native population had declined in the past but that its future decline was inevitable. The myth of the Vanishing American accounted for the Indians' future by denying them one, and stained the tissue of policy debate with fatalism.

When the government turned from the segregationist philosophy behind the Removal and Trade and Intercourse Acts of the 1830s to the assimilationist philosophy behind the Dawes or General Allotment Act of 1887, and then to the philosophy of cultural relativism and self-determination, embodied in the Indian Reorganization Act of 1934, more than national conditions had been transformed. Attitudes toward the Indian had also changed, and nothing registered this more sensitively than the fluctuating popularity and successive reevaluation of the Vanishing American as a master explanation for the red man's destiny in what had become a white man's world.

ACKNOWLEDGMENTS

My chief intellectual debt is to William H. Goetzmann, who directed the dissertation at the University of Texas (1970) on which this book is based. I also wish to thank the following who have helped me in ways they may not even know: Donald L. Weismann, Robert M. Crunden, Bruce T. Dippie, Meta Butler, Raymund Paredes, June Belton, F. Joy McBride, James D. McLaird, Charles W. Cowan, Alison MacLennan, Jim Keefer, Jeanne Cannizzo, David T. Stafford, William C. Hine, Paddy Tsurumi, Arlene McLaren, Angus McLaren, Terry Eastwood, Wesley T. Wooley, Phyl Senese, and Alfred N. Hunt. Grants by the University of Victoria President's Committee on Faculty Research and Travel allowed me access to a number of libraries and, in particular, to obtain the photographs used here as illustrations. I am grateful to the art galleries, archives, libraries, and historical societies that were so cooperative in providing the necessary prints, and to Professors Barbara S. Groseclose and William H. Gerdts for directing me to pertinent works.

The scholarly activity in American Indian studies has stepped up dramatically since I began my investigation of white attitudes and United States Indian policy back in 1966. I am already beholden to a number of recent monographs and undoubtedly the poorer for not having had the opportunity to read others that will have appeared since my manuscript was finished. It is a pleasure, then, to acknowledge my debt to the scholars, past and present, whose works are so essential to a study such as mine. Due to the exigencies of academic publishing today, I regretfully have had to greatly curtail my notes. But I would like to mention some recent, related works that might be of interest to readers of *The Vanishing American*: Robert F. Berkhofer, Jr., *The White Man's Indian: Images of the American Indian from Columbus to the Present* (New York, 1978); Ronald Sanders,

Lost Tribes and Promised Lands: The Origins of American Racism (Boston, 1978); H. C. Porter, *The Inconstant Savage: England and the North American Indian, 1500–1600* (London, 1979); Ronald T. Takaki, *Iron Cages: Race and Culture in Nineteenth-Century America* (New York, 1979); Karen Ordahl Kupperman, *Settling with the Indians: The Meeting of English and Indian Cultures in America, 1580–1640* (Totowa, N.J., 1980); Bernard W. Sheehan, *Savagism and Civility: Indians and Englishmen in Colonial Virginia* (London, 1980); Frederick Turner, *Beyond Geography: The Western Spirit against the Wilderness* (New York, 1980); Richard Drinnon, *Facing West: The Metaphysics of Indian-Hating and Empire-Building* (Minneapolis, 1980); Ray Allen Billington, *Land of Savagery, Land of Promise: The European Image of the American Frontier in the Nineteenth Century* (New York, 1981); and Lee Clark Mitchell, *Witnesses to a Vanishing America: The Nineteenth-century Response* (Princeton, 1981).

Blake and Scott, who are both much younger than their father's book, were an inspiration in themselves, while Donna, to whom this book is dedicated, was more than encouraging, more than patient, and more than understanding. She actually believed, as the years rolled by, that one day I would finish.

A NOTE ON NUMBERS

There are in the United States today about 1.4 million Indians, Eskimos, and Aleuts according to the 1980 U.S. Census Bureau tally. This figure, up 71 percent from the 1970 total, marks the first time the native population has passed the million mark in the official census count, and confirms the trend observed in 1970, making Indians one of the fastest-growing minority groups in the United States.[1] But the census data must be used cautiously. In 1970, anyone who declared his or her race to be American Indian and indicated a tribe was reported by the census as Indian. Since the Bureau of Indian Affairs counts only Indians living on or near the reservations for whom the federal government provides direct services, its figures are much lower than the Census Bureau's. Some estimates, however, greatly exceeded the census total, ranging as high as 15 million Indians.[2]

Where Indian population is concerned, exact figures have always been elusive. Their continuing imprecision allows us to regard Indian population counts for what they are: subjective estimates reflecting the desire to be (or not to be) considered Indian, as well as white assumptions about what an Indian is and what his ultimate destiny will be. What we have here is a numbers game—"truly one of the most fascinating . . . in history,"[3] according to a recent student—for, baldly stated, the expansion and shrinkage of Indian population estimates correlate with changing attitudes about the native American's rights and prospects. Consequently, estimates must be understood in relative rather than absolute terms.

In a popular version of the Indian numbers game, the starting point is the accepted estimate for aboriginal population at the time of Columbus's arrival. A high pre-Columbian population means a marked drop in Indian numbers after the arrival of the white man. Indians then could be seen as a wasting race, perhaps congenitally inferior, doomed to disappear through the operation of natural laws. Or they could be seen as the victims of white aggression and disease. The first interpretation, racial in nature, freed the white man from past blame and implied the futility of trying to save the "red man" since, realistically, he had no future. The second, environmentalist interpretation challenged white Americans as a matter of Christian duty and national honor to remedy a situation for which, inadvertently or otherwise, they were responsible.

A low pre-Columbian population implies, on the other hand, a reasonable stability in Indian numbers since the arrival of the white man. Since the white man could not be blamed for wasting the native peoples, the "century of dishonor" existed more in the overheated imaginations of reformers than in fact. At the same time, such an estimate refuted the theory of inevitable racial atrophy. It exposed the Vanishing American as a pernicious fallacy, and butressed the view that Providence had not intended Indians to disappear upon contact with white civilization. They could coexist with it or exist within it.

After 1900, when it was established that the Indian population was on the upswing, another variable received increasing attention in the numbers game—the growing percentage of mixed bloods and the relative decline of full bloods in the native population. Statistics showed that Indians were rapidly amalgamating with whites. For official purposes Indian numbers might be on the increase, but, in fact, the pure aboriginal stock, which could never be replenished, was disappearing. Many Americans naturally applauded this news, since it underlined the efficacy of the government's assimilationist program. But it also inspired regrets among those who took the position that the distinctive Indian cultures were a precious heritage.[4]

Where does the situation stand today? Fifteen years ago Henry F. Dobyns advanced a Western Hemisphere population estimate that has already altered our understanding of pre-Columbian America, and has convinced some historians that the traditional version of the European colonization of the New World is not merely misleading but false. There were,

Dobyns contends, at least 90 million people living in the Western Hemisphere when Columbus arrived, 10 million of them in the area now bounded by the United States.[5] Such figures contradict our impression of a vast, sparsely settled land mass, occupied in the North by scattered tribes whose total numbers never exceeded 1 million (the standard estimate, give or take a few hundred thousand), and whose claims to the soil were as limited as their ability to use it productively. If Dobyns is even close, the "virgin land" was actually a "widowed land," and the European onslaught in the New World nothing less than the destruction of a people. "Europeans did not find a wilderness here," Francis Jennings has written. "Rather, however involuntarily, they made one."[6] If we accept Dobyns's estimates for pre-Columbian times, it is obvious the white man triggered a staggering reduction in native numbers and that the Vanishing American is a precise encapsulation of historical experience.

Dobyns's figures, like those advanced before them, are, of course, estimates. They have been critically scrutinized and scaled downward, perhaps by as much as one-half, by other scholars friendly to his approach.[7] Dobyns's methodology drives home the point that all estimates are necessarily relative rather than absolute. Dobyns derived his totals by multiplying the lowest figure for any given Indian population (based on an actual enumeration) by a depopulation factor of 20 (or, for an outside projection, 25), representing the decrease due to disease and other causes related to white advance. Irrespective of the validity of his depopulation factors—and they are highly controversial—Dobyns's estimates can only be as accurate as the census counts. However Dobyns's figures are modified, they remain important as a reminder that the idea of a "bold, but wasting" race will not soon be put to rest. And, if they are even approximately correct, they suggest why the idea took hold in the first place and found such acceptance that by the time the United States came into being, the native American was already commonly thought of as the Vanishing American.

For nearly 300 years white Americans, in our zeal
to carve out a nation made to order, have dealt
with the Indians on the erroneous, yet tragic,
assumption that . . . [they] were a dying race.

—JOHN COLLIER, *Commissioner of Indian Affairs, 1938*

PART ONE

AND THEN THERE WERE NONE
A "Bold, but Wasting Race" of Men

What can be more melancholy than their history? By a
law of their nature, they seem destined to a slow, but
sure extinction. Everywhere, at the approach of the
white man, they fade away. We hear the rustling of their
footsteps, like that of the withered leaves of autumn,
and they are gone for ever. They pass mournfully by us,
and they return no more.

—Justice Joseph Story, "Discourse, Pronounced at the
Request of the Essex Historical Society, September 18, 1828,
in Commemoration of the First Settlement of Salem, Mass."

If these aboriginal nations of America should continue
to waste away, as they have done since the country was
occupied by Europeans, in a few generations to come,
they will scarcely be found, except in the pages of history, and in the traditions and monuments which they

may leave behind. The causes of this rapid decrease are not difficult to be explored . . .

—*Biblical Repertory and Princeton Review*, Vol. X (October 1838), p. 513

CHAPTER ONE

THEIR POWER HAS BEEN BROKEN:
The Indian After the War of 1812

A few months after the Founding Fathers met in convention to draft a new Constitution, a Philadelphia magazine carried some lines by Philip Freneau "occasioned by a visit to an old Indian burying ground":

> By midnight moons, o'er moistening dews;
>   In habit for the chase arrayed,
> The hunter still the deer pursues,
>   The hunter and the deer, a shade!
>
> And long shall timorous fancy see
>   The painted chief, and pointed spear,
> And Reason's self shall bow the knee
>   To shadows and delusions here.[1]

Even in 1787 the Indian seemed a spectral presence. His eastern hunting grounds were graveyards now, and from the perspective of the seacoast society in which Freneau moved—Philadelphia, Charleston, and New York—he could be viewed with detachment as a legitimate American ghost. Like all of the dead past, the Indian was unthreatening, as John Adams suggested in a nostalgic letter to Thomas Jefferson. "Aaron Pomham the Priest and Moses Pomham the King of the Punkapaug and Neponsit Tribes, were frequent Visitors at my Fathers house at least seventy Years ago," Adams recalled.

I have a distinct remembrance of their Forms and Figures. They

3

were very aged, and the tallest and stoutest Indians I have ever seen. . . . There was a numerous Family in this Town, whose Wigwam was within a Mile of this House . . . and I in my boyish Rambles used to call at their Wigwam, where I never failed to be treated with Whortle Berries, Blackberries, Strawberries or Apples, Plumbs, Peaches, etc., for they had planted a variety of fruit Trees about them. But the Girls went out to Service and the Boys to Sea, till not a Soul is left. We scarcely see an Indian in a year.[2]

Adams remembered the "Time when Indian Murders, Scalpings, Depredations and conflagrations were as frequent on the Eastern and Northern Frontier of Massachusetts as they are now in Indiana, and spread as much terror," but the years had dimmed the terror and the Indian was associated in the East with fond childhood memories of treats of whortleberries.

EIGHTEENTH-CENTURY EXPECTATIONS FOR THE INDIAN

Americans who bothered to reflect on the subject entered the nineteenth century firmly convinced that race was not an ultimate limiting factor in human achievement. That seminal document of the Enlightenment, John Locke's *An Essay Concerning Human Understanding* (1690), had set forth the theory that people began life with a *tabula rasa*, a mind like "white paper, void of all characters, without any ideas." "How comes it to be furnished?" Locke asked, and answered, "In one word, from experience." No innate ideas, capacities, advantages, or disadvantages distinguished one race from the other. Enculturation alone accounted for whatever observable differences marked the human varieties. It followed that humans were literally created equal, and that the races shared an identical potential for improvement.

The Republic was conceived in an intellectual milieu that simply assumed the transforming power of environment. Thus Indians, like others, could become civilized and enjoy the fruits of education and Christianity. "Let it not be said, that they are incapable of improvement," one of Jefferson's contemporaries wrote in 1798. "Natural History . . . teaches us, that the physical differences between nations are but inconsiderable, and history informs us, that civilization has been constantly preceded by barbarity and rudeness."[3]

Despite facing stiff Indian opposition to further westward expansion, the fledgling United States government by the latter 1790s had adopted a relatively conciliatory policy in its dealings with the natives. Government officials could afford to be benign. A major victory over the northwestern tribes at the Battle of Fallen Timbers in 1794 had redressed earlier setbacks in establishing control over the region and had resulted in a substantial cession of Indian land north and west of the Ohio River. American land hunger in the area was temporarily satisfied. To the south, meanwhile, the Cherokees, Chickasaws, and Creeks, under unremitting governmental pressure, reluctantly ceded lands in Georgia and Tennessee.

Both Washington and Jefferson expressed confidence in the Indian's powers of improvement; Jefferson, in particular, favored a policy of complete assimilation. Racial amalgamation seemed the perfect solution. Once the Indians abandoned the perilous existence of the hunter and became cultivators of the earth as God intended, they would have no further need for vast tracts of wilderness. "While they are learning to do better on less land," Jefferson explained, "our increasing numbers will be calling for more land, and thus a coincidence of interests will be produced between those who have lands to spare, and want other necessaries, and those who have such necessaries to spare, and want lands."[4] The Indian could be transformed into an American farmer, and transformed willingly.

THE IMPACT OF THE WAR OF 1812

Jefferson had badly underestimated the tenacity with which the tribes would cling to their own ways of life. In a message to Congress delivered on June 1, 1812, President James Madison commented on "the warfare just renewed by the savages on one of our extensive frontiers," and pointed an accusing finger at the British for complicity in stirring unrest.[5] On June 18, just ten days before John Adams wrote his mellow letter to Jefferson about the absence of Indians in his neighborhood, Congress declared war on Great Britain, and the Indian problem returned to public prominence. Many tribes elected to fight by the side of the British, an alliance that reversed

American optimism about the Indians' capacity for civilization. The hand of friendship, extended in vain, was now withdrawn in anger. Whatever their environment, it was assumed that some men and women were apparently depraved from birth.

Previous wars, too, had occasioned thorough reconsiderations of the Indian character. After the tribes uprose in Virginia in 1622, for example, Samuel Purchas insisted that, by proving themselves "unnaturall Naturalls," they had forfeited their "remainders of right" and were deserving of whatever punishment the colonists meted out.[6] "Our hands which before were tied with gentleness and fair usage, are now set at liberty by the treacherous violence of the Sauvages," one Virginian announced with relish.[7] The European image of the Indian oscillated between the noble savage and the bloodthirsty devil. War made the latter view generally acceptable, and the War of 1812 was no exception. Jefferson's dream of racial harmony was one of its first victims.

The tarnishing of the Indian's image after 1812 can be traced in the changing mood of Madison's annual messages to Congress. In the first, in 1809, he reported that "our Indian neighbors," under a "just and benevolent system," had remained at peace and were rapidly advancing toward civilization. By 1811, when the sky was black with war clouds, he referred to "several murders and depredations committed by Indians" on the northwestern frontier, and to "the menacing preparations and aspects of a combination of them on the Wabash, under the influence and direction of a fanatic of the Shawnee tribe." Two days later General William Henry Harrison defeated the Shawnees at Tippecanoe, but the fighting had just begun in earnest. The country was embroiled in war when Madison gave his second Inaugural Address in 1813. He damned the British for procuring Indian allies "eager to glut their savage thirst with the blood of the vanquished and to finish the work of torture and death on maimed and defenseless captives." By 1815 he noted that efforts were under way to reopen relations with the tribes. The following year he was "happy" to observe that tranquility had been restored in the Northwest and that the work of civilization could be resumed. "Our Indian neighbors" were back in the government's good graces.[8]

Still, the war and Tecumseh's "conspiracy" to unite all the western tribes in a grand alliance to oppose American expansion had shattered the comfortable illusion that the Indians would gladly exchange land for civilization. Writing early in 1814, six months before the United States and Britain opened formal peace negotiations, Washington Irving had detected a hardening of "popular feeling" toward the Indian and beseeched his countrymen to exercise restraint. "The enormities of the Indians form no excuse for the enormities of the white men," he cautioned, yet some Americans still discussed "the *policy* of extirpating thousands." Unless cool heads prevailed, the nation would "lay up, in a moment's passion, ample cause for an age's repentance."[9] During the peace talks, a British minister accused the United States government of a total disregard for Indian land title, "thereby menacing the final extinction of those nations." Stung, the American ministers defended their government's "humane and liberal" Indian policy.[10] But the exchange indicated a growing awareness that the War of 1812 had permanently altered Indian-white relations in North America.

A TURNING POINT IN INDIAN-WHITE RELATIONS

Historians commonly refer to Pontiac's Rebellion, a postscript to the bitterly contested French and Indian War of 1756–1763, as the last significant Indian resistance to American advance. While the issue momentarily hung in doubt, the argument goes, the elimination of the French presence by treaty in 1763 had doomed Pontiac to defeat. Thereafter the Indian "menace" would never again be of national consequence. However, as long as British and Indian interests continued to coincide, particularly in the Old Northwest, and as long as ownership of the area south of the Great Lakes and north of the Ohio River remained uncertain, the outcome of the American-Indian struggle was less obvious to contemporaries. American settlers could still see a Redcoat behind every redskin.

The War of 1812 brought their fears to a head. But on October 5, 1813, with his British allies in ignominious flight, Tecumseh fell near the forks of the Thames, in present-day Ontario. Less than six months later, Andrew Jackson crushed the Creeks at Horseshoe Bend, in what would soon become the state of Alabama, virtually ending Indian resistance in the South. Though the Seminoles remained defiant and British "agents" were thought to be lurking among the palmettos inciting them to violence, few could elevate the situation in Florida into a grave national threat. For all practical purposes, the land east of the Mississippi River had been secured. The treaty concluded with Britain in 1814 paved the way for the Convention of 1818, which established the basic boundary between British territory and the United States, leaving only its eastern and western extremities to future negotiation. The fear of a determined British-Indian offensive was quieted at last.

In December 1818, John C. Calhoun, who as Secretary of War had charge of Indian affairs, reported to Speaker of the House Henry Clay that "helplessness has succeeded independence" among the tribes on the western frontier. "The time seems to have arrived when our policy towards them should undergo an important change," he said. "They neither are, in fact, nor ought to be, considered as independent nations. Our views of their interest, and not their own, ought to govern them."[11] Calhoun's proposal for a basic realignment of policy was half a century ahead of its time, but his analysis of the Indians' situation was widely accepted. Speaking a month later, Clay commented that when the colonies were established, "we were weak, and . . . [the Indians] were comparatively strong; . . . they were the lords of the soil, and we were seeking . . . asylum among them." Now the positions were reversed:

We are powerful and they are weak: . . . to use a figure drawn from their own sublime eloquence, the poor children of the forest have been driven by the great wave which has flowed in from the Atlantic ocean to almost the base of the Rocky Mountains, and, overwhelming them in its terrible progress, has left no other remains of hundreds of tribes, now extinct, than those which indicate the remote existence of their former companion, the mammoth of the New World![12]

The Indians' days as a valuable ally in the struggle for continental mastery were over. William Clark, who had been active in Indian affairs since the heroic 1804–1806 overland expedition to the Pacific, wrote in 1826 that before 1815 "the tribes nearest our settlements were a formidable and terrible enemy; since then their power has been broken, their warlike spirit subdued, and themselves sunk into objects of pity and commiseration."[13]

Whatever rights the Indians enjoyed in the future would be at the discretion of the government. Native title to the soil, based on the right of occupancy, a legalism understandable when the tribes could resist expansion and had to be placated, was now vulnerable. By siding with the British, the ungrateful Indians had forfeited any claim to sympathy. The country owed them nothing; its sense of fair play was now their sole protection.[14]

THE MISSIONARY FAITH IN INDIAN CAPACITY

The long-term ramifications of the War of 1812 for Indian-white relations were initially obscured by public and private efforts to prove that Americans had in fact been "humane and liberal" in their dealings with the natives. In the vanguard were the missionary societies. They had never wavered in their faith that the Indians could be saved. "However the various denominations of professing Christians may differ in their creeds and general doctrines," the House Committee on Indian Affairs reported in 1824, "they all unite in their wishes that our Indians may become civilized."[15] Their principal worry, as Robert Berkhofer has pointed out, was one of priorities: Which should come first, Christianity or civilization?[16]

It was an old problem. The Jesuits had championed the preeminence of conversion. Their Jansenist critics contended that the Indians must be "Frenchified" first. The Virginia Company's charter, true to the Elizabethan mission of saving the Indians from heathenism and Catholicism alike, had assumed that civilization would be the natural offspring of Protestantism. To the Puritans, absorbed in their own exclusive mission, civilization must clear the way for the Word, not vice versa. Education and inducements to industry would curb the savages' dangerous individualism and bring them within those restraints of civil society, the sole protection from man's natural depravity. At best, the Puritans had been lukewarm missionaries. John Eliot dedicated himself to uplifting "the red man," urging the "praying Indians" to congregate in "towns," cut their hair, dress, and live like the Puritans. Before they could find God, they would have to become Englishmen. In the Great Awakening of the 1720s "conversion was everything and civilizing nothing," Roy Harvey Pearce has written.[17] By the time of the Revolution, evangelical enthusiasm had waned, leaving unsettling doubts about the practicality of efforts to improve the Indian by conversion or civilizing.

But the Second Great Awakening beginning in the 1790s again aroused interest in conversion of the natives, and the War of 1812, which occasioned the Indians' fall from official favor, gave a dynamic urgency to this missionary work. More broadly based and better financed, aided by improved transportation and inspired by the dream of a network of stations across the West, the missionary societies pressed deeper into the interior. God's work was the nation's work as well. The societies that stressed skills such as farming and husbandry, rather than the nobler but less practical goals of indoctrination and instruction, won new respect. Even a skeptic conceded in 1828 that "if any effort on our part could check or arrest the downward career of this race, if any extensive or valuable benefits could be extended to them, they would accrue from the benevolent exertions of that class of men, who go among them to teach the elements of the useful arts, and the principles of the Christian religion."[18]

But if the missionaries never doubted the Indians' capacity for improvement, "the great mass of the community" did not share their optimism. "There seems to be a deep rooted superstition . . . that the Indians are really *destined*, as if there were some fatality in the case, never to be christianized, but gradually to decay till they become totally extinct," a religious writer commented.[19]

Extermination as policy was unthinkable, but a fully rounded version of the Vanishing American won public acceptance after 1814. By its logic, Indians were doomed to "utter extinction" because they belonged to "an inferior race of men . . . neither qualified to rise higher in the scale of being, nor to enjoy the benefits and blessings of the civilized and Christian state."[20] A popular convention, premised on a moralistic judgment, had become natural law. Romantic poets, novelists, orators, and artists found the theme of a dying native race congenial, and added those sentimental touches to the concept that gave it wide appeal. Serious students of the Indian problem provided corroboration for the artistic construct as they analyzed the major causes hurrying the Indians to their graves. Opinion was virtually unanimous: "That they should become extinct is inevitable."[21]

CHAPTER TWO

THE ANATOMY OF THE VANISHING AMERICAN

"The present hour has but one oracle for the Indians," a Virginia professor wrote near midcentury. "It is wo! wo!"[1] A simple formula accounted for this situation. Coming in contact with civilization, Indians surrendered what was good in their racial character and absorbed what was bad in that of the whites. The universal law of civilized progress ordained that savages could hold no area permanently their own. Where American progress would stop, Jefferson noted in 1824, "no one can say. Barbarism has, in the meantime, been receding before the steady step of amelioration; and will in time, I trust, disappear from the earth."[2]

Sensitivity about the United States' moral stature among the nations of the world made it difficult for Americans to admit to a deep complicity in the Indians' destruction. It was easier to indict Indians for their own ruin, thereby washing the white man's hands of responsibility. An even more satisfactory explanation held that the fate of the aborigines was predestined. Their demise reflected no discredit on American institutions or morality, nor on the Indians, but, rather, reflected the wishes of the same benevolent Providence who swept clean the shores of Plymouth Bay to make room for His pilgrims years before. One could deplore the fact that the Indian was earmarked for extinction; but one could not alter it. "These things seem mysterious," a Bostonian conceded in 1841, "but it would be impious to murmur at the decrees of fate."[3]

THE RHETORIC OF DOOM

To make their case, poets, novelists, and essayists adopted a stylistic strategy that summed up Indian fate in images drawn from nature. The Indian was at the sunset of his existence; night was about to swallow a race fated to vanish "as the snow melts before the sunbeam,"[4] or "like the morning dew, insensibly and mysteriously to disappear, before the lights of civilization and christianity."[5] "Like a promontory of sand, exposed to the ceaseless encroachments of the ocean, they have been gradually wasting away before the current of the white population, which set in upon them from every quarter," a Georgia senator observed in 1825.[6] "One by one they perish, like the leaves of the forest that are swept away by the autumn winds; melancholy shrouds them; they die of sadness, and are effaced from the earth by an inexorable destiny," Eliza Lee mourned twenty-two years later.[7] In an address delivered before the Cambridge Phi Beta Kappa Society in 1815, William Tudor, Jr., declared that the Indians were vanishing "like snow before the vernal influence," and their disappearance reminded him of the "sublime allegorical painting of Guido, in which Apollo encircled by the hours, is chasing night and her shadows over the surface of the globe." It could almost represent "the extinction of our savage precursors before the dawn of science and cultivation."[8]

William Cullen Bryant helped define the Vanishing American theme for poets in a much-admired 1824 composition, "An Indian at the Burying-place of His Fathers":

> They waste us—aye—like April snow
>   In the warm noon, we shrink away;
> And fast they follow, as we go
>   Towards the setting day,—
> Till they shall fill the land, and we
> Are driven into the western sea.[9]

Citing Bryant as his inspiration, Isaac McLellan, Jr., published "Hymn of the Cherokee Indian," which opened with a burst of similes suggesting an additional debt to the magnificent coronach for Duncan in Sir Walter Scott's *The Lady of the Lake* (1810):

> Like the shadows in the stream,
> Like the evanescent gleam
> Of the twilight's failing blaze,
> Like the fleeting years and days,
> Like all things that soon decay,
> Pass the Indian tribes away.[10]

G. W. Cutter, writing in the 1840s, concluded "The Death of Osceola" with a bouquet of images:

> Like snow beneath thy fiery glance—
> Like dew in thy garment's ray—
> Like bubbles that o'er the ocean dance—
> Our tribes are swept away!
> Father of Heaven! We faint—we fall,
> Like leaves on some lonely flood;
> And the earth beneath our conquerors' hall
> Still reeks with thy children's blood![11]

In this and dozens of similar verses, poets seemed less concerned with the causes of the Vanishing American than with the opportunity to exercise their descriptive powers and to appeal to popular sentimentality.

The same could be said of the orators who mentioned the First American in public addresses commemorating milestones in the nation's progress from wilderness to civilization. In an Independence Day address in 1825 Charles Sprague, a Boston banker and an amateur poet, included several lines that entrenched themselves in nineteenth-century school readers and anthologies. "Roll back the tide of time," he commanded his audience of proper Bostonians:

Not many generations ago, where you now sit, circled with all that exalts and embellishes civilized life, the rank thistle nodded in the wind, and the wild fox dug his hole unscared. Here lived and loved another race of beings. Beneath the same sun that rolls over your heads, the Indian hunter pursued the panting deer; gazing on the same moon that smiles for you, the Indian lover wooed his dusky mate. Here the wigwam blaze beamed on the tender and the helpless, the council-fire glared on the wise and the daring. Now they dipped their noble limbs in your sedgy lakes, and now they paddled the light canoe along your rocky shores. Here they warred; the echoing

whoop, the bloody grapple, the defying death-song, all were here.
. . . Here, too, they worshipped. . . .

And all this has passed away. Across the ocean came a pilgrim
bark, bearing the seeds of life and death. The former were sown for
you, the latter sprang up in the path of the simple native. Two
hundred years have changed the character of a great continent, and
blotted forever from its face a whole, peculiar people. . . . The
Indian, of falcon glance, and lion bearing, the theme of the touching
ballad, the hero of the pathetic tale, is gone! and his degraded
offspring crawl upon the soil where he walked in majesty. . . .

As a race they have withered from the land. Their arrows are
broken, their springs are dried up, their cabins are in the dust. Their
council-fire has long since gone out on the shore, and their war-cry
is fast dying away to the untrodden west. Slowly and sadly they climb
the distant mountains, and read their doom in the setting sun. They
are shrinking before the mighty tide which is pressing them away;
they must soon hear the roar of the last wave, which will settle over
them forever.[12]

The easy sweep of the language, the inspired phrases, and
the comforting euphemisms anesthetized the listener's conscience. The "still small voice within" was lost amid a forest of
conventional images. Autumn leaves dropping from the trees.
The mist rising. The morning dew dissipating in the heat of
the day. The setting sun. The ocean's all-consuming waves.
Such figurative prose obscured a harsh reality. The Indian,
like the seasons, was meant to pass, but not to return again.

The Vanishing American became a habit of thought. Navy
Lieutenant George Falconer Emmons in 1852 indignantly
charged that "lawless whites" were waging a "war of extermination" on the tribes in California and Oregon. The Indians
"are falling by tens, fifties, and hundreds, before the western
rifle." Still, his righteous anger was neutralized by his conclusion: "It is melancholy to see them melting away so rapidly;
but it does not appear to be intended that divilization should
prevent it."[13] A natural law was in operation, and no mortal
could alter its course. The "inexorable destiny" of the Indians,
like that of the wilderness with which they shared an almost
symbiotic relationship, was to recede before civilization's advance. Their fate had important implications for white Americans self-consciously searching for a national identity.

INDIAN ORIGINS AND THE AMERICAN IDENTITY

Few subjects intrigued eighteenth- and nineteenth-century Americans of a philosophical bent of mind more than the question of Indian origins. So many preposterous theories were propounded and ardently championed that John Adams grumbled, "I should as soon suppose that the Prodigal Son, in a frolic with one of his Girls made a trip to America in one of Mother Careys Eggshels, and left the fruits of their Amours here, as believe any of the grave hypotheses and solemn reasonings of Philosophers or Divines upon the Subject."[14] Yet popular writers could speak of the necessity of "tracing the descent of these once mighty nations, and of solving the great problem of the settlement of America."[15]

It is worth pondering why native origins should constitute a "great problem" for Americans. The answer seems to lie in the search for a distinctive national identity. Obviously, the recentness of civilization's penetration into the wilderness went a long way toward explaining the differences between the American and the European, the former progressive, the latter stagnant and time-bound. Without a past of its own, however, America lacked moral grandeur, its character remained distressingly two-dimensional; thus the desire to locate indigenous roots that might reach back to a New World antiquity, a lost heritage distinctively American. The Indian, as the First American, was necessary to any such attempt at self-definition. He *was* the American past. In 1846, nine years after Emerson delivered his "literary Declaration of Independence" at Harvard, Henry R. Schoolcraft, perhaps the most eminent ethnologist of the day, read his own manifesto before the New Confederacy of the Iroquois in Aurora, New York. "We have drawn our intellectual sustenance . . . from noble fountains and crystal streams. We have all England, and all Europe for our fountain head." But, he added, it was time that Americans produced a culture "characteristic of the land that gave us birth." Not surprisingly, the Indian was to be the starting point:

And where, when we survey the length and breadth of the land can a more suitable element for the work be found, than is furnished by the history and antiquities and institutions of the free, bold, wild, independent native hunter race? They are relatively to us what the ancient Pict and Celt were to Britain or the Teuton, Goth and Magyar to continental Europe.[16]

Four years later, the venerable Daniel Webster was urging Congress to purchase George Catlin's celebrated gallery of Indian portraits as "an *American* subject . . . a thing more appropriate for us than the ascertaining of the South Pole, or anything that can be discovered in the Dead Sea or the River Jordan."[17]

Even Americans who found a link with paint-daubed natives demeaning settled on the Indian antiquities in their search for a usable past, simply denying that they were Indian. Thus, late in the eighteenth century and throughout most of the nineteenth, the "myth of the mound builders" flourished. Its principal tenets were that a vanished race, probably white, had thrived in the valley of the Mississippi centuries ago, constructed the mounds that dotted the region, then perished at the hands of the "red savages." Here was a reply to those who dismissed the United States as a country without a history. "Europeans have described the general features of our scenery, as harsh and savage, and our landscape, as destitute of moral interest," Timothy Flint complained in 1827:

We have, it is said, no monuments, no ruins, none of the collossal remains of temples and baronial castles, and monkish towers, nothing to connect the imagination and the heart with the past, none of the dim and deep recollections of the times gone by, to associate the past with the future.

But the United States, far from "wanting those golden links of the chain of association," had "monuments innumerable"—her prehistoric mounds.[18] Another writer maintained that the United States alone on all the globe exhibited a "perfect union of the past and present; the rigor of a nation just born walking over the hallowed ashes of a race whose history is too early for a record, and surrounded by the living forms of a people hovering between the two."[19] As Andrew Jackson was to contend, the legendary mound builders could also serve as justification for displacing the Indians, since they had displaced an earlier people.

The denial of America's Indian heritage implicit in the mound-builder myth persisted in the face of an awesome burden of evidence to the contrary. But the insistence that the United States' dual tradition, Old and New World, be white did not obviate the peculiar merits of the native American. "No part of our globe has presented specimens of savage nature which will bear a comparison in body or mind with our American Indians," an essayist boasted in 1834. A young country out to establish its position in the world could not afford to miss an angle; in the United States, a legion of writers would assert, even the savages were a cut above the average.[20]

THE VANISHING AMERICAN AS AMERICA'S NOBLE SAVAGE

One attraction of the Indian theme was the stamp of approval given it by European literati enamored of the "noble savage." Although many *philosophes* dismissed the noble savage ideal as an absurd contradiction in terms, since the time of Columbus a broad spectrum of opinion—from Spanish clerics and French Jesuits through eighteenth-century deists, skeptics, and primitivists—had found in the noble savage an appealing conceit and a versatile tool in their attacks on the established order and conventional wisdom.

The noble savage is commonly associated with Jean-Jacques Rousseau, though his particular contribution was the elaboration of the idea, already old when he was writing, that mankind once enjoyed a "Golden Age," a bright morning of existence marked by an innocence and contentment never since recovered. Rousseau recognized that the "pure state of nature" beloved of contemporary thinkers was a philosophical abstraction, but the temptation remained to accord it a literal existence in the remote past or in the present somewhere far away. The "infant society" of known savages hardly represented a pure state of nature. But, even tainted, it had peculiar advantages, striking, as Rousseau argued in his *Discourse upon the Origin and Foundation of the Inequality among Mankind* (1755), a "just Mean between the indolence of the primitive State, and the petulant activity of Self-love" that characterized the civilized state. It represented "the real Youth of the World"—or as close an approximation of it as man would ever witness again—and "all ulterior Improvements" were illusory, for natural man epitomized the human species at its happiest.

The noble savage's primary virtue was innocence of civilized failings. It was this innocence that made the savage a favorite satiric device in the eighteenth century. Like the visitor from abroad whose letters home provided running critiques of French or English society, the noble savage transported into a European setting was a detached observer of the life around him. Because innocent, and thus unaware of the motives behind what he saw, he spoke in the spirit of curiosity, not malice, and his criticisms consequently were all the more devastating. For example, l'Ingénu, the hero of Voltaire's 1767 tale of the same name, could provide a telling critique of French life, especially its religious factionalism, because his upbringing as a Huron in touch with the eternal verities of nature allowed him to slice through artifice to get at truths hidden from all but the most observant Frenchmen. Besides its use in satire, the noble savage convention served didactic ends. In Rousseau's *Emile, ou l'education* (1762) and Bernardin de Saint-Pierre's *Paul et Virginie* (1788), the concept affirmed the feasibility of revitalizing civilized beings by exposing them to the wonders of nature.

To turn from Rousseau's natural man and Voltaire's l'Ingénu to Chateaubriand's noble savage Chactas near the beginning of the nineteenth century is to turn from a philosophical to an emotional construct. Chactas, the Natchez hero of *Atala*, is a convert to Roman Catholicism, and as passionately devoted to his new religion as he is to the beautiful mixed-blood maiden Atala, who in order to escape temptation and preserve her purity poisons herself. The distraught Chactas is left behind to mourn her, and the Florida wilderness resounds not with the carefree shouts of nature's children at play, but with the sound of sobbing beneath the soughing pines. The twin strains of exoticism and melancholy deeply tinctured Romantic thought, and when the Chateaubriands went "to the depths of the woods" to discover nature's innocents they found instead, not surprisingly, projections of their own anguished soul-searching.

American authors in the early 1800s who favored the Indian as a national subject were inclined to write within the imported conventions of Romanticism. Their environment, of course, left its own stamp upon their work. Civilization was cutting rapidly into the wilderness; behind it stretched a growing area of settled land and a burgeoning population disposed to idealize what was almost always best appreciated from a distance. One part of the national character, progressive and practical, rejected the noble savage out of hand. "Let us never undervalue the comfort and security of municipal and social life, nor the sensibilities, charities and endearments of a Christian home," Cincinnati's Timothy Flint, an ardent booster of the West, wrote in 1827. "The happiness of savages steeled against feeling, at war with nature, the elements, and each other, can have no existence, except in the visionary dreaming of those, who have never contemplated their actual condition."[21] Another part of the national character embraced the noble savage as a refined and purer version of the true American, a cleanly chiseled self-portrait of what "that new man" might be, or might have been. Philip Freneau, sometimes called the progenitor of the entire band of nineteenth-century writers on the American Indian, believed that "Nature's ruder child" could teach civilized man "one great Truth":

> That, through the world, wherever man exists,
> Involved in darkness, or obscured in mists,
> The *Negro*, scorching on *Angola's* coasts,
> Or *Tartar*, shivering in *Siberian* frosts;
> Take all, through all, through nation,
>   tribe, or clan,
> The child of Nature is the *better* man.[22]

Since Americans had made their choice—civilization over savagery, cities and fields over forests and unplowed prairies—the noble savage most often appeared in American literature as a variation on the brooding, ill-starred creature of Romantic thought. A sense of personal tragedy had been superseded by an awareness of impending racial doom. Freneau's tribute to "Nature's ruder child" appeared in an 1822 poem, "On the Civilization of the Western Aboriginal Country," which told how Nature has two wheels "constantly for play":

> She turns them both, but turns a different way;
> What one creates, subsists a year, an hour,
> When, by destructions wheel is crushed once more.

No art, no strength this wheel of fate restrains,
While matter, deathless matter, still remains. . . .[23]

The Indians were destined to "disappear with the animals they hunted, and the forests that sheltered both." America's noble savage was not Rousseau's natural man, then, nor l'Ingénu, nor even Chactas; but a doomed figure about to succumb "before the spirit of civilization."[24]

THE VANISHING AMERICAN IN LITERATURE

The demand for a truly national literature raised in the United States in the years after the War of 1812 was answered in the 1820s, the first decade in which the Indian figured prominently in American fiction. Some forty novels published between 1824 and 1834 included Indian episodes, constituting what G. Harrison Orians termed a "cult of the Vanishing American."[25] The tenor of this cult is summed up in the title of its solitary masterpiece—*The Last of the Mohicans* (1826)—for its appeal was to that awareness of fleeting time so dear to the Romantic temperament. As Orians noted, several related novels could have been titled "The Last of . . ." leaving the name of the particular tribe to be filled in—the Narragansetts, Pequots, Cochi, Yemassees. But it was James Fenimore Cooper's work, and his concern with the clash of civilization and wilderness in America, that set the style for the genre.

The theme is established early in *The Last of the Mohicans*, when Uncas is introduced to the reader by his father. "Where are the blossoms of those summers!" Chingachgook cries:

Fallen, one by one. So all of my family departed, each in his turn, to the land of spirits. I am on the hilltop, and must go down into the valley; and when Uncas follows in my footsteps, there will no longer be any of the blood of the Sagamores, for my boy is the last of the Mohicans.

Subsequently this theme is advanced by casual references to Uncas, particularly in the scenes with the Delaware sage Tamenund, whose memory stretches back to the time when "the children of the Lenape were masters of the world." Tamenund is a symbol of decayed power—a living reminder of the fate that has befallen his people. Thus, his confusion of Chingachgook's Uncas with the Uncas of his youth is especially poignant. "Is Tamenund a boy?" he wonders:

Have I dreamt of so many snows—that my people were scattered like floating sands—of Yengeese, more plenty than the leaves on the trees! The arrow of Tamenund would not frighten the fawn; his arm is withered like the branch of a dead oak; the snail would be swifter in the race; yet is Uncas before him as they went to battle against the palefaces! Uncas, the panther of his tribe, the eldest son of the Lenape, the wisest Sagamore of the Mohicans! Tell me, ye Delawares, has Tamenund been a sleeper for a hundred winters?

But the Delawares' fate is relentless, and, "before the night has come," Tamenund has "lived to see the last warrior of the wise race of the Mohicans."

With Uncas's death at the hands of the evil Huron Magua the theme is rounded out; only Chingachgook remains, truly the last of his kind. So it is left for him, an older man deeply conscious of change, to mourn what has been lost. "As for me, the son and the father of Uncas, I am a blazed pine, in a clearing of the palefaces. My race has gone from the shores of the salt lake, and the hills of the Delaware. . . . I am alone." As the final link in an immemorial chain, Chingachgook is fiction's most memorable Vanishing American.[26]

The Last of the Mohicans made an immediate impression on the reading public. Well before the names of its major characters entrenched themselves in the American vocabulary and artists committed its most memorable scenes to canvas, reviewers had critically analyzed its presentation of the Indian. William Gardiner wrote in the *North American Review* that "Mr. Cooper's Indians are somewhat of a visionary order," but he deemed them infinitely superior to the "mere creations of the poet's brain" that had previously passed for Indians in literature. He dismissed Uncas as a complete fabrication. Chingachgook, occupying the middle ground between the extremes of noble savage and red devil, was "drawn far nearer to the life," while Magua, though "one of those licensed instruments of romance, which belong rather to the diabolical orders of creation, than to any tribe of the human species, savage or civilized," was "a well conceived and well sustained . . . somewhat exaggerated character."[27] With only minor modifications these judgments remained standard. Contemporary reviewers realized that Magua was just as implausible as Uncas, but they reserved their critical shafts for the noble savage. Consequently, "Mr. Cooper's Indians" became a nineteenth-century synonym for any positive depiction.

Why the innocuous Uncas should have occasioned scornful denunciation is problematical. As an individual, he has no more life than the Greek statuary to which Cooper likens him. However, as the representative of a doomed race he is memorable. And here, precisely, seems to be the source of critical dissent. By introducing a personal element into the universal law decreeing the extinction of savagery, the noble Indian denied Americans the comforting sanction of simple inevitability.

When the Indian is depicted as a red devil, that fiend of the captivity narrative and the frontier romance, his passing is not mourned. "Of such a race of miscreants we are almost ready to say—'Perdition catch their souls!'" Joseph C. Hart exclaimed in his 1834 novel *Miriam Coffin.* They inspired a literature of their own dedicated to the proposition that savagery begets savagery, what Herman Melville referred to as "the metaphysics of Indian-hating." One does, however, mourn the passing of the noble savage. Of "a truly godlike Indian" in *Miriam Coffin,* Hart was willing to say "with fervour—'REQUIESCAT IN PACE!'"[28] Such an Indian is a judgment on New World civilization. The Vanishing Americans in literature were dying not of their own vices, but of the white man's. Uncas and Magua epitomize a savagery that must disappear before civilized progress; and both consequently are destroyed, although one represents natural virtue and the other, evil. They are as distinct as they are similar, then, and the distinction is as significant as their common ground of doomed savagery.

The dichotomy was basic to American thought. The settlers of the New World, who had tacitly repudiated the Old and then had asserted the moral superiority of the society they were hewing out of the woods ("Not such as Europe breeds in her decay"), could never escape the fact of the wilderness. As they destroyed it, they mourned it. They were aligned with the dreamers of man's Golden Age; their mood, too, was elegiac and burdened with a yearning as pure as it was hopeless. Elémire Zolla's study of the Indian in American letters argues that the eighteenth century's heritage, a blind devotion to progress, was "the chief culprit, the actual agent of the slaughter" of the Indian and his spirit by European man. Progress, he argues, banishes the old as obsolete, "while at the same time it represses the love, so congenial to man, of that delicate, wise patina that time deposits on the things of this world."[29] However, Zolla misses the crucial point that nostalgia and progress were happy companions. Indian remnants *were* the American past, even if they had to be whitened into respectability; while the Indian in the act of vanishing before civilized progress elicited a full range of emotional responses—sympathy, regret, sadness, despair—if not that *emotional empathy* that Zolla alone recognizes as an acceptable criterion for judging writings about the Indian.

The elegiac tone that suffuses the Leatherstocking tales reflected Cooper's own doubts about the virtue of progress and the superiority of a civilized life. *The Pioneers* (1823) with its aging white hunter, Natty Bumppo, and its Chingachgook near dissolution at his death (another victim of rum, the white man's tomahawk), and *The Prairie* (1827) with its sunset imagery and its vision of the westward drive of empire eliminating the wilderness where Natty roamed, both suggest Cooper's early misgivings. But it was in the last two Leatherstocking novels, *The Pathfinder* (1840) and *The Deerslayer* (1841), that Cooper was fully aware that the American wilderness was vanishing, and with it, a younger, simpler America. Throughout the 1840s a new set of real Indian and wilderness adventures distracted the nation, and by decade's end the great push westward had culminated at the Pacific. In his introduction to the revised edition of *The Last of the Mohicans*, written the year before his death in 1851, Cooper observed that the Delawares were the first tribe to be dispossessed, and the "seemingly inevitable fate of all these people, who disappear before the advances, or it might be termed the inroads of civilization, as the verdure of their native forests falls before the nipping frost, is represented as having already befallen them." Something vital was being lost to Americans, "a life fast dying out," an army officer's wife wrote, "and soon to fail forever in the suffocating atmosphere of encroaching civilization."[30]

GEORGE CATLIN AND THE THEORY OF VICES AND VIRTUES

Americans who mourned the disappearing wilderness and the Vanishing Indian were forced to reconcile their ideal with the real. Some observers on encountering the Indian were jarred out of their belief in natural man and natural virtue; others decided that while the noble savage may have existed in the past, or might still exist elsewhere, those with whom they were familiar fell far short of perfection. The key to reconciling expectation and actuality was in building backward from the present reality to the past ideal, letting the gulf between serve as a measure of civilization's deleterious effects. Assuming that the Indian was once noble, then it followed that the degraded contemporary specimens proved contact with the white man inimical, confirming the theory that the Indians were doomed to perish before civilization's advance. The noble savage substantiated a naturalistic interpretation of savagery's inevitable defeat.

Even "that subtle savage" Magua was once a good Indian. Cooper attributed his fall to liquor in particular. It was the coming of the white man that ended Magua's twenty-year idyll in the forests and made him a "rascal," for Magua, like all "real" Indians, was a victim of the ruthless law of "vices and virtues."[31] This law, which wormed its way into virtually every discussion of the Indian question in the nineteenth century, can be defined in a sentence: "By mixing with us . . . [the Indians] imbibe all our vices, without emulating our virtues— and our intercourse with them is decisively disadvantageous to them."[32] The red devil, then, was simply a fallen noble savage. To survive, the noble savage must remain uncontaminated by contact with the white race.

No man in his time cleaved more precisely to this line of reasoning than George Catlin, a self-taught Philadelphia portrait painter, who, like many young men of his day, responded to the lure of the West. A devout admirer of the noble savage (he was himself "at least *semi-indianized*," one reviewer noted with mixed emotions),[33] Catlin attempted a personal verification of the vices and virtues equation—The Noble Savage + Civilization = The Degraded or Bloody Savage—by establishing that the relatively pure Indian was indeed noble, and did manifest many of the fabled primitive virtues. Catlin had a mission in life, to become *the* painter of the uncorrupted Indian, erecting, as he so ingenuously said, "a monument to a dying race, and a monument to myself."[34]

The frontispiece to the first volume of Catlin's *Letters and Notes on the Manners, Customs, and Condition of the North American Indians* (1841) shows an artist dressed in the buckskin garb of the prairie traveler, brush in hand, capturing on canvas the image of an elaborately costumed *beau sauvage*. That painter— Catlin, of course—is a man at work realizing his dearest ambition; his drawing is a study in contentment. As if the illustration alone were not sufficient, Catlin went on to offer a version of his life's mission so compressed and romanticized that it acquired in his telling the aura of a creation myth. Inspired by a delegation of "some ten or fifteen noble and dignified-looking Indians" who were visiting Philadelphia, he remembered, he resolved on "snatching from a hasty oblivion what could be saved for the benefit of posterity," and so embarked for the Far West in 1830, "to extend a helping hand to a dying race."[35] Over the next six years, "with great difficulty, and some hazard to life," he visited forty-eight different tribes and produced an extensive pictorial record (approximately 470 portraits and genre pieces) of native life as lived in the "uncivilized regions of their uninvaded country."[36]

"Uncivilized" and "uninvaded" conveyed a special meaning to Catlin. He divided all American Indians into two categories, the corrupted and the uncorrupted. Of the 2 million Indians alive, he estimated, about 1.4 million were already debased through contact with the white man. It was his task to introduce Americans to the shrinking minority still existing in a "wild and unsophisticated state." People formed their opinions about Indians from a brief exposure to the "drunken, naked and beggared" types encountered on the frontier. "But amongst the wild Indians," he insisted, "there are no beggars—no drunkards—and every man, from a beautiful natural precept, studies to keep his body and mind in such a healthy shape and condition as will at all times enable him to use his weapons in self-defence."[37]

Catlin's mission was not merely personal, but national. The wild Indians were "melting away at the approach of civilization," and if future Americans were to know them, it would only be through the work of artists like himself. This idea had received official endorsement in the 1820s when James Barbour, Secretary of War, and Thomas L. McKenney, who was instrumental in procuring for the War Department an extensive collection of Indian portraits, deemed it their generation's duty to preserve a graphic record of the Indian to meet posterity's inevitable question: *What sort of a being was the red man of America?*[38] Catlin was preparing an answer, for, "phoenix-like, they may rise from the 'stain on a painter's palette,' and live again upon canvas, and stand forth for centuries yet to come, the living monuments of a noble race."[39] His ringing affirmation held cold comfort for the Indians. Like most of his contemporaries, Catlin had written them off in the end.

There is something almost callous about the enthusiasm with which artists and writers went about their self-appointed task of preserving not the Indian, but a *record* of the Indian. The value of that record—in mercenary as well as scientific and aesthetic terms—resided in the fact that it could never be duplicated. Thus, Catlin's father wrote in 1838 that George "mourns the dreadful destiny of the indian tribes by the small pox . . . but unquestionably that shocking calamity will greatly increase the value of his enterprize & his works."[40] That same year in a catalog of his Indian Gallery, Catlin drew attention to a painting of the interior of a Mandan earth lodge:

Reader, the hospitable and friendly Mandans, who were about 2400 in number when I was amongst them and painted these pictures, have recently been destroyed by the small pox. It is a melancholy fact, that only thirty-one are left of the number . . . their tribe is extinct, and they hold nowhere, an existence as a nation, on earth.

Nearly 20 of their portraits can be seen on the walls, and several other paintings of their games and amusements. I have also a vocabulary of their language, and full notes on their manners and customs, which will shortly be published.[41]

Throughout the years that followed, whenever and wherever Catlin promoted his gallery as a unique and irreplaceable record of Indian life, he had to regard his visit to the Mandans and their subsequent sad fate as a stroke of personal good fortune.

The Vanishing American validated Catlin's entire endeavor. His mission to the distant tribes was justified by the degradation of the nearer Indians; its urgency derived from these same Indians, since they established beyond doubt the fate that awaited those who roamed in ignorance far beyond the frontier. At the end of *Letters and Notes on the Manners, Customs, and Condition of the North American Indians* Catlin appended a tabular statement comparing the Indian's character in a "primitive and disabused state" to that which followed on contact with whites. It diagrammed the theory of vices and virtues:

Original	Secondary	Original	Secondary
Handsome	Ugly	Independent	Dependent
Mild	Austere	Grateful	Grateful
Modest	Diffident	Happy	Miserable
Virtuous	Libidinous	Healthy	Sickly
Temperate	Dissipated	Long-lived	Short-lived
Free	Enslaved	Red	Pale-red
Active	Crippled	Sober	Drunken
Affable	Reserved	Wild	Wild
Social	Taciturn	Bold	Timid
Hospitable	Hospitable	Straight	Crooked
Charitable	Charitable	Graceful	Graceless
Religious	Religious	Cleanly	Filthy
Worshipful	Worshipful	Brave	Brave
Credulous	Suspicious	Revengeful	Revengeful
Superstitious	Superstitious	Jealous	Jealous
Warlike	Peaceable	Cruel	Cruel
Proud	Humble	Increasing	Decreasing
Honest	Honest	Faithful	Faithful
Honourable	Honourable	Stout-hearted	Broken-hearted
Ignorant	Conceited	Indolent	Indolent
Vain	Humble	Full-blood	Mixed-blood
Eloquent	Eloquent	Living	Dying
		Rich	Poor
		Landholders	Beggars

So a work whose first volume opened with an image of the artist and the unspoiled Indian closed by equating the noble savage, the fallen savage, and the Vanishing American.[42]

THE LAW OF CIVILIZED PROGRESS

In his day, few men were more tolerant of cultural practices that they could not comprehend than Catlin. And no one was more caught up in the Indians' fate—it made his heart bleed to even think about it. But for all that, he was not about to deny reality. In the Indians' displacement and decline, he too beheld the "grand and irresistible march of civilization." "All this is *certain*," he said: "Man's increase, and the march of human improvements in this New World, are as true and irresistible as the laws of nature."[43] Civilization's advance was awesome and destructive, inevitable and right.

No idea was more uniformly acceptable to Americans of the nineteenth century than universal human progress. It was the rule of life, and Western civilization was its agent. Thus the position of the Indian, as civilization's antithesis, the embodiment of savagery, was fatally compromised. As an essayist put it, "Who will hesitate in deciding the question which shall retire before the other?"[44] Could the Indian be civilized? Was he a hunter out of necessity because he lived in a forest environment, or was he fundamentally different, *intended* by God to be a hunter? Because the Bible said, "Be fruitful and multiply, and fill the earth, and subdue it; and have dominion over the fish of the sea, and over the fowl of the heaven, and over every living thing that moveth upon the earth," people who preferred searching for game to tending flocks and turning over the sod were naturally suspect. Both the Indian and the wilderness would have to be "subdued" and made "fruitful." But the savage's mind, an impenetrable mystery, was closed to change and improvement. Even the threat of extinction could not shake its complacency.

The Indian was confined to a lower state of social development (savagery, savagism, or barbarism, depending on the commentator), and this reality fixed the perimeters for achievement. Edward Everett defended a conventional parallel between the ancient Greeks and the Indians by arguing that both represented degrees of barbarism quite distinct from civilization. Civilization and barbarism "are not themselves different degrees of the same thing," he explained. "There appears to be an essential difference between them, which makes the highest point of barbarism a very different thing from a low degree of civilization."[45] America's first Ph.D. (1817), professor of Greek at Harvard, editor of the *North American Review*, and a man of imposing oratorical skills, Everett was also an influential spokesman for realpolitik. In an article published in 1823, he brought together the main points of the case for civilization's rightful displacement of savagery.

The issue was simple. To establish civilization, the forests which sustained savagery had to be cleared away. Thus, "the very first step to feed and support the newcomers aims at the extinction of the savages." Nothing could be done about this. "The Europeans came; and—by causes as simple and natural, as they are innocent—the barbarous population . . . has been replaced by one much better, much happier." Everett had no patience with those who grew maudlin. The red race perished "by the unavoidable operation of natural causes." Proximity to the white man was invariably fatal. "It is not necessary to exterminate a savage tribe—place the germ of civilization in their soil—and such is its living principle, such the *vis conservatrix* of the arts of civilized life, that it will strike root, shoot up, and spread."[46] And so savagery would be displaced.

Three years earlier, in 1820, Edward Everett and his brother John had counseled against government involvement on the Indian's behalf. If the red man could change from savagery to civilization on his own, well and good; if not, "leave him to the operation of his character and habits; do not resist the order of providence, which is carrying him away, and when he is gone, a civilized man will step into his place."[47] Everett, who as a congressman from Massachusetts more than once displayed an unhappy knack for compromising himself, would have occasion to regret these words in 1830 when, in reply to his damnation of Indian removal, Georgia's Richard H. Wilde read them aloud to the House of Representatives. Everett could only squirm in his seat. A few years later he was back to insisting that it was "obviously the purpose of Providence"—a "moral necessity"—that civilization should displace savagery. Indian life being minimal, their "removal from one tract of country to another is comparatively easy."[48] Because he was the "representative of a *condition*," the Indian could not be saved.

Philosophical generalizations, and the rhetoric in which they were couched, constituted one level of the belief in the Vanishing American; it was also sustained by a series of specifics advanced by students of the Indian problem as the major causes of native decline. Whether these causes were seen as the preordained means to an end, or simply as facts of life, they added up to the same thing. The Indians were dying out.

CHAPTER THREE

THE PATHOLOGY OF THE VANISHING AMERICAN

John Heckewelder, the Moravian missionary whose *Account of the History, Manners, and Customs of the Indian Nations* (1818) served as a principal source for James Fenimore Cooper, wrote of the Mohicans eight years before Cooper would immortalize them as representative Vanishing Americans:

This once great and renowned nation has almost entirely disappeared, as well as the numerous tribes who had descended from them; they have been destroyed by wars, and carried off by the small pox and other disorders, and great numbers have died in consequence of the introduction of spirituous liquors among them. The remainder have fled and removed in separate bodies to different parts, where they now are dispersed or mingled with other nations.[1]

The Mohicans were but one vanished tribe. History confirmed the suspicion that several others had also disappeared, and it was obvious that the destructive principles at work in the past were still operative. In New England, writers chanted the names of tribes long departed like some exotic litany. "We in Massachusetts see the Indians only as a picturesque antiquity," Ralph Waldo Emerson confided to his journal in 1845: "Massachusetts, Shawmut, Samoset, Squantum, Nantasket, Narranganset, Assabet, Musketaquid. But where are the men?"[2]

Things were no better to the south. In his *Notes on the State of Virginia* (1785), Thomas Jefferson had discussed the tribes of the old Powhatan Confederacy and, by correlating a population estimate made by Captain John Smith in 1607 with a count taken by the State Assembly in 1669, determined that in the space of sixty-two years the tribes enumerated had shrunk to one-third their original strength. Another grim litany followed:

Very little can now be discovered of the subsequent history of these tribes severally. The *Chickahominies* . . . attended the treaty of Albany in 1685. This seems to have been the last chapter in their [tribal] history. . . . There remain of the *Mattaponies* three or four men only, and [they] have more negro than Indian blood in them. They have lost their language, have reduced themselves, by voluntary sales, to about fifty acres of land . . . and have from time to time, been joining the Pamunkies. . . . The *Pamunkies* are reduced to about ten or twelve men, tolerably pure from mixture with other colors. . . . Of the *Nottoways*, not a male is left. A few women constitute the remains of that tribe.[3]

Some writers did contend that no tribes had disappeared after the founding of the Republic.[4] Nevertheless, the history of the original colonies, Virginia and Massachusetts, offered a grim prognosis.

Jefferson, despite the evidence he cited, remained cautious. His environmentalism, adhered to with some consistency where the Indian was concerned, would not allow him a theory based on racial predestination. Moreover, in his *Notes* he was at pains to refute the widespread opinion, advanced by Comte Georges Louis Leclerc de Buffon and other European intellectuals, that the New World environment was deleterious to flora, fauna, and men, producing small, sickly specimens of each. Buffon had cited Indian decline in Spanish America as evidence for his theories that the native American was congenitally inferior to the European, and, lacking even the desire to propagate, consequently doomed by a sexual inertia that amounted to racial suicide. Environmentalism could cut both ways, then, and by insisting on the vitality and high aptitude of the North American Indian, Jefferson was forced to deal with the problem of the Vanishing American. He considered it "most probable" that the survivors of many defunct tribes had retired to the west and been absorbed into other tribes. "Different appellations for some of the tribes" would also create the false impression that those once known under a discarded name had disappeared.[5] But, while Jefferson's *Notes* were frequently cited in subsequent examinations of the Indian question, his caveats were seldom remembered, and his population chart, along with other preliminary investigations of the subject, was referred to as proof positive that the Indians had already suffered a marked decrease in population and were still losing ground daily.

The great question, of course, was *why* the Indian should be vanishing, and the reasons given by Jefferson—"spirituous liquors, the small-pox, war, and an abridgement of territory to a people who lived principally on the spontaneous productions of nature"—were scripture to believers in the Vanishing American.

ALCOHOL AND INDIAN DECLINE

"We speak the result of some observation, that wherever the white man comes in contact with the Indian, there the latter is sure to obtain the means of ruinous, and long-continued, and frequent indulgence in drunkenness," an essayist asserted in 1828.[6] And if one discounts D. H. Lawrence's misreading of motives, the formula which he derived from "Old Daddy [Benjamin] Franklin" is psychologically acute: "Rum + Savage = 0."[7] That equation represents a tradition as old as Indian-white contact in North America, and as current as the modern stereotype of the "whiskey Indian."

For the Indians, alcohol brought with it a whole train of destructive consequences—quarrels disruptive of family and social life, the breakdown of traditional moral sanctions, impaired health due to exposure during bouts of drinking, maiming, prostitution, venereal disease, murder, and a lowered birth rate. A Jesuit priest in Canada in 1637 informed his superior that the rising number of deaths among the natives "is attributed to the beverages of brandy and wine, which they love with an utterly unrestrained passion, not for the relish they experience in drinking them, but for the pleasure they find in becoming drunk. . . . As they drink without eating, and in great excess, I can easily believe that the maladies which are daily tending to exterminate them, may in part arise from that."[8] Tribal leaders over the centuries have struggled with the effects of intoxicating liquors on their people, and the phenomenon of Indian alcohol addiction—characterized by a pattern of compulsive or pathological drinking—has inspired an extensive professional literature. In the 1970s, scientists at the Oklahoma Center for Alcohol-Related Research entered a thorny area of controversy by suggesting that Indians might have a genetic intolerance to distilled spirits;[9] two Canadians pointed to the possibility that hypoglycemia, exacerbated by severe stress and nutritional deficiencies, accounts for the Indian's susceptibility to strong drink;[10] while an anthropologist, discounting physiological explanations in favor of the notion of cultural determination, argued that Indian drinking is an assertion of Indianness before an indifferent or hostile world.[11]

In the early nineteenth century, however, Indian drunkenness was explained away as just another of those providential causes operating to clear the path for civilization. "The inordinate indulgence of the Indians in spirituous liquors is one of the most deplorable consequences, which has resulted from their intercourse with civilized men," Lewis Cass wrote in 1827.[12] Governor of Michigan Territory from 1813 to 1831, Secretary of War under Andrew Jackson, Secretary of State under James Buchanan, and himself the unsuccessful Democratic candidate for the presidency in 1848, Cass made his original reputation as a man of action leading an Ohio volunteer regiment and then a regular army brigade against the British in the northwestern theater of the War of 1812. As a self-confessed authority on the American Indian ("I know the Indians thoroughly," he advised George Catlin),[13] Cass was one of those nineteenth-century Americans regarded by their contemporaries as "Indian experts." He exerted weighty influence on the nation's Indian policy, and his views, advanced between 1826 and 1830 in a series of articles in the *North American Review*, were always given an attentive hearing.

Though Cass properly deplored the effects of alcohol on the Indian, he felt that the problem went deeper than strong drink. "Among other nations, civilized and barbarous, excessive ebriety [drunkenness] is an individual characteristic, sometimes indulged and sometimes avoided," he observed. "But the Indians in immediate contact with our settlements, old and young, male and female, the chief and the warrior, all give themselves up to the most brutal intoxication, whenever this mad water can be procured."[14] The Indian's alcoholism was, in effect, biologically induced, his extremely low resistance proof of some racial defect ("a national idiosyncracy," Cass would much later term it).[15]

Drunkenness was, in microcosm, the entire Indian problem: upon contact with the white race, the Indian exchanged his virtues for civilized vices. Against these vices the Indian had no defense. The government, try as it might to staunch the flow of spirits into Indian country, was doomed to failure. The Indian *wanted* liquor. Cass remembered how a venerable chief of the Potawatomies, during the negotiations at the Treaty of Chicago in 1821, begged the commissioners to give his people alcohol, saying, "Father, we care not for the money, nor the land, nor the goods. We want the whiskey. Give us the whiskey."[16] The traders competed to satisfy the Indian's craving. "Little does the spirit of commerce care how many Indians die inebriates, if it can be assured of beaver skins," Henry Schoolcraft, Cass's friend and himself a recognized Indian expert, lamented in 1829.[17] Laws and regulations alone could not stop the flow of liquor into Indian country. The government might as well attempt to arrest the law of civilized progress, for Indian drunkenness was its direct result. Cass did remark that the "revolting scenes" of Indian drunkenness were fortunately "confined to the vicinity of the settlements, where spirituous liquors can be more easily procured."[18] Indians remote from the settlements were still innocent of alcohol. At a time when the government was pondering a general policy of removing the eastern tribes west of the Mississippi, far away from white society, Cass's remarks were of more than casual interest.

DISEASE AND INDIAN DECLINE

Modern authorities who favor a high estimate of pre-Columbian Indian numbers have consistently maintained that "disease in epidemic form" was "the greatest factor in [native] depopulation."[19] If we accept a hemispheric estimate of 50 to 75 million population (such as was advanced by H. J. Spinden at a time when the orthodox figure was 7 to 10 million), or the even higher projection of Henry F. Dobyns of between 90 and 112.5 million, only devastating epidemics, Dobyns has argued, can explain such "tremendous mortality."[20]

Since the Pilgrims arrived to find that a "wasting plague" introduced earlier probably by English traders had nearly wiped out the local native population,[21] Anglo-Saxons were aware of the deadly effects of their own diseases imparted to the New World natives. The devastation they suffered only fortified the suspicion that they were constitutionally inferior or "feeble." Civilization was to advance with a minimum of resistance, and disease was to be its cutting edge. "The vast preparations for the protection of the western frontier are superfluous," an observer wrote in 1838 after smallpox had raged among the western tribes. "Another arm has undertaken the defense of the white inhabitants of the frontier; and the funeral torch, that lights the red man to his dreary grave, has become the auspicious star of the advancing settler, and of the roving trader of the white race."[22]

Smallpox epidemics, occurring among the tribes with increasing frequency as the eighteenth century neared its end, doubtless helped usher in the full-blown theory of the Vanishing American in the second decade of the nineteenth century. With Edward Jenner's discovery in 1797 that a cowpox culture would safely and effectively immunize humans against smallpox, all-out vaccination programs were urged as the Indian's one hope for survival, and became government policy after an epidemic in 1831–1832 decimated the Pawnees and other tribes along the Platte River.[23] The western tribes remained highly suspicious of vaccination, while they were healthy, turning to it only as a last, belated resort. As a consequence a series of epidemics between 1836 and 1840 ravaged tribes along the West Coast from Alaska to California, and swept across the Southwest. A particularly virulent epidemic devastated the Upper Missouri tribes in 1837, nearly annihilating the Mandans before racing upriver as far as the country of the Blackfoot.

Although thousands of Indians in every afflicted area perished, the virtual extinction of the Mandans, a well-known, sedentary people, most profoundly impressed contemporary observers. Both Catlin and Schoolcraft regarded the destruction of the Mandans as symbolic of the Indian's fate. With a measure of foresight, Catlin had paid particular attention to the Mandans on his trip to the West in 1832. With a measure of hindsight (since his letters from the Indian country did not appear in book form until 1841, permitting ample time for selective revision), he observed that they were a "strange, yet kind and hospitable, people, whose fate, like that of all their race is sealed; whose doom is fixed to live just long enough to be imperfectly known, and then to fall before the fell disease or sword of civilizing devastation."[24] Prophecy or not, the remark was unerringly accurate. Schoolcraft, in turn, rated smallpox, "scourge to the aborigines," just below "ardent spirits" as a cause of Indian decline. He recorded incidents arising from the epidemic of 1837, including the attempts to warn other tribes of the danger after the Mandans were infected. The tribe was reduced from 1,600 to 31 souls, Schoolcraft wrote; the Minnetarees, Arickarees, Assiniboines, Crows, and Blackfeet all suffered heavy losses. Granting everything that could be asked on the "score of excitement and exaggeration," he concluded that not fewer than 10,000 Indians (Catlin had suggested 25,000, exclusive of the Mandans) perished of the disease in a matter of weeks. Villages deserted by the fleeing tribes were left inhabited only by a few stray wolves "fattening on the human carcasses that [lay] strewed about."[25]

The government, as Catlin pointed out, had made "repeated efforts" to persuade the western tribes to be vaccinated, but had failed to overcome superstition and suspicion.[26] The epidemic of 1837 also showed that the policy of removal and isolation then under way would prove ineffective in the end. The tribes living west of the Mississippi River, farther from any white settlements than the removed eastern tribes would be, had contracted smallpox from a fur company steamboat. Civilization would not be denied.

WARFARE AND INDIAN DECLINE

Warfare, either interracial or intraracial, was ranked high as a cause of Indian depopulation.

Hostilities between red and white remain a touchy subject since they bring into sharp focus the white man's role as a direct factor in Indian decrease. Contemporary discussions tended to minimize or skirt the issue, creating a historical vacuum that has too often been filled with exaggerated estimates of the number of Indians "massacred" by United States troops in pursuance of the government's "genocidal" Indian policy. The available data will not sustain the charge of wholesale slaughter. One estimate is that, between 1789 and 1898, Indians killed some 7,000 white soldiers and civilians and in turn suffered losses in the area of 4,000 dead—a fraction of one percent of the total number of Indians who lived during this period.[27]

Such figures overlook the disruption and destruction of tribal life itself, however, and the attendant, depressing effects on Indian population caused by persistent military pressure. A recent study of the New England tribes contends that between 1620 and 1750 almost 10,000 Indians perished through warfare with the white man, 2,950 killed outright, 795 dying from wounds in battle; and 6,000 lost through capture, enslavement, famine, exposure, and permanent removals consequent to defeat. If the total depopulation of New England's tribes in this 130-year period amounted to 36,000 Indians (a standard figure, though as suspect, it should be added, as any other estimate), warfare accounted for more than 25 percent of the total, and was a substantial factor in Indian decline.[28]

Indian warfare also meant intertribal conflict. "Their own ceaseless hostilities have, more than any other cause, led to the melancholy depopulation, traces of which are everywhere visible through the unsettled country," Lewis Cass wrote. Twenty years before Lewis and Clark journeyed to the West, for example, there were nine Mandan villages on the Missouri, four of them recently abandoned; by 1805, only three were occupied; and by 1826, one. The Arickarees had suffered a similar reduction.[29] It did not occur to Cass that the introduction of horses and firearms and the crowding together of tribes recoiling from white pressure to the east—conditions which exacerbated the traditional intertribal enmities—were directly linked to civilization's advance. For him, the cause of Indian

warfare, itself a cause of Indian depopulation, could be readily surmised: some "strong exciting" racial principle impelled
"ceaseless hostilities."[30] The cause, then, lay in the Indian's
nature, and predisposed him to self-destruction.

Intertribal warfare also fostered an unfavorable impression
of native character, accentuating its negative attributes: ferocity,
cruelty, a warlike spirit ever ready to be ignited by revenge.
Civilized men made "war without passion";[31] Indians were said
to relish the prospect of battle. "Glory and distinction appear
to be the idols of their hearts," an officer who accompanied
the Yellowstone expedition in 1819 observed.[32] Among the
tribes along the Missouri, he discovered an intricate system of
social ranking based on martial exploits, and he noted that a
young man was not considered ready for marriage until he
had won his first honors in battle. If war was the Indian's
consuming passion, the morality of the white conquest could
be seen in a new light. All the legalistic hairsplitting over Indian
title, for example, was pointless if, as Edward Everett thought,
the natives "hunted and fished in the streams and forests of
this country, merely, by the right of the strongest."[33] The
Indians themselves provided precedent for their displacement
by force of arms.

Intertribal warfare was symptomatic of a larger cause of
Indian decline: traditional tribal enmities. Tribal divisions—
and, also, intertribal factions—often cut deeper than racial
differences, and had been ripe for exploitation since the day
Hernando Cortés found willing allies in the Aztec tributaries
and proceeded to bring Montezuma's empire down. A similar
scenario was repeatedly enacted in North America. King Philip's
defeat, for example, was significantly expedited by "friendly"
Indians who, in serving the Puritans as guides and soldiers, set
a pattern that would persist until the end of the Indian wars
more than two centuries later. Whenever European powers
clashed with the natives or with one another over conflicting
New World ambitions, Indians were sure to be involved—
to their detriment, it always seemed.[34] Divisiveness, rooted in
the very concept of tribalism, fatally compromised the Indian's
ability to resist white advance.

LOSS OF LAND AND INDIAN DECLINE

In the abridgment of Indian territory, suggested by Jefferson as a fourth cause of Indian decrease, American interests were obviously involved. The result was a web of legal and moral complications. Though the Indian's fondness for war might justify a course of military conquest, most Americans preferred to base their case on higher laws: the superior claims of civilization, the Biblical injunction to till the earth and the theory of the Indians' improper usage of the lands they occupied.[35] "The Indian disappears before the white man, simply because he will not work," Albert Gallatin asserted in 1836. "There was nothing to prevent the Indian from reaching the same state of agriculture and population [as the white man], but his own indolence." If the Indians were to be saved, "they must be deeply impressed with the conviction that their ultimate fate depends exclusively on themselves." "Inveterate indolence," then, and not the white man's aggressive expansion, was the real culprit in the Indian's decline.[36]

The contributors to the *North American Review* were relentless in pursuing this line of reasoning. Nathan Hale, for example, pointed out in 1819 that if the Indians' title to occupancy of the soil were to be acknowledged, then their competency to alienate it, and the corresponding right of a civilized nation to acquire it, would have to be conceded. The fact that the tribes were now virtually landless—"they have at last deprived themselves of their homes and country," Hale wrote—did not mean that any "undue advantage was taken of their ignorance and weakness." A superior race who "knew better" than the Indians how to "improve the bounties of providence" had simply displaced an inferior and indolent one. Hale did regret the pressure of American settlers on the remaining Indian land. While the extinction of the red men was inevitable, "this cannot excuse us for pressing upon them with indecent haste. If they must perish, let them die a natural and not a violent death."[37] It was one of those nineteenth-century arguments resting on a belief in the Vanishing American. It drove home the point that the abridgment of territory contributed significantly to aboriginal decline, yet assumed that the fault lay not with the white man who hungered for Indian land, but with the Indian who recklessly misused it.

The issue was best understood as a morality play about virtue (civilization) and vice (savagery). Virtue rested on an agricultural base, vice on a hunting base. To advance, the former had to level the forests on which the latter relied, thereby applying, as Edward Everett pointed out, "the most effectual check" to savagery's increase.[38] The Indian's inability to perceive the necessity of settling down, tending his herds and becoming a happy yeoman, was part of an unmalleable nature riddled with imperfections—a thirst for alcohol, a susceptibility to disease, an addiction to war—that made his disappearance certain. The abridgment of tribal territory was an effect, not a cause, of the Indian's downfall.

Some writers did connect the loss of lands with other causes of Indian depopulation, notably the creation of new wants. As their territory shrank before white encroachment and the game disappeared, the Indians found themselves cut off from their customary sources of food, as well as from the furs needed to buy trade goods, particularly whiskey. Forced to seek more productive hunting grounds, the tribes retreated westward, colliding with other groups, creating new frictions, irritating old ones, and adding a previously unknown desperation to intertribal warfare, which was now fought with the deadlier weapons of civilization's arsenal. "Society has advanced upon them like a many-headed monster, breathing every variety of misery," Washington Irving wrote. "Before it went forth, pestilence, famine, and the sword; and in its train came the slow, but exterminating curse of trade. . . . It has increased their wants, without increasing the means of gratification." Irving imagined the Indians as beggars at the white man's banquet. "The whole wilderness blossoms like a garden, but they feel like the reptiles that infest it."[39]

Irving, the romantic, was supported by hard-headed officialdom. Americans had come to realize that civilization's major attraction for the Indians was materialistic. Indeed, the Indians historically had often chosen alliances on the basis of gifts offered and goods provided in trade by the competing European powers. The British decision following the French and

Indian War to encourage Indian self-sufficiency by abandoning the expensive policy of gift-giving on the northwestern frontier contributed to Pontiac's 1763 rebellion. Trade with the Indians, a colonial official had noted earlier, was "the foundation of their alliance or connexion with us . . . the chief cement which binds us together." Consequently, trade "should undoubtedly be the first principle of our whole system of Indian politics."[40] The neglect of this principle had proven a costly mistake the American government would try to avoid by making certain that regulated trade was the cornerstone of federal Indian policy.

Trade with the white man was an insidious blessing. It created new wants that eventually became necessities and, Lewis Cass argued in 1826, directly led to the Indians' disappearance. Greed for "cloths, guns, and other tempting articles" drove them to hunt not for food, but for the furs and skins with which to purchase white goods. Firearms made the slaughter of game (as it made intertribal warfare) so efficient that the remaining animals were forced to retreat "from the circle of destruction, which advanced with the advancing settlements."[41] The Indians had sacrificed essentials for luxuries to their own detriment. As Benjamin Franklin had stated in his influential "Observations Concerning the Increase of Mankind and the Peopling of Countries" (1751), "Foreign luxuries and needless manufactures, imported and used in a nation, do . . . increase the people of the nation that furnishes them, and diminish the people of the nation that uses them."[42] The Indians proved that this rule applied to uncivilized nations as well.

THE CASE OF THE CHEROKEES

Friends of the Indian, looking for any hopeful evidence to counter the bleak doctrine of racial decay, turned to the semicivilized tribes of the Southeast, particularly the Cherokees. Here was an Indian nation that was progressing steadily toward civilization, prospering and on the increase. The Cherokees were the crucial exception that *disproved* the rule of Indian decline.

But those who had already made up their minds were unimpressed. The Indians were vanishing in accordance with a higher law, and, they maintained, there could be no exceptions. One Virginia gentleman dismissed the claims of the Cherokees' admirers by pronouncing it "a mistake to imagine a nation civilized because it has black cattle, or plants a few potatoes in the weeds, or spins a gross of broaches of very indifferent cotton." Farming, the great panacea for the Indian's ills in nineteenth-century humanitarian thought, had neither civilized the Cherokees nor ensured their perpetuity. If they were to survive, it would be by blending into the white population, losing their color and forgetting all their savage habits. Such would be "the euthanasia of the Cherokees."[43]

Writing thirteen years later, in 1830, with the pressures of the Cherokee question and President Jackson's inflexible stand on a removal policy at a head, Cass was more abrupt and sweeping. The Cherokees were "in a state of helpless and hopeless poverty," all told a "wretched race." In presenting the official figures on Indian population, he noted that precision was both "unattainable" and, since the principal facts were "indisputable," quite "unimportant." "The Indians have gradually decreased since they became first known to the Europeans," he wrote, and "there is no just reason to believe, that any of the tribes, within the whole extent of our boundary, has been increasing in numbers at any period since they have been known to us." So well entrenched was the notion of the Vanishing American that Cass simply dismissed the evidence for Cherokee increase with the remark: "That the Indians have diminished, and are diminishing, is known to all who have directed their attention to the subject."[44]

At the time Cass was writing, acrimonious dispute had engulfed the Cherokees, and his refusal to even consider the possibility of Indian progress appears both partisan and self-interested. Yet he was merely expressing the accepted opinion of his contemporaries. Nothing directly could be done to save the Indians in the East, but they might at least have the opportunity to pass their final years in comfort, far from that civilization which, rapidly bearing down on them, would soon destroy them where they were.

PART TWO

ISOLATION
Indian Policy Before the Civil War

Andrew Jackson to the Creek Nation, March 23, 1829:

Friends and brothers, listen: Where you now are, you and my white children are too near to each other to live in harmony and peace. . . . Beyond the great river Mississippi, where a part of your nation has gone, your father has provided a country large enough for all of you, and he advises you to remove to it. There your white brothers will not trouble you; they will have no claim to the land, and you can live upon it, you and all your children, as long as the grass grows or the water runs, in peace and plenty. It will be yours forever.

Speckled Snake, Creek chief, in reply:

Brothers! I have listened to a great many talks from our great father. But they always began and ended in this—"Get a little further; you are too near me."

—*Niles' Weekly Register*, Vol. XXXVI (June 13, 1829), p. 258; (June 20, 1829), p. 274

CHAPTER FOUR

MAKING GOOD NEIGHBORS:
Segregation in Indian Policy

Until the second half of the nineteenth century, United States Indian policy, in keeping with the British policy that preceded it, was committed to the separation of Indians and whites. Closely regulated contact, officials reasoned, would best secure peaceable relations between the races at a time when the pressure of white settlement was engendering bad feelings and periodic hostilities. "The deep rooted prejudices, and malignity of heart, and conduct, reciprocally entertained and practised on all occasions by the Whites and Savages will ever prevent their being good neighbours," the Secretary of War reported in 1787. Consequently, "either one or the other party must remove to a greater distance, or Government must keep them both in awe by a strong hand, and compel them to be moderate and just."[1] To some extent the government's posture would be that of a referee. The "cherished object" of federal Indian policy remained constant: the civilization and "ultimate incorporation" of the Indians into the body politic.[2] But during the Republic's first century, segregation of the races was the rule in practice.

By the 1820s, when white expansion carried settlers to the banks of the Mississippi River, the existing intercourse laws had proved ineffective. Isolation of the Indians east of the river was no longer possible. Yet, as everyone knew, unless the Indians were isolated from civilization and its vices they would in short order be destroyed. "Experience has clearly demon-

47

strated that independent savage communities can not long exist within the limits of a civilized population," President James Monroe remarked. "Pressed . . . on every side by the white population," their government and morals would soon crumble since the change would be "too rapid to admit their improvement in civilization."[3]

Conflicting proposals were offered to resolve the dilemma. Some advocated an intensive civilizing program as a form of shock therapy for what was probably a terminal patient anyway; others, a strict noninterference in tribal affairs. The result was vacillation. Henry Schoolcraft, who had wide experience among the northwestern tribes, complained in 1828 that Indian legislation "is only taken up on a pinch. It is a mere expedient to get along with the subject. . . . Nobody knows really what to do." By the next decade, the old system of separation had emerged triumphant under a new guise, and Schoolcraft noted with satisfaction in 1838 that "it is now evident to all, that the salvation of these interesting relics of Oriental races lies in colonization west. . . . Public sentiment has settled on that ground; sound policy dictates it; and the most enlarged philanthropy for the Indian race perceives its best hopes in the measure." Segregation would remain the keynote of federal policy.[4]

THE CONCEPT OF INDIAN COUNTRY

At the heart of the American government's regulatory policy was the concept inherited from the British of Indian country, a shrinking area of land conceded to the natives for purposes of occupancy. With Pontiac's rebellion as an object lesson, the initial guidelines had been set down in the Royal Proclamation of 1763, which reserved for the exclusive "use" of the Indians "all the land and territories lying to the westward of the sources of the rivers which fall into the sea from the west and northwest," with certain specified exceptions. The proclamation also stipulated that in the future only the imperial government could negotiate for or acquire Indian lands, though any British subject would be permitted to trade with the Indians after obtaining a license. It was not the Crown's intention to make the Appalachian watershed a permanent barrier to white advancement westward. The proclamation simply established the fact that the Indians were not to be "molested or disturbed" in the possession of their western hunting grounds. Once stability had been restored, the Crown would seek through treaty and purchase to define a more exact—and, for white interests, more favorable—boundary line. By 1768 temporary connecting boundary lines had been drawn the length of the western frontier, a formal attempt to separate the races and rationalize the process of frontier advance.

In the year of American independence, John Dickinson's draft of the Articles of Confederation made provision for regulating the Indian trade and honoring the existing boundaries. But these provisions were not adopted in the version of the articles finally ratified in 1781. The Confederation government was left to construct its Indian policy on a piecemeal basis. The idea of a boundary was supplemented by a British proposal to create an Indian barrier or buffer state in the Northwest between the United States and British North America. Nevertheless, the Northwest Ordinance, enacted by Congress in 1787, was silent on both the boundary line and the barrier state. It was scrupulous in its regard for Indian rights, pledging the government's "utmost good faith" in all dealings with the natives: "In their property, rights, and liberty, they shall never be disturbed, unless in just and lawful wars . . . ; but laws founded in justice and humanity, shall from time to time be made for preventing wrongs being done to them, and for preserving peace and friendship with them." In the new Constitution even then being drafted in Philadelphia, however, the Indian was mentioned only twice. Article I, Section 3, of the Constitution provided that "Indians not taxed" be excluded from the census count for purposes of apportioning representatives and taxes among the states. Article I, Section 8, stipulated that Congress would have the power "to regulate commerce with foreign nations, and among the several States, and with the Indian tribes."[5]

It was a significant juxtaposition that found the Indians following "foreign nations" and "the several States" in this clause, for the status of the tribes, as contemporaries liked to point out, occupied an anomalous middle ground. Were the tribes independent nations, each one to be dealt with by treaty, or "domestic dependent nations," analogous to yet different from the states? The treaty system, a carryover from the colonial administration, remained in effect until 1871, when it, and the "legal fiction" of tribal autonomy, were ended by congressional fiat. In turn, the concept of a separate Indian state surfaced periodically, notably during the peace negotiations after the War of 1812 when the British ministers demanded as a *sine qua non* to further discussions the creation of a permanent Indian buffer state between Canada and the United States.[6] By 1878, however, with mounting opposition to the establishment of an Indian territory in the area of present-day Oklahoma, the idea had run its course.[7]

The constitutional provision for regulating the Indian trade— an explicit admission of its significance in official thinking— was embodied in a series of Trade and Intercourse Acts passed between 1790 and 1834. The first, to apply for two years only, dealt with the licensing of traders, the sale of Indian lands, and the punishment of crimes committed in Indian country by non-Indians. In effect, it served to set aside an area of Indian country, to protect it from intrusion and, by segregating the Indians, to preserve peace along the frontier. The government's regulatory function was underscored in the legislation that followed in 1793 (no white settlement permitted on Indian lands), in 1796 (a detailed definition of Indian country), in 1799 and in 1802 (the first permanent Trade and Intercourse Act, by which the President was empowered to act "from time to time" to stem the liquor traffic in Indian country). These legislative acts provided the foundation for American Indian law, reflecting a rather passive and noncommittal approach.[8]

INDIAN CIVILIZATION AND THE ACT OF 1819

One of the subordinate purposes of the Trade and Intercourse Acts was the promotion of civilization and education among the Indians. Even within the framework of a separatist policy, the higher values of a Christian society were to be fostered by transforming the wandering hunter into a sedentary farmer, thereby teaching the primacy of private property. The seeming contradiction between method and putative goal—segregation in the present, assimilation in the future—was satisfactorily resolved by the theory of the Vanishing American. In the long run, the Secretary of War observed in 1792, the natives would have to accept "the blessings of civilization, as the best means of perpetuating them on the earth."[9] But civilization was most deadly to the Indians when they had had no opportunity to build up an immunity to its vices through a gradual exposure to its virtues. Past efforts to elevate the Indians had floundered because they did not recognize this fundamental principle. The Indians were "called upon to take one bold stride from the savage to the civilized state," a writer observed in 1816. "They could not advance by a slow progression; and they were utterly incapable of going over the ground in any other way."[10]

Accepting the need for an intermediate step between savagery and civilization, the Baptist missionary Isaac McCoy began in 1823 to advocate the removal of the eastern Indians to a colony west of Missouri, the land to be provided by the federal government and each Indian to receive title to an individual plot or, in legal parlance, an allotment in severalty. Thus would segregation and civilization be reconciled. McCoy's scheme eventually assumed grandiose proportions—a permanent state composed of educated, Christian Indians, with himself its spiritual and temporal ruler as superintendent. The core idea of isolating progressive Indians from their regressive or resistant brethren and from the representatives of white civilization as it manifested itself on the border was as old as the "praying towns" founded by John Eliot in Massachusetts nearly two centuries before. But McCoy's dream, of Christian Indian communities in the West—halfway houses for the fully assimilated Indians of the future—had a special relevance in the 1820s since it corresponded to the government's evolving policy, justified on humanitarian as well as practical grounds, of removing the eastern tribes beyond the Mississippi.[11]

Other philanthropists and missionaries saw isolation as a temporary measure that afforded no permanent solution to the Indian problem. The Indians' future could be assured only by introducing them at once to civilization. If they had the capacity for improvement, they could improve where they were. Since the beginning of the century, Protestant missionaries had been experimenting with the establishment of "model Zions"—small settlements or stations in the wilderness where Indian children would be congregated, free from the contaminating influences of home and instructed in Christian values through daily exposure to education and industry.[12] The manual-labor boarding school would eventually entrench itself as the primary instrument in Indian education.

Practical endeavors of this sort were always welcome and, some argued, worthy of federal support. Late in 1818, for example, a memorial to Congress reported the success of the Society of Friends in weaning the natives from their savage ways by sending "persons of exemplary habits" to reside among them and teach them, by example, the skills of agriculture and milling.[13] *Niles' Weekly Register* was greatly impressed by the Quaker endeavor. Although critics might say "that we have no right to legislate for the civil or moral government of the Indians," *Niles'* said, the "urgency of the occasion" justified "such laws as may be *honestly* established and faithfully administered, for their own benefit." The editorial concluded by calling for a "code of laws calculated to accomplish the purposes hinted at."[14]

President Monroe, in his annual message for 1818, remarked that to civilize the Indians, "and even to prevent their extinction," it was "indispensable that their independence as communities should cease, and that the control of the United States over them should be complete and undisputed." He called on Congress to adopt "some benevolent provisions,"[15] and on March 3, 1819, signed into law a bill providing for "the civilization of the Indian tribes adjoining the frontier settlements." It appropriated the sum of $10,000 annually for the employment of "capable persons of good moral character" to instruct the Indians in agriculture and to teach their children reading, writing, and arithmetic. Although the act was a modest measure, it marked the beginning of formal government involvement in tribal internal affairs. It entailed a long-term commitment, and thus stands as a landmark in American Indian legislation.[16]

While the missionary societies were initially slow to take advantage of the new act, Jedidiah Morse, a representative of the Northern Missionary Society of New York, and an early applicant for a grant from the civilization fund, enthusiastically endorsed the government's initiative. The public's eyes, he wrote, "are directed, as they sh[oul]d be, to the Government to take the lead in . . . [Indian civilization]—to form the plan, & to propose the measures & means for its accomplishment, & I fully believe they are ready, to a great extent, vigorously to co-operate." In 1820 Morse obtained federal support for a personal tour of the neighboring tribes, undertaken "to acquire a more accurate knowledge of their actual condition, and to devise the most suitable plan to advance their civilization and happiness."[17] In his report to the Secretary of War, completed in 1822, Morse warned that the certain fate of the frontier Indians would be "miserably to waste away for a few generations, and then to become extinct forever . . . unless we change our policy towards them; unless effectual measures be taken to bring them over this awful gulf, to the solid and safe ground of civilization."[18] The government had moved in the right direction in 1819, and it was imperative that it not stop now.

THE FACTORY SYSTEM

The Indian civilization act went against the grain of those who opposed the extension of federal authority into areas outside its stipulated jurisdiction as a violation of both constitutional and laissez-faire principles. They urged Congress to refrain from trying to preserve the Indians, and allow the laws of nature to take their course. The Vanishing American was invoked to explain why the government should not attempt to prevent the Indian from vanishing. It would be an exercise in futility. Any hope would lie in the efforts of dedicated missionaries trained in the practical arts and willing to impart them as a prelude to conversion. It was not the business of government to meddle.[19]

Obviously, to the extent that the regulatory provisions of the Trade and Intercourse Acts protected the natives from harmful contact with the white man and retarded their decline, the government was already involved on their behalf. For example, the government denied liquor (one of the "most unrelenting and most murderous" of the "plagues" bringing "blight" and "mildew" on the red race)[20] to the Indians in Indian country. Although American fur companies complained that the ban on liquor gave a decided advantage to their less scrupulous British and independent rivals in the Indian trade, the government was adamant. Federal actions also affected the Indians in other ways. Many treaties negotiated by the government in this period attempted to establish boundaries between the tribes in the hope of ending internecine warfare. The stringent regulation of contact between white and red lessened the likelihood of border warfare with the settlers, checked the spread of social diseases among the tribes, and might help prevent epidemics. President Jefferson's instructions to Meriwether Lewis included the sentence: "Carry with you some matter of the kine-pox; inform . . . [the Indians] with whom you may be, of it's [sic] efficacy as a preservative from the smallpox; & instruct & encourage them in the use of it."[21] Yet for all these partial initiatives, deep-seated resistance to specific programs of Indian improvement remained.

The Indian trade offered an acceptable area for experimentation in governmental efforts at benevolent control. Years before, Benjamin Franklin had urged that Indian friendship be cultivated by carefully managed commerce. "Publick trading houses would certainly have a good effect towards regulating the private trade, and preventing the impositions of the private traders," he wrote in 1751, "and therefore such should be established in suitable places all along the frontiers."[22] Franklin's advice was taken belatedly with the passage of an act in 1795 establishing trading posts or factories throughout Indian country to offer the natives an attractive array of quality goods at cost.[23] The factory system was a nonprofit venture, but it was not charity. It put the national interest first, and frankly sacrificed private interests in the process. Contented Indians in the present would mean generous land cessions in the future. The natives in the Northwest and Southwest had gravitated to the British and Spanish spheres; they would have to be won over to the American side if the frontiers were ever to be made safe.

Of the twenty-eight government trading posts, some thrived, but the system could never escape the charge that in purposely underselling private traders in order, as Jefferson said, to "drive them from the competition,"[24] the government was trampling on free enterprise. Since the War of 1812 established that the Indians felt no obligation to fight for those from whom they bought, the theory behind the factory system was discredited, and private fur traders lobbied all the more strenuously to abolish it. If they were to offset the British trade advantage among the northwestern tribes, they would have to be allowed to compete freely. In the Southwest, waning Spanish strength and the defeat of the Indians had eliminated the need for government conciliation of the tribes through trade.[25] The factory system had outlived its usefulness. Charges of corruption and mismanagement against the Superintendent of Indian Trade administered the *coup de grâce*. The factory system was terminated under fire in 1822.

Two years later, a resolution was before the House of Representatives inquiring into the "expediency of repealing" the 1819 civilization act. In response, the Committee on Indian Affairs prepared a report recommending its continuance. Indian civilization was a "work of great national importance":

Such is their condition, at present, that they must be civilized or exterminated; no other alternative exists. He must be worse than a savage, who can view, with cold indifference, an exterminating policy. All desire their prosperity, and wish to see them brought within the pale of civilization.[26]

The act was saved, but the committee's opinion on the Indian's future did not carry the day. One week after the report was made, President Monroe proposed that it would "promote essentially the security and happiness of the tribes within our limits if they could be prevailed on to retire west and north of our States and Territories on lands to be procured for them . . . in exchange for those on which they now reside."[27]

CHAPTER FIVE

A MAGNANIMOUS ACT OF INTERPOSITION: Indian Removal

Thomas Jefferson's hope that the tribes would willingly become farmers and amalgamate with the white population, thus releasing wilderness tracts to white settlement, had floundered on the rock of Indian resistance and was dashed by the War of 1812. But Jefferson had devised an alternative plan. In an 1803 draft of a possible amendment to the Constitution, written in anticipation of the acquisition of Louisiana Territory, he proposed to grant Congress the power "to exchange the right of occupancy in portions [of Louisiana] where the U.S. have full right for lands possessed by Indians within the U.S. on the East side of the Mississippi."[1] Meriwether Lewis, who was assigned to test the feasibility of such an exchange for the President, endorsed it as a policy "of primary importance to the future prosperity of the Union."[2]

The Louisiana Purchase would secure the nation's agrarian destiny. At the same time, setting the area off as the exclusive province of Indians and fur traders, thus "condensing instead of scattering our population," would allay the fear that expansion was stretching republican institutions perilously thin.[3] The removal scheme complemented Jefferson's vision of a string of sister republics friendly to the United States running from sea to sea. And it would alleviate the embarrassment of 1802 when the federal government, in exchange for Georgia's western lands, bound itself by compact to extinguish existing Indian title in the state, despite the "solemn guarantees" previously made to the indigenous tribes. With both motivation and opportunity at hand, a removal policy was outlined in the Louisiana Territorial Act of 1804. But such a grandiose scheme was premature—the Cherokees, for example, solidified their "sense of national identity" in opposing it[4]—and removal was dropped on the official level, though scattered voluntary emigrations from the Southeast and the Northwest were negotiated with growing frequency after the War of 1812.

THE GEORGIA-CHEROKEE CONTROVERSY

The situation in Georgia that first gave impetus to Jefferson's removal plan became increasingly irksome in the decades that followed. The government was disinclined to act on the 1802 compact, and Georgia grew restive. Which solemn promise would the government see fit to honor? The promise to the Indians had been made first, but the issue was Indian rights versus state rights.

The Georgia question was further complicated by the fact that the Creeks and Cherokees were, by contemporary standards, highly advanced, and the Cherokees, especially, constantly acclaimed as the model of a civilized Indian nation. If the commitment to civilizing the Indian was serious, the promise to the Cherokees would have to be honored.

Despite setbacks suffered in the 1790s, the Cherokees had entered the nineteenth century politically divided but endowed with sophisticated leaders and capable of pulling together to resist white pressures to assimilate or to remove. Possessors of fifteen million acres, they had abandoned the chase and adopted an agricultural mode of life. They were rich in livestock and slaves. Many dressed in whites' attire, and some wrote and spoke fluent English. Christianity had made satisfactory progress among them. Their educational, judicial, and legislative systems were often praised. After 1821, they even had an eighty-five-symbol syllabary of their own, and in 1828 began publication of the *Cherokee Phoenix*, a newspaper printed in New Echota, Georgia, capital city of the Cherokee Nation. But every enthusiastic report on Cherokee progress elicited a dour rebuttal from white spokesmen. Progress applied to a mere handful of shrewd half-breeds, they insisted. It had not touched the great mass of pure-blood Cherokees who, exploited by their leaders, were more ignorant and degraded than the average frontier Indian.[5]

By the 1820s the civilization of the Cherokees and the other southeastern tribes, far from being a source of white congratulation, obviously presented an obstacle to expansionist ambitions. The Cherokees, recognizing that their land was essential to their nationhood, in 1819 made the death penalty the punishment for any unauthorized cession to the American government. Through the 1820s they were united in the defense of their homeland, and thus a formidable foe since they had acquired a handsome measure of civilization's own cunning and were prepared to fight their dispossession with delaying tactics and an arsenal of legal weapons far more effective than bows and arrows.

The challenge before the Cherokees was clear. The administration of James Monroe had revived the removal scheme in 1817. Removal would simultaneously advance the nation's progress westward, "which the rights of nature demand and nothing can prevent," and its duty "to make new efforts for the preservation, improvement, and civilization of the native inhabitants," Monroe explained. It would resolve the conflicting interests of all three parties to the Georgia dispute by satisfying the Georgians, saving the Indians, and rescuing the federal government from its predicament. Although Monroe considered emigration to be in the Indians' best interest, he abjured the use of force as "revolting to humanity and entirely unjustifiable."[6] In one of the last acts of his second administration, "breathing," a critic would say, "the language of the purest benevolence,"[7] Monroe charged Congress with the task of providing for the removal of the tribes.

The Senate passed a removal bill on February 23, 1825, but the House failed to concur. President John Quincy Adams was less enthusiastic than Monroe about the emigration policy. A New England realist cut from the same cloth as Edward Everett, he had never sentimentalized Indians; he remained a hard-liner on the subject of aboriginal title, but he was a scrupulous legalist: the government's promises to the Indian must be honored. Nothing less than the nation's credibility was at stake. Under Adams, the push for Indian removal was temporarily stymied.

But in 1827 the Cherokees confounded some defenders and infuriated Georgians by drafting a constitution modeled on that of the United States, making them an independent nation with sovereignty over territory in Georgia, North Carolina, Tennessee, and Alabama. The Georgia legislature responded with a series of measures circumscribing Indian rights within its borders. Because the issue coincided with the mounting excitement over states' rights occasioned by the tariff controversy in South Carolina, it was explosive. Georgia asserted its sovereign power to legislate on all matters under its jurisdiction and, buoyed by the belief that the government had reneged on the 1802 compact, dared federal authorities to uphold Cherokee claims to independence from state law. Faced with Georgia's defiance, the grave nature of the states' rights issue, and the fact that the case, for all the emotion it engendered, was "prejudged," Adams grudgingly endorsed voluntary removal as the only practical course open to the Indians.[8]

In 1829 the Georgia-Cherokee controversy reached a head with the inauguration of Andrew Jackson as President and the discovery of gold inside Cherokee territory. The Georgia legislature, encouraged by Jackson's evident sympathy with its proposition,[9] announced its intention to place the Cherokee lands under state jurisdiction effective June 1, 1830. Although the Cherokees fought back, Jackson had been urging the southeastern tribes to emigrate, and his position was clear. Those that would not remove "must be subject" to state laws.[10]

In his first annual message, Jackson proposed that an "ample district west of the Mississippi, and without the limits of any State or Territory," be set aside for those Indians who agreed to emigrate. There the government would guarantee their right of occupancy. They would be taught the arts of civilization, and could raise up "an interesting commonwealth, destined to perpetuate the race and to attest the humanity and justice of this Government."[11] Congress was requested once again to implement a removal policy.

ANDREW JACKSON AND THE CASE FOR REMOVAL

Andrew Jackson was one of the most persuasive spokesmen for the viewpoint that only removal could save the Indians from racial extinction. He relished the role of Great White Father, Michael Rogin has argued,[12] and set himself up as the true friend and protector of his red children, acting in their best interests when they could not perceive them. "The fate of the Mohegan, the Narragansett, and the Delaware is fast overtaking the Choctaw, the Cherokee, and the Creek," he warned Congress in 1829. It was incumbent on the American government to do something to forestall this calamity. "Humanity and national honor" demanded as much. Immediate incorporation had been tried to no avail. The law of vices and virtues had blasted the natives, while the government, professing a desire to improve them, had "lost no opportunity to purchase their lands and thrust them farther into the wilderness."[13]

Jackson proposed *first* to thrust the Indians into the wilderness, and *then* to reclaim them in their isolation. It would be "an act of *seeming* violence," an appreciative supporter wrote in congratulation. "But it will prove in the end an act of enlarged philanthropy. These untutored sons of the Forest, cannot exist in a state of Independence, in the vicinity of the white man. If they will persist in remaining where they are, they may begin to dig their graves and prepare to die."[14]

There is something appealing in the image of Andy Jackson, rough-hewn frontier democrat, champion of the common man, hero of the battles of New Orleans and Horseshoe Bend, assuming the presidency with a western vigor and disregarding the legalisms and nice distinctions that had mired his Atlantic-seaboard predecessors in uncertainty. Here was a fit companion to Davy Crockett, willing to act boldly on the principle Be sure you are right, then go ahead. From a different perspective, Jackson was merely the descendant of Nathaniel Bacon and the Paxton Boys, a prototypical westerner who had no regard for Indian rights.

Of course, Jackson was not the actual architect of general removal. The venerable concept of a separate Indian country provided the policy's foundation, and a humanitarian rationale was its cornerstone. In his seminal message of 1825, President Monroe had summed up this rationale concisely when he said that removal "would not only shield . . . [the Indians] from impending ruin, but promote their welfare and happiness." Were they to remain in the East, their "degradation and extermination" would be inevitable; but were they to emigrate westward, they would be saved, and in time become a "civilized people." This was the "powerful consideration" which Americans could offer the Indians as an inducement to relinquish their lands. It was, Monroe thought, a consideration of "sufficient force to surmount all their prejudices in favor of the soil of their nativity, however strong they may be."[15]

This gift of civilization—the ultimate gift, to the whites' way of thinking—had its drawbacks. It always seemed to please the donor more than the recipient. Defenders of slavery in the nineteenth century habitually suggested that civilization was more than fair compensation for the Negroes' labor. Even in servitude, their condition was superior to that of free Negroes in barbarous Africa. So, too, the Indians' fabled freedom was illusory. Only the civilized Christian could be free. In exchange for their lands, the Indians would be given the opportunity to become civilized, and space, by serving as a buffer between the tribes and white society, would ensure them the time needed to make the adjustment.

Because of the popular acceptance of the theory of the Vanishing American, the humanitarian argument for removal was not easily refuted. Jackson's plea for support was directed to those most likely to oppose the measure:

May we not hope . . . that all good citizens, and none more zealously than those who think the Indians oppressed by subjection to the laws of the States, will unite in attempting to open the eyes of those children of the forest to their true condition, and by a speedy removal to relieve them from all the evils, real or imaginary, present or prospective, with which they may be supposed to be threatened.[16]

CONVERTS TO REMOVAL: LEWIS CASS, JAMES BARBOUR, THOMAS L. MCKENNEY

Some influential citizens, like Lewis Cass, were stirred from a lethargic acceptance of the status quo in Indian affairs to become active advocates of removal. Others, like James Barbour, who had vacillated between assimilation and segregation, were won over to the emigrationist viewpoint. Most impressively, a few, Thomas L. McKenney among them, who had been committed to the immediate civilization and incorporation of the Indians, renounced that position and avowed the necessity of colonization in the West.

Long before he became an Administration spokesman as Jackson's Secretary of War, Lewis Cass had inclined toward removal but cautioned against its immediate adoption on the pragmatic grounds of Indian resistance, and in 1826 professed to find the "whole subject . . . involved in great doubt and difficulty." He could only advise perseverance in the existing regulatory policy. "It is better to do nothing, than to hazard the risk of increasing . . . [the Indians'] misery."[7] As late as February 1828, a congressman referred his colleagues to Cass's *North American Review* articles for "an unanswerable array of facts and arguments against this plan of Indian colonization."[18] When in January 1830 Cass announced his conviction that removal was the "only means of preserving the Indians from that utter extinction which threatens them," he did not contradict his earlier opinions. He continued to maintain that the Indians had never yet managed to become civilized, but he now attributed their failure—and their subsequent decline—to the fact that no change could occur "so long as they occupy their present situation." Removal was the obvious answer. By the time civilization again surrounded the Indians, either they would have advanced sufficiently to coexist with whites "without danger to them and without pain to us," or they would have "yielded to their fate" and disappeared. In the meantime, the Indians were perishing where they were, and "speedy and entire removal" was essential if even a "remnant of this race" was to be saved.[19]

Cass was a born realist, and his conversion to removal was characteristic. Barbour and McKenney, however, were a different matter. Both had been committed to the civilization of the Indian *in situ*, and Barbour, as Secretary of War, listened with dismay to Secretary of State Henry Clay's opinions, advanced during a cabinet meeting late in 1825, that the Indian was by nature incapable of civilization, "essentially inferior to the Anglo-Saxon," "rapidly disappearing," and "destined to extinction" probably within fifty years.[20] President Adams, who recorded the discussion in his diary, feared that Clay's prediction was all too plausible, and began to press for voluntary removal rather than the assimilation policy still favored by Barbour, who had long held that the Indian tribes were sovereign nations before the law, "without any legislative superior, though we claim a right of regulating their trade, and a kind of pre-emptive right of purchasing their lands."[21]

In a report prepared for the House Committee on Indian Affairs in February 1826, Barbour expressed his personal qualms about removal. Removal would contradict everything the government had stood for, and undo everything done in the past to encourage the Indians' early civilization. "They have been persuaded to abandon the chase—to locate themselves, and become cultivators of the soil—implements of husbandry, and domestic animals, have been presented them. . . ." Yet when the Indians did as told, Barbour charged, "*you* send *your* Agent to tell them they must surrender their country to the white man, and re-commit themselves to some new desert, and substitute as the means of their subsistence the precarious chase for the certainty of cultivation." In the accompanying bill, which he had drafted at the committee's request, Barbour supported individual—in contradistinction to tribal— removals on a strictly voluntary basis, eventual allotment in severalty in order to secure inviolable title to the new lands, and establishment of a territorial government in the West for the colonized tribes. Nothing was to be done without the Indians' "own consent." Only in this way could the policy be made palatable. "I am cheered with the hope, that much good may be effected with comparatively little injury," Barbour commented. "Our difficulties in their present form, will be diminished, or entirely removed."[22] It was the perfect Freudian slip.

James Barbour's halfway covenant with removal represented a compromise; Thomas L. McKenney's conversion to the policy was a startling about-face. As Superintendent of Indian Trade under the old factory system, and head of the amorphous

Office of Indian Affairs from 1824 to 1830, McKenney was intimate with all aspects of Indian affairs. "His knowledge of the Indian character, and of our Indian relations in general, is not surpassed by any other individual in this nation," a Congressman declared in 1828.[23] In his time, McKenney was known as one of the Indians' warmest friends. He brought a Choctaw boy into his home and raised him as his own son while Superintendent of Indian Trade. In the face of skepticism and ridicule, he was unwavering in his affirmation of the Indian's capacity for improvement, and, as head of the Office of Indian Trade, had devoted an inordinate amount of time to humanitarian work, even to the neglect of the primary duties of his office. McKenney believed education was the key to civilizing the Indian, and he actively encouraged missionary activity among the tribes, awaiting the day when they would "constitute a portion of 'our great American family of freemen.'"[24]

Nevertheless, in the summer of 1827, while on a tour among the tribes of the South (including the Cherokees, whom he had considered "a civilized people" two years before),[25] McKenney experienced a "sudden change" in his "opinion and . . . hopes."[26] In his report for 1828 he recommended withdrawing the Indians to a new area where they might get a fresh start, safe from civilization.[27] The timing was suspiciously fortuitous. McKenney had managed to hold office under three previous Presidents, Madison, Monroe, and Adams. He survived under Jackson as well. His sincere interest in Indian welfare was incontestable, but when opinion drifted strongly in the direction of removal, McKenney, who was chronically short of funds and dependent on his government salary, shifted with it, provided that any removal be entirely voluntary. He clung to this requirement to justify his defection from the ranks of the assimilationists. By 1830 the Jackson Administration viewed his insistence on choice as obstructionist, and this was a factor in his dismissal from office.

Though McKenney would be at pains to distinguish between the noncoercive Indian colonization plan he had endorsed and Jackson's policy, the fact remains that he was implicated in how removal worked out in practice. He had put his reputation on the line, and drawing on the goodwill built up over the years, urged his fellow reformers to follow him to removal's promised land. In a widely circulated address to the Indian Board, for the Emigration, Preservation, and Improvement of the Aborigines of America—a New York City society he was instrumental in founding in 1829 as a means of countering the anti-removal propaganda of the American Board of Commissioners for Foreign Missions and other religious bodies—McKenney dismissed the possibility of the Indians' becoming civilized in the East and elaborated on the reasons for his own change of mind. "We once . . . thought it practicable to preserve and elevate the character of our Indians, even in their present anomalous relations to the States; but it was 'distance that lent this enchantment to the view,'" he said. "We have since seen for ourselves, and that which before looked like a flying cloud, we found, on a near inspection, to be an impassable mountain. . . . If the Indians do not emigrate, and fly the causes, which are fixed in themselves, and which have proved so destructive in the past, they *must perish!*"[28]

THE CASE AGAINST REMOVAL

Despite the prominent defectors from their ranks, many champions of Indian rights were unmoved by the arguments for emigration. They saw in removal just another device to break solemn treaties and to pry land from the Indians. Men like Edward Everett and John Quincy Adams stressed the inviolability of the government's legal obligations to the Indians, and, though both suffered the humiliation of having their own tough words on the relative merits of civilization and savagery turned against them during the removal debates, they stood firm. Other opponents of removal were more concerned with the Indians' salvation, racial and spiritual, and it was left to them to controvert the humanitarian rationale behind the emigration policy. But because they themselves shared at least partially in the premise of the Vanishing American, they were reduced to insisting that the southern tribes were the exceptions proving that the rule of decay need not be universal.

The anti-removal case was simple. Once the savage had survived the critical period of adjustment to civilization, he was out of mortal danger and could advance without jeopardy. The tribes in the South were *prima facie* evidence that it was not impossible for Indians to take these crucial first steps. Removal was deplorable because it was directed at the very peoples who, in showing that Indians *could* coexist with white men, proved the policy unnecessary.

Out West, Indians who had made the difficult transition from hunting to farming would be tempted to abandon the plow, take up the bow and arrow again, and resume a roaming existence. Men who had advanced in the civilized arts would be put in close contact with their wild brethren. Even if they resisted the inducements to revert to old ways, they would almost certainly be forced to fight the indigenous tribes in order to reestablish an agricultural-pastoral life. Moreover, as Edward Everett told Congress in 1830, "if the lands to which you remove them are what you describe them to be, you may as well push back the tide in the Bay of Fundy, as keep out the white population." The territory west of the Mississippi that was offered the Indians in exchange for their own would not be "a permanent home," but a "mere holding-place—a half-way house on the road to the desert."[29] If, on the other hand, as some claimed from personal knowledge, the western lands were as barren and unattractive as the region they bordered— the "Great American Desert"—then, while their title might indeed be secure from white cupidity, the Indians would never succeed as farmers.[30]

Either way, "another removal" would "soon be necessary," Jeremiah Evarts, corresponding secretary of the American Board of Commissioners for Foreign Missions, argued in the last in a series of influential essays that he wrote for the *National Intelligencer* under the pseudonym William Penn. For, "if the emigrants become poor, and are transformed into vagabonds, it will be evidence enough, that no benevolent treatment can save them, and it will be said they may as well be driven beyond the Rocky Mountains at once. If they live comfortably, it will prove, that five times as many white people might live comfortably in their places."[31] It was as though an already delicate, even precarious experiment was being deliberately jeopardized by the introduction of a new and complex set of variables.

Confronted with the Vanishing American, the anti-removal

forces could only reiterate the principle that no emigration take place without the willing consent of the Indians involved. The tribes affected must be presented with a choice between two equal alternatives: to go West, with title to the lands in the new location guaranteed; or to remain where they were, again with all property and civil rights protected by the government. "If the Indians remove to better their condition, it is manifest that their removal should be voluntary," Evarts insisted.[32]

But even the argument for voluntary removal was undermined by the belief in the Vanishing American. A Tennessee congressman likened the Indians who refused to move to a man about to commit suicide by taking "a slow poison, which must, ere long, destroy him":

Shall we not act with the same caution toward these children of the forest that we would with the miserable suicide? Is it our duty to consult their will in such a matter? . . . These poor beings are incapable of understanding their own true interest, or choosing what will be most for their benefit. Let us act for them. . . .[33]

What did the anti-removal spokesmen have to offer in reply? Peleg Sprague, a Whig senator from Maine, argued that if the Indians' existence "cannot be preserved" and "it is the doom of Providence, that they must perish," at least "let it be in the course of nature; not by the hand of violence. If in truth they are now in the decrepitude of age, let us permit them to live out all their days, and die in peace; not bring down their gray hairs in blood, to a foreign grave."[34]

Removal, in contrast, was a dynamic and potentially positive policy, embracing, as one advocate insisted, a "salutary principle" that was "sufficiently potent to check the tendencies to decay and dissolution."[35] If it failed in the end to civilize the Indians, it would at least shelter them from immediate danger. Lewis Cass, in his first report as Secretary of War, put the Indians' options into a proper Jacksonian perspective: "If they remain, they must decline and eventually disappear. . . . If they remove, they may be comfortably established, and their moral and physical condition meliorated. It is certainly better for them to meet the difficulties of removal, with the probability of an adequate and final reward, than, yielding to their constitutional apathy, to sit still and perish."[36]

THE REMOVAL ACT AND INDIAN POLICY IN THE 1830s

Just two months after Daniel Webster, recognizing the explosive states' rights issue embodied in the South Carolina tariff controversy, delivered an emotional plea for "Liberty *and* Union, now and forever, one and inseparable," the Senate began consideration of the removal bill. Another sectional dispute was at boiling point.

A report from the Committee on Indian Affairs recommending the removal policy had come before the Senate on February 22, 1830, and a bill enacting the committee's recommendations on April 6. It passed on April 24. During debate, the opponents of Indian emigration sought to extract the teeth from the removal bill by obtaining a guarantee that the rights of the Indians would be protected should they decide not to move westward. Such efforts were fruitless. On the day of the bill's passage, the Senate rejected two proposed amendments. The Senate bill was before the House of Representatives on April 26, and though the final vote was close, the measure passed without substantial modification on May 26. That same day, the Senate, again ignoring protests, approved the amended version, and two days later President Jackson signed into law "an act to provide for an exchange of lands with the Indians residing in any of the States or Territories, and for their removal West of the river Mississippi."[37]

The removal act testified, section by section, to the fact that the government had made the Indians' decision for them. The only hint of an alternative to removal was the statement that land west of the Mississippi was to be "divided into a suitable number of Districts, for the reception of such tribes or nations of Indians as may choose to exchange the lands where they now reside, and remove there." The silence about this "choice" was lost in the barrage of rhetoric on the protection of Indian rights *after* removal had been completed. The President was to assure the tribes that the United States would "forever secure and guaranty to them, and their heirs or successors, the country so exchanged with them." Indians who agreed to remove were to be compensated for all improvements on their personal property, aided and assisted in the actual emigration and resettlement, and "protected, at their new residence, against all interruption or disturbance" by other Indians and whites. For those who remained behind, there were no promises. The states themselves would have to decide how best to interpret their rights and ameliorate their condition.[38] Removal was the ultimate means to an established end. Along with four other measures passed in the 1830s, it constituted a functioning isolationist policy.

In 1832 Congress issued a general prohibition against the introduction of liquor into Indian country—a restriction that, in one form or other, remained in force until 1953—and formally created the post of Commissioner of Indian Affairs. It was an act of lasting consequence. The commissioner was charged with "the management of all Indian Affairs"—a crucial phrase since, as one expert on Indian law pointed out in 1953, "little by little 'the management of all Indian Affairs [of the federal government]' has come to be read as 'the management of all the affairs of Indians,'" and, backed by more than 2,200 regulations, the commissioner's powers have grown awesome.[39]

On June 30, 1834, two more important Indian acts were signed into law. One, heavily influenced by Lewis Cass, then serving as Secretary of War, provided for the organization of what would be known as the Bureau of Indian Affairs, giving a legal basis to an office that had existed for a decade under the War Department's aegis but without statutory authority. The other was a comprehensive revision of the Indian Trade and Intercourse Act of 1802. "Indian country" was redefined as that area to which the Indian title was yet unextinguished outside the boundary of any existing state or territory. Other procedures relating to the licensing of traders, the liquor traffic, and crimes committed by non-Indians in Indian country were modified. The fourth major piece of legislation, passed on January 9, 1837, regulated the disposition of proceeds from the sale of Indian lands ceded to the government by treaty, and provided one means of funding the Indian Service.

The system of Indian isolation was compromised at the outset when a third bill introduced in 1834, organizing the Western Territory to provide a government for the colonized Indians, was rejected by Congress. Territorial status, with a delegate to represent Indian interests, would have given the tribes real protection against further encroachment on their lands. McKenney, for one, urged the creation of an Indian territory, with title in fee simple, as the only feasible plan "for the protection, preservation, and future well-being of the remnants of this ill-fated race."[40]

But this was to assume that the removed Indians had a future. When Jared Sparks, as editor of the *North American Review*, read the pro-removal essay submitted by Cass in October 1829, he confessed himself persuaded. Removal *was* the answer. But, Sparks continued candidly, "After all, this project only defers the fate of the Indians. In half a century their condition beyond the Mississippi will be just what it now is on this side. Their extinction is inevitable."[41] The very clause in the removal act promising emigrant tribes that the United States would "forever secure and guaranty to them, and their heirs or successors, the country so exchanged" included a standard proviso that implied more than legal precaution: "*Provided always*, That said lands shall revert to the United States if the Indians become extinct, or abandon the same."[42]

THE VANISHING AMERICAN AS RATIONALE FOR REMOVAL

"It is impossible to destroy men with more respect for the laws of humanity," Alexis de Tocqueville concluded after an examination of United States Indian policy in the 1830s.[43] The bitterness of his observation reflected first-hand knowledge of the removal process, of last-ditch resistance and needless suffering, of a callous obsession with economy rather than human values—an astonishing parsimoniousness on the part of the federal government in view of the real estate bonanza it was reaping—of, in short, a succession of "trails of tears" created by the massive dislocation of thousands of America's native peoples. De Tocqueville's understanding penetrated to the ambivalence at the core of Indian policy. Noble motives always seemed to serve opportunistic ends.

By the terms of the removal policy, unassimilable Indians would be transported to a remote sanctuary where they might live on, while white settlers would acquire the lands left vacant. The conviction that the Indians were doomto to die if they remained where they were gave removal its humanitarian veneer. William Lumpkin of Georgia piously decried the efforts of some congressional colleagues "to defeat the best and most reasonable plans which can be devised for the salvation of the poor, perishing, and afflicted aborigines of this country."[44] A congressman from Florida echoed Lumpkin's concern: "They are rapidly melting away—no one can deny this—and the question is, how is this doom to be averted?"[45] Removal was the answer—as fast and as far away as possible from the constituencies represented by the two gentlemen.

The Cherokees, in waging their paper war against removal, recognized that they were dealing with an unquestioning acceptance ("no one can deny this") of the concept of the Vanishing American. "It is frequently said that the Indians are given up to destruction; that it is the will of heaven that they should become extinct, and give way to the whiteman," the *Cherokee Phoenix* protested in 1829. Cherokee progress refuted such a contention. Rather,

the causes which have operated to exterminate the Indian tribes, that are produced as instances of the certain doom of the whole aboriginal family . . . did not exist in the Indians themselves nor in the will of Heaven, nor simply in the intercourse of Indians with civilized man; but they were precisely such causes as are now attempted by the state of Georgia; by infringing upon their rights; by disorganizing them, and circumscribing their limits.

White injustice, not inevitable destiny, made the red man droop "like the fading flower before the noon day sun."[46] The belief in the Vanishing Indian was the ultimate cause of the Indian's vanishing.

EXPANSION AND THE RESERVATION SYSTEM

Removal was a solution geared to the Jacksonian predilection for isolating society's misfits—the poor, the criminal, the insane—in order to reform them, as well as to what Daniel Boorstin has called the "vagueness of the land."[47] As long as the American West was Louisiana Territory, and as long as that territory remained the province mainly of fur trappers and Indians, conditions were suitable for isolationism. But in

1818, seven years before Missouri's Thomas Hart Benton delivered his famous peroration in the Senate calling for the erection of a "statue of the fabled god, Terminus" on the ridge of the Rocky Mountains marking an absolute limit to American expansion,[48] an essay in *Niles' Weekly Register* had argued that there could be no permanent barrier to western expansion short of the Pacific.[49] The Great American Desert would be crossed, Benton's "convenient, natural, and everlasting boundary" of the Rockies would be surmounted. In the 1830s George Catlin could still wander around the far western "fairy-land" and dream of a permanent wilderness reserve where the Indians and the buffalo might live wild and free, but his fantasy, like the whole mirage of isolation as a long-term solution, evaporated before the expansionist energies of the next decade.[50]

A term like "manifest destiny" scarcely does justice to the magnitude of what happened in the 1840s. Emigrant traffic on the overland trail to Oregon had been brisk after 1842, and the burgeoning American population in the Pacific Northwest enabled the government to end joint occupation with Great Britain and negotiate a favorable treaty dividing Oregon along the forty-ninth parallel. A month before the Senate ratified the Oregon Treaty, in June 1846, the United States declared war on Mexico. The result was an overwhelming victory that reconfirmed the annexation of Texas and added a huge area of western land to the Republic. The Mormon exodus to their New Zion in the Great Salt Lake Basin, a movement away from the United States when it began in 1846, had become part of the process of the settlement of the American interior as a result of the Mexican cession; while the ill-starred Donner party, which spent the winter of 1846–1847 snowbound in the Sierras, denoted the trickle of immigration into California that would swell into a flood in 1849 when the full impact of the discovery of gold in the former Mexican territory registered nationally. Twenty-four years after he advocated raising a statue of Terminus on the crest of the Rockies, Senator Benton capped the decade of the 1840s by proposing the construction of a railroad from the Mississippi to the Pacific shore.

Americans were understandably dazzled by what they had accomplished in a few short years. Some were also understandably alarmed. In the course of realizing its manifest destiny, the United States had been profoundly changed. Traditional concerns about the dangers of spreading republican institutions over an unmanageably large area were dwarfed by the more pressing issue of slavery expansion into the newly acquired western territories, a controversy that helped precipitate the Civil War.

Western expansion naturally had a direct bearing on Indian relations as well. In his report for 1846 the Commissioner of Indian Affairs noted "the increasing importance of that remote but interesting country" to the west, and subsequent developments suggested he was right.[51] For one thing, the territory added to the Union in the 1840s created an extensive interior and a series of administrative headaches with which the existing bureaucratic structure was unequipped to deal. Consequently, Congress in 1849 established a new executive department, the Department of the Interior, charged, among other duties, with the management of Indian affairs. The transfer of the Indian Bureau from the War Department led to some grumbling in the Senate, but a future Secretary of War, Jefferson Davis, framed the reply that would serve proponents of civilian jurisdiction over Indian affairs for the next three decades. In the past, Davis declared, Indians were best left under the watchful eye of the War Department. Now, "happily for them, honorably for us, the case has greatly changed, and is, I hope, before a distant day, to assume a character consonant with the relations of guardian and ward, which have been claimed by us as those existing between our Government and the Indian tribes."[52]

Americans at mid-century were aware that western expansion had fatally compromised the isolationist policy. "The whites can no longer be kept out of the Indian country," the chairman of the House Committee on Indian Affairs reported in 1853. "The plains and prairies to the Rocky mountains have nearly ceased to echo the lowing of the buffalo; the crack of the emigrant's whip, the merry jest and joyous laugh of the Caucasian man, now ring through the vast wilderness."[53] But what was to be done with the Indians?

The government had been concerned enough about this question to take an unusual step in 1847 when, after ten years of intermittent lobbying on his part, it granted Henry Schoolcraft $5,000 to "collect and digest such statistics and materials as may illustrate the history, the present condition, and future prospects of the Indian tribes of the United States."[54] Schoolcraft, a geologist, mineralogist, and explorer long active in Indian affairs, launched into his project without delay. It eventually cost the government some $100,000 and took a decade to "complete." The six massive volumes published between 1851 and 1857—praised more for their bulk than their content, and undoubtedly more looked at (they were beautifully printed and illustrated) than read—were untidy compilations of Indian miscellanea flawed by Schoolcraft's own enthusiastically eclectic approach to ethnology. Their great shortcoming was a failure to fulfill the promise to provide expert guidance "to enable government to perform its high and sacred duties of protection and guardianship" over the native tribes.[55] Indian affairs in the 1850s were in a period of transition, and Schoolcraft was left with no accurate guideposts to follow. He recognized the need to "meet and solve the problem of Indian colonization . . . and not let action creep up on us as a mere contingency," but he could not shake the conviction that colonization was still the best policy. So, with a crisis at hand, he fell back on the familiar, recommended that "other colonies of refuge" be established for the "weak, flying, and perishing tribes," and, due to "the limitation of the work," simply omitted the crucial section that was to have crowned the final volume: "Indian Policy and the Indian Future."[56]

Schoolcraft's failure was symptomatic of a national one. Americans were quick to perceive that new circumstances had altered their relationship with the natives, but were unable to develop a far-reaching policy based on this perception. "On the general subject of the civilization of the Indians, many and diversified opinions have been put forth; but, unfortunately, like the race to which they relate, they are too wild to be of much utility," the Commissioner of Indian Affairs complained in 1851. "The great question, How shall the Indians be civilized? yet remains without a satisfactory answer."[57]

One of the contributors to Schoolcraft's work, the Reverend David Lowry, a missionary among the Winnebagos, closely anticipated the direction of post–Civil War Indian reform.

Writing in 1848, he dismissed removal as bad policy on both practical and philanthropic grounds. It was plain to him that settlement west of the Mississippi would "soon meet the tide rolling eastward from the Pacific." Consequently, future removals would be impossible, while the tribes that had already been relocated out West were foredoomed, the victims of a misguided benevolence based on the erroneous assumption that the Indian was "born to be a hunter" and could not be improved. "That Indian children, at a very early period, receive impressions in favor of this mode of living, I admit," Lowry wrote, "but these impressions result from example—they are not *innate.*" Having rejected its underlying premise, Lowry was free to dismiss the Vanishing American as a dangerous fallacy. It had "found its way to the bench of the Supreme Court . . . and to our halls of legislation, and prevented the enactment of good and salutary laws." Just keep the Indian where he was; surround him with positive influences and force him to become "a tiller of the soil," and in short order "the superstitious savage" would emerge "an enlightened man and a Christian."[58]

Lowry was not alone in urging the government to abandon its traditional policy of isolating the Indians. "A temporizing system can no longer be pursued," the Secretary of the Interior conceded in 1851. "The policy of removal, except under peculiar circumstances, must necessarily be abandoned; and the only alternatives left are, to civilize or exterminate them. We must adopt one or the other."[59] But the government was opting for more of the same. Indian segregation would be continued, in a modified form: instead of a solid area of Indian country west of the frontier line there would be a series of small Indian countries scattered across the West, each under federal jurisdiction and the provisions of the Trade and Intercourse Acts. Thus while continental expansion made a shambles of the concept of a separate Indian country, the reservation system, rather than a program for Indian assimilation, emerged as the official "alternative to extinction," the only means of saving "our colonized tribes from being injuriously pressed upon, if not eventually overrun and exterminated, before they are sufficiently advanced in civilization . . . to be able to maintain themselves in close proximity with, or in the midst of, a white population."[60]

Reservations were a natural consequence of the government's reluctance to go beyond isolationism. Removal had failed to protect what the government could not—the sanctity of Indian title—while the events of 1846 left no doubt that a barrier as artificial as Indian country would not long withstand the pressures of white expansion. As early as 1848 government officials were agitating for a corridor through Indian country to permit settlers access to the Far West, a mere passageway. But it meant that Indian country in the traditional sense of a barrier state was finished. It meant additional removals. And it meant, finally, that the generations of undisturbed peace promised the tribes in exchange for their eastern lands— generations in which to work out their own destiny at their own pace—would be, in truth, a precious few years.

The reservation system had won support in government circles by the late 1840s. It was not, however, fully implemented until 1853. The turbulent circumstances of California's early years under the American flag led to an appalling destruction of its native population. Reservations were the solution for Indians trapped within the borders of a sovereign state swarming with whites and with nowhere else to go (Oregon, New Mexico, and Utah Territories having indicated their adamant opposition to any removals north or east). Eighteen treaties negotiated in 1851 set aside large tracts of land in California as reservations for the exclusive use of the Indians, but all were rejected by the Senate. The next year, the state's Superintendent of Indian Affairs proposed a system of small "military reservations" where the tribes would be invited to assemble for protection and to acquire the rudiments of civilization. Subsequently, Congress authorized the creation of five such reservations in California. No treaties were involved; the Indians were in effect guests of the federal government. But the reservation idea had taken hold, and by 1863, with a few large reservations substituted for many small ones, it was regarded as "the fixed policy of the government."[61]

RACE AS AN AMERICAN FACT

The persistence of isolationism as a guiding principle in Indian policy long after it had outworn its usefulness suggests that it fulfilled certain psychological needs among whites that ran deeper than mere expediency. For the Indian problem was not the only racial question to cause Americans anguish in the first half of the nineteenth century.

Schemes for colonizing Negro freedmen in Africa or the West Indies had proliferated in the last decades of the eighteenth century. Then, with the Louisiana Purchase, attention was redirected westward. But the War of 1812 exposed an expansionist zeal that squelched the hope of colonizing manumitted slaves in the West even as it dispelled the lingering faith in the Indians' early incorporation into American society and propelled the country toward a policy of removal. Nine days after President Jackson called on Congress to enact a measure providing for Indian removal across the Mississippi in order "to preserve this much-injured race,"[62] Henry Clay told the Frankfort (Kentucky) African Colonization Society that the area west of the Rocky Mountains was unsuitable for its purposes because it would soon be engulfed by the onrushing "wave of the European race."[63] Blacks would find no shelter in the American interior; they would have to be returned to their African homeland. For the freedman and the Indian, then, segregation remained a white objective through the middle of the nineteenth century, the one to be separated by an ocean, the other by a river.

The inability to cope with the permanent fact of a triracial (or multiracial) America, the persistent dream of a white man's country miraculously freed from the curse of race, constituted a nineteenth-century American tragedy. The Civil War, to borrow Arthur Schlesinger's arresting image, was the act of violence that finally broke a logjam in the nation's affairs.[64] It abruptly ended the practice of human slavery on American soil and opened the way to a possible new era in race relations. But old habits of thought persisted, outliving the institution of slavery. The Civil War did serve, however, as a dividing line between dominant philosophies in Indian affairs. Before 1860, segregation was still the rule; after 1865, assimilation was increasingly the order of the day.

The Vanishing American had defied the prophecies of the past. Whites had shed their rhetorical tears in vain. The Indian's continued presence was a fact that could not be evaded. One had to explain it, then act on it, shaping a policy in accordance with its implications. Geography could no longer offer an escape. As a consequence, the United States in the 1870s and 1880s, reluctant heir to a legacy of social activism and racial egalitarianism, was left to deal with the unprecedented problem of the Non-vanishing American.

PART THREE

THE NON-VANISHING AMERICAN

. . . the extinction of the Indian race is not, from the nature of things, an inevitable necessity. It can be preserved.

—"Our Indian Tribes," *Boston Review*, Vol. II (September 1862), p. 523

. . . the belief that the Indian belonged to a doomed race, and that he was incapable of civilization, was so prevalent and so firmly intrenched in the minds of our people as to make them palliate national injustice as the inevitable adjunct of a conclusion that was unavoidable.

—Herbert Welsh, "The Indian Question Past and Present," *New England Magazine*, N.S., Vol. III (October 1890), p. 261

CHAPTER SIX

RED, WHITE, AND BLACK

Emancipation, David Donald once argued, was the killer of the abolitionists' dream.[1] Caught up in the momentous events of their day, they enjoyed an unaccustomed celebrity, and, patricians for the most part, assumed a leadership role that satisfied a personal need for social consequence. The means to an end became an end in itself. Then suddenly it was all over. With emancipation, Donald contended, the abolitionists no longer had a purpose. In fact, many abolitionists were deeply engaged in the freedman's cause after the Civil War—particularly the passage and ratification of the Fourteenth and Fifteenth Amendments.[2] Still, organized abolitionism was a dead letter by 1870. No comparable reform movement emerged to take its place.

Certain elements of abolitionist thought carried over to Indian affairs, and certain abolitionists became involved in the campaign for Indian policy reform. The *National Anti-Slavery Standard* in 1869 asserted that "the Indian question is not any more difficult than the slavery question, and it is not very different from it,"[3] and other veterans of the crusade against slavery joined Wendell Phillips in the mid-1870s in warning that "except for the negro, no race will lift up at the judgment seat such accusing hands against this nation as the Indian will."[4]

Nevertheless, the Indian and Negro "problems," even for those who defined them as such, were never really analogous. Before the Civil War, missionaries to the slave-owning civilized tribes in the South consistently maintained that their evangelical duty to convert the heathen took precedence over other

81

considerations, and they averted their eyes from what their northern brethren regarded as the moral abomination of slavery. Once the Indian had been made into a good Christian, his imperfections—including slaveholding—could be corrected. Abolitionism was not the missionaries' concern: "The temporal good of alleviating slavery was ephemeral; the spiritual good of saving souls was eternal."[5] Once one accepted that slavery was an abomination, the solution was self-evident: end it. The simplicity of the abolitionist goal of emancipation finally overcame disagreements and inconsistencies among those who pursued it, uniting them in a single, commanding purpose. The Indian problem, in contrast, was incredibly complex. Indignation and moral fervor were lost in a maze of contradictory proposals. Different tribes meant different problems to different people. In such a muddled situation, the abolitionist experience was of qualified usefulness. Goodwill was not enough.

THE THEORY OF DISTINCT RACIAL TYPES

One neglected explanation for the difficulty of melding activity on the Negro's behalf with Indian reform is that the black man and the red man, apart from their shared experience as outcasts in a white man's country, had always been regarded as antipodes in racial character. They presented a study in contrast that had achieved sharp definition by mid-century in a theory that endowed the concept of the Vanishing American with its harshest meaning ever. The "American school" of ethnology, chiefly inspired by Samuel George Morton's *Crania Americana; or, a Comparative View of the Skulls of Various Aboriginal Nations of North and South America* (1839), was dedicated to a theory of polygenesis or multiple creations, and the consequent permanent inequality of the various types of mankind, who were endowed by their Creator with certain unalienable traits. Morton's work argued that the skull conformations of the human types had been constant over the millennia, pointing to the unavoidable conclusion that present differences between the types had existed since the Creation. The so-called varieties of man were actually separate species. The Caucasian type stood highest on the ladder of merit; the Negro was permanently restricted to the bottom rung.

In freeing the study of race from the shackles of religious orthodoxy, the American school performed a service to science in the United States. But, from the earliest, tentative conclusions of Morton to the most uninformed generalizations of his disciples, polygenesis was necessarily directed to another end equally antagonistic to pure science: the defense of the South's "peculiar institution."[6] The American school's most representative work, *Types of Mankind; or, Ethnological Researches*, by J. C. Nott, a medical doctor resident in Mobile, Alabama, and George R. Gliddon, a well-known lecture-circuit Egyptologist, appeared in 1854.

Types of Mankind was conceived as a monument to the memory of Morton, who had died three years before. The section written by Nott, in particular, was a summation of the American school's tenets. He deftly disposed of the question of man's origins in a few sentences, contending that the observable differences among the human types could only be accounted for by original differences—that is, by independent creations. The "inherent love of primitive locality" and the "instinctive dislike" and "repugnance" entertained toward foreign lands and peoples demonstrated the "fixedness of the unhistoric types of men." The American Indians illustrated this point. Even with destruction staring them in the face, they had resisted the government's attempts to remove them to an area of comparative safety. Their unreasonable attachment to a specific locale also demonstrated the limitations of their native intellect, the seat of their inability to become civilized. "It is as clear as the sun at noon-day, the last of these Red men will be numbered with the dead," Nott asserted. "To one who has lived among American Indians, it is in vain to talk of civilizing them. You might as well attempt to change the nature of the buffalo."[7]

Writers in the 1820s, having located the causes of the Indian's decline in his savage nature, and having declared that decline a law of the universe, nevertheless were unable to abandon the Christian precept of the brotherhood of man and went on to propose plans for the Indian's improvement. By the tenets of the new science, however, that inconsistency was resolved. A lower race could not be raised to the level of a higher one for the excellent reason that it was not environment but biology that permanently separated the two. A frankly racist argument now accounted for the Vanishing Indian. Americans who were pleased to learn from science that God had actually created a species of black men for the express purpose of serving as their slaves found no difficulty in understanding that He had also created the Indian, "this sketch in red crayons of a rudimental manhood[,] to keep the continent from being a blank until the true lord of creation should come to claim it."[8]

Southerners unbothered by the heretical implications of polygenesis could find much to admire in the American school's teachings. Some westerners, too, recognized the convenience of the doctrine of separate creations, though older rationales for displacing the savage would serve just as well. But the appeal of the theory of hyman types did not rest on its immediate usefulness, nor was the appeal sectionally limited. Dr. Morton, after all, was a respected physician in Philadelphia. Louis Agassiz, professor of natural history at Harvard, was a convert, and it was one of Massachusetts' distinguished sons, Oliver Wendell Holmes, who likened the Indian to a red crayon sketch. Even that Boston Brahmin, Francis Parkman, readily embraced the premise of innate racial differences.

Parkman prepared himself for his life's work of recording the history of the French and English in North America by going west in 1846 "to see the Indians, glean their traditions, and study their character for the benefit of 'Pontiac,'" the biography he was then contemplating. Parkman searched for those "true Simon pure" Indians,[9] those "living representatives of the 'stone age,'" who would afford him an insight into "the Indian character"—a character he believed to be shared by all the natives "north of the Mexican territories." He spent six months on the Oregon Trail, one with a camp of Oglala Sioux, and concluded that the Indian was a "thorough" savage ruled by uncontrollable passions, especially vengeance; a braggart and liar; a stoic; a man of limited mental range; childlike and capricious; yet, withal, beautiful in physique and possessed of a martial ardor that saved him from "lethargy and utter abasement." Indian independence, Parkman believed, was encouraged from childhood by a laxity of parental supervision and discipline, resulting in "that wild idea of liberty and utter intolerance of restraint which lie at the foundation of the Indian character."

In the end, frustrated in his attempt to further penetrate the Indian mind, Parkman decided that "an impassable gulf lies between . . . [a civilized white man] and his red brethren. Nay, so alien to himself do they appear, that, after breathing the air of the prairie for a few months or weeks, he begins to look upon them as a troublesome and dangerous species of wild beasts."[10]

Parkman's assessment of his Oglala hosts served him for a lifetime in his literary endeavors.[11] Since the Indian was a distinctive racial type, one *could* serve for all. Parkman's contemporaries agreed. Romantic racialists, to use George Fredrickson's term,[12] they assumed the variant types of mankind to be different in character and often turned to comparisons to emphasize the salient features of each. Morton himself made the conventional distinction between red and black. "It must be borne in mind that the Indian is incapable of servitude, and that his spirit sunk at once in captivity, and with it his physical energy," he wrote, while "the more pliant Negro, yielding to his fate, and accommodating himself to his condition, bore his heavy burthen with comparative ease."[13] The Indian could live only in freedom, the Negro, only in slavery. In slavery, then, there was hope for the Negro; for the Indian, given the law of civilized progress, there was none. *DeBow's Review*, an influential vehicle for the teachings of the American school, explained to its readers in 1854:

It is otherwise with the negro than with the Indian. The former, in the state of slavery for which he is created, under the favoring care of a superior race, cannot be civilized or made a white man by any length of culture, but his condition can be ameliorated, and he indirectly enjoy the benefits of civilization. But the stern, proud Indian cannot be enslaved. The type of the savage beasts among whom he lives, like them he will disappear before the new tide of human life now rolling from the East, and with the buffalo, will have vanished the red man of America.[14]

The French visitor Alexis de Tocqueville had said it all before

when he commented, "The servility of one dooms him to
slavery, the pride of the other to death."[15]

Freed blacks would perish because of a racial inability to
withstand the competitive stresses of the capitalist system. Only
Negro slaves would live on—and only as long as they remained
slaves. As for the Indians, there was no hope at all. Free and
independent by nature, they were doomed by their own best
qualities. This idea of dark races magically melting away before
the white man when they no longer served his purposes is
immensely suggestive. "One might say that the European is to
the other races of man what man in general is to the rest of
animate nature," de Tocqueville noted in the journal he kept
during his American tour. "When he cannot bend them to his
use or make them indirectly serve his well-being, he destroys
them and makes them vanish little by little in front of him."[16]
Whites valued blacks as slave labor; once freed, they were no
longer useful and so were denied a future.

Shortly after the Civil War, James A. Garfield candidly
confessed that he "would be glad" if the former slaves "could
be colonized, sent to heaven, or got rid of in any decent way."[17]
The wish was father to the thought: in the opinion of some
postbellum racial theorists, the freedmen *were* declining in
numbers according to prediction, and one could speak confidently of the "vanishing Negro." Since what the white man
wanted of the Indian was his land, not his labor, theories about
his racial destiny had a different cast. The native would have
to disappear to free the land for the settler, and the idea of the
Vanishing American owed much of its popularity to this simple
realization. As long as the Indians held what the whites coveted,
it was convenient to believe that God intended their extinction; after they had surrendered their most desirable lands, it
was equally easy to assume that they were now disappearing
through a natural absorption. Either way, they were doomed
as a distinct racial type. Thus would Negroes and Indians no
longer of use to the whites "vanish little by little."

FREDERICK DOUGLASS AND HENRY HIGHLAND GARNET ON
BLACKS AND INDIANS

White Americans could not be blamed because their wishes

and God's will coincided so nicely. Indeed, partial corroboration could be found in the most unlikely quarter, the writings of two prominent black abolitionists, Frederick Douglass and Henry Highland Garnet, who made revealing contributions to the discussion of racial destiny at mid-century.

Nettled by the demeaning comparison commonly drawn between their own race and the Indian, both men urged southern slaves to rebel. *"Rather die freemen than live to be slaves,"* Garnet counseled in 1843.[18] At the same time, anxious to silence the agitation for African colonization, both men accepted the conventional distinction between red and black, but interpreted its significance differently. In contrast to the Indian race, which was daily wasting away, "the history of the Negro race proves them to be wonderfully adapted to all countries, all climates, and all conditions," Douglass told an audience at Western Reserve College in 1854:

> Their tenacity of life, their powers of endurance, their malleable toughness, would almost imply especial interposition on their behalf. The ten thousand horrors of slavery, striking hard upon the sensitive soul, have bruised, and battered, and stung, but have not killed. The poor bondman lifts a smiling face above the surface of a sea of agonies, *hoping on, hoping ever*. His tawny brother, the Indian, dies, under the flashing glance of the Anglo Saxon. *Not* so the Negro: civilization cannot kill him. He accepts it—becomes a part of it.[19]

Garnet had made substantially the same point six years earlier by conjuring up the familiar image of the Vanishing American. "The Red men of North America are retreating from the approach of the white man," he advised his listeners. "They have fallen like trees on the ground in which they first took root, and on the soil which their foliage once shaded. But the Colored race, although they have been transplanted in a foreign land, have clung to and grown with their oppressors, as the wild ivy entwines around the trees of the forest, nor can they be torn thence."[20]

The adoption of such tactics, however understandable, was self-defeating. If the Negro thereby gained a rung on the Indian, the white man was still perched on top of the racial ladder. The important distinction had never been that between the Indian and the Negro, but that between the Anglo-Saxon and all others.[21] Later, embittered by the realization that though the black man might be a permanent entity therein, America would remain a white man's country, Douglass passively and Garnet actively revised their views on Negro colonization.[22] It was tacit admission that there was no escaping racial stereotypes at home.

RACIAL STEREOTYPES IN THE POPULAR CULTURE

A content analysis by Morton Cronin of 543 Currier and Ives lithographs issued between 1835 and 1902 showed some interesting tendencies. Of the thirty prints dealing with the Negro that he examined, twenty-three were humorous depictions of the follies and pretensions of the comic "darky"; of the thirty-two Indian prints, only two were meant to be funny, and neither at the expense of the Indian. "The Indian," Cronin concluded, "was recognized as a dignified human being, with a legitimate life of his own, to a far greater extent than was the Negro. Above all, he was taken seriously."[23]

The checkered careers of red and black in popular music, poetry, theater, and fiction corroborate Cronin's findings. Certainly the graphic arts alone provide ample evidence of the extent to which the contrasting images of the two races won general acceptance. It was a case of the banjo-eyed, ear-to-ear-grinning "colored boy" hitching post versus the stern, sharp-featured cigar-store Indian, his celebrated stoicism rendered, as it should be, in wood. These antithetical stereotypes persisted. Negroes made good subjects because they were "natural born humorists," a how-to manual advised aspiring cartoonists in 1928. They say "side-splitting things with no apparent intention of being funny," and are easily caricatured by their "love of loud clothes, watermelon, chicken, crap-shooting, fear of ghosts, etc." The best that could be said for the red man as a cartoon subject was that "even the stoical Indian is not without his humorous side."[24]

When the Indian was used for comic effect, the joke usually involved a play on names (Sitting Bull, for example, became Recumbent Bison)[25] or firewater and its lurid effects on "nature's child." In 1890 Currier and Ives issued a typical two-part gag. In the first print, a tenderfoot and a scout are shown nipping from a jug, oblivious to the five warriors creeping up on them; in the sequel, they are tied together ("Aw!, I dont want to hunt Injuns anymore, I want to go home!" the tenderfoot bawls) while four whooping braves, waving their weapons in the air and draining the last drops from the jug, prance around them. In the original sketch the fifth Indian lay sprawled on the ground in a drunken stupor, but he was deleted from the finished print.[26] The Indian, always dangerous, was never to be sneered at.

Even as Indian barbarism was being systematically eliminated on the North American continent, the Indian served as an honored symbol for the United States, while the Negro, with few exceptions, remained an object of contempt. He deserved to be a slave, the argument went, because he had acquiesced in a condition no self-respecting white would endure for a moment. "He came as the basest of criminals—he came as a slave; for submission to slavery is a crime even more heinous than the crime of murder; more odious than the guilt of incest; more abominable than the sin of devil-worship," Hinton Rowan Helper wrote shortly after the Civil War. A notorious racist, Helper was nevertheless expressing a commonplace when he accused the Negro of being "so bestial and so base as to prefer life to liberty."[27] Some whites at mid-century professed to find much to admire in the blacks' meek, uncomplaining nature. "Of a singularly docile species, with a better memory of benefits than of injuries," they exhibited virtues that the strong, aggressive, all-conquering Anglo-Saxon lacked and desperately needed in order to establish a truly Christian society.[28] But Thomas W. Higginson, himself a radical abolitionist, sliced through the hypocritical cant when he wrote in 1861: "If the Truth were told, it would be that the Anglo-Saxon despises the Negro because he is *not* an insurgent, for the Anglo-Saxon would certainly be one in his place."[29]

Indians, in contrast to blacks, were invariably described as ferociously independent and proud—"perfect republicans," one early admirer put it.[30] A Puritan divine might distinguish between civil liberty, which was liberty within the essential restraints of society to do right, and natural liberty, which was the liberty of the Indian and was merely license to do wrong.

The nineteenth-century American too might consider the Indian's brand of liberty a form of anarchy that, carried to its logical conclusion, always proved self-destructive. Still, the love of liberty was a precious asset—and a "little Indian" would always be a welcome component in the national character. As an autochthonic type, the native American became a popular national symbol.

Contrary to those eighteenth-century European theorists who maintained that the New World environment was deleterious, Americans had actually produced the healthiest and happiest natives on earth. "They live to be a hundred and fifty years old, and are seldom sick," a Spaniard wrote in 1505,[31] and, if anything, the North American natives were superior to their southern counterparts. The "pure" Indian glowed with robust vigor. Moreover, since informed opinion held that a disease and its sovereign remedy were always found in close proximity, it followed that the natives, who were indigenous to the New World and read nature like a book, possessed secret medicinal lore of great value. Patent-medicine companies in the nineteenth century, working loving variations on this theme, peddled Old Sachem Bitters, Modoc Oil, Seminole Cough Balsam, Nez Percé Catarrh Snuff, and a whole line of Kickapoo cure-alls. The promotional literature for such products used the Indian to symbolize that salubrious, out-of-doors life-style that Americans had enjoyed in their pioneering youth. Any white who envied nature's children their stamina or their sculpturesque physiques could emulate them with a swig of some wondrous concoction, and youth itself would be restored.[32]

In the middle of the eighteenth century, when the American colonists were becoming aware of themselves as a people, they chose the figure of an Indian princess to represent their sense of differentness. Revolutionary propaganda frequently portrayed America as an Indian maiden, befeathered and often bare-breasted, defying Britannia's tyranny.[33] Though the Indian princess was eventually replaced by other national symbols, notably the lanky figure of Uncle Sam, the link between the red man and core American values had been established before there was a United States. A popular account of America published in 1776 and widely circulated in England noted prophetically: "The darling passion of the American is liberty and that in its fullest extent; nor is it the original natives only to whom this passion is confined; our colonists sent thither seem to have imbibed the same principles."[34]

Plumed profiles graced United States coinage as early as 1854, when a homely Liberty exchanged her customary turban cap for an Indian headdress on the one- and three-dollar gold pieces. The change was probably related to southern opposition to the old headgear, a Phrygian liberty cap, which, one contemporary wrote, "derived from the Roman custom of liberating slaves, thence called freedmen and allowed to wear this cap."[35] It might be fitting for a nation of former slaves, the argument went, but such a cap was hardly an appropriate symbol for a people "who were born free and would not be enslaved."[36] In the same period, sculptor Thomas Crawford, who was commissioned to execute a monumental statue of Liberty (or, as he called it, *Freedom Triumphant in Peace and War*) to crown the nation's Capitol in Washington, D.C., was persuaded against his better artistic judgment to abandon the liberty cap. Instead, in accordance with the wishes of Secretary of War Jefferson Davis, who had insisted that "American liberty is original, and not the liberty of the freed slave," Crawford gave Freedom a helmet with "an eagle's head and a bold arrangement of the feathers, suggested by the costume of our Indian tribes."[37]

Through the 1850s, symbolic content was scrutinized in the sculptures, bas-reliefs, frescoes, and paintings commissioned by the government to ornament the newly renovated and expanded Capitol. Illustrative of the touchiness of the times was a midwestern congressman's denunciation of a statue of an Indian youth straining under the weight of a bowl as an "utter falsification of Indian character": When did we ever make a hewer of wood and drawer of water of an Indian? We have broken his heart, but never his spirit; never has he bent his back to be the menial of the white man."[38]

In 1905 Augustus Saint-Gaudens proposed to act on President Theodore Roosevelt's suggestion that he use an Indian head to represent Liberty on the ten-dollar U.S. gold eagle. Regulations forced him to modify his concept and place a headdress on a feminine profile of the goddess instead.[39] But the Indian received direct tribute in two of the United States' most popular coins, the Indian-head penny (1859–1909) and the famous buffalo nickel (1913–1938), as well as the gold quarter and half eagle (1908–1929). The year after the nickel went into circulation, a full-face portrait of the Sioux warrior Hollow Horn Bear dignified the fourteen-cent postage stamp—a fitting companion to Chief OnePapa, who since 1899 had glared out from the five-dollar silver certificate, as well as all the other Indians who commonly decorated the borders of American commemorative stamps. No Negro's face has ever been impressed on regular American coinage; until 1940, no American stamp honored a black person's achievements. The national iconography clearly reveals the distinction so sharply drawn in the 1850s between the "submissive, obsequious, imitative negro" and the "indomitable, courageous, proud Indian."[40]

WHITE ATTITUDES TOWARD RED AND BLACK AFTER THE CIVIL WAR

Americans after the Civil War were still certain of the basic distinction between red and black. A Maryland poet compressed it into a few lines of a verse titled "Lay of the Last Indian":

> . . . they've gone—they have passed,
> Like the dew from the spray,
> And their name to remembrance
> Grows fainter each day;
> But for this they were forced
> From their ancestors' graves;
> They dared to be freemen,
> They scorned to be slaves.[41]

The generation that "fought to free the slave" and ratified the Fourteenth and Fifteenth Amendments could not easily ignore the question of Indian citizenship. It seemed elementary justice that something comparable be done for the original American. Benson J. Lossing, a facile and prolific historian with a large readership, argued in an 1870 article, "Our Barbarian Brethren," that the teaching "of all history, and of our own experience as a nation," framed a simple answer to the question "What is to be their destiny?": *"Make the Indian a citizen of the republic, wherever he may be, and treat him as a man and a brother."*[42]

For a brief time, Americans in the 1870s seemed to share in Lossing's benign mood. One western clergyman, conceding that the "savages of America are as capable of civilization as the savages of Africa," envisioned a grand American amalgam:

It has pleased Almighty God to bring to the shores of America and to bestow upon us as a free gift, the passion of the French, the calm logic of the Teuton, the Scotchman's perseverance, the fiery eloquence and sturdy sinews of the Irishman, the Englishman's great head and purse, the Negro cheerfully toiling under the torrid sun, the patient industry of the Chinese, the Spaniard's gravity, and the indomitable spirit of the Indian warrior—the excellencies of all the families of the earth combined in our American nationality.[43]

Thomas Nast, the premier political cartoonist of the decade, gave visual form to the case for Indian citizenship. In what his editors at *Harper's Weekly* deemed a "spirited cartoon," Nast made a "manly plea" for justice toward the red man. His drawing showed a blanket-draped warrior being turned away from the polls, while behind him a collection of ethnic stereotypes cast their ballots. "Move On!" the caption read: "Has the native American no rights that the naturalized American is bound to respect?"[44] But a reversal in sentiment was evident in Nast's own work by 1876, when his depictions of the Indian took on a biting edge. His later insistence that the ballot, "the great protector of the age," was the "quickest and cheapest way" of civilizing the Indian, like the Negro, the German, and the Irishman before him, was heavy with disdain.[45]

The press of economic concerns had turned the public's attention away from social problems. The atmosphere of goodwill and humanitarian optimism that prevailed when Ulysses S. Grant took office had dissipated before he left it, and the election to decide his successor resulted in a compromise that abandoned Negroes to their own devices in a nation grown weary of self-recrimination and increasingly willing to accommodate itself to the expedient vision of a white man's country.

By 1880 moral retrenchment had become full-scale retreat. The traditional ideal of the open society, of the United States as a haven for the Old World's "wretched refuse," the "huddled masses yearning to breathe free," was beginning to crumble. In the Chinese Exclusion Act of 1882, the United States for the first time in its history shut "the golden door" on a whole race. The act was a temporary measure that, like so many others of its sort, became permanent. Already plagued with two racial problems, white Americans were not about to admit a third. In the same period, the Supreme Court in a series of decisions dismantled most of the progressive legislation of the Reconstruction period and laid the foundation for Jim Crow segregation in the South.

Yet, at the very time racism and nativism were forging an alliance with profoundly conservative implications for American society, the United States government finally disowned the isolationist philosophy that had dominated Indian affairs since the 1820s, and in 1887 committed itself fully to a program of Indian assimilation. Nativism apparently connoted a greater respect for the native.

Because he was the First American, the Indian was different. He could not be lumped indiscriminately with America's other minorities. That rigid, unyielding character and native love of freedom that doomed him for one generation of Americans was, for the next, the very reason he *had* to be preserved. In calling for a "wise and comprehensive" policy in 1876, the Commissioner of Indian Affairs remarked, "We cannot afford to allow this race to perish without making an honest effort to save it."[46] For concerned humanitarians, the issue was on the line. Here was another commitment that could no longer be deferred.

CHAPTER SEVEN

CAN HE BE SAVED?
Environmentalism and Evolutionism

If the Indians were "doomed to decay," a clergyman wrote in 1875, why "waste mind and material" upon them? "If averse to civilization, why cast such a pearl before such swine?"[1] In the 1870s two schools of thought, one religious in orientation, the other scientific, were ready with their different answers.

ENVIRONMENTALISM AND THE INDIAN

Before the War of 1812 and for two decades after, outside (i.e., British) interference in American Indian affairs had served as a handy scapegoat for the nation's inability to civilize the red man. Judge James Hall, writing at the end of the 1830s in defense of the Indian's capacity for improvement, indicted the English for conniving to keep the tribes restive in order to block the United States' westward advance, monopolize the fur trade, and harass the young Republic. Thus Hall simultaneously vindicated the government's Indian policy ("benevolent, fore-bearing, and magnanimous," its "declared purpose" had always been "to secure . . . [the natives'] friendship—to civilise them—to give them the habits and arts of social life—to elevate their character, and increase their happiness") *and* the Indians' full human potential for advancement in the future.[2] Past failure had been a matter of practical application, not of intent or of irremediable circumstance.

   With the outbreak of the Civil War, American Anglophobia

found new outlets. Supplying rifles to frontier Indians seemed paltry business compared to the charge that England was working hand in glove with the Confederacy to undermine the Union cause by providing warships and a northern sanctuary for Southern sympathizers. While the 1862 Sioux uprising in Minnesota—an unusually bloody conflict just below the Canadian border—stirred residual suspicions about British meddling with American Indians, an alternative explanation for the Indian's past failure to become civilized still had to be devised. The errors of previous policy were part of the problem. "The practice of removing tribes has of course retarded their improvement," one writer flatly declared in 1860. The Indians' "isolated condition and the smallness of their numbers have precluded the mutual intercourse, imitation, and rivalry which have been powerful aids to civilization in more populous states."[3] Policy reform was obviously necessary. But why had even Jeffersonian benevolence with its goal of racial amalgamation not succeeded in winning a substantial number of red converts to white civilization?

Despite opinion to the contrary, the argument went, Indians had never actually rejected civilization. Never having been exposed to it, they had never had the opportunity. It was the warped, perverted version of civilization that had proven so lethal. The Indian had always met the white man along the troubled frontier, where the representatives of civilization were unrepresentative—what one Catholic essayist described as "the scum and dregs of society; a motley collection of adventurers and fortune-hunters with one aim and purpose in life—that of enriching themselves in any way that offers."[4] The law of vices and virtues had done its deadly work, exactly as tradition maintained, but not because of some innate deficiency in Indian racial character. To the contrary, the Indians were at birth "beautiful blanks"[5] waiting for the values of their social environment, whatever they might be, to be impressed on them. Their decay was "a present fact," a religious writer conceded in 1875, but "not a necessary doom; . . . the reason our civilization has not commended itself to them may be due to the faulty presentation thereof."[6]

Far from proving that the Indians were incapable of becoming civilized, the law of vices and virtues proved that they were receptive to change. The error of the past had been in isolating Indians *from* good models and *with* the worst that society afforded. Civilization was not the Indians' nemesis; it was their savior. But should they fail to civilize—that is, should the nation fail to *make* them civilize—then, given the logic of vices and virtues, there could be no alternative but the old one: racial extinction.

PATERNALISM AND THE INDIAN

"Civilize or die" was a venerable byword in American Indian affairs, and its meaning was grim as long as opinion held that the Indians could not become civilized. By the 1870s, however, "civilize or die" meant something quite different, and even the meekest humanitarian could utter the phrase without flinching since it implied no more than the government's duty to civilize the Indians in order that they might live on. The "terrible alternative" made it a compelling appeal "to the Christian philanthropist . . . to come forward with all those appliances of Christian civilization which alone have proved sufficient to save dying nations."[7] Two paths lay open to the United States: one, the path of honor, the other—associated with the frontier "scum and dregs of society"—of dishonor. For a nation under God there could be no choice. The Indians must be civilized. The tribes would have to perish so that the individual Indian might survive. "The conviction is now as firmly cherished through our nation at large as it ever was by the most ruthless body of the earliest colonists, that the land must be rid of savages," Massachusetts' George E. Ellis wrote in 1882. "While this conviction holds unqualified, civilization is substituted for extermination as the method for realizing the conviction."[8]

Through the alchemy of duty, the diverse elements in reformist thought about the Indian were transformed into a hard-line paternalism that interpreted the phrase "wards of the government" literally. As barbarism was to civilization, so the barbarian was to the civilized man: child to parent or, more precisely, guardian. The essence of paternal authority was firmness tempered with justice. "You should use them as a wise and firm disciplinarian would deal with children," a former Secretary of the Interior explained. "Your purpose, command, promise or threat must be made simple, clear, and easily understood."[9] The right to be savages would have to be "emphatically denied" the Indians.[10] Disabused of past errors and free to develop in a healthy and progressive environment, they would then rapidly advance to the maturity of civilization. While they remained on their reservations and labored to improve themselves, they would be showered with rewards in the form of annuities. Stray from their reservations, however, and they would immediately feel the corrective sting of the Great Father's military arm.

Paternalism set the tone for the controlled environment that would transform the savage.[11] The environmentalist philosophy encouraged efforts on the Indian's behalf. At the same time, it had its limitations. Former slaves, on being granted the privilege of American citizenship ("the highest boon that can be conferred on mortal man," according to one Texas senator)[12] were expected to rise to the occasion and become self-supporting members of society at once. When this did not happen, many reformers lost patience, disparaged the race, and abandoned blacks in their struggle for economic opportunity and social equality.

This insistence on almost magical solutions was implicit in the assumption that the Indian's mind was a *tabula rasa*, and Indian culture a compendium of erroneous ideas, superstitions, and practices to be willingly thrust aside under the light of civilization. Another school of thought, grounded in evolutionary theory, was prepared to explain why such expectations were naïve.

HUBERT HOWE BANCROFT ON EVOLUTION AND THE INDIAN

The Englishman Herbert Spencer's evolutionary doctrines, advanced between 1862 and 1896 in a succession of books directed at the educated layman, found a particularly warm reception in the United States. In Spencer's scheme, at least as it unfolded through the early 1880s, the universe was still visualized as a teleological construct, subject to the laws of evolutionary progression from "incoherent homogeneity" to "coherent heterogeneity." Since life had meaning and purpose, since natural and social developments occurred within a grand design, in the distance, dim but certain, was a final, perfect resolution. For the student of the Indian question, Spencerian evolution offered one great lesson: the gap between savage and civilized man was more apparent than real. By the law of growth through change, true for all life, there could be no ultimate cleavage. A writer, who can stand for many, put the matter succinctly: "Civilization is a thing of growth, with its roots in barbarism, and is as much the rightful inheritance of the savage as of the saint."[13]

This was the idea that in the 1870s informed the work of an energetic Californian named Hubert Howe Bancroft, who undertook the task of assembling and schematizing a sizable portion of American history, that of the Far West from Alaska to South America. His grand synthesis—quite as ambitious as Spencer's ten-volume *Synthetic Philosophy*—involved a well-organized assault on a formidable body of written materials. In 1869, with a team of assistants under his direction, the former merchant buried himself in a library of 16,000 books, some 1,200 of them about the American Indian. He emerged late in 1874 with the publication of the first of five volumes on *The Native Races of the Pacific States of North America*. In his memoirs Bancroft totaled up the man-hours invested in this work and, with the pride of an old soldier showing off his battle scars, wrote, "There had been expended on the *Native Races* labor equivalent to the well-directed efforts of one man, every day, Sunday excepted, from eight o'clock in the morning till six at night, for a period of fifty years."[14]

The commanding theme of *The Native Races* was similar to that of another of Bancroft's works—social progress—though George Bancroft ("with whom, by the way, I am in no way related," Hubert Bancroft felt called upon to mention)[15] based his optimism on a romantic vision of America's manifest destiny. Hubert Bancroft, in contrast, adhered to Spencer's evolutionary outline for inevitable social advancement. In discussing the three major theories of human origins, he summarized the teachings of the two special-creation schools, mono-

genism and polygenism, with "they say" and "they claim."
When he came to the evolutionary school of gradual development from a lower type, he stated its arguments without
such hedging. Darwinism was the new order and, as Bancroft
observed, "old-time beliefs have had to give place." In his first
volume, he provided a capsule statement of his theme: "Human
nature is in no wise changed by culture. The European is but
a white-washed savage."[16] In Volume Two, *Civilized Nations*,
the implications of this remark were explored in standard
Spencerian terms.

Bancroft developed his major ideas in a chapter titled
"Savagism and Civilization" that demonstrated just how far the
theory of evolution had carried opinion since Schoolcraft
pondered the alphas and omegas of society at mid-century.
"The terms Savage and Civilized, as applied to races of men,
are relative and not absolute terms," Bancroft explained. "At
best, these words mark only broad shifting stages in human
progress: the one near the point of departure, the other farther
on toward the unattainable end. This progress is one and
universal, though of varying rapidity and extent." Thus civilization was most usefully defined as the "measure of progres-
sional force implanted in man." This force operated as a
dialectic in which good and evil were opposed, while "extrinsic
force"—for instance, necessity in the form of war—acted as an
"iron hand," compelling mankind to improve. War, to continue
the example, forced savages to suppress their individual freedom and unite for the commonweal, thereby taking the first
step toward civilization.[17] Bancroft had arrived by his own
route at Spencer's militant phase of social organization.

Since civilization was rooted in savagery, questions about a
particular people's inherent capacity for improvement were
senseless. Progress was the "ultimate natural and normal state
of man," and civilization a "predestined, ineluctable, and eternal
march away from things evil [i.e., savagism] toward that which
is good." Consequently, all life was growth—being was becoming—and humanity was destined one day to be both "good
and happy"—relatively speaking, of course.

By Spencerian law, direct interference in the process of social
evolution could do no good and might cause harm. Thus

Bancroft cautioned that though the savage state is in all respects the "perfect germ" of the civilized state, "it must not be forgotten that civilization cannot unfold except under favorable conditions":

Often has the attempt been made by a cultivated people to civilize a barbarous nation, and as often has it failed. True, one nation may force its arts or religion upon another, but to civilize is neither to subjugate nor annihilate; foreigners may introduce new industries and new philosophies, which the uncultured may do well to accept, but as civilization is an unfolding and not a creation, he who would advance civilization must teach society how to grow, how to enlarge its better self; must teach in what direction its highest interests lie.

The Central and South American Indians served as incontrovertible proof of the ruinous consequences of misguided efforts to graft civilization onto simpler social organizations. While the primitive nations of North America lingered on, those to the south, subjected to "fanatical attempts to substitute by force foreign creeds and polities for those of indigenous origin and growth," had "withered at the first touch" of the European.[18]

Since direct interference in Indian affairs had succeeded only in supplanting native virtues with civilized vices, indirection was the rule. To promote Indian advancement, try altering the environment, not the man. This evolutionary view harmonized with the environmentalist contention that conditions at the time of contact between red and white were the primary cause of Indian degradation. The fundamental difference was in what the two schools of thought proposed to do to improve the situation. While the environmentalists devised plans for immediate and perhaps drastic corrective action, the evolutionists recommended a modified version of laissez faire. Since necessity was the father of progress, they argued, it must be allowed free operation to compel the Indians to become civilized. In practice, this might mean the suspension of annuities for uncooperative tribes on the reservations, and a sound thrashing by the troops for those off.

From the standpoint of Indian progress, the destruction of wild game, especially the buffalo, could only be construed as a positive good. Scarcity and hunger would force all the plains tribes to rely on the government's bounty, and would hasten the realization among them that they would have to labor—to farm or raise stock—if they were to prosper. "Viewed as a civilizing agent, labor is man's greatest blessing," Bancroft insisted.[19] By labor, he meant the *need* to labor, and there was nothing indirect or subtle about the means he had in mind. Whenever evolutionists and humanitarians discussed the Indian question, they agreed that coercion was part of the answer. For the fainthearted who might waver in this conviction, the "white man's burden" coupled with a hint of "survival of the fittest" should prove sufficient persuasion.

But there was no need to issue dire warnings. The crisp message that all *had* to progress because of a force inherent in human nature—indeed, in all life and all social organizations— was enough. For Bancroft, progress was a certainty, and no one was excluded.[20] That was the important point.

LEWIS HENRY MORGAN AND EVOLUTIONARY PROGRESS

Pruned of Spencerian mysticism, the evolutionary faith became a sequential theory of social advancement in the hands of a man renowned in the often jealous circles of post-Civil War American science as the nation's foremost ethnologist, Lewis Henry Morgan. While still a young Rochester, New York, lawyer dabbling in ethnology, Morgan in 1851 published the most sophisticated treatise on an American Indian tribe to appear to that time, *League of the Ho-de-no-sau-nee or Iroquois*. He joined the American Association for the Advancement of Science five years later and, as his ethnological concerns deepened, frequently read papers at its annual meetings. In 1876 he presided over the first "Permanent Subsection of Anthropology," and in 1880, the year before his death, served as the association's president.[21]

Morgan's early interest in kinship studies had become a preoccupation by 1859. He circulated an extensive questionnaire to informants around the world, and undertook field trips during four successive summers, the last a major expedition up the Missouri to the foot of the Rockies. The result, *Systems of Consanguinity and Affinity of the Human Family*, completed in 1865 and published in 1870 after extensive revision, is commonly regarded as Morgan's most substantial work. In his own time, it earned him the respect of the scientific community but aroused only moderate interest. Although it advanced a mass of evidence to support the theory of the Asian origins of America's natives, its accumulation of data did not satisfy either its author or its readers. *Systems* was too specialized and esoteric to excite an age of amateur anthropologists who preferred sweeping explanations. They awaited a grand synthesis in the manner of Darwin and Spencer. In 1877 Morgan fulfilled this expectation with the publication of *Ancient Society; or, Researches in the Lines of Human Progress from Savagery through Barbarism to Civilization*. A ringing sentence in the preface stated the book's thesis: "The history of the human race is one in source, one in experience, one in progress."

Ancient Society is a monument to the systematic mind. Human development, for Morgan, described an upward path from savagery through barbarism to civilization—three "distinct conditions . . . connected with each other in a natural as well as necessary sequence of progress." These basic divisions further divided into seven "ethnical periods," each characterized by a particular technological development. Morgan tabulated them, along with their distinguishing features:

I. Lower Status of Savagery	From the Infancy of the Human Race to the commencement of the next Period.
II. Middle Status of Savagery	From the acquisition of a fish subsistence and a knowledge of the use of fire, to etc.
III. Upper Status of Savagery	From the Invention of the Bow and Arrow, to etc.
IV. Lower Status of Barbarism	From the Invention of the Art of Pottery, to etc.
V. Middle Status of Barbarism	From the Domestication of animals in the Eastern hemisphere, and in the

	Western from the cultivation of maize and plants by Irrigation, with the use of adobe-brick and stone, to etc.
VI. Upper Status of Barbarism	From the Invention of the process of Smelting Iron Ore, with the use of Iron tools, to etc.
VII. Status of Civilization	From the Invention of a Phonetic Alphabet, with the use of writing, to the present.

All pertinent data about advances in the arts of subsistence, government, language, the family, religion, house life and architecture, and the idea of property were reduced to their simplest form and filed under the appropriate heading, and the larger argument developed with a constant reference back to this schemata.[22]

Although Morgan insisted that his ethnical periods were "provisional" and merely represented degrees of "relative progress," his language and argument tended to the opposite conclusion. For one thing, he assumed that human advance *had* to take place in sequence. Since each step, or period, was necessary to the next, it was, in effect, an absolute. Humans could not transcend these periods; they were bound by them as by the cycle of life. Human experience, Morgan was certain, had "run in nearly uniform channels." Thus "human necessities in similar conditions have been substantially the same; and . . . the operations of the mental principle have been uniform in virtue of the specific identity of the brain of all the races of mankind." This argument for parallel cultural development approached biological determinism, since men in different ethnical periods were assumed to have different innate capacities, and a "gradual enlargement of the brain itself, particularly of the cerebral portion," was credited to cultural progress. It was even possible to make scientifically valid value judgments about the races based on their levels of attainment, or ethnical periods. The Aryan family enjoyed an "intrinsic superiority," Morgan found, while the "inferiority of savage man in the mental and moral scale, undeveloped, inexperienced, and held down by his low animal appetites and passions," was "substantially demonstrated" by fossil remains and cultural artifacts.[23]

The meaning of Morgan's scheme for the American natives was as clear as their place within it. At discovery, the Indians represented "three distinct ethnical periods"—Upper Savagery and Lower and Middle Barbarism. By all evolutionary logic, they possessed the ability to rise to a civilized level. At the same time, by the logic of progressive development, they could make the transition to civilization only by gradually changing over the "long protracted ethnical periods" that intervened. For even the most advanced Indians, there would be a slow passage through Upper Barbarism; the rest were sentenced to an indefinite wait. "Human progress, from first to last, has been in a ratio not rigorously but essentially geometrical," Morgan wrote. Based on the theory of continually accelerating progress, "the period of savagery was necessarily longer in duration than the period of barbarism, as the latter was longer than the period of civilization." Assuming that man had existed for 100,000 years, Morgan thought it likely that 60,000 years had been spent in savagery, 35,000 in barbarism, and only 5,000 in civilization, a "conclusion of deep importance in ethnology."[24]

Evolutionary progress through a series of prescribed ethnical periods offered social theorists an appealing blueprint since it assured ultimate improvement. For nineteenth-century anthropologists, it was a universal law that gave coherence and significance to their studies. The comparative method assumed that the hierarchy of existing cultures reflected accurately all stages of human social evolution. In studying primitive cultures, civilized scholars were studying their own antecedents. Put differently, to understand civilization and how it had evolved, one had to understand the primitive—and that was the task of the anthropologist. Even the reformer could make a selective use of Morgan's theory. For example, Morgan's stress on private property as a civilizing factor nicely complemented the environmentalist program for saving the Indian.

But Morgan's overall view seemed hopelessly obstructionist.

One could encourage the primitive to prosper, but one could not make the primitive civilized. Present efforts would have to forgo present results, a thought no reformer could abide. Consequently, when a comprehensive new Indian policy was enacted in the 1880s, Morgan's hierarchy of progress was accepted, but an almost mystical civilizing power was attributed to education and practical instruction in agriculture.[25] The Indians, through the medium of private ownership of their lands, were expected to break in at the level of American farmers and were allowed twenty-five years to complete the remaining steps to civilization. Such a concession to evolutionary gradualism seemed woefully inadequate to those who were speaking in terms of eons. "Like the successive geological formations, the tribes of mankind may be arranged, according to their relative conditions, into successive strata," Morgan noted in a telling image. "Time has been an important factor in the formation of these strata; and it must be measured out to each ethnical period in no stinted measure. Each period anterior to civilization necessarily represents many thousands of years."[26]

Near the end of *Ancient Society*, Morgan wrote that "with one principle of intelligence and one physical form, in virtue of a common origin, the results of human experience have been substantially the same in all times and areas in the same ethnical status. . . . No argument for the unity of origin of mankind can be made, which, in its nature, is more satisfactory."[27] Evolutionism, like Christian humanism, precluded the possibility that the Indians were vanishing through some innate flaw in their racial character.[28] Informed opinion was agreed that they could become civilized. It remained only for a practical demonstration of Indian capacity to carry the mass of opinion before it.

CHAPTER EIGHT

HE CAN BE SAVED:
Agriculture and Education

In his annual message for 1870, President Ulysses S. Grant observed that the "subjects of education and agriculture are of great interest to the success of our republican institutions, happiness, and grandeur as a nation."[1] This was a routine but revealing lead-in to a discussion of the recent operations and future goals of the Bureau of Education and the Department of Agriculture.

AGRICULTURE, PRIVATE PROPERTY, AND THE INDIAN

Even the casual student of United States history is forcibly struck by the importance placed on agriculture in the American value system. Jefferson's influential *Notes on the State of Virginia* (1785) contained a glowing tribute to "those who labor in the earth." J. Hector St. John de Crèvecoeur's *Letters from an American Farmer* (1782) also remains a cherished artifact of the agrarian myth: the independent yeoman was a model citizen, his virtues the essential virtues of a free and enlightened people enjoying the blessings of a republican form of government. Cradled in the arms of bountiful Mother Nature, he imbibed her goodness daily. Simple, direct, self-sufficient, and morally circumspect, he was beholden to no one and at liberty to act on his conscience without reference to any higher authority save the Father of Us All. The American farmer was, as Crèvecoeur said, *the* American.[2]

Both of America's racial problems seemed amenable to an agrarian solution, though each presented a complication. The Negro was favorably disposed to farming, but had no land; the Indian had the land, but had no inclination to farm. After freeing the slaves, the government had committed itself to a program of land redistribution in the South, but it was abandoned without a fair trial and subsequently mocked as an idle fancy—"forty acres and a mule"—of credulous blacks and irresponsible carpetbaggers. The black man would be an agricultural worker, all right—but on someone else's farm. For the Indian, land was not the issue (though *arable* land would prove another matter). It was enough that the western tribes had acres to spare. "Every Indian may own a homestead!" The Commissioner of Indian Affairs trumpeted in 1885. "Contrast his situation with that of millions of white families in the country, to say nothing of the larger number of homeless people in the Old World, and of the negroes of the Southern States. What a heritage!"[3] The problem was a reluctant heir. The plains Indian had no agricultural experience, and exhibited a positive hostility toward farming for a living. The Indian must be presented with the alternative of survival as a farmer or extinction as a huntsman, and, a reformer insisted, "It is for you and me to say which it shall be."[4]

For the southern Negro, agriculture would define a humble role in life as a member of a permanent American peasant class; for the landed Indian, it would facilitate eventual mergence with white society. But events proved agriculture to be an outmoded solution to social problems. The farmer's glory days had ended with the Civil War and the subjugation of the South. The passing of the old order was reinforced as urban centers mushroomed and the locus of population in the United States shifted from the country to the city.

Yet in the postwar period government policy opted for the farming life as the shortest route to civilization for the Indians. Yesterday's savages, today's farmers, tomorrow's citizens. Back in the halcyon days of agriculture *Niles' Weekly Register* had confidently projected the path of Indian progress: "From ploughmen they will become moralists—and from moralists the transit will be easy to the sublime tenets of religion."[5] Even in the 1880s Americans were still prepared to accept such statements at face value. "It is our purpose to make the Indians farmers," a leading reformer wrote in 1883. "It is in the natural order of progress for them to pass from a nomadic to an agricultural state."[6]

The Indian farmer would be able to feed himself, thus reducing a burden on the public treasury. He would get a rudimentary training in the precepts of civilization and Christianity, which placed a premium on the virtue of industry. Best of all, he would have no need of his extensive wilderness hunting grounds. Henry R. Schoolcraft once estimated that 50,000 acres were required to feed a single hunter—a figure, an amused reviewer pointed out, that meant the whole United States could have sustained only 38,245 Indians.[7] Whatever the actual acreage involved, it was enormous in comparison to the small plot of land that would comfortably sustain the cultivator. Such traditional concerns, however, were overshadowed late in the nineteenth century by the fact that the Indian had been deprived of his hunting lands and now had no choice but to farm. Provision for implements, seed, and instruction had been a standard item in past Indian treaties. Now it constituted general policy.

Agriculture's value as a solution to the Indian problem stemmed from a second great consideration. "Common property and civilization cannot co-exist," the Commissioner of Indian Affairs asserted in 1838,[8] a dictum certain to appear in any discussion of the Indian question. Without a just appreciation of private property, no one could be induced to labor. Without labor, and the habits it inculcated, mankind could not progress. Yet progress was the only security. "The Indian will never be reclaimed till he ceases to be a communist," George Ellis stated. "He will be a vagabond and a pauper so long as he is not an individual proprietor and possessor, with a piece of land held by him in fee, with tokens of his own interest and ownership."[9] Agriculture was the means to a higher end. Its natural corollary was the division of tribal lands into individual holdings. The agrarian solution, it followed, *meant* allotment in severalty; thus agriculture afforded an ideal method of arousing a healthy respect for private property.

Lewis Henry Morgan was left to corroborate conventional wisdom with scientific law. "It is impossible to overestimate the influence of property in the civilization of mankind," he wrote, and a separate section of *Ancient Society* was devoted to the "Growth of the Idea of Property." A "feeble impulse aroused in the savage" became a "tremendous passion in the splendid barbarian of the heroic age." The idea of property was a "controlling influence" in the later stages of social evolution, and "its dominance as a passion over all other passions marks the commencement of civilization."[10]

Morgan went on to comment that the desire for property had become an "unmanageable power" among civilized men and, in words that made his book a bible for Marxist thinkers, concluded that it carried within it "the elements of self-destruction." The idea was intriguing, suggesting a stage beyond civilization when everyone would share in a spirit of mutual dependence that transcended the selfishly personal and completed the process of social evolution. Morgan's "next higher plane of society" was not to be confused with savage or barbaric communalism, though it would be a much-improved "revival . . . of the liberty, equality and fraternity of the ancient gentes."[11] Tribal values were, in embryonic form, the values of the future.

The implications of Morgan's remarks and the tribal ethic could make no impression upon the America of Jay Gould, John D. Rockefeller, Andrew Carnegie, and J. P. Morgan. Francis Parkman had glumly remarked in 1875 on "that frenzy of speculation and that race for wealth which have created an atmosphere where the scholar and the thinker find it hard to breathe."[12] Big business was supreme, the Republican Party was entrenched in national office, and, though the occasional depression might rock the boat, the ship of state was committed to a course of unprecedented material growth. While the farmers watched its progress uneasily and fought a rear-guard action to retain their traditional primacy in the nation's councils, the values of the Gilded Age, from rags-to-riches to survival of the fittest, bore down upon their own. The simple farming life would have no significant part in the future.

Already dependent upon eastern capital and thus the national economy with all of its fluctuations, the farmer would have to make another concession to progress by adopting the costly technology of the day, or be left permanently behind. Political protest gave vent to frustration and anger at oppressive economic conditions and the concomitant degradation of the old Jeffersonian ideal. Not the least of the ironies of the government's agrarian-based Indian policy was its timing—the Indians to be made into individualistic, self-sufficient yeomen just when white farmers were taking collective action to secure a fair share of the nation's wealth. Yet the agricultural solution to the Indian problem was adopted precisely because it would break up existing tribal units. By the mere act of grasping the handles of a plow, the Indians would become civilized men and useful citizens.

After the Indian was allotted land in severalty, the Reverend John C. Lowrie wrote, "then should follow the encouragement of farming, stock raising, &c., the fostering of schools, and especially the encouragement of the religious and benevolent agencies of our Missionary Boards."[13] While the order might vary, the components rarely did: any plan that looked to the final solution of the Indian problem would have to include individual ownership of a plot of arable land and a Christian education. Byron M. Cutcheon, a congressman from Michigan and a friend of efforts to uplift the Indian, ended a speech in 1886 to the applause of his colleagues by urging a three-step solution to the Indian problem: "First, self-support; secondly, ownership of property and citizenship, and third, education; and now abide these three, self-support, citizenship, and education, and the greatest of these is education."[14]

EDUCATION AND THE CARLISLE EXPERIMENT

Should the initial emphasis be placed on training the Indians in civilized skills—from stock-raising and farming to horse-shoeing and rudimentary mechanics—in order that the ground might be prepared for planting the seeds of Christianity and culture, or would a knowledge of the Gospel purify savage souls and thus render them more receptive to the teachings of civilization? To the public the answer was obvious. Practical instruction should precede more esoteric efforts. In 1819, when the government first circulated its conditions for apportioning the annual $10,000 Indian civilization fund among participating missionary societies, it stipulated that an acceptable "plan of education, in addition to reading, writing and arithmetic, should in the instruction of boys, extend to the practical knowledge of the mode of agriculture, and of such of the mechanic arts as are suited to the condition of the Indians; and in that of the girls, to spinning, weaving, and sewing."[15] But with Indian education in the hands of missionaries until 1876, when the government appropriated $20,000 for "the support of industrial schools, and other educational purposes," the actual order of priorities remained uncertain.[16] Even after 1876, the religious emphasis of certain government Indian schools made training in self-sufficiency a secondary consideration. In 1879, for example, employees of the industrial boarding school on the Puyallup reservation in Washington were advised that they were teachers "of a barbarian race, whom the Govt. desires to Civilize as speedily as possible," and that "the highest & only true form of Civilization is Christian Civilization—as Civilization without Christianity is only cultured barbarism."[17]

The second question—Where should the Indians be educated?—elicited two contrary responses: in their own domain, or at a boarding school, preferably far from the reservation. Opponents of the off-reservation boarding-school system, which isolated the Indian from the tribe, rested their case on the principle of retrogression. The Indian student who was educated away from home became a person without a people, unacceptable alike to civilized white folk and to his ignorant reservation brethren. In theory, such an Indian would bring enlightenment to the tribe; in fact, on returning, he invariably reverted to savage type. "The present scheme of taking a few boys and girls away from the camps to put them in school where they are taught English, morals, and trades, has nothing reprehensible about it, except that it is absolutely of no consequence so far as solving the Indian problem is concerned," the artist Frederic Remington asserted in 1889. Isolated and lonely, the returned students "go back to the blanket, let their hair grow, and forget their English. In a year one cannot tell a schoolboy from any other little savage. . . ."[18] Those who supported off-reservation boarding schools consistently maintained that the Indian could progress only in an environment conducive to progress. The most influential spokesman for this viewpoint, a man who was to dominate the field of Indian education for a quarter of a century, was Richard Henry Pratt, an officer of the United States Cavalry.

On November 1, 1879, the doors of Carlisle Indian School opened to its first class of 137 students, drawn from more than a dozen tribes. Captain Pratt had realized one part of his dream, and, like another soldier before him, General Oliver O. Howard, instantly established himself as a leader in race education. Howard, in conjunction with his duties as head of the Freedmen's Bureau, had helped found Howard University in 1867, becoming its president two years later. Ordered to the Southwest as President Grant's "peace commissioner" to the hostile tribes in 1872, he thereafter fancied himself an authority on Indians. He championed a tough policy tempered with paternal benevolence, and advocated education as the surest means of improvement for the Indian as for the black. Another officer renowned for his humanitarianism, General George Crook, sarcastically recalled that Howard "told me that he thought the Creator had placed him on earth to be the Moses to the Negro. Having accomplished that mission, he felt satisfied his next mission was with the Indian."[19] But when the title "Red Man's Moses" was eventually bestowed, it went not to Howard but to Captain Pratt.[20] He was, one admirer wrote, "the man chosen by God to do just this work."[21]

Pratt, commissioned as a second lieutenant in the newly formed black Tenth United States Cavalry Regiment in March 1867, was assigned to duty on the southern plains and immediately confronted with the fact of a triracial America. His first patrol in Indian Territory introduced him to a detachment of able Cherokee scouts and to his Negro troopers, whose "ready obedience and faithful performance of duty" earned his respect. Race, Pratt decided, was a meaningless abstraction. All men *were* created equal, and he deplored the inconsistency by which reservation Indians were barred from civil society and

Negroes received second-class status even in the nation's military, black enlisted men being restricted to all-Negro regiments under the command of white officers like himself. Looking back on his first patrol many years later, Pratt said it taught him that "all gross injustices to both races . . . are primarily the result of national neglect to give the opportunities and enforce the safeguards of our Declaration and Constitution."[22]

The flaws preventing American perfection were not other races, Pratt maintained, but "race problems" that could be eliminated by extinguishing all distinctions based on race, which, in turn, could be eliminated by extinguishing race through a program of total assimilation. Like General Howard, Pratt was imbued with a sense of mission. In 1880, as a lowly brevet captain, he wrote a confidential letter to the President criticizing General of the Army William T. Sherman's opposition to his activities. "I know I am at this time 'fighting' a greater number of 'the enemies of civilization' than the whole of my regiment put together, and I know that I am fighting them with a thousand more hopes of success," he declared. "Knowing as I do that I am supremely right, it would be wicked to falter, even though pressure to that end came in threats from the General of the Army."[23]

Pratt's active involvement in Indian education began in 1875. In the aftermath of conquest of the southern plains tribes, a small-scale removal full of irony took place. Seventy-two warriors prominent in the fighting were sent from an area adjacent to Indian Territory where the Five Civilized Tribes resided to the old Southeast—specifically, a prison at Fort Marion near St. Augustine, Florida. Pratt accompanied the Indians as their jailor, and in their confinement far from familiar surroundings recognized an ideal opportunity to conduct an experiment. Education would be their salvation, and the success he achieved in a three-year span only confirmed him in the opinion that the final solution to America's Indian problem was simple. Since assimilation was the government's ultimate goal, all efforts should be directed toward preparing the Indians for civilization through education.

When in 1878 the Indian prisoners were released, twenty-two refused to return home. In his efforts to place them elsewhere, Pratt approached Hampton Normal and Agricultural Institute in Hampton, Virginia, an academic and manual labor school for Negroes under the supervision of General Samuel C. Armstrong since opening in 1868. Armstrong, another prominent army officer–race educator, had commanded a regiment of Negro troops during the Civil War, and after the war had served as an agent to the Freedmen's Bureau headquartered at Hampton. Impressed by the need to prepare former slaves for their new role in life, he had secured the support of the American Missionary Association for a school for Negroes that would emphasize industrial education. Hampton Institute was the result. Though his experience was limited to the black man, Armstrong proved receptive to the notion of educating red and black together. Seventeen Indian students were accepted, and shortly after, many more. Pratt himself was placed on a special detail to recruit Indian pupils for the institute, and the Hampton experiment was soon attracting favorable attention. According to one journalist, it affirmed the capacity of even "the rudest savages of the plains for mechanical, scientific, and industrial education, when removed from parental and tribal surroundings and influences."[24]

But Pratt was not completely satisfied. While he admired General Armstrong's devotion to the welfare of his charges, he disagreed with Armstrong's "tenacious" insistence on segreated racial education. Not only were the students at Hampton effectively cut off from outside society, but within the institute social intercourse between red and black was curtailed. They were separately quartered, and ate at their own tables. Interracial mingling of the opposite sexes was positively discouraged. "Trouble might come of it," Helen Ludlow, a faithful worker and longtime propagandist for Hampton, noted. "None ever has. The effort is to build up self respect and mutual respect. And we believe that education of the mind and heart tends to individual morality and race purity."[25] Red-black contact was mostly limited to the classroom, where, one observer noted, the essential differences between the two races appeared in high relief. Negroes were "light-hearted and happy," "easily moulded" and "anxious to be moulded"—in a phrase, pliable and openly receptive to instruction. Indians, in contrast, were "no race with long years of servitude behind them, and with the instincts of servitude burned into them by the fearful laws of heredity." Nevertheless, wary, stoical, taciturn, and cold as the Indian pupil might seem, behind his inscrutable "red mask" was a desire to learn just waiting to be kindled by the teacher. "If we treat him as we would treat the negro, we shall fail," the observer warned, for "far more than the negro he needs *fine* natures to deal with him."[26] But the potential was there.

Hampton, then, was an experiment—not only in Indian education, but in the education of Indian and Negro side by side. It was an ambitious undertaking, acquiring its tone from Armstrong's unswerving devotion to "the gospel of work and self-help" within a rather isolated setting.[27] Both races, Armstrong believed, "are to be in the main, agricultural people, but can become good mechanics. A few should be fitted for higher spheres: many can teach common schools."[28] These assumptions became truisms in Negro education in the postbellum era. In particular, they are identified with Hampton's most famous graduate and Armstrong's most fervent disciple, Booker T. Washington, who would promote a doctrine of black accommodation to the segregated social structure in the South. Armstrong's viewpoint would also leave its mark on Indian education in the same period, but a mark much less profound. For one thing, governmental policy was moving away from segregation for Indians and toward integration. For another, Captain Pratt was a thoroughgoing assimilationist.[29]

To Pratt's mind, segregation was always a mistake. Complete assimilation should be the only object of race education. Thus Pratt began to search for an alternative to Hampton. Showing a skill at lobbying, he enlisted the support of Secretary of the Interior Carl Schurz, a celebrated immigrant success story who listened patiently while Pratt explained that "the Indians need the chances of participation you have had and they will just as easily become useful citizens. They can only reach this prosperous condition through living among our people."[30] Schurz was won over, and with his backing the crusading captain gained congressional approval of his plan for converting the abandoned cavalry barracks at Carlisle, Pennsylvania, into classrooms for Indian students. Captain Pratt, father *and* midwife to the experiment, remained with the Carlisle Indian School on permanent detail to the Bureau of Indian Affairs until his retirement in 1904.

Carlisle steered a middle course between "literary and industrial training." "By half-day school and half-day work," Pratt told a military audience in 1885, "we give to the boys practical instruction in some one branch of mechanics, as carpentry, blacksmithing, wagonmaking, harness-making, tinsmithing, shoemaking, tailoring, printing, painting, baking and agriculture; and to the girls a knowledge of all kinds of sewing, cooking, house and laundry work."[31] Pratt could have been reciting the curriculum recommended by the government in 1819. As for "literary" skills, the English language, in keeping with the aim of preparing the Indians for incorporation into white society, was deemed most essential. The Carlisle philosophy was augmented through a system of "outings"; Indian students were boarded with white families during the summer months, earning a small allowance and getting an introduction to civilization on a personal, workaday basis. Such outings were, Pratt liked to say, "a way out"[32]—out of savagery and into civilization, since they "enforced participation, the supreme Americanizer."[33] They also helped break down white prejudice toward the Indians.

For Pratt, segregation was the enemy. He considered isolation totally responsible for the Indians' past failure to become civilized. Still, his belief in physical proximity as the ultimate civilizing device was carried to extremes. It ignored as an article of faith any attachment to a nonwhite culture. It could not brook the obstructionism of scientific opinion that cultural change was necessarily gradual. Indeed, Pratt's passion for interracial elbow-rubbing led him to argue that slavery, for all its evils, had one redeeming feature: by providing a coercive environment wherein blacks were forced to labor, and thus to improve, it served as a classroom in American civilization. The Indians, lacking similar compulsory stimulation, had lagged in their racial development.[34]

Pratt also had to contend with the argument that students sent back to their tribes to act "as a little leaven"[35] would more likely prove "a waste of new cloth and new wine"[36] by reverting to savagery. To succeed, Pratt admitted, the Carlisle concept would have to be universally applied. "Partial effort invites partial failure," he wrote.[37] But day schools and other alternatives to the distant boarding schools were not the answer. If the government made a determined effort to educate all Indian children in institutions like Carlisle there would soon be no reservations to return to. The problem of reversion would disappear with the opportunity for it. The integration of red into white would occur naturally.

Secretary Schurz, who visited Carlisle in February 1880, concurred with Pratt in an article published the next summer, though he reached his conclusions by a different route. He commended Carlisle and similar endeavors, and confessed himself struck by the urgency of the work. Yet he recognized in the pressures of white settlement out West a valuable prod to civilization. "Knowledge and skill are in immediate demand" among the tribes, Schurz said. It was "no longer to be apprehended" that the returned student would "relapse into savage life. He will be a natural helper, teacher, and example to his people."[38]

Pratt went beyond assimilation in his thinking. He interpreted the Declaration of Independence literally, and tried to convert its ringing phrases into action. He was a pure Lockean environmentalist. The Indian, he insisted, "is born a blank, like all the rest of us. . . . Transfer the savage-born infant to the surroundings of civilization, and he will grow to possess a civilized language and habit."[39] For Pratt, nurture was everything, nature nothing.

Physical appearance was an obsession at Carlisle, and the school delighted in sending out packets of photographs showing students on their arrival, garbed in native costumes, their faces apprehensive or unexpressive; then, a few months or years later, bathed, combed, and dressed in whites' clothing. As one of Pratt's admirers observed:

Anyone who has seen a group of Apache children as they arrived at Carlisle, with all the characteristics of the savage, not only in their dress and manner, but visibly stamped upon their features in hard lines of craft, ferocity, suspicion and sullen obduracy, and has also seen a year later the same children neatly dressed, with their frank intelligent faces, not noticeably unlike in expression those of wholesome and happy boys and girls of our own race, must be convinced that education under suitable conditions is the true solution of the Indian problem, and that if all the Indian children could be placed under the same influences as the few hundred at Carlisle, that problem would disappear within ten years.[40]

Such a simplistic insistence on overnight transformations could scarcely fail to arouse the scorn of social scientists steeped in the theory of evolution. John Wesley Powell, as chief of the government's Bureau of Ethnology, considered denouncing the Hampton and Carlisle experiments as ethnologically unsound, but refrained out of respect for the selfless zeal that had gone into them.[41] Nevertheless, the bureau's position on Indian education was known, and Pratt denounced the anthropologists as "the most insidious and active enemies of Carlisle's purposes."[42]

Pratt disliked the Bureau of Ethnology but detested the Bureau of Indian Affairs. Its sole purpose, he perennially complained, was self-perpetuation at the expense of Indian assimilation.[43] This brought him full circle to the major point of contention: on- versus off-reservation education. Pratt conceded that "all educational work for the Indians is good," but added that the "system of removing them from their tribes and placing them under continuous training in the midst of civilization is far better than any other method." Indian youth must be given "opportunities to acquire our civilization in the environment of civilization."[44] Pratt's critics were just as stubborn. They tenaciously clung to the theory of "back to the blanket," their position encompassed in the question raised about Hampton and Carlisle by a skeptical officer: "But what is to become of the Indian youths after completing their education at these places?"[45]

Outside the bounds of Pratt's vision of Indian progress and total integration, the education of a select handful of children in the East did seem self-indulgent. Certainly it offered no solution to the massive Indian problem out West. During Pratt's twenty-four years as superintendent, a total of 4,903 Indian children attended Carlisle. Such efforts clearly had to be supplemented by broad programs to uplift the many. Elaine Goodale, a teacher of Indians who was later to marry the noted Sioux doctor Charles A. Eastman, and later yet to write the standard biography of Pratt, gravitated from qualified approval to stout opposition to the off-reservation system. She admired Pratt's passionate commitment, characterizing him as a man making "much good work possible by eloquently insisting upon glorious impossibilities."[46] But "far better than another Carlisle," she maintained in 1890, would be the "application of Carlisle methods to a vast series of elementary schools scattered all over the Indian country, ready to become, at the earliest possible moment, an integral part of our common school system."[47]

In the years after his retirement Pratt found his program repudiated. In 1918 the Bureau of Indian Affairs closed Carlisle. But his achievement was substantial. When he died in 1924, his pallbearers were former students, and two years later several hundred graduates contributed to a monument in Arlington National Cemetery "in loving memory" of the "Friend and Counsellor of the Indians."[48] More than any other individual, Pratt had been responsible for shifting the starting point in the debate on Indian education from "if" to "how." Herbert Welsh, a philanthropist prominent in the influential Indian Rights Association, thought that "probably nothing has done so much to change the current of public opinion as to the possibility of civilizing Indians as the experiments in the education of Indian youth at the Carlisle and Hampton schools."[49]

To the question "Are the Indian races of North America capable of receiving a Christian civilization?" Bishop Henry Whipple of Minnesota had responded in 1864, "We answer, unhesitatingly, Yes."[50] Now secular opinion could add, unhesitatingly, Amen. "Capacity of the Indian no longer needs demonstration," the President told Congress in 1888. "It is established."[51]

Proponents of agriculture and education assumed that the Indian could farm and could learn. Thus the theory of the Vanishing American was demonstrably false. Congressman Cutcheon, Pratt's warmest champion in the House of Representatives, dismissed the idea that the Indians are "fast fading away" as "a delusion and a snare":

They are capable of taking on civilization; of being educated; they are capable of self-cultivation; they are capable even of the highest civilization attainable by any race except the Caucasian [a reservation that must have left Pratt gnashing his teeth]. They are not going to vanish; they are not going to be obliterated.

The concept of the Vanishing American was not so easily dismissed, nevertheless. Now it was invoked to impress the public with the need for immediate action. In the same speech in which he denied the Indians were doomed to disappear, Cutcheon warned that "civilization, like the atmosphere, is pressing upon them on every side. The Indian question must be solved for weal or for woe, and it must be solved within the next twenty years—in fact, it must be solved at once."[52]

The element of fatalistic inevitability in the Vanishing American was receding, to be replaced by a heightened concern that the Indian not be allowed to disappear out of mismanagement or apathy. The changing significance of the theory was partly the result of a determined campaign to push beyond rhetoric to fact and thus expose the Vanishing American for what it was: a cultural tradition, based on emotion, self-interest, and error, not logic or moral necessity, and serving ends that were deplorable and wicked.

CHAPTER NINE

THE CONVENIENT EXTINCTION DOCTRINE:
A Crusade Against the Vanishing American

A few writers who were anxious to establish the Indian's ability to become civilized perceived uneasily that the assumption of racial atrophy was too pervasive and self-serving to be ignored. It presented a real obstacle to reform. As far back as 1789, President Washington's Secretary of War had observed that the opinion that it was "impracticable" to civilize the natives was "probably more convenient than just."[1] By removing the Indian's fate from mortal hands, it stultified normal, humane concern. One veteran Episcopalian missionary termed all discussions of the Indian's probable fate "beside the question, and dangerous, because they drown the call of present duty."[2] It did not matter whether the Indian was destined to live or die; the nation's duty was the same. This attitude, in one form or another, prevailed in the postbellum period. But even a confident affirmation of Indian potential could not convince skeptics or carry the day for a dynamic civilizing policy. That power belonged to fact alone, and it would take fact to successfully challenge the Vanishing American.

THE REFORMER CRITIQUE

The assumption that the Indian need not vanish provided a common bond between evolutionary science and traditional theology. Both agreed on the crucial issue of the Indian's

inherent abilities. Since we all rose from savagery, Benson
Lossing observed, it follows that had we treated the Indians as
men like ourselves, "they might have acquired as clear a charter
for permanent existence as other children of the All-Father."[3]
Scientific objectivity was amplified by missionary zeal. The
implications of the vanishing-race theory had never squared
with Christian doctrine. Committed to the enlightenment of
the aborigines, missionaries never embraced a theory that
would doom the object of their good works, and thus the good
works themselves. They never faltered in their belief that the
Indian could be saved. Through the dark years after the
War of 1812, they clung to that faith in relative isolation; by
mid-century, secular converts were joining their ranks. When
a frontal assault on the Vanishing American was mounted,
Christian humanitarians were in the vanguard.

In 1862 the *Boston Review*, a journal "devoted to theology
and literature," carried one of the strongest early statements
arguing that "the extinction of the Indian race is not, from the
nature of things, an inevitable necessity. It can be preserved."
The anonymous author set out to correct "some wrong impressions" that tended to discourage efforts on the Indians' behalf.
By "wrong impressions" he meant the body of thought that
constituted the Vanishing American, and he began his dissec-
tion by asserting that "exaggerated estimates" of the Indians'
numbers in the past had led uncritical writers to assume a
drastic decline in light of the relatively small existing Indian
population. A more cautious estimate of original Indian numbers would show that the decrease was "not so great as is
generally supposed," and would discredit the notion that the
"mere contact of civilization must be fatal to the race." A "truly
Christian civilization" would immeasurably improve the red
man. The real causes of the Indians' depressed condition were
not those racial attributes advanced by Vanishing American
theorists. Rather, they were a product of circumstances: the
influence of medicine men, which turned the superstitious
tribesmen away from the teachings of Christianity, and thus
from civilized redemption; "improvidence and indolence"; and,
especially, the corrupting presence of unprincipled white men,
"a set of vampires who disgrace the name of man."

The *Boston Review*'s writer was not advocating a wholesale rejection of the Vanishing American. He regarded the "fact that the Indian . . . 'disappears'" as "beyond dispute," insisting only that it "remains to be proved" that this was "due to a radical incompatibility between his character and the claims of civilization." By separating all natives into two classes based on "their adoption or rejection of labor and letters," he isolated one group that would justify the missionary faith and another that would fulfill the prophecy of doom. The former proved that "there is in the Indian a vigorous life, and that he, as well as the Saxon or the Gaul, is susceptible of civilization and enlightenment." As for the latter, they were destined to "speedy extinction" unless they even more speedily abandoned their old habits. "Their only choice is civilization or extinction," the reviewer commented, "and this must be made at once."[4]

The Vanishing American could now serve as a spur to action. But this new reading of an old truism invalidated its premise, that the Indian's decline was grounded in racial *necessity*. Thus others, who were more interested in scientific fact that in the reformer's arts of persuasion through coercion, attacked the theory as unsound, a fallacy from start to finish. They too hoped to clear the path for reform, but by completely eliminating the Vanishing American, not merely by reinterpreting its significance. The theory had been reiterated until it cast a "kind of fatal spell which has hung over the mind of the American people in relation to the Indian, paralyzing their sense of common humanity, as they have steadily absorbed his domain."[5] It was a supreme rationale for Manifest Destiny. Before real progress in Indian policy reform might be expected, it would have to be laid to rest. This was the purpose of the campaign against the Vanishing American that reached its climax in the 1870s.

SELDEN N. CLARK AND THE STATISTICAL CRITIQUE

Francis A. Walker, superintendent of the ninth census, in 1873 reported with evident surprise the "possibility that the Indian may bear restriction as well as the negro has borne emancipation." Fatalism had proven largely wrong. He documented this "opinion contrary to the general belief" in a footnote, maintaining that an Indian tribe "reaches its minimum when it attains the point of industrial self-support . . . thereafter it tends to increase, though less rapidly, doubtless, than is usual with white communities." Walker produced census figures from several reservations to support his contention, and felt it "entirely safe to say that the civilized and semicivilized tribes are holding their own, if not actually increasing in numbers."[6] His cautious conclusions adumbrated those in a pamphlet compiled by an obscure Bureau of Education employee and first distributed in 1877. Selden N. Clark's *Are the Indians Dying Out?: Preliminary Observations Relating to Indian Civilization and Education*, today virtually unknown, in its time created a minor sensation.

Clark was associated with John Eaton, Commissioner of the Bureau of Education and a representative of the Department of the Interior at the Centennial Exposition in Philadelphia. His assignment was to prepare a statement on Indian numbers for the catalog describing the official Indian display at the fair. In particular, Clark was to investigate the various estimates of Indian population advanced between 1789 and 1876. He stated his assumptions plainly:

The solution of the problem of Indian civilization depends greatly on the conclusions reached respecting Indian population. If, as is generally believed, the Indians are a vanishing race, doomed to disappear at a not remote period, because of their contact with civilization . . . then the efforts in behalf of their civilization will assume, in most minds, a sentimental aspect. . . . But, on the contrary, if it is shown to be true that the Indians, instead of being doomed by circumstances to extinction within a limited period, are, as a rule, not decreasing in numbers, and are, in all probability, destined to form a permanent factor, an enduring element of our population, the necessity of their civilization will be at once recognized, and all efforts in that direction will be treated as their importance demands.

Clark printed eighteen aggregate figures for Indian population in the United States, all advanced since Washington's presidency and all different, some strikingly so. Lewis Cass, Henry Schoolcraft, and Walker himself had contributed to the confusion. Three concurrent estimates indicate the margin of imprecision: 1820: 471,036; 1825: 129,366; 1829: 312,930.

Estimated at 400,764 in 1853, the Indian population dipped to 254,300 in an 1860 report, rose to 305,068 in 1875, and the next year was fixed at 291,882. Clark's point was irrefutable. Population estimates were obviously highly unreliable, and virtually worthless as indicators of the Indian's racial destiny.[7]

The most serious errors were the original ones, he contended. Spanish, French, and English settlers had wildly overestimated the total aboriginal population on the North American continent; their guesses had become the standards against which all subsequent enumerations were measured. A glance at the history of the Cherokees, Seminoles, Sioux, and the tribes of Alaska and California, as well as an extended consideration of the Iroquois Confederacy, established the thesis that estimates of Indian population "almost invariably exceed the true number." When the inflated estimates were compared with later, more accurate enumerations, an alarming drop in Indian population was always indicated.[8]

Although Clark admired Walker's work with the 1870 census, he nevertheless referred to it as a case in point. Walker had set the native population of Alaska at roughly 70,000; since then, relatively reliable figures suggested a total nearer 25,000. "It is highly probable that an actual enumeration will reduce these figures as low as 20,000, perhaps still lower," Clark noted, "and when that is done it is to be hoped, but hardly to be expected in the light of past experience, that nobody will gravely point to the forty or fifty thousand difference between the census estimates of 1870 and the numbers ascertained by actual enumeration, and inform us that the Indians of Alaska are rapidly dying out, and will in a few years become extinct." Clark formulated a general law to cover any genuine decline: "Actual enumeration always reduces the estimated number of Indians by a much greater ratio than any or all causes reduces [sic] their actual numbers."[9]

Beginning in 1874, the Bureau of Indian Affairs in its annual reports had undertaken to include vital statistics reflecting the birth and death rates of the tribes. While the returns were yet too fragmentary to afford a basis for general conclusions, a definite trend had emerged: births for each year exceeded deaths. Thus "whatever positive evidence the figures afford is not in favor of the theory of a rapid decrease of the Indian population from natural causes." Clark had had no opportunity to investigate these "natural causes," and he advanced his ideas cautiously. Nevertheless, he closed his treatise with a personal statement whose implications could not be mistaken. Years of studying a multitude of facts, he wrote, had convinced him that "the usual theory that the Indian population is destined to decline and finally disappear, as a result of contact with white civilization, must be greatly modified, probably abandoned altogether."[10]

GARRICK MALLERY AND THE SCIENTIFIC CRITIQUE

Reformers often complained that the reports on the Indian question prepared under government auspices were foredoomed to obscurity.[11] Clark's *Preliminary Observations* proved an important exception. Even before it was issued in pamphlet form, Garrick Mallery, an officer in the U.S. Geological Survey and one of the more active of the government ethnologists, learned of it and, through him, Clark's views won over a coterie of influential true believers.

At the 1877 meeting of the American Association for the Advancement of Science, convened in late August in Nashville, Tennessee, Mallery, who was a student of aboriginal pictographs and sign language, read a paper on "The Former and Present Number of Our Indians." Despite the oppressive summer heat, northern scholars were in attendance, and several heard Mallery's paper. He delivered it again in substantially the same form that December before the Philosophical Society of Washington, and he minced no words in coming to his main point. He meant, by discrediting the traditional overinflated estimates of Indian population, to discredit the theory of the Vanishing American, which, he said, consisted of three "correlated propositions":

1st, That the native population on the arrival of the first colonists was very large; 2d, That it is now rapidly becoming extinct; and 3d, That the cause of that extinction is an innate characteristic or defect of the race, rendering impossible its civilization or even existence with civilized environments.

The huge discrepancies in population estimates that apparently established a dramatic decline were "often but the result of accurate information succeeding vague guesses." But instead of accepting the one set of figures as accurate and the other as false, "the whole world" believed both, and "accounted for the diminution by rhapsodies about decadence, and a profound theory manufactured to suit false premises, that what they called the red race was *ferae naturae*, and could never be tamed nor exist near civilization." Moreover, Mallery charged, "this has not been wholly an error of honest ignorance, but of wilful determination."[12]

Mallery did not go beyond Clark's statistical data to support his conclusions, but he did expand on the reasons for the pervasive inaccuracy in estimating Indian population in the past. Early explorers and settlers, following the coastline and the rivers inland, met the Indians "precisely where they were the most numerous and stationary." From these encounters, they assumed that the same population density prevailed everywhere, and thus their estimates of the total native population were enormously distorted. Too, "aboriginal brag" inspired tribes to claim a size and an importance which they had never enjoyed. This exaggeration was magnified by "their utterly confused synonymy," by which a single tribe was known under many names. White men naturally assumed that each name designated a different tribe, and accordingly added each one into the population total. When the repetitions were subsequently discovered and dropped from later counts, "absolute extinction" seemed to have befallen certain "tribes." The "combination and absorption" of different tribes into one another also "swelled the wail of extirpation." Even the destructive effects of "constant wars" and "strange diseases" on Indian population had, in Mallery's opinion, been wildly overestimated in the past.[13]

Specific instances when studied in the clear light of scientific objectivity refuted the Vanishing American theory. The Iroquois, for example, numbered two thousand more than in the years before the American Revolution—which hardly corroborated Schoolcraft's "ex cathedra dictum, that 'the red man withers at the touch of civilization,'" Mallery acidly observed.

Where tribes had actually been decimated—in California and Oregon—the "crime was not accomplished by white civilization, but by white barbarity." As for the notion of vices and virtues and the belief that Indians had never made substantial progress in civilization, Mallery delivered an *ex cathedra dictum* of his own in line with evolutionary thought: "It is silly to expect a sudden improvement among any people by the *presto change!* of political conjuration, when their old modes of life are forbidden and none furnished instead."[14]

Mallery's bluntness far surpassed Clark's. The

"blight" and "withering" or *ferae naturae* theory is proved absolutely false, and . . . though some temporary retrogradation must always be expected among individual tribes at the crisis of their transition from savagery or barbarism to more civilized habits, yet now, the number of our Indians is on the increase and will naturally so continue, unless repressed by causes not attributable to civilization, but to criminal misgovernment, until their final absorption into the wondrous amalgam of all earth's peoples, which the destiny of this country may possibly effect. Neither from views of their physiological, religious or sociological characteristics should they be regarded as an exceptional or abnormal part of the human race, or so treated in our national policy.

"Only those legislators and officials who are prepared to encourage downright murder," Mallery concluded, "can neglect their duty under the Satanic consolation of the convenient extinction doctrine."[15]

One of Clark's and Mallery's earliest converts, Edward Howland, in an article in *Harper's Monthly*, remarked: "That the Indians are surely destined to remain with us would seem to be the opinion of those best able to judge."[16] Others who were won over included a former Commissioner of Indian Affairs[17] and the first head of the Bureau of Ethnology.[18] Mallery's facts and statistics, a journalist said for them all, "appear to give the death blow to the commonly accepted 'blight' and 'withering' theory."[19] Ironically, in his casual tribute to the assimilationist ideal revered by Captain Pratt and the reformers generally, Mallery had espoused a philosophy that would breathe a new life into the Vanishing American. Assimilation was a sentence to cultural death after all, and the Indian as Indian was still destined to disappear.

ARMY SUPPORT FOR THE VANISHING AMERICAN

"The well-informed persons who suppose that the Indian race in the United States is declining, and destined before long to become extinct, are diminishing in number faster than the Indians are," the *New York Times* confidently proclaimed in 1878.[20] But resistance was tenacious. The emotional power of the Vanishing American could not be denied; popular opinion still invoked it, even if informed opinion did not. George Ellis, in *The Red Man and the White Man in North America* (1882), was at pains to present the most recent findings on Indian population. The old assumptions about Indian decline "are now largely, if not universally, discredited," he wrote. Yet he said in the same work:

If I am competent to infer from the mass of what I have read, the consenting opinion and judgment of the very large majority of men of actual knowledge and practical experience of the mature Indians is that they cannot be civilized,—that the race must perish either by violence or decay. The final catastrophe, it is said, has been forecast, prepared for, and is steadily advancing to its dismal close.[21]

Ellis's confusion about what the majority of Americans thought on the subject of the Indian's destiny was symptomatic of a transitional period. Similar confusion was apparent in other quarters as well.

Paradoxically, although "race educators" like Samuel Armstrong, O. O. Howard, and Richard Pratt, humanitarians like George Crook and Nelson Miles, and ethnologists like Garrick Mallery and John Wesley Powell, army officers all, were in the forefront of the campaign to foster a more enlightened public opinion on the Indian and Indian policy, some of their brother officers who had served on the frontier were among the most intransigent devotees of the "red devil" stereotype and of the Vanishing American theory. Their viewpoint could be as myopic as that of Brigadier General James H. Carleton, who in 1865 wrote that the Indians were decreasing "very rapidly" from many causes, but most particularly those "which the Almighty originates, when in their appointed time He wills that one race of men—as in lower animals—shall disappear off the face of the earth and give place to another race. . . . The races of the mammoths and mastodons, and the great sloths, came and passed away: the red man of America is passing away!"[22]

The depressing odds with which the Mallerys and the Clarks had to contend were illustrated a few years after they published their observations on Indian population when the Military Service Institution of the United States in 1880 assigned "Our Indian Question" as the topic for its annual essay contest. Of nine papers received, five were published in the institution's *Journal*. The gold medal went to Colonel John Gibbon, best known for his part in the expedition against the Sioux that added a sad but thrilling note to the nation's centennial celebration when General George A. Custer's command won immortality in utter defeat. Gibbon began with the assertion that the Indian was "a *wild animal*" who was "*bound to disappear from this continent*":

Philanthropists and visionary speculators may theorize as they please about protecting the Indian . . . and preserving him as a race. *It cannot be done*. Whenever the two come in contact . . . the weaker *must* give way, and disappear. To deny this is to deny the evidence of our own senses, and to shut our eyes to the facts of history.[23]

A younger officer, Lieutenant C. E. S. Wood, as aide-de-camp to General Howard in 1877, had demonstrated an ear for figurative language in jotting down Nez Percé Chief Joseph's eloquent surrender speech disavowing war "from where the sun now stands." In his essay on "Our Indian Question" he reached for the perfect metaphor: "The green plant does not flourish in the dark, and the Indian sunlight has been fading for many years." The Indian was doomed to be crushed by the onrushing "ball of civilization"; he was the oil to civilization's water, incapable of mixing or intermingling; he was the thoughtless man caught along a narrow beach by the rising tide. "Too late he sees the inexorable cliffs behind him and endeavors to beat back the waves," Wood wrote. "Little by little they rise higher and higher, following him to his last and highest refuge, then slowly but oh how surely they creep up, up, to chin and mouth, a few struggles and they laugh and leap above his grave." Finally, the Indian's end was necessary and right, a decision made by a higher power:

Men know that nature has a retribution all her own. Therefore let his annihilation not come upon him corruptly as by firing his forests and tented dwelling places; nor suddenly as a frost in the night; but let it steal upon him with all the tenderness of sleep; so that no man can say: now the beginning of the end has come. Let him die from among us as by a euthanasia so kind that it is as if Nature—his mother—placed her foot upon his cradle and rocked him to his grave.[24]

EAST VERSUS WEST ON THE INDIAN QUESTION

The military had no monopoly on the debate over the Vanishing American. The clash of conflicting views about the Indian's probable destiny was more sharply limned in regional terms. From the beginning of American history there had been an east and a west to Indian affairs, a fact decisively demonstrated by Bacon's Rebellion in Virginia in 1676. After a party of Tidewater planters massacred a group of peaceful Susquehannocks in 1675, hostilities had flared along the Potomac. But colonial officials in the relative safety of Jamestown seemed indifferent to the situation on the western frontier. The Indians around Jamestown, a contemporary reported, were "absolutely subjected, so that there is no fear of them," and remoteness dictated the government's response.[25] Perhaps a string of forts could be erected on the frontier to forestall such unpleasantries in the future. That was the farsighted solution, and that was what the government proposed to do. But the frontiersmen wanted swift, punitive action against the Indians; since the colonial officials were unwilling to act decisively, they took matters into their own hands. Nathaniel Bacon, an ambitious planter with good connections, was made general of a volunteer army, which he promptly led against several bands of friendly Indians and then against the government itself. Bacon's Rebellion has been seen as the forerunner to revolution. In another sense, it was only the most dramatic acting out of western grievances against easterners and their detached viewpoint on the Indian problem.

As Americans pushed westward through the nineteenth century, the dividing line moved with them. The east became proportionately larger, and its views proportionately more dominant in shaping policy. Boston and Philadelphia in particular were hives of pro-Indian activity; from them emanated a potent, philanthropic pressure that westerners dismissed as naïve sentimentalism. Frontier attitudes toward the Indian ranged from the contempt of a Mark Twain to the hatred that periodically found expression in a cry for extermination. There was nothing very theoretical about the western viewpoint: the Indians were in the way and would have to go. "This is God's country," a Dakota newspaper explained in 1874:

He peopled it with red men, and planted it with wild grasses, and permitted the white man to gain a foothold; and as the wild grasses disappear when the white clover gains a footing, so the Indian disappears before the advance of the white man.

Humanitarians may weep for poor Lo, and tell of the wrongs he has suffered, but he is passing away. Their prayers, their entreaties, can not change the law of nature; can not arrest the causes which are carrying them on to their ultimate destiny—extinction.

The American people need the country the Indians now occupy; many of our people are out of employment; the masses need some new excitement. . . .An Indian war would do no harm, for it must come, sooner or later.[26]

So vivid was the contrast between eastern and western attitudes that few writers on the Indian question failed to mention it. One experienced observer pictured the states "divided into two great parties, one crying for blood, and demanding the destruction of the Indians, the other begging that he may be left in his aboriginal condition, and that the progress of civilization may be stayed."[27] These views, another writer noted, were conditioned "by contact, cupidity and prejudice, on the one hand; and enthusiasm, benevolence and remoteness, on the other."[28] The pertinent point was that easterners had solved their problem by moving the Indians out of the way, and had "long since forgotten the savage war whoop";[29] while in the West, "the Indian question is a live question," men live in "constant danger," and their "only appellation" for the Indians is "red devils."[30]

The western Indians, despised by settlers eager to dispossess them and travelers who saw them only as degraded beggars and prostitutes, were often damned for falling short of the Cooper prototype. Westerners assumed that Cooper, being an easterner, was simply ignorant, and they gleefully embroidered

Twain's contrast between the pure noble savage of romance
and philanthropy and the "real" Indian, "truly . . . nothing but
a poor, filthy, naked scurvy vagabond, whom to exterminate
were a charity to the Creator's worthier insects and reptiles
which he oppressess."[31] A little soap and water, Twain was
fond of saying, was all it would take to finish him off.[32]

Cooper's Indians offered a convenient vehicle for the venting
of a sometimes pathological hatred. Bill Nye, a humorist who
made his reputation as a journalist in Laramie, Wyoming
Territory, between 1876 and 1883, loathed Indians and their
eastern champions about equally. He produced some amusing
parodies of such Cooperian conventions as "The Aged Indian's
Lament": "Warriors, I am an aged hemlock. The mountain-
winds sigh among my withered limbs. A few more suns and I
shall fall amid the solemn hush of the forest, and my place will
be vacant. I shall tread the walks of the happy hunting grounds,
and sing glad hallelujahs where the worm dieth not and the
fire-water is not quenched." Some of Nye's columns, however,
were merely glosses on an unfunny text, since in his opinion
the only good Indian was a dead one. "Somehow live Indians
do not look so picturesque as the steel engraving does. The
smell is not the same, either," he commented in one sketch.
"A dead Indian is a pleasing picture. . . . The picture of a wild
free Indian chasing the buffalo may suit some, but I like still
life in art. I like the picture of a broad-shouldered, well-formed
brave as he lies with his nerveless hand across a large hole in
the pit of his stomach."[33]

In time, Cooper and Cooper's Indians became code words
for the easterner and his sentimental view of the noble red
man. Satirical references to Cooper's creations became so
commonplace that one critic, writing in 1889, felt called upon
to insist that "they are . . . heroic figures, no doubt, and yet
taken from life, with no more idealization than may serve the
maker of romance."[34] A few defenders went further. The
problem was judging who was at fault, Cooper or the current
crop of Indians for discrediting his portrayal of the old-time
woodland warrior. At least one writer decided that Cooper's
were the real Indians, "the representatives of their race," while
the savages who roamed the West pillaging and burning as

they went were obviously "ignoble types," blemished copies of the authentic Uncas prototype.[35]

Ironically, Cooper's severest critics were often as literal-minded as his most unabashed champions. They rejected Uncas, but in their denunciations created a stereotype squarely in the Magua tradition. When Twain added to his catalog of Indian vices a heart that was "a cesspool of falsehood, of treachery, and of low and devilish instincts,"[36] he could have been describing Cooper's "cunning Huron," the perfect red devil, who sat like "the Prince of Darkness, brooding on his own fancied wrongs, and plotting evil."[37] In the nineteenth century, white thought on the Indian rarely transcended the literary conventions of noble savage and bloody savage. Western realism was no exception. Eastern sentimentalism would always distinguish between the savage and savagery; western realism simply assumed they were the same. Consequently, the Vanishing American found a home in the West.

Ambrose Bierce, a brilliant satirist active in San Francisco from 1868 to 1909, first defined "Aborigines" in his sardonic *Devil's Dictionary* as "considerate persons who will not trouble the lexicographer of the future to describe them," then later went beyond this in an oft-quoted definition: "Persons of little worth found cumbering the soil of a newly discovered country. They soon cease to cumber; they fertilize."[38] The Indian was dying out, and deservedly so. If fate required an extra push, so be it. A "few miserable savages" should not be permitted to retard the progress of civilization:[39] "The destiny of the aborigines is written in characters not to be mistaken. The same inscrutable Arbiter that decreed the downfall of Rome has pronounced the doom of extinction upon the red men of America."[40] Eastern opinion may have undergone a reversal on the subject of Indian numbers and Indian destiny, but western opinion was hardly about to concur.

A classic confrontation between the two views took place in the Senate on March 30, 1882, when George F. Hoar of Massachusetts and Preston B. Plumb of Kansas squared off over the Indian question. During a routine debate on the education provisions in the Indian appropriation bill, Hoar took the opportunity to express his conviction that books, not bullets, would most honorably and expeditiously terminate the Indian question. Citing Clark, "an accomplished statistician," Powell, "perhaps our most accomplished ethnologist," and Mallery, he informed the Senate that the "best statistical authorities declare that the Indians are not a perishing or dying race." Pratt's work at Carlisle confirmed the Indian's capacity for civilization and a "very high degree of intellectual development." An extended examination of expenditures made between 1789 and 1872 on the Indian, and particularly on miliary campaigns against him, revealed that a sum total of "a thousand million dollars" had been spent. Yet, Hoar charged, no end was in sight. A dedicated program of Indian education, in contrast, would require only a fraction of that amount, and would settle the Indian problem "in ten years, perhaps in five."[41]

Plumb began his rebuttal with the traditional rejoinder that easterners had acquired a scrupulous conscience where the Indian was concerned rather late in time, in fact only well after they had disposed of their own indigenous population. "A century of dishonor," that catch phrase of the reformers, neatly excluded all dealings with the Indian before the creation of the Republic. But in colonial times, easterners too had seen the Indian question in its true light, as a "struggle for race supremacy." "The white race was contending with the red race for the mastery," Plumb explained, "and with the inevitable result . . . foreordained from the beginning, that the red race shall give way." Ancestors and, for that matter, old opinions, might be an embarrassment, but they could not be denied. Georgia's Richard Wilde had impaled Massachusetts' Edward Everett with his earlier uncharitable views on Indian rights during the removal debates in 1830. Similarly, Plumb confronted Hoar with the "words of an honored son of Massachusetts now living"—Oliver Wendell Holmes—to the effect that "the red race is a provisional one":

The Indian, according to this theory, is not designed to improve, and increase, and fill the land, but simply to make things ready for the Anglo-Saxon; and the people who landed at Plymouth Rock and at other places on that bleak coast acted on that principle long before Mr. Holmes spoke, and when he said the red was a provisional race he spoke of a race that had already been destroyed by his own people.

The correct end of policy, Plumb thought, was to make the Indian self-supporting so that he might be placed "beyond pauperism" and "off the hands of the Government."[42] The Carlisle system and allotment in severalty offered no solution, since the Indian could not accomplish in a generation what the white race took twenty generations to do. As always, evolutionary conservatism dictated that the red race be left largely to its own devices. And from Plumb's perspective, as he made abundantly clear on an earlier occasion, this meant that the Indian would vanish in the end. "He is simply here to get out of the way at the proper time."[43]

Apparent in such debate is the fact that, increasingly, the Indian's capacity for civilization had become the point of departure, not the issue at stake. A few die-hards would never yield. But beneath the loud disagreement on particulars, a consensus was forming. Those who dismissed the Vanishing American as a fallacy made one concession: that during the transition period from barbarism to civilization the Indian population was unstable and tended to decline. Those who asserted the continuing validity of the Vanishing American gravitated to the position that only the Indian race and culture, and not the individuals who constituted them, were fated to disappear. For disputants of both persuasions, assimilation offered a broad area of agreement. Even the melodramatic Lieutenant Wood, doom-monger nonpareil, paused long enough to say that "the Indians should be assimilated to the whites. . . . Natural forces will . . . draw them toward the same condition," he thought, "and predominance of race will quietly complete the transformation."[44] When the old rhetoric was employed, it clearly had a new and different meaning.

All told, the campaign against the "convenient extinction doctrine" enjoyed only mixed success. It never entirely supplanted the belief that one morning the world would awaken to find not an Indian alive. In 1912 a magazine expounded on the "sentimental regret" with which Americans viewed the "approaching extinction of the Red Man" and the general interest that was manifested in the relics of "this dying race."[45] When an anthropologist wrote in to correct the impression that the Indians were dying out, the editors commented that his "assertion comes as a considerable jolt to the current sentiment, which pictures the red man as a tragic figure expatriated and fast vanishing from his native plains and woods."[46]

The battle, in short, was never really won. But the work of Clark, Mallery, and their colleagues was part and parcel with the larger movement that effected a minor revolution in white thinking about the Indian, clearing the way for the comprehensive reform measure of 1887. After almost a century of nationhood and over half a century of subscribing to the theory of the Vanishing American, white Americans had reached two conclusions: the Indians were not vanishing of innate necessity, but *would* vanish in the near future unless something was done to ameliorate their condition; and while the Indians would continue to exist as individuals and even increase in numbers, they were moving to certain cultural extinction. Inclusion rather than seclusion thus became the new orthodoxy, and the Indian problem attained an unaccustomed simplicity. The Vanishing American was a "present fact," one western clergyman acknowledged, but environment, not race, was entirely responsible, and all the talk about laws of decay was just so much "erudite nonsense." "How shall we save the small remnant left of the Indian race? This is *the* Indian question of today."[47]

The Last of the Mohicans, oil by Asher B. Durand, 1857, one of several American artists who found inspiration in James Fenimore Cooper's novel, *The Last of the Mohicans.*
Courtesy of the White House Collection, Washington, D.C.

G. Catlin.

"The Author painting a Chief, at the base of the Rocky Mountains," sketch by George Catlin fulfilling his mission to preserve a pictorial record of a vanishing race.
George Catlin, *Letters and Notes on the Manners, Customs and Condition of the North American Indians* (New York, 1841)

"'Move On!' Has the Native American No Right that the Naturalized American is Bound to Respect? The Other Nationalities May Vote, but Not the Original American," sketch by Thomas Nast
Harper's Weekly (April 22, 1871)

"Give the Natives a Chance, Mr. Carl [Schurz]. The Cheapest and Quickest Way of Civilizing Them," sketch by Thomas Nast
Harper's Weekly (March 13, 1880)

"An American Indian contemplating the progress of Civilization," sketch by an unknown artist, ca. 1847. A warrior, displaced by civilization, surveys a world no longer his own; the paraphernalia of savagery are scattered about him, his unstrung bow and an animal's skull signify the end of the hunter's life.
S. G. Goodrich, *A Pictorial History of the United States, with Notices of Other Portions of America* (rev. ed., Philadelphia, 1847)

"The Course of Empire," sketch by an unknown artist, 1867, of the Indians retreated before the inexorable advance of emigrants and the railroad.
Harper's New Monthly Magazine 35(June 1867)

Across the Continent. "*Westward the Course of Empire Takes Its Way,*" Currier & Ives lithograph (1868) from a drawing by Frances F. Palmer. The railroad leaves two warriors behind in its smoke, implying that the nation holds no future for the Native Americans.
Courtesy of the Amon Carter Museum, Fort Worth, Texas

The red man's forest falls to the white man's axe, sketch by an unknown artist (ca. 1858). In the first half of the nineteenth century the paramount symbol of progress in America was the pioneer leveling the forest. The Indian could neither arrest nor join the new order.
John Frost, *The Indian: On the Battlefield and in the Wigwam* (Boston, 1858)

Morning of a New Day, painting by Henry F. Farny, 1907. A wandering band of Indians need only glimpse below to sense that civilization has arrived.
Courtesy of the National Cowboy Hall of Fame and Western Heritage Center, Oklahoma City, Oklahoma

Sitting Bear Signing the Declaration of Allegiance to the U.S. Government,
photograph © 1913 by Rodman Wanamaker. Indian Inspector James McLaughlin,
who disliked the pomp of the ceremony, stands watching on the left as Sitting Bear,
and Arickaree, "signs" the document in a scene set up to prove that yesterday's
savages will be tomorrow's good citizens, during Rodman Wanamaker's Expedition of
Citizenship to the North American Indian.
Courtesy of the American Museum of Natural History, New York

Presenting the Flags at
Pauma, photograph © 1913
by Rodman Wanamaker. The
American flag-raising was
staged 169 times during
Wanamaker's expedition, led
by Joseph K. Dixon (standing
to the right holding the flags).
An assistant prepares to play
a recording of an
inspirational message from
President Woodrow Wilson.
Courtesy of the American Museum of
Natural History, New York

"A class of Indians in Fort Marion, with their teacher (Mrs. Gibbs)," sketch by Zotom, a Kiowa prisoner at Fort Marion, Florida, 1877. Captain Richard H. Pratt used his experience with Indians at Fort Marion as a guide in planning white education for Indians at Hampton Institute and Carlisle.
From *1877: Plains Indian Sketch Books of Zo-Tom and Howling Wolf* (1969); courtesy of Northland Press, Flagstaff, Arizona

Tom Torlino (Navajo) as he arrived at Carlisle and after four years at Carlisle, Carlisle School photographs, 1882 and 1885. Carlisle distributed before-and-after photographs of its students to show Indian progress after a proper education.
Courtesy of the Cumberland County Historical Society, Carlisle, Pennsylvania

"Move On, Maroon Brother, Move On!" sketch by Frederick Opper in *Bill Nye's History of the United States* (London, 1894). Opper's drawings illustrated a *satiric history*, in which Nye caustically remarked that "the real Indian has the dead and unkempt hair of a busted buggy cushion filled with hen feathers. He lies, he steals. . . ."

"On His Way to Join the Cave-bear, the Three-toed Horse, and the Ichthyosaurus," Sketch by Frederick Opper.

"Pigeon's Egg Head [The Light] going to and returning from Washington (1831–32)," sketch by George Catlin. Catlin wrote: "Black and blue cloth and civilization are destined, not only to veil, but to obliterate the grace and beauty of Nature." George Catlin, *Letters and Notes on the Manners, Customs and Condition of the North American Indians*, vol. II (New York, 1841)

The White Man's Gift, oil by an unknown artist, 1840. Liquor was the devastating vice that civilization gave the native in exchange for his natural virtues. This painting may have been inspired by Lydia Sigourney's 1836 poem, "First Gift to the Indians at Albany."
Courtesy of Kennedy Galleries, Inc., New York

Unnaturalized. Naturalized." Sketch by Henry Worrall.

Henry Worrall earned a substantial reputation in Topeka, Kansas, as an expert caricaturist by 1869. He contrasts the sentimental eastern version of the noble red man to the frontier version of reality.

W. E. Webb, *Buffalo Land: An Authentic Account of the Discoveries, Adventures, and Mishaps of a Scientific and Sporting Party in the Wild West* (Philadelphia, 1872)

Many Tailfeathers, Blackfoot, photograph by Arthur E. McFatridge, 1912.

McFatridge spent seventeen years as an Indian Bureau official in the West. "One spring day in 1912," he recalled, "I photographed a tired old man dressed in shabby white man's clothing . . . this was Many Tailfeathers, once an honored chief of his people."

McFatridge Collection of Indian Photos, courtesy of Dorothy McBride, Billings, Montana, and the Montana Historical Society, Helena

The Twilight of the Indian, wash drawing by Frederic Remington, 1897. The most popular western illustrator in the 1890s, Remington gloried in the clash between white civilization and, as he saw it, red savagery. At the end of the century he waxed nostalgic about the disappearance of the "Old West," in this work illustrating yesterday's buffalo-hunting warrior reduced to farming for a living.
Courtesy of the R. W. Norton Art Gallery, Shreveport, Louisiana

Visions of Yesterday, oil by William R. Leigh, 1943. Leigh unites the symbolic elements of Remington's *The Twilight of the Indian* and Charles Russell's "The Last of His Race" to produce an allegorical statement on the vanishing American.
Courtesy of the Woolaroc Museum, Bartlesville, Oklahoma

A Vision of the Past, oil by E. Irving Couse, 1913. Couse first visited Taos, New Mexico, in 1902 and was one of the founding members of the Taos Society of Artists. Although he generally portrayed Pueblo life, this painting of a sculpturesque group of men dreaming of a way of life the boy will never know is a rendition of a theme that by 1913 was closely identified with the plains Indians of prereservation days.
Courtesy of The Butler Institute of American Art, Youngstown, Ohio

The Last of Their Race, oil by John Mix Stanley, 1857. The Indians have been driven to the ocean in a scene that closely anticipates the theme of James E. Fraser's allegorical sculpture *The End of the Trail.*
Courtesy of the Buffalo Bill Historical Center, Cody, Wyoming

"The Last of His Race,"
sketch by Charles M.
Russell, 1899. Russell,
Montana's celebrated
"cowboy artist," went west in
1880, rode the open range,
and spent a winter with the
Blood Indians of southern
Alberta. His work thereafter
concentrated on "the West
that has passed," with the
Indian serving as the symbol
of his own deep sense of
loss.
Courtesy of the Montana Historical
Society, Helena

Ishi, last of the Yahi Indians,
August 29, 1911
Courtesy of the Lowie Museum of
Anthropology, University of
California, Berkeley

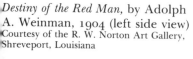

An Appeal to the Great Spirit,
sculpture by Cyrus E. Dallin, 1908
Courtesy of the Museum of Fine Arts,
Boston, gift of Peter C. Brooks and others

Destiny of the Red Man, by Adolph
A. Weinman, 1904 (left side view)
Courtesy of the R. W. Norton Art Gallery,
Shreveport, Louisiana

The Dying Chief
Contemplating the
Progress of Civilization,
sculpture by Thomas
Crawford, ca. 1855
Courtesy of the New-York
Historical Society, New York

The End of the Trail,
sculpture by James E.
Fraser, 1915
Courtesy of the National
Cowboy Hall of Fame and
Western Heritage Center,
Oklahoma City

The Sunset of a Dying Race,
photograph © 1913 by
Rodman Wanamaker
Joseph K. Dixon, *The Vanishing Race:
The Last Great Indian Council* (Garden
City, N.Y., 1913)

"The Vanishing Race,"
photograph by Edward S.
Curtis, ca. 1900
Edward S. Curtis, *The North American
Indian: Being a Series of Volumes
Picturing and Describing the Indians of the
United States and Alaska* (New York,
1907–30)

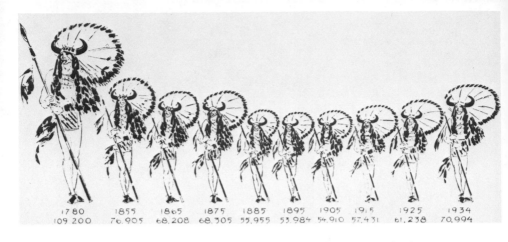

1780	1855	1865	1875	1885	1895	1905	1915	1925	1934
109 200	76,905	68,208	68,305	55,955	53,984	54,910	57,431	61,238	70,994

How the Plains Indian population has changed, graph from *Natural History* 34
(September 1934)

Symbol of the United Native
Americans, Inc., San
Francisco. A 1960's update of
The End of the Trail.

PART FOUR

ASSIMILATION
Indian Policy Through World War I

The whole thing is changed; the Indians in their relations to the Government, and the Government in its duty to them. They are no longer held in the light of enemies or treaty-making powers; they are wards, children in their minority, to be cared for as such, and fitted to become citizens, by education, civilization, and a practical knowledge of industrial pursuits.

—"Indian Extermination or Civilization," *Republic*, Vol. II (May 1874), p. 316

In the judgment of the great mass of the American people the time has come when the policy of keeping the Indians together in their tribal organizations and restraining and controlling them by bayonets and shotguns must be abandoned and a new era inaugurated— an era of the allotment of lands to the Indians in severalty, an era of education, an era in which they shall be enabled and required to qualify themselves for the duties of American citizenship, and to support themselves by industry and toil.

—Rep. Bishop W. Perkins of Kansas, December 15, 1886, in the *Congressional Record*, 49th Cong., 2nd sess., p. 191

CHAPTER TEN

IN SEARCH OF THE ONE TRUE ANSWER:
Indian Policy After the Civil War

"When the existing [reservation] system was adopted," President Grover Cleveland told Congress in December 1886, on the eve of the most important revision of federal Indian policy since the founding of the Republic,

the Indian race was outside of the limits of the organized States and Territories and beyond the immediate reach and operation of civilization, and all efforts were mainly directed to the maintenance of friendly relations and the preservation of peace and quiet on the frontier. All this is now changed. There is no such thing as the Indian frontier. Civilization, with the busy hum of industry and the influences of Christianity, surrounds these people at every point. None of the tribes are outside of the bounds of organized government and society. . . .

The case for a complete overhaul of Indian policy could not have been made more succinctly. In the fifty-two years since the passage of the final Trade and Intercourse Act, the United States had been transformed, and with it, the position of the Indian in American life. The West was won; the wilderness and its Indian population were now confined to "reservations" for their own protection. The short-term, expedient approach to the Indian problem, followed since colonial times, was no longer viable. The land was used up, and the Indian had stubbornly refused to vanish. Now, more than ever before, the

President warned Congress, a comprehensive, planned solution to the problem of the Indian's continuing presence was a need "pressing in its importance."[1]

The sense of an impending crisis in Indian affairs had been mounting since the 1840s when continental expansion fatally compromised the theory of Indian isolation out West. But it was one thing to recognize the crisis and another to remedy it. The only point of substantial agreement among those concerned with the Indians' welfare in the years immediately after the Civil War was the desire for better, fairer, and more effective treatment. Some thought that this would necessarily entail their enfranchisement; thus citizenship was the desired goal. Others called for forty acres and a mule; first make the Indians farmers, and then they would be ready for civilization and citizenship. Some counseled that the Indians would have to be approached as two (civilized and uncivilized) or three (civilized, semicivilized, and uncivilized) distinct problems, each requiring a different solution. Disciples of evolutionary science maintained that the Indians would have to ascend gradually from one ethnical period to another. Those with less patience insisted that the Indians had to be civilized at once if they were to be saved for the future. Most army officers urged the transfer of the Indian Bureau from the Department of the Interior to the War Department, arguing that the Indians would advance only if back under military control, "whipped into submission," and compelled to civilize.[2] Most philanthropists opposed transfer for the reason that "Bibles, and not bayonets, are the proper instruments by which to reclaim savages and confer the blessings of civilization."[3] Some advised that the Indians be kept apart from society, on their reservations, and there slowly trained in the arts of civilization; others, in increasing numbers, argued that only when the reservation was subdivided and the Indians fully incorporated into American society would there be progress.

THE DOOLITTLE COMMITTEE

Aware that the absence of a single guiding light in Indian affairs continued to pose a formidable obstacle to the reform almost everyone agreed was mandatory, the government periodically tried to assert leadership and correct this deficiency. In 1865, for example, Congress appointed a special joint committee to "inquire into the condition of the Indian tribes and their treatment by the civil and military authorities." Headed by Senator James R. Doolittle of Wisconsin, it compiled evidence by circulating a questionnaire that drew twenty-seven responses, eleven of them from army officers, the rest from civilians connected in some way with the Indian Bureau. The committee members also fanned out across Indian country to conduct first-hand investigations. A traveler who encountered Doolittle and another member en route to the Southwest to undertake their portion of the field work expressed the hope that a "more intelligent and effective Indian policy" would reward their efforts. "Whoever shall discover and cause to be put in practice a policy towards our Indian tribes, that shall secure protection alike to them and the whites, and stop indiscriminate massacre on both sides, will prove the greatest of national benefactors."[4]

But the Doolittle committee failed to meet expectations. Its report, submitted after the elapse of nearly two years, consisted of a bulky appendix of uneven and conflicting evidence prefaced by a report proper of only ten pages. First, the committee concluded, the Indians everywhere except in Indian Territory were decreasing in numbers. Twenty of the twenty-seven respondents to the questionnaire supported this view, and several thought the decline irreversible. The committee was less pessimistic, though its recommendations offered little that was fresh and no clear direction for future policy development. Five inspection districts were to be created in Indian country, and five boards of inspection appointed, each composed of an assistant Commissioner of Indian Affairs, one army officer, and one person nominated by the religious bodies. The three would report, respectively, to the Secretary of the Interior, the Secretary of War, and "the government." The boards were to try to visit all the tribes in their jurisdiction every year, hear their complaints, and examine the day-to-day conduct of Indian affairs.[5]

Instead of proposing an innovative departure from past

practice, the Doolittle report called for more of the same, closely supervised to restore integrity to the Indian Service, which, its critics maintained, was a sink of corruption. Indeed, in the early 1860s scandals and rumored scandals had rocked the bureau, and civilian reformers and army officers alike spoke knowingly of an "Indian Ring" that robbed the public treasury with one hand and the government's red wards with the other, impeding every attempt to solve the Indian problem since success would mean the end to a lucrative spoils system.[6] Structured on the checks-and-balances principle, the proposed boards of inspection were designed more to satisfy the government's critics than to meet the pressing needs of the Indians.

Subsequent efforts to revamp federal Indian policy were equally unfruitful, and the Commissioner of Indian Affairs was left to complain in 1876, as his predecessors had for thirty years, that the "fundamental difficulty in our relations hitherto with Indians has been the want of a well-defined, clearly understood, persistent purpose on the part of the Government."[7] The achievement of the 1870s would be a negative one: the exhaustion of several false starts, and the gravitation to a single ruling concept, the allotment of Indian lands in severalty, as the only policy capable of meeting the existing crisis and leading the Indians to citizenship and full assimilation.

PRESIDENT GRANT'S PEACE POLICY

On March 3, 1871, President Grant signed into law an act of considerable symbolic importance. The United States, just five years short of the hundredth birthday of its independence, had elected to abandon the treaty system, the modus operandi of government-Indian relations since the creation of the Republic. "No Indian nation or tribe within the territory of the United States shall be acknowledged or recognized as an independent nation, tribe, or power with whom the United States may contract a treaty," the act declared, adding that existing treaties were unimpaired by its terms.[8] An "absurd" anachronism[9] and a "cruel farce"[10] had been eliminated, principally out of political motives since the House of Representatives resented footing the bill for the rash of Indian treaties ratified by the Senate shortly after the Civil War. The abandonment of the traditional way of conducting business with the natives also served notice that the position of most of the tribes had undergone a dramatic change since the eighteenth century. Their dependency had long since eclipsed their status as "nations," domestic or otherwise. With congressional repudiation of the treaty system, Indians were now in law what they were in fact, wards of the federal government, and theory was aligned with the reality represented by the program of Indian improvement Grant had initiated upon taking office in 1869.

In his inaugural address Grant had sounded a venerable theme, calling for a policy that would facilitate the Indians' "civilization and ultimate citizenship."[11] Unlike most of his predecessors, however, Grant proposed to *do* something. That very year, perhaps with the Doolittle committee report in mind, he appointed the Board of Indian Commissioners, composed of eminent philanthropists serving without pay.[12] The board was expected to act both as a watchdog of and an advisory body to the Indian Bureau, which continued to labor under public suspicion. Besides creating the board, Grant, at the instigation of a delegation of Quakers, implemented the novel policy of inviting interested Christian sects to nominate men of their choosing as Indian agents.

Originally, it had been Grant's intention to appoint army officers as agents. His reasoning was simple. An officer-agent would continue to be responsible to the War Department, commissioned in the military for life and, therefore, not subject to the shift of political fortunes. His and the nation's best interests would coincide. He would work to establish peace on the plains and in the desert in order that he might one day enjoy duty stateside. His appointment would be economical—he was already on the government payroll—and, bound by the code of military honor, he would be virtually incorruptible. The army officer had no short-term interest in the Indian, with the desire for a quick return on some past political investment ever foremost in his mind. Thus the scandal of corruption in the administration of Indian affairs would be ended, and integrity would be restored to the service.

But Grant's hopes were dashed in 1870 when Congress

passed a law forbidding the employment of army officers as Indian agents. Humanitarians were opposed to the idea on principle, and Congress was not about to relinquish its control over patronage as valuable as the Indian agencies. Grant responded by adopting the Quaker plan across the board, and throwing it open to all denominations.

The "Quaker Policy" was soon oversubscribed, and considerable bickering broke out among the participating sects dissatisfied with the reservation quotas assigned them. The interdenominational squabbling was a portent. But Grant had a larger vision, his "Peace Policy." Its keynote was recognition of the fact that the Indians were, as he said, "wards of the nation (they can not be regarded in any other light than as wards)." Civilization was rapidly descending on the last wild tribes, and the only alternative to their extinction was a system that would place "all the Indians on large reservations, as rapidly as it can be done," and there give them "absolute protection." With the promise of individual allotment of the lands and territorial status in the future, Grant rounded out his Peace Policy.[13]

"Conquest by kindness," representing the "Quaker" in the policy, was to be the preferred method of inducing the tribes to settle on their reservations. But, as an officer pointed out at the time, persuasion would have to be backed with force. "Give to the Indians sugar and coffee, furnish them with plows and seeds, but let them at once and forever understand that the hand that feeds can, and if need be, will, strike," Colonel George Ward Nichols wrote. "The benefits of the arts of peace may be taught the red man, but the saving grace of our reform movement is, 'The iron fingers in a velvet glove.'"[14] For administrative purposes, all Indians would thenceforth fall into two categories: reservation Indians, under civilian management, and hostile Indians, under army jurisdiction.

THE ARMY AND THE INDIAN QUESTION

The question of army jurisdiction in itself sparked a prolonged bureaucratic wrangle. The army had only reluctantly accepted the transfer of the Indian Bureau to the new Department of the Interior in 1849, and after the Civil War many officers persistently agitated for the bureau's return. The transfer question, as it was called, involved a mixture of motives. Following Appomattox, the army had tumbled out of public favor. In a nation anxious for sectional reconciliation, it was a painful reminder of divisiveness. For southerners under Reconstruction, the army became a hated symbol of northern oppression. In Congress, it was constantly assailed by Democrats who found a formidable weapon in the need for economic retrenchment during the severe depression of the 1870s. Maintaining peace in the trans-Mississippi West was the army's chief *raison d'être*, all that stood between it and lower pay, slower promotions, and further cuts in manpower and budget.[15]

A parade of high-ranking officers stepped forward in the 1860s and 1870s to argue that civilian control had proven inefficient and notoriously dishonest, basing the case for transfer on the same arguments Grant had used in his abortive attempt to appoint army officers as Indian agents. More provocative was the army's charge that civilian mismanagement had been directly responsible for most of the hostilities along the frontier. The Indians, systematically starved by corrupt agents busily lining their pockets with annuity monies, were armed with the latest weapons by corrupt traders, who also plied them with the firewater that fueled their war spirit. Transfer would put the army in control of the whole situation, and end its frustration at being brought in after the civilian bureau had so badly bungled things that war was the only recourse. Divided—and often overlapping—jurisdiction was anathema, then, no matter how neat it might seem in theory. It complicated affairs from the top down to the bottom, and led to interminable quarrels between the officers and agents in the field. Of more consequence, it created a *"divisum imperium"*[16] that fostered the impression of weakness in the Indian mind, thereby encouraging resistance. But if the hand that fed were also the hand that punished, the Indians would quickly learn to respect the authority of the government, and would think twice about creating disturbances. As it was, Richard I. Dodge said for a legion of officers, "the Indian is in the position of a wilful boy, with a powerful but henpecked father, and an indulgent, weak mother."[17] Undivided paternal rule was the answer.

The transfer issue became a preoccupation with certain

military men, its currency as a public question waxing and
waning over the years until it eventually faded out due to
inertia and changed circumstances. As long as Indian wars
were being fought, however, the issue was alive—and not
without reason. The army was placed in an unenviable position.
On the one side were westerners, favorable to transfer, demanding protection and urging extermination of the savages.
On the other were concerned easterners, Indian-less and
shocked by such frontier barbarism, insisting that chastisement
be used only sparingly, as a supplement to the policy of
containment and enlightenment. The army could expect only
criticism from eastern philanthropists, yet could not satisfy
western opinion either, faced as it was with the hopeless task
of patrolling a vast region where it could not touch the Indians
on their reservations and, experience showed, usually could
not catch them off. The army's dilemma was summed up by
General William T. Sherman in 1870: "There are two classes
of people, one demanding the utter extinction of the Indians,
and the other full of love for their conversion to civilization
and Christianity. Unfortunately the army stands between and
gets the cuffs from both sides."[18]

For all its difficulties, the army was a vital factor in post–Civil
War Indian policy. The conquest of the western tribes proved
a long, drawn-out affair. A succession of Indian outbreaks in
the 1860s and early 1870s embarrassed a nation eager to
proclaim its material and moral progress as it neared the
hundredth anniversary of its independence, and Sioux and
Cheyenne war cries along the Little Big Horn rudely interrupted the eagle's proud birthday scream during the centennial
summer. One Indian war followed another until the end of
the decade, by which time all the plains tribes were subdued
and the Modocs, Nez Percé, and Utes had joined General
Custer in making their last stands.

In the southwestern desert, scattered bands of Apaches
resisted well into the 1880s, but by 1891, with Wounded Knee
serving as a pathetic closing act, America's Indian wars were
over. They had provided the background to policy debate
through the years, lending urgency to the humanitarian interest
in the Indian by making extermination a frightening prospect,

and it was their gradual cessation that, by effectively removing the army from an active role in decision-making, freed eastern reformers to mold a new Indian policy in accordance with their cherished objectives, untroubled by an *object* capable of meeting coercion, philanthropic or otherwise, in kind. At last the Indian everywhere was a ward in fact as in theory, and this was a consideration of profound consequence to policy formulation. The army itself had made transfer a dead issue.

RESERVATIONS AND CONCENTRATION

In its humanitarian dedication to civilizing the Indian, Grant's Peace Policy could not be faulted. Nevertheless, it suffered from a glaring defect. Even as Americans of every persuasion were becoming convinced that the segregation of the Indian was neither desirable nor possible, the Peace Policy adhered to the outmoded isolationist philosophy represented by the reservation system.

To its supporters, the reservation system was the most efficient method of bringing the wandering tribes into a permanent relationship with the government and tying them down to a fixed abode. To that extent, the reservation was an essential part of any program of Indian civilization, and it might yet provide for that isolation that had justified removal as a humane policy. The Trade and Intercourse Acts still applied on the reservation, and contact between red and white was thus legally circumscribed. At a time shortly after the Republican Party had revived the scheme of Negro colonization in Central America or Haiti, a few enthusiasts were prepared to push the notion of Indian segregation to its logical extreme. All of America's native peoples should be relocated on islands— perhaps Isle Royale in Lake Superior, Angel Island in San Francisco Bay, Santa Cruz or Santa Catalina off the coast of California, "desirable" islands in the Atlantic near the East Coast, or maybe even "some small West Indian island . . . where tropical nature will feed them without expense to the Government."[9] It did not matter where the islands were located, really, so long as the principle was adopted. Inasmuch as "the first step to a good and moral influence upon the Savage is the removal of the causes of corruption, it is clear that this may be effected where the nature of the reservation assists."[20]

To their detractors, reservations were already islands—islands of barbarism in the sea of American civilization. But they were intended as something more, and President Grant, in proposing the Peace Policy, had in mind what two special commissioners meant by a reservation: not "a pen where a horde of savages are to be fed with flour and beef," "supplied with blankets," and "furnished with paint and gew-gaws by the greed of traders," but rather "a school of industry and a home for these unfortunate people."[21] On the reservation, safe from the destructive vices of frontier society, the Indians would prepare for the day when, sufficiently advanced, they could receive a portion of the tribal estate for their own and assume the duties and privileges of American citizenship.

It was a pleasant scenario, but not everyone was convinced that the government had drafted it correctly. Isolation was a mirage, experience showed. Accept this, and the elaborate rationale for the reservation system began to crumble. It was an expedient, and its success would depend on two factors: how long the reservation could last, and how long it would take the Indians to become civilized. Reservations, like Indian country before them, would be in the way eventually, and the Indians would have to move on. Tell them, Samuel Bowles wrote in 1869, "you must not leave this home we have assigned you; the white man must not come hither; we will keep you in and him out; when the march of our empire demands this reservation of yours, we will assign you another; . . . so long as we choose, this is your home, your prison, your playground." But when empire came marching, *where* could the Indians be moved? Since Bowles believed the Indian was destined to die out anyway, the question did not unduly trouble him. "All we can do is to smooth and make decent the pathway to the grave," he insisted.[22]

However, the problem of administering the reservation system was less simple. A succession of treaties in the 1860s had sprinkled reservations over the broad West, far from one another and well beyond the reach of efficient management and protection from the incursions of white trespassers. Now each individual reservation was subject to the same pressures that had beset Indian country, with the added difference that "the smaller the reservation, the speedier the Indians become extinct."[23]

This difficulty had been perceived early on, and a solution proposed: the concentration of all the tribes in one or more large "districts," with the possibility of territorial status in the near future. The scheme was facilitated by the fact that the civilized nations occupying Indian Territory had compromised their treaty rights by supporting the Confederacy in the war, and were now vulnerable to retaliatory action. By 1867 the Commissioner of Indian Affairs was urging "preservation by gradual concentration on territorial reserves" as the only alternative to "swift extermination by the sword, and famine."[24]

A commission appointed that year to treat with the western tribes and, as one of its tasks, investigate the concentration plan, expressed its preference for an assimilation policy, but reluctantly endorsed consolidation. The tribes east of the Rockies should be gathered into two districts, the existing Indian Territory and another bounded on the north by the 46th parallel, the east by the Missouri River, the south by Nebraska, and the west by the 104th meridian, with the eventual object of breaking them down into "one homogenous mass."[25] Removal once again would constitute the means to a noble end.

Concentration's advantages were obvious. Besides centralizing and simplifying Indian management, it would throw large tracts of desirable land open to the ever-pressing settlers. For those concerned that civilization would soon engulf the existing reservations to the detriment of the Indians, it would eliminate the issue. Thus while the current of events and opinion ran counter to the Peace Policy's segregationist theory, isolation through concentration might still serve as a bridge between past and future.

FRANCIS A. WALKER AND THE CASE FOR CONCENTRATION

Though President Grant first recommended the concentration of the western Indians in Indian Territory in 1869, and dutifully mentioned it in subsequent annual messages to Congress, the most outspoken champion of the idea was Francis A. Walker. Superintendent of the ninth and tenth censuses, president of the Massachusetts Institute of Technology from 1881 to 1897, an economist and statistician of international reputation, and an important early theoretician of immigrant exclusion, Walker, after completing the 1870 census, served as Commissioner of Indian Affairs from November 1871 to December 1872. He had already exhibited a level-headed interest in the Indian question, aptly summing up the dilemma of policymakers in 1870:

Unless they be Indians or soldiers on the war-path, or philanthropists by the Atlantic sea-board, Americans do not pretend to be otherwise than confused when the Indian is spoken of. As a people we have not been able to solve "the Indian question," or it would not any longer be the loud-echoing question that it is. We should be greatly obliged to any one who would convince us of the true answer and let us get rid of it.

For his part, Walker was convinced that the reservation system was the "true answer" to the problem.[26] While his tenure as commissioner was too brief for him to exert a decisive influence on policy, he brought a plausible case for concentration before the public in an 1873 article on "The Indian Question" in the *North American Review*, reprinted the following year as a book along with his unusually thorough official report for 1872.

Walker argued that two distinct Indian questions presented themselves: one involving the hostiles, the other, Indians already settled on reservations. This bifurcation, basic to the Peace Policy, meant that two different solutions were in order. Asserting that the primary consideration in the first instance was the safety of the frontier, Walker advocated a "policy of temporizing" rather than direct military intervention. That is, the Indians should ostensibly be pampered and their whims catered to. For those who found this thought repugnant, Walker stressed that "there can be no question of national dignity involved in the treatment of savages by a civilized power." In reality, the government was simply "playing" with the Indians, biding its time, awaiting the day when "their power of resistance shall have departed" and they were reduced to wardship. More consequential—and difficult—was the other question: "What shall be done with the Indian when he shall be thrown helpless on our government and people?"[27]

First, Walker countered the popular opinion, which, captivated by the theories of vices and virtues and reversion to savage type, supposed inevitable extinction. Indian civilization was not "altogether impossible," he argued, a fact that made it incumbent on the government to encourage the Indian's improvement. For this purpose, the reservation system should be made "the general and permanent policy of the government." Thus Walker called for a renewed effort at total "separation and seclusion" for "the good of both races." His old-fashioned appraisal was modern only in recommending the concentration of America's western Indians on "one or two grand reservations," with two perhaps the more desirable plan.[28] The Trade and Intercourse Acts, thoughtfully revised and stringently enforced, would yet secure the desired isolation.

Walker was fully aware that his position was unpopular, but he regarded seclusion as an acceptable alternative to assimilation. Service against the South in the Civil War and a debilitating confinement at Libby, the notorious Confederate prison in Richmond, Virginia, had not made him an advocate of racial equality, and a trace of distaste at the prospect of unrestricted intermingling colored all his writing. The future "philosopher of immigration restriction" was a natural-born segregationist.[29]

He reaffirmed his position on Indian isolation in an article published in 1874 opposing the persistent reformer demand for Indian citizenship. In it, he analyzed at length the advantages and disadvantages of the "two antagonistic schemes," separation and assimilation, disarming potential critics by frankly conceding that "times have indeed changed, and it is fitting that we should change with them." By change, however, Walker meant retrenchment, and he went on to explicate the benefits that would be secured by concentration. Retention of the traditional tribal structures would lighten the burden of governing the Indians and would preserve their virtues. Immediate citizenship and allotment, in contrast, would only divest them of their lands and leave them supplicants upon the government's charity, a prospect particularly onerous for the western states. Thus the nation's "sacred duty" was clear: "To cut off a reservation sufficient for the wants of this unfortunate people . . . ; to hedge it in with strict laws of non-intercourse, turning aside for the purpose railway and highway alike; and, upon the soil thus secluded, to work patiently out the problem of Indian civilization. . . ."[30]

THE CHEYENNE AND PONCA REMOVALS

Despite Walker's exertions, the concentration scheme went down to defeat before an imposing array of critics. Though the Commissioner of Indian Affairs was still flirting with the idea as late as 1885,[31] for practical purposes it had become a dead issue. The western states bordering on Indian Territory were not about to welcome an influx of wild tribes as near neighbors, and Missouri, Texas, Kansas, and Arkansas formed a powerful bloc in Congress against every proposed removal. The government's enthusiasm for the Quaker Policy had waned by the middle of the 1870s, and after President Grant left office the appointment of agents returned to the hands of interested politicos rather than participating Christian denominations. The resulting dilution of religious authority on the reservations, once hopefully conceived of as "Christian workshops," led many reformers who had earnestly supported the Peace Policy's isolationism to advocate instead a program of assimilation. Most of all, the forced removal of northern tribes to Indian Territory awakened uneasy memories of the 1830s, and two incidents in particular evoked the shame of the "Trail of Tears."

In 1878 a band of Northern Cheyennes, sent to Indian Territory the previous year in keeping with the concentration policy and as punishment for their involvement in the Sioux War of 1876, tried to return to their homeland. Some were captured and imprisoned in Nebraska; when they escaped out of fear of being sent back south, they were tracked down and many of them killed. The inhumanity of the end result underlined removal's intrinsic inhumanity. The policy was at fault, and the eastern press was prepared to blame its bloody outcome on the nation's "disgraceful conduct" in implementing it.[32]

If the Cheyennes had to some extent forfeited sympathy by their recalcitrance in the past and the raiding they did on their trek north, the same was certainly not true of a second removed tribe, the Poncas. Indeed, the Poncas' was a textbook case in the miscarriage of justice. Indian policy often suffered from a fault endemic to programs geared to maximum bureaucratic convenience: unruly tribes received preferential treatment while those renowned for their peacefulness and cooperation were either taken for granted and ignored or, far worse, exploited. In order to pacify the powerful Sioux, the government in 1868 had ceded them an area of land that inadvertently comprised the Ponca reservation created by treaty ten years before; in order to *keep* the Sioux pacified, the government in 1877 removed the Poncas to Indian Territory. Uprooted and unable to adjust to the new climate, the Poncas initially suffered a heavy loss of life. One band that had resisted the move all along returned north in 1879, creating a complex legal situation involving a feisty, sympathetic Nebraska newspaperman, a federal district judge, an army general, the Secretary of the Interior, a young Omaha woman with the appealing name Bright Eyes, and an eloquent Ponca chief named Standing Bear. Egged on by a smoothly orchestrated propaganda campaign, national indignation soared.[33]

Boston, in particular, was swept away by the Poncas' cause. The city's mayor, the pastor of Old South Church, prominent residents like Wendell Phillips and Henry Wadsworth Longfellow, the president of Amherst College, the governor of Massachusetts, and one of the state's powerful senators all did their bit. Not since the removal controversy had the Bay State been so caught up in the Indian question. Before the furor settled down, the Commissioner of Indian Affairs had been replaced and President Rutherford B. Hayes had contritely jotted in his diary that "a great and grevious [*sic*] wrong" had been committed.[34]

For the Poncas, there was a relatively happy ending: those who chose to remain in Indian Territory *and* those who chose to return to their old Dakota reservation were accommodated. Moreover, the concentration-through-removal policy had been permanently discredited. "In showing up the Ponca case," the reformer William Justin Harsha wrote in 1882, "a grievous system of wrongs has been so effectually disclosed that no inspector will ever again attempt the removal of a tribe of Indians against their will."[35]

HELEN HUNT JACKSON AND THE REFORM APPEAL

The lesson taught by the Ponca incident was simple. Only when Indians enjoyed the rights of citizenship and owned their land in severalty with legally impeccable titles would they have any protection against trespass and usurpation.[36] Overnight, reform organizations like the Boston Indian Citizenship Committee and the Women's National Indian Association (Philadelphia) sprouted in the East, most of them committed to the new verity of assimilation through allotment in severalty.[37] In a nation preoccupied with other matters, the most difficult obstacle faced by Indian reformers had always been public apathy. Only loud, organized protest would alert Congress to the need for a comprehensive policy reform, and only concerted, unrelenting pressure would make Congress act. The Poncas served to focus attention on Indian rights and transform ordinary citizens into reformers. Bright Eyes expressed the hope that a book on the trials and tribulations of the Poncas would enter "every home in the land," wherein alone resided power sufficient "to remedy the evil."[38] Constant agitation was imperative to keep the moral issue at the forefront and the nation's conscience in perpetual ferment. "Agitate! Agitate!" a Boston minister urged. "On the Indian question, Congress will go no further than it is forced to go by public opinion. Public sentiment must smite the laggard sails of our national legislature; otherwise this whole matter will lie in a dead calm, even while Indians starve to death."[39]

If agitation was the order of the day, the perfect agitator proved to be an aspiring Harriet Beecher Stowe of the Indians,[40] Helen Hunt Jackson.

The daughter of an Amherst professor, Helen Maria Fiske had led the sheltered life typical of a girl of her class and breeding. She married young and began to raise a family. But when her husband drowned, leaving her widowed and on her own at the age of thirty-five, she turned to writing for a livelihood. A prolific contributor of poems, travel sketches, and short stories to the popular periodicals, "H.H." (Helen Hunt) supported herself until the necessity was removed with a second marriage twelve years later, in 1875, to a Colorado Springs banker and railroad man. Casting about for an interest to fill her newly idle hours, she encountered the Indian problem first in the excitement that swept Colorado following the White River Ute uprising in September 1879, and later that fall at a lecture in Boston by Standing Bear. From that time until her death in 1885, she was, in her words, "a woman with a hobby," passionately dedicated to the Indian's cause.[41] Her indictment of American Indian policy, published in 1881 as *A Century of Dishonor*, remains a classic muckraking polemic.

Writing in the heat of moral outrage, Helen Hunt Jackson saw it as her role to confront the nation with a record of duplicity in its dealings with the Indian so repugnant that no citizen could ignore it. An aroused national conscience was her sole purpose; all else would follow. She was to be a purifier administering the purgative that would flush the American system clean of a century's accumulation of foul deeds, clearing the way for a healthy diet of honesty, good faith, and high principles in Indian affairs. Her crusader zeal, like Carry Nation's, was not *for* something but *against* something. "There is a disposition in a certain class of minds to be impatient with any protestation against wrong which is unaccompanied or unprepared with a quick and exact scheme of remedy," she explained.

This is illogical. When pioneers in a new country find a tract of poisonous and swampy wilderness to be reclaimed, they do not withhold their hands from fire and axe till they see clearly which way roads should run, where good water will spring, and what crops will best grow on the redeemed land. They first clear the swamp. So with this poisonous and baffling part of the domain of our national affairs—let us first "clear the swamp."[42]

An exposé of the nation's past crimes, then, would do more good than a thousand reasoned proposals for solving the Indian problem; Americans must first be aroused before they would take action against the outrages.

The root cause of the "century of dishonor," Jackson said,

was a legal one centering on Indian title to the land. Once Europeans had acknowledged the Indians' right of occupancy of the soil, retaining the right of sovereignty for themselves, as civilized men they were bound to respect Indian title. By negotiating treaties with the tribes, the United States had acquiesced in the old system. In time the treaties had proven an inconvenience no longer justified by the need to placate the natives. But treaties did not exist at the convenience of one party, and Americans were still legally and morally bound to honor them. Faithlessness in repeatedly breaking their solemn promises to the Indians damned the United States as "wicked," and invited punishment before the tribunal of world opinion as well as "that more certain natural punishment which, sooner or later, as surely comes from evildoing as harvests come from sown seed." A recitation of wrongs followed, tribal case histories illustrative of the crime of treaty-breaking. Like a ritual cycle, the same story was repeated over and over. "It makes little difference . . . where one opens the record of the history of the Indians; every page and every year has its dark stain."[43] The text climaxed with the chapter "Massacres of Indians by Whites," which drove home the terrible lesson that treaty-breaking at sword's point disgraced a civilized Christian nation, dragging it down to a level far below that of ignorant savagery. The cumulative effect on the reader, Jackson hoped, would be a boiling sense of indignation, a cry of "Shame!" and a resolution to prevent such injustices from ever recurring.

For practical reformers, Jackson's insistence on the right to criticize destructively put her book in a curious light. George Manypenny's *Our Indian Wards* had appeared the year before *A Century of Dishonor*. While it contained its own quota of white abuses, it was specifically intended as a rebuttal to the constant criticism directed at the civilian Bureau of Indian Affairs by various army officers. Manypenny, who had headed the bureau in the 1850s, defended it and the government policy it administered, and attacked the military for its atrocities. Thus *Our Indian Wards* stood as a counterargument to demands that the bureau be transferred back to War Department control. *A Century of Dishonor* had no such concrete purpose. Helen Hunt Jackson pointedly disavowed efforts to uplift the Indians through immediate and general citizenship or allotment in severalty, and denounced any "sovereign and instantaneous panacea for all their ills."[44]

Jackson was no wild-eyed reformer. It was American dishonor that concerned her, not Indian rights per se. On such matters as the legal superiority of civilization's claims to those of savagery, she could be unexpectedly hard-headed. To question that superiority, she maintained, was "feeble sentimentalism."[45] But her identification with the pioneer who drained swamps, leveled forests, and plunged on heedless of consequences, made clear the distinction between the abolitionist movement, where the moral issue and its practical solution had been obvious, and Indian reform, where the moral issue was reasonably apparent but its practical solution was not. At least allotment in severalty offered a plan of operation, one of Jackson's critics wrote.[46] She offered none, and her unremitting war on the Secretary of the Interior over the Ponca problem was divisive at a time when the Indian reform movement desperately needed a united front.

But in the larger perspective, Helen Hunt Jackson's role in policy reform was substantial. *A Century of Dishonor* attracted a wide and influential readership. It was crammed with damning details that could be held up to public scrutiny—and opprobrium—by the preacher and the editor alike. It stirred a lethargic populace, and while Theodore Roosevelt muttered about "foolish sentimentalists,"[47] others joined in the fight for Indian reform. Stragglers, under the spell of her California Indian love story, *Ramona* (1884), were also brought into the fold. Helen Hunt Jackson died before she could discern any lasting results from her labors. But others now echoed her pleas for the rebirth of a sense of justice and expressed their determination to prevent a second "century of dishonor."[48] The movement for Indian reform was well under way.

By 1880 the diverting side issues had all been thrashed out— the Quaker Policy, with its church-nominated agents; the transfer issue; and the Peace Policy, with its overarching concept of reservation sanctuaries, reduced in number by removal and concentration to a few large blocs of land, patrolled on the outside by the army and supervised within by humanitarians dedicated to the work of Indian enlightenment. Most of the western tribes were now on the reservations, their power of resistance broken. But despite a decade of experimentation, the Indian problem remained unsolved.

Those with the firmest grasp of the situation had reached a few basic conclusions: History demonstrated the temporary nature of an isolationist policy, and only assimilation, the government's long-deferred goal, offered a permanent solution. No law could restrain the settlers pushing at the borders of the reservations. They wanted the Indian lands, and they would have them. "*All reservations*"—of Indian lands, race, or culture—"are only necessary evils or but temporary expedients," a pioneer missionary insisted. Safety for 250,000 widely dispersed natives in a nation of 50 million could be found "only if the smaller people flow in with the current of the life and ways of the larger."[49] Assimilation would be policy's end, allotment in severalty its primary means.

CHAPTER ELEVEN

A NEW ORDER OF THINGS:
The General Allotment Act

By the 1880s the allotment of Indian lands in severalty was an accepted feature of American Indian policy, though only on a tribe-by-tribe basis. In the post–Civil War years one respected spokesman after another came out in favor of a general allotment policy as the single, far-reaching measure commensurate to the problem—"the key with which to unlock the whole question," a Kansas legislator told his colleagues early in 1877, "the first decisive step in the solution of the Indian difficulty."[1]

The Commissioner of Indian Affairs in his annual report for 1876 had urged adoption of a comprehensive allotment policy, and President Hayes and his successors concurred. Carl Schurz, Secretary of the Interior from 1877 to 1881, a liberal reformer of long standing, was a warm advocate. Writing in the *North American Review*, he rejected the theory behind concentration as untenable, and in a single sentence stated the principal tenets of an allotment policy:

What we can and should do is . . . to fit the Indians, as much as possible, for the habits and occupations of civilized life, by work and education; to individualize them in the possession and appreciation of property, by allotting to them lands in severalty, giving them a fee simple title individually to the parcels of land they cultivate, inalienable for a certain period, and to obtain their consent to a disposition of that part of their lands which they cannot use, for a fair compensation, in such a manner that they no longer stand in the way of the

161

development of the country as an obstacle, but form part of it and are benefited by it.[2]

Led by several well-organized reform groups, public opinion concurred. Best of all, allotment in severalty was a policy that spanned sectional divisions in its appeal.

AN EAST-WEST CONSENSUS

In colonial times, when England attempted to protect native title, it had found that the Crown's American subjects regarded Indian lands as free for the taking. A student of the Iroquois land frontier has argued that the British effort to honor Indian title was a potent grievance that bred a spirit of rebellion in the colonies—especially since the Crown showed itself ineffectual in enforcing its own decrees.[3] The United States government fared little better. In 1789 the Secretary of War conceded that while legislators could pass prohibitive measures, "the disposition of the people of the states to emigrate into the Indian country cannot be effectually prevented."[4]

Through the nineteenth century, policy was made in the East, but its fate was determined out West. The army was often put in the position of tryig to enforce policy on a vast frontier where the white population chose to ignore the law and resist its implementation. In the end, expediency always dictated that the government back down. This predictable process—omnivorous white land hunger gobbling up weakly protected Indian-holdings—was behind those official reversals and broken treaties that Helen Hunt Jackson deplored. The Ponca incident illustrated the government's perpetual inability to protect the tribal domain and fostered demands for a wholesale revision in Iridian tenure, from communal to individual ownership. Reformers like William Harsha felt that law "must go before the granting of land in severalty."[5] Most were convinced that only when each Indian owned his own parcel of land in fee simple would the white man accept his title as valid. Until that day, no Indian land was safe from encroachment and eventual appropriation.

The East-West split on the Indian question had been exacerbated by the Peace Policy, with its stalemate between force and suasion, might and benevolence. The beauty of a general policy of allotment in severalty was that it managed to accommodate both East and West. It appealed simultaneously to humanitarian instincts and overt self-interest. In 1879 the Commissioner of Indian Affairs echoed the sentiments expressed by the Secretary of War exactly ninety years before: "The experience of the Indian Department . . . goes to show that the government is impotent to protect the Indians on their own reservations, especially when held in common, from the encroachments of its own people, whenever a discovery has been made rendering the possession of their lands desirable by the whites."[6] The commissioner was affirming in the strongest possible terms the need for a general allotment policy. On the one hand, it would encourage Indian civilization while protecting Indian title; on the other, it would break up and redistribute the huge tracts of tribal land westerners coveted. From the outset, those who urged the subdivision of the reservations had been at pains to elucidate allotment's advantages for white settlers. Only a stipulated acreage would go to each Indian family. What remained of the reservations after allotment—in most cases, a sizable portion—would be thrown open to white settlement. Left unsaid was the fact that past experience showed that the great preponderance of land actually allotted to the Indians would also wind up in white hands, thereby completing the sweep of the reservations.

The homesteader would get the land, and the Indian the benefit of close association with an enlightened white population of trustworthy farmers. The Carlisle "outings" would be duplicated in a natural setting, and "we will soon find the Indians upon their homesteads advancing in civilization," Senator Joseph E. Brown of Georgia predicted in 1881:

Under the benign influence of the Christian denominations, we shall see Sunday schools and churches planted among them; and instead of roving bands without fixed habitations, goaded to desperation by injustice and wrong, spreading death and destruction in their pathway, we shall find them in the comfortable homes of civilized man, not only a Christian people but many of them cultivated and honorable citizens.[7]

So rapidly would the Indians progress that they would require only a brief wardship period during which their titles were inalienable, no more than fifty years at the outside, and some said ten years would be sufficient.[8]

Westerners were less hostile to allotment than to earlier programs; the allotment policy also enjoyed the warm, but not unqualified, support of eastern advocates of reform. Indeed, tough words were directed at its provisions for the sale of unallotted Indian lands, and three members of the House Committee on Indian Affairs in 1880 damned general allotment as a "pretext . . . in the name of Humanity, and under the cloak of an ardent desire to promote the Indian's welfare by making him like ourselves," to "get at his lands and occupy them."[9] Some doubted the suitability of most reservation lands for agriculture. Others fretted that past treaties should be honored before new commitments were made. Some clergymen and missionary societies, dreaming of a return to the "Christian workshop" theory of the Grant years, were only grudgingly reconciled to immediate assimilation. But there was nothing in severalty, finally, to divide the friends of the Indian as removal had divided those of an earlier generation. All agreed that the Indian could be civilized, and that education, agriculture, and private property would work the transformation.

Indians would at last be given opportunity to demonstrate their capacity for improvement. In a positive environment, exposed only to good influences, they were bound to flourish as they labored in their fields and milked their cows, safe from the bad influences infesting the reservations.

THE EVOLUTIONISTS' CRITIQUE: L. H. MORGAN
AND J. W. POWELL

Those who took an evolutionary view of things shook their heads in dismay at the naïve expectations of the reformers. Science taught that man rose through a series of immutable ethnical periods, as Lewis Henry Morgan had been at pains to explain. One could not skip a period or progress at an accelerated rate. Each level involved a set time before a culture was ready to take the next step upward. At best the Indians were middle barbarians, two removes away from civilization, and most of the recently conquered western tribes were actually three or four ethnical periods behind white American society.

This did not mean that a philosophy of laissez-faire was the necessary corollary of evolutionism. Herbert Spencer had counseled reformers to curtail their expectations and unite "philanthropic energy with philosophic calm"[10]—to be patient, in short. Many who admired Morgan's scheme were supporters of the reservation-concentration policy. If Indians were isolated and protected, they could be encouraged to improve on their particular ethnical level, slowly and in accordance with the universal laws of social evolution.

Morgan himself had long believed that assimilation and absorption offered the only hope for preserving a remnant of the Indians; he recognized that allotment in severalty would eventually be necessary. Still, he confessed in 1859 that he was "yet afraid of it,"[11] and when he sat down to outline a comprehensive Indian policy in 1876, allotment played no part in it. Solutions would have to conform to the abilities and needs of each grade of Indians. Thus a factory system was the answer for tribes settled on reservations, and a pastoral system for those still roaming on the plains. The plains tribes, who owned their own herds of horses and were thus already partially pastoral, could be induced to raise domestic cattle as a substitute for hunting buffalo.[12] With an assured food supply and the acquired experience necessary for advancement to the next level of cultural attainment, they might one day graduate to a factory system.

Morgan's factory system was based on the philosophy of self-help. Any number of "staple articles" could be produced on the reservation, from rasberry jam to trinkets for the tourist trade, as the Ojibwa had been doing under a white factor since 1848. The reservations, "places of stagnation and death," would become hives of industry, and the Indians, aroused from their torpor, would demonstrate a willingness "to improve their condition" if a factor could be found "to stand efficiently and intelligently between their fabrics and the markets of the country."[13] Beginning with a different premise, Morgan had arrived at a scheme for economic development on the reservations that directly anticipated certain New Deal programs, especially the Indian Arts and Crafts Board. To round out his plan, he urged the creation of a separate Department of Indian Affairs to give undivided attention to the experiment proposed.[14]

Morgan's policy demanded "patience and forbearance." Indians were at "a low stage of barbarism, immensely below the plane of civilization." Time alone could raise them, though it might be reduced by "the usual incentives to human action."[15] In 1878, when the transfer issue flared again, Morgan restated these principles and advised additional patience. "We wonder that our Indians cannot civilize; but how could they, any more than our own remote barbarous ancestors, jump ethnical periods?" he asked. "They have the skulls and brains of barbarians, and must grow towards civilization as all mankind have done who attained to it by a progressive experience."[16]

One unexpected tribute to Morgan's influence appeared in *Catholic World*, where an article expressing an abhorrence of the "Let the fittest survive" ethic propounded by crude frontiersmen and the "modern illuminati" nevertheless based its case against allotment on elementary evolutionary principles. "The sun does not burst upon the world all of a sudden in its meridian splendor," the author wrote:

So in the moral order after the gloom of savagery comes the first ray of enlightenment to the mind: too much light would daze and stupefy. Man's mental grasp is very finite, and he must acquire knowledge by degrees. The Indian in many respects is but a child, and in his development must be treated accordingly. And yet his ill-advised well-wishers would have trained and developed him into a full-blown civilized American citizen whilst at present the bud is still in embryo. They are too eager for progress.... Patience ... is needed with the Indian; he cannot pass from a savage life into a full-developed civilization in a single generation.[17]

Catholic missionaries had traditionally enjoyed an advantage over their Protestant rivals among the western tribes, and they jealously guarded their prerogatives during the trying years of the Quaker Policy. On the whole, they were as unenthusiastic about allotment as they were suspicious of the motives of the "tight little group of dedicated men and women"—overwhelmingly Protestant, a Jesuit historian has noted[18]—who were touting it in the 1880s. The *Catholic World* essayist's evolutionary arguments were another strategy in defense of a reservation system that, for all its defects, favored the church's missionary work. The restatement of Morgan's views in a sectarian discourse on the Indian question attests to the weight they carried and the respect commonly accorded them.

John Wesley Powell, an avid reader of Morgan's "great work,"[19] *Ancient Society*, most directly injected evolutionary ideas into the debate over Indian policy. One-armed, fierce-visaged, magnificently bewhiskered, Powell was to some of his contemporaries a neo-Renaissance man. Famed for his daring journey down the Colorado River in 1869, he relished the pleasures of a contemplative life, and preferred the title of professor to colonel.[20] Powell was a scientist by inclination, delving into zoology, botany, geology, and anthropology, and dabbling in physics, chemistry, and psychology. One flattering colleague stated that Powell and Francis Bacon had laid "the modern foundation of science."[21] At the behest of Professor Joseph Henry of the Smithsonian Institution, Powell had collected Indian vocabularies while exploring along the Colorado, and a subsequent assignment as special commissioner to the Ute and Shoshone tribes strengthened his interest in native cultures.

As first director of the Bureau of Ethnology, Powell was in a position to influence policy formulation. Indeed, the bureau was created in 1879 largely at his instigation. Ethnological research, he had argued in a letter to the Secretary of the Interior in 1878,[22] offered more than esoteric information of interest to specialists; it offered the opportunity to put American Indian policy for the first time on a scientific footing. Congress might better formulate a wise, long-range program of Indian management if it had reliable data and understood something of the nature of cultural change.

The government had bought similar arguments in the past. Lewis and Clark, Jedidiah Morse, Lewis Cass, and Henry R. Schoolcraft had all conducted ethnological investigations under federal auspices. Schoolcraft's project, the most extensive of the lot, had proven a costly fiasco, and should have alerted policymakers to the difficulties of bending anthropology—even Schoolcraft's amateur brand—to utilitarian ends. But Powell convinced the government to undertake a much larger commitment, a permanent Bureau of Ethnology, which he defended on the grounds that previous ventures into applied anthropology had failed not because the concept lacked merit, but because earlier students were ignorant of the laws of evolutionary development.

Ironically, if Schoolcraft's work was ruinously handicapped by the lack of an organizing ethnological principle, the bureau's work under Powell would be limited in its usefulness for the opposite reason: it organized the data along theoretical lines too inflexible to accommodate administrative realities. Taking his text from Morgan, Powell explained to a Congress seeking guidance on how to modify existing policy in order to expedite Indian assimilation that "savagery is not inchoate civilization," but "a distinct status of society, with its own institutions, customs, philosophy, and religion; and all these must necessarily be overthrown before new institutions, customs, philosophy, and religion can be introduced."[23] The concept of private property ran counter to the social system and the religion of the tribesmen. Only when the acquisitive instinct had superseded the communal would the Indian accept allotment. A prolonged exposure to civilized modes of living would be necessary.

Asked to comment directly on the general allotment bill, Powell pointed out that the Indian family organization or gens, the fundamental unit of tribal government, had no counterpart in civilized society. Consequently, a civilized value such as private property had no basis in the Indian social structure, and allotment in severalty was "opposed to the customary laws, traditions and religion of primitive tribal society." Before an allotment policy could be successfully implemented, the Indians would have to adopt the civilized family's form, recognize the value of individual property and the right of lineal inheritance, and abandon the pursuits of savagery. (At other times, Powell advocated the substitution of English for the bewildering variety of Indian tongues, steeped in barbaric associations, as a crucial part of the transformation.) Changes would have to take place "slowly and contemporaneously." Allotment in severalty was a good idea, but the individualization of Indian title made no sense apart from a thorough reformation of the

Indian character.[24] Thus, Powell favored tbe kind of reservation factory system proposed by Morgan, and predicted for the Indians a slow advancement and then gradual absorption by the white population.

Since Powell was the head of a bureau created to advise Congress on the scientific management of Indian affairs, his ideas should have exerted a commanding influence. But he had forfeited a leadership role to his evolutionary views. "The attempt to transform a savage into a civilized man by a law, a policy, an administration, through a great conversion, 'as in the twinkling of an eye,' or in months, or in a few years, is an impossibility clearly appreciated by scientific ethnologists who understand the institutions and social condition of the Indians," he bluntly stated in 1878,[25] and he had experienced no change of mind by 1881 when he gave as his opinion that "savagery cannot suddenly be transformed by the magic of legal enactments into civilization."[26] For their part, reformers and statesmen, their hearts set on an early, sweeping reformation of policy, found ethnology too obstructionist to be taken seriously.

Social evolutionists were always uncomfortably aware that parallel evolution, however neat theoretically, was frequently belied by experience. Morgan, for one, recognized that cultural diffusion blurred the precise divisions between ethnical periods, and Powell, influenced by his friend Lester Frank Ward's "dynamic sociology," concluded that there were three kinds of evolution, tbe third of which, "anthropic evolution," was "the result of the exercise of human faculties in activities designed to increase happiness and through which the environment is adapted to man."[27] Human evolution, the argument went, had long since transcended the animal level of survival of the fittest. Now consciousness determined being, and the environmental forces that once shaped man had become instruments at his disposal to achieve predetermined ends. In short, ideas had a dynamic, creative potential of their own that rendered Spencerian determinism and strict evolutionary parallelism inoperative in human affairs. Obviously "anthropic evolution" could be carried only so far before it discredited Morgan's unilinear model in *Ancient Society*—a model that, to the faithful, was not a theory but a law of life. They were in the position of trying to reconcile what they observed with what they believed to be true. Thus a field worker like Adolph F. Bandelier, Morgan's confessed disciple, struggled to get in line with his master's teachings on subjects where he had much the superior command of the data and the data were contradictory.[28] Some evolutionists simply asserted their theories as fact. Others expanded and contracted them to suit the occasion.

Occasionally, it seemed as though the social evolutionists wanted to have it both ways. At one meeting of the Anthropological Society of Washington in 1881, Powell heard Lester Ward press his conviction that "positive social action" was in no way ruled out by the evolutionary laws at work in nature. In fact, Ward contended, state regulation historically enjoyed a record of success that disproved the Spencerian contention "that all attempts at government regulation had proved failures or resulted in an excess of evil to society." In response, Powell ruefully conceded that "nine-tenths of the legislation of the world" ignored evolutionary doctrine, and admitted that he too approved government regulation of industry. Exactly three weeks later at a meeting of the same society, Powell listened to a paper that argued that there are "well marked stages of progress, corresponding to Mr. Morgan's periods," and that "attempts to leap over these . . . or to substitute progress in one category for that in another, ignoring the intermediate ones, have been fatal in several ways." Powell heartily agreed. All off-reservation experiments in Indian education, "conducted in ignorance or disregard" of broad ethnological principles, he said, were doomed to failure.[29] Apparently, immutable laws changed with the circumstances.

Because of the theoretical uncertainty, some social evolutionists saw no problem in endorsing an allotment-assimilation policy. Alice C. Fletcher, a pioneering student of the Omahas, concluded that private property had historically stimulated industry and civilization and would continue to do so. She recommended compulsory educational programs for Indian children and advocated allotment in severalty as the surest means of promoting Indian progress,[30] positions that earned her the revealing complement from a reformer that "her philanthropy swallowed up her anthropology."[31] Since the alternative was extinction, to Fletcher and a few others direct interference in the evolutionary process was an acceptable "last resort to save the race."[32]

Most social scientists were unwilling to compromise their evolutionary principles, and their conviction that all real change for the Indian was slow—achingly slow—precluded their having a decisive role in policymaking. While they spoke knowingly of progressive development through prescribed ethnical periods, of barbaric skulls that could not absorb civilized teachings, and of peoples who lagged centuries behind and were still in the infancy of cultural growth, reformers looked anxiously at the Indians' present situation and concluded that immutable natural laws would have to be ignored. Secretary Schurz spoke for all of them when he wrote, "It is true that the transition from the savage state to the pastoral is less violent than that from the savage state directly to the agricultural, but this does not prove that the latter is impossible." Moreover, an evolutionary transition "would necessarily require a considerable time . . . not interfered with by extraneous circumstances," and time was precisely what the Indian did not have.[33] The social-gospel movement and a presentiment of progressivism had captured the reformers. The government could and must act positively to ameliorate the Indian's precarious condition. Even as Schurz was explaining why immediate action was imperative, the debate over a general policy of allotment in severalty was under way in Congress.

THE ALLOTMENT ACT

Although general allotment bills were introduced in both bodies of Congress in 1879, and though other measures came before the House in the following years, the Senate alone gave the matter a thorough public airing. Approval was granted with a minimum of fuss once it was taken up in earnest.

The first bill to receive extended consideration came before the Senate on January 20, 1881. The issue most controversial was Indian citizenship. The bill provided for the Indian allottee to be made a citizen upon receiving title in fee simple to his homestead, having demonstrated his ability to manage his land during a twenty-five-year trust period. Both Massachusetts senators, loyal to the Fourteenth Amendment and undoubtedly responsive to the Boston Indian Citizenship Committee's lobby, contended that the Indian should be made a citizen directly on taking out his allotment.[34] One could become civilized only by fully participating in civilization.

The prospect of immediate Indian citizenship did not strike most western representatives as an attractive one, and Richard Coke of Texas, the bill's sponsor, as well as George H. Pendleton of Ohio, headed off the issue. Pendleton argued that the Coke bill was too important to be encumbered by extraneous considerations, however worthy. Nothing less than the fate of a race hung in the balance.[35] But the question of immediate Indian citizenship would not fade out. It was invigorated by the persistent fear that the Indian during his trusteeship would be in a legal twilight zone, neither citizen nor ward, deprived of the protection of tribal law, and barred from that of federal or state law, "a defendant," Massachusetts' George F. Hoar asserted, but not "a plaintiff" in the courts of the land.[36]

Though the Coke bill did not pass the Forty-sixth Congress, when it came before the Forty-seventh the Senate approved it without debate. The House failed to take action. In the Forty-eighth Congress it found Senate favor again, and failed of consideration again in the House. In the next Congress, Senator Henry L. Dawes of Massachusetts introduced what came to be popularly known as the Dawes Act. It passed on February 25, 1886, won House approval almost a year later, and was signed into law by President Grover Cleveland on February 8, 1887.

REACTIONS TO ALLOTMENT

The General Allotment Act was the culmination of years of sustained effort. Indian rights groups and government officials hailed the dawning of a new day in American-Indian relations. "There can be but little doubt that this is one of the most vital and important steps ever taken by Congress in its dealings with the Indians," the influential Indian Rights Association reported to its members. "It may be said to make an era; to be the beginning of a new order of things. In its very nature it is a new departure on the part of Congress."[37] Just over half a century after the Removal Act and the revised Trade and Intercourse Act went into effect, the nation had finally abandoned its isolationist policy.

Two episodes during the allotment debates suggest how completely national developments had discredited isolationist theory over the years. The most outspoken congressional opponent of allotment in the early 1880s was a Colorado senator named Henry M. Teller. "If I stand alone in the Senate," he dramatically declared in 1881, "I want to put upon the record my prophecy in this matter, that when thirty or forty years shall have passed and these Indians shall have parted with their title, they will curse the hand that was raised professedly in their defense to secure this kind of legislation."[38] The frequency with which this prediction has been quoted by historians attests to its accuracy. Still a confirmed critic, Teller rejoined the Senate discussion over allotment in 1886, after a three-year stint as Secretary of the Interior. But, accepting the inevitable, he now insisted that the bill's great fault was that it did not go far enough. It was based on the old "false idea . . . that it is absolutely necessary for the preservation and welfare of the Indian that he be isolated from the white man, that he be kept from contact with civilization."[39] Only a system of opening alternate quarter sections of Indian land to worthy white settlers would accomplish the goal of thoroughly integrating the red man into American life. If the country wanted assimilation, there was no point in going only halfway.

During the removal debates of the 1830s majority opinion had decreed that distance alone could save the Indians—and satisfy the Georgians clamoring for their land. Now a westerner, shrewdly aware of the growing scarcity of good farmland, could extol the merits of allowing every Indian a white neighbor and, in his eagerness to facilitate an arrangement so obviously advantageous to both races, could scornfully dismiss "the stupid idea that the red man will be overcome by the vices of civilization, and will be destroyed by contact with civilization and with Christianity."[40] To complete the historical irony, it was not Senator Dawes or Hoar of Massachusetts, nor any of their northeastern colleagues, who stepped forward to deliver the most stirring plea for an allotment policy, but Senator Joseph E. Brown of Georgia. In the past, he told his colleagues, removals had driven the Indians "from one point to another," retarding their progress in the name of encouraging it. Allotment would wed end and means. He concluded, "I do not believe there is any other plan that will ever solve this Indian question short of their extermination from the continent."[41]

By the terms of the Dawes Act, the President was empowered to allot in severalty part or all of any reservation that he considered "advantageous for agricultural and grazing purposes," in the amount of one quarter section to each head of a family, and in smaller quantities to children over eighteen, orphans, and those yet in their minority. The Indians were to choose their allotments themselves or, if they failed to do so within four years of the President's ordering allotment on their reservation, have them chosen for them by agency officials. The President was to hold the title in trust for twenty-five years or longer, at his discretion. At the end of the trust period, the Indians, who became citizens of the United States as soon as they took out their patents, were to receive title to their land in fee simple, provided that they had demonstrated sufficient industry during the trust period. Indian lands not allotted were to be disposed of by the government to "actual settlers" in plots not exceeding 160 acres, and proceeds from the sale were to be held in trust for the Indians, "subject to appropriation by Congress for . . . [their] education and civilization." Indians who were allotted land were to be given preference for employment in the government's service. Several tribes, most notably the Five Nations in Indian Territory, were exempted from the act's allotment provisions.[42]

Certain features of the original Coke bills had been lost along the way to passage. The measure before the Forty-eighth Congress had empowered the President to issue trust patents for entire reservations, with clear title to go to the tribes after twenty-five years. Thus those reservations unsuited to allotment in the near future would be legally protected from white incursion. Moreover, allotment was not to apply to a reservation until consent of two-thirds of the adult males thereon had been secured, though individuals could take out allotments at any

time without having to obtain tribal approval. While acknowl-
edging that the bill's end was "tribal disintegration" and the
"blotting out of the reservations as fast as it can be safely done,"
the Indian Rights Association had endorsed its flexibility:
"There is neither a compulsion of the majority nor the slightest
disregard of the wants of the minority."[43] The same could not
be said of the Dawes Act. It stands as a pure product of the
reformer mind of the age—hostile to every vestige of tribalism,
coercive, well-meaning, certain that the Great Father knew
what was best for his red children.

In the process of saving the Indian, something had been
sacrificed. Later critics would charge that the Dawes Act was
cold-bloodedly predicated on the assumption of future Indian
decline. Put differently, the act made no provision for possible
increases in the native population. That is why after a reservation had been allotted there was "surplus" land to sell to
white settlers. The Indians would have no subsequent need for
it, the reasoning went, since their numbers were decreasing.
Yet the act's authors believed that allotment in severalty would
arrest Indian decline. That was one of the selling points.
Consequently, past population projections were irrelevant. As
wandering red hunters became stable, sedentary red farmers,
they would experience the same rate of natural increase as
whites. And when their numbers rose, one fact would become
starkly evident: their rightful patrimony had been dispersed,
leaving future generations landless. Seen in this light, allotment
in severalty was an internally inconsistent, ill-conceived, and
short-sighted policy, not a grand panacea.

But there was another consideration. Perhaps allotment in
severalty was just the means to an end, the assimilation of the
Indians into white society. Accept this, and apparent difficulties
evaporated. There would be no future shortage of land for the
Indians because after they were absorbed there would be no
Indians in the conventional sense.

A "century of dishonor" had been redressed. Slight modifications and improvements on the original allotment act were to
be admitted in the future when the need for change was
conclusively demonstrated, but the prototype was fundamen-

tally sound. It was in this spirit tbat Francis E. Leupp, Commissioner of Indian Affairs from 1904 to 1909, could write a year after leaving office, "The Indian problem has now reached a stage where its solution is almost wholly a matter of administration."[44]

CHAPTER TWELVE

A MATTER OF ADMINISTRATION:
Indian Policy's Confident Years

The Indian Rights Association in 1887 celebrated the passage of the Dawes Act as a great advance toward the association's "general policy of gradually making the Indian in all respects as the white man."[1] This was the government's policy too.

Until the 1920s no dramatic activity in Indian affairs compared with that which preceded the passage of the Dawes Act. There was no comparable clash of views over policy, its ends, and the best means to attain them. "The Dawes policy was based upon a few simple propositions which have been so carefully thought out and are so unanimously accepted by every man and woman whose opinion on the Indian question is of any value," one journal stated in 1892, that it "would no more give space at this day to arguing them than it would allow its pages to be wasted in a discussion of the question whether or not the earth is round and revolves around its solar centre."[2] As the century neared its end, Dawes himself claimed "undivided public support" for the allotment-assimilation policy.[3] While the consensus was never *that* perfect, there was agreement in principle that assimilation should be achieved forthwith, thereby resolving the Indian problem. "Modern observation and thought have reached the conclusion that allotment of land in severalty, and citizenship, are the indispensable conditions of Indian progress," a Connecticut senator summed up in 1895.[4] Consequently, the crowning legislative achievement of the assimilationist epoch was the passage in 1924 of an act granting citizenship to all American Indians.

THE HEIRSHIP PROBLEM AND LEASING

Between allotment in severalty and the granting of citizenship were a series of adjustments on the Dawes prototype. These constituted the burden of Indian legislation for a third of a century. For example, administrative discretion regarding the trust period for allottees was increased so that the period could be continued beyond the twenty-five years originally provided for or shortened whenever the Secretary of the Interior was satisfied with an individual Indian's competence to manage his own affairs. Legislation made it possible for any Indian to apply for a pro-rata share of his tribe's funds, thus effecting the same end as allotment in severalty, the individualization of those common holdings that sustained tribalism.

While the intention of such legislation was in harmony with assimilation, modifications introduced complications. Most disturbing, they permitted an expanding administrative authority over the Indians inimical to the Dawes Act's core concept of Indian self-sufficiency. As the heirship problem emanating from allotment in severalty burgeoned with each passing year and the legal tangle grew more intricate, the government's role increased accordingly. In 1910 the Secretary of the Interior was empowered to deal decisively with the problem created when an allottee died intestate—a common occurrence, since all deceased Indians who held only a trust patent to their allotments were deemed to have died intestate. Beginning in 1910, restricted Indians could draw up wills disposing of their allotments, which offered one defense against the fractionizing of holdings. However, the wills had to be approved by the Secretary of the Interior, who could accept or reject but could not modify them—an absolute authority that forced the secretary to reject outright many documents that had only minor defects and to probate the estate as though there were no will. His administrative authority was further amplified by the provision that if no competent heir wished the estate sold off, its disposition was left entirely in the secretary's hands. He could order its partition among competent heirs, lease it and pay the revenue to the heirs, or order it sold even if none of the heirs agreed. Bureaucracy had an intimate and continuing

involvement in Indian affairs where the Dawes Act had fore-
seen only the healthy autonomy of red citizens attaining their
majority.[5]

Like the proponents of removal sixty years earlier, allotment's
supporters had assumed the disappearance of the Indians.
Thus the allotment policy in theory was a model of simplicity:
the land would be parceled out to those concerned, the surplus
would be sold off, and that was that. There would be no second
round, because there would be no landless claimants in the
future demanding a fair share. Similarly, there could be no
heirship problem. The scarcity of heirs alone would ensure
this. The persistent belief in the Vanishing American was
partially responsible for this myopia. Experience belied it, but
failed to shake the public's confidence.

The one significant deviation from the spirit of the Dawes
Act was introduced early and remained to plague the assimilationists. In 1891 the government provided for the leasing of
unallotted or tribal lands, as well as of individual allotments
where "age or other disability" prevented working them personally. Leasing attested to the hostility toward "exceptional-
ism" evident in Indian policy throughout the 1890s.[6] Even
Senator Dawes, firmly opposed to leasing in 1890, had modified
his position by 1894 when leasing's terms were broadened to
include any who due to "inability" could not work their own
allotments. The very popularity of this provision served notice
that something was amiss. Prior to 1894, the Commissioner of
Indian Affairs approved only six leases; that year alone, nearly
300 leases were validated, and from 1895 through 1900 the
number approved in a single year shot up from 330 to 2,500.[7]
Clearly, leasing vitiated the whole purpose of the twenty-five-
year trust period, making a mockery of the notion that the
Indians would utilize the opportunity to improve their farming
skills in preparation for the day they received clear title to their
lands and assumed the duties and privileges of citizenship.

THE CASE FOR GRADUALISM

If the Dawes Act was so wise in theory and right in practice,
why did the Indian not improve faster? What was retarding

his progress now? "What concerns us to-day," Frances Campbell Sparhawk wrote in 1906, "is to find out what is the matter with tbe Indian, what keeps him from assimilating with his surroundings, why we cannot absorb two hundred and fifty thousand Indians into all our millions and never know where they are."[8]

The obvious answer was also one of the most popular. Original projections as to the time required to make the transition from savagery to civilization had been much too optimistic. Not surprisingly, those who accepted the evolutionary notion of progress through measured stages were most vocal in pointing out this blind spot in reformer hopes. "Our notions of land ownership have developed through thousands of years," George Bird Grinnell, an expert on the plains Indian culture, argued, and it had been absurd from the outset to expect a primitive Indian to grasp the concept of "private monopolies" entailed in allotment in severalty. Thus the Dawes Act was a failed panacea. "In many cases allotment has proved the greatest misfortune that could come to the Indians, and . . . it is often an absolute bar to their progress."[9]

Confused by the government's latest policy, the Indians had been dispossessed of what was rightfully theirs through a combination of "the greedy man, on the one hand, and the fanatic, on the other," the novelist Hamlin Garland insisted.[10] Garland, who had visited a number of the western reservations in the 1890s and become interested in the problem of integrating the red man into white society, in 1902 secured a position as supervisor of an Indian renaming project designed to bring the translations of Indian names on the tribal rolls into conformity with standard American practice so that each allottee, upon receiving his grant of land, might begin with a "decent and reasonable name."[11] Renaming would clarify family relationships and facilitate government bookkeeping.

Though the project was unabashedly ethnocentric and made Garland a collaborator in the assimilation policy, he could still denounce the Dawes Act on evolutionary principles. Since allotment was "being carried to the bitter end by those who believe a Stone Age man can be developed into a citizen of the United States in a single generation," he wrote, it "has failed of expected results." Garland's explanation for this failure rested partly on his own boyhood experiences. Farming, which presented "a sombre phase of civilized life," went against the Indian's sociable, gregarious nature. "As a boy, I hated the solitary labor of the Western farm, and I would not condemn even a convict to such life as is involved in a lonely cabin on the plains."[12]

Garland's position had already found support in an unlikely quarter. Grover Cleveland, in the second half of his bifurcated presidency, expressed doubts about the wisdom of the measure he had proudly signed into law in 1887. Agrarian protest had intervened, and the white farmer's economic distress had dampened his enthusiasm for the Dawes Act. Allotments, he now argued, "should be made sparingly, or at least slowly, and with the utmost caution."[13] Grinnell, too, insisted it was "folly" to imagine that the Indian could farm successfully in the arid West.[14] Allotment simply invited failure, and consequently retarded the Indian's progress by convincing him that "work was useless because work in the white man's way brought him no return."[15]

Francis E. Leupp, who became Commissioner of Indian Affairs in 1905, agreed. In an address to the Anthropological Society of Washington, he noted that the government, after the initial blunder of making the Indians indolent and dependent by providing them with rations on their reservations, had compounded its error by veering too sharply in the opposite direction in the hope that "each and every Indian if given an allotment would be made into a self-supporting farmer." This was a hope "as absurd in its application," Leupp told his audience of anthropologists, as if each of his listeners "should be set down upon 40 or 80 or 160 acres or so of land and expected to make a living from the soil."[16] Leupp believed that the Indians must be taught to labor, to work their own way out from under the fostering care of the mistaken reservation system. If he had not, he would never have been Theodore Roosevelt's commissioner. But Leupp always counseled a proper respect for evolutionary truths. "A people reared to war or the chase," he remarked on another occasion, "could not be turned into farmers or laborers overnight."[17] That had been the fallacy of the Dawes Act.

These arguments pointed to one conclusion: allotment in

severalty should be slowed down. If cultural change were to "take" in any meaningful sense and the Indian be fully prepared to assume his duties as a citizen, the government would have to continue its wardship responsibilities for more than the one decade or the one generation optimistically predicted in 1887. Garland condemned the "sink or swim" philosophy of those reformers who wanted to throw the Indian onto his own resources by immediately opening all the reservations and removing special protections. "The reservation is still an 'isle of safety' to the Northwest tribes," he maintained.[18] Grinnell, in turn, urged that the patents issued to Indians in the future be inalienable for life, or perhaps even a hundred years. Restraint was essential, he felt, to prevent the "grave wrong" that was being done "under the guise of a benevolent policy."[19] Leupp conceded that it would be "a blessed day for the red race and for the whole country when the last vestige of the reservation system disappears," but that fact did not obviate the necessity of providing some "bridge" to transport the Indian from his recent roaming past to self-sufficient citizenship.[20]

Garland, Grinnell, and Leupp did not oppose ultimate Indian assimilation, nor, for that matter, did they disagree with the principle of allotment in severalty. But their arguments, which constituted a minority report on Indian policy, did tend to a conservative conclusion, requiring not only a prolongation of the government's supervisory powers over the Indians, but an amplification of those powers at the very time when the Indians, clear title in hand, were supposed to be enjoying unrestricted American citizenship.

THEODORE ROOSEVELT AND THE GRADUALIST APPROACH

The minority viewpont was distinguished by its commitment to gradualism. The Indian problem was a practical one and could best be solved by concentrating on day-to-day realities. This viewpoint had its heyday under Theodore Roosevelt, who has been unfairly characterized as the most anti-Indian President since Andrew Jackson. If Jackson was the prototypical frontiersman, Roosevelt, according to this interpretation, was an Eastern pretender, a pale, pampered schoolboy raised in the lap of luxury who proved his masculinity on a ranch in the Dakotas, at the Battle of San Juan Hill, and on several well-publicized hunting trips and safaris. His views on the Indian question, consistent with his cowboy image, are usually adduced from some remarks he made during a lecture in New York in 1886. "I don't go so far as to think that the only good Indians are the dead Indians," he is quoted as having said, "but I believe nine out of every ten are, and I shouldn't like to inquire too closely into the case of the tenth. The most vicious cowboy has more moral principle than the average Indian."[21] Roosevelt's later attacks on "foolish sentimentalists" like George Manypenny and Helen Hunt Jackson, and his respect for such recounters of massacres, mutilations, and tortures by "our wild Indians" as Colonel Richard I. Dodge, merely confirmed the impression that he had fully absorbed the frontier viewpoint. Andy Jackson had returned to the White House.

But Roosevelt's ideas were far more complicated than his image. He was, as he saw it, a realist working for causes too often dominated by idealists. For example, he was a prominent conservationist of the hunter-sportsman variety, advocating tough game laws and the creation of forest reserves in keeping with the philosophy of wise-use resource management. If he had little sympathy for the aesthetic preservationists who would simply close off wilderness areas, he had none at all for those interests, mostly western, that demanded the unrestricted right to exploit America's remaining natural resources. Thus he was eastern rather than western in his stance on conservation.[22] Similarly, in Indian affairs, despite his popular image, he belonged within the hard-headed eastern tradition of Edward Everett and Francis Parkman. He did not subscribe to exterminationist doctrine and, for that matter, had more than the ordinary respect for Indian cultures. But he operated on a simple premise: the Indian was a savage, the Anglo-Saxon a civilized man. Civilization always had priority over savagery. One could accept this without either hating the Indians or mourning their fate. And one could admire their good qualities without feeling the need either to preserve them or ruthlessly crush them out, recognizing that time would render native cultures increasingly anachronistic until one day they vanished of their own accord.[23]

In Roosevelt's views are the outlines of the gradualist position. It did not reject the goal of Indian assimilation, as Roosevelt made clear in 1892 when he recommended that each Indian be given a piece of land and "thrown loose to shift for himself, as a citizen amongst other citizens, as soon as he can be prepared for the ordeal." The "as soon as" was the crucial qualifier. Roosevelt elaborated:

It must not be done too quickly, for he will then be helpless and perish, nor must it be delayed too long, for he will then become accustomed to being petted and cared for and will be too weak to stand when finally left alone. When it is done, we must be prepared to see a great many of the Indians sink under the strain. . . .

. . . We must protect and guard them up to a certain point; but all the while we must be fitting them as we best can for rough contact with the world.[24]

As President, Roosevelt had the opportunity to put his ideas into practice. After winning a personal mandate in 1904 he chose as Commissioner of Indian Affairs his old ally from the battle for civil service reform in the 1890s, Francis Leupp. Their views on Indian affairs harmonized perfectly,[25] and together they forged a policy embodying their convictions about the need to prepare the Indians for eventual emancipation from the reservation system while retaining those safeguards essential to shield an inexperienced people from the perils of a hard world.

Leupp's immediate predecessor, William A. Jones, convinced that the Indian must be compelled to work, in 1901 introduced a "compulsory labor law" on the reservations ordering the agents to strike all able-bodied males from the free-ration roll and provide them with work instead.[26] It was a move Roosevelt and Leupp agreed with in principle; indeed, in 1892 Roosevelt had urged that nothing be given even the wildest tribesmen "except upon performance of work on their part."[27] But in practice, the principle seemed altogether too arbitrary and harsh. Better to establish a labor bureau that would find employment off the reservation for Indians willing to "cut the leading-strings" and stand on their own two feet.[28] Jones's compulsory labor law was like similar measures intended to rush the Indians into civilization. They stripped the Indian of self-respect. Consequently, Roosevelt and Leupp opposed haircut regulations, blanket bans on Indian ceremonials and dances, rules about clothing and dwellings, and decrees proscribing the native arts and languages.

Roosevelt thought that the short-hair rule among the semicivilized tribes would be a "misfortune," that many of the Indian dances were "perfectly proper to keep up and even encourage," and that a student of the southwestern cultures was probably right in believing that teachers in the reservation schools "should encourage instead of discouraging" the perpetuation of Indian songs and poetry "not merely for the good it will do them, but for the chance that great good will be done thereby in the end to the whites."[29] The practice of forcing the Indians to assimilate because, in the words of an earlier commissioner, "in requiring this we do not ask that they concede anything of real value to themselves,"[30] was rejected as insensitive and wrong-headed. It smacked of the Carlisle philosophy of "kill the Indian to save the man"—a philosophy which Leupp, who believed that "pride of race is one of the saving graces," dismissed as so much "prattle."[31] Given his long, acrimonious dispute with Richard H. Pratt over Indian education, this was, perhaps, an intentional pun.

FRANCIS LEUPP, RICHARD PRATT, AND INDIAN EDUCATION

Pratt was an expert propagandist. With packets of before-and-after photographs, public recitations by gifted students, passionate speeches and a plethora of catchy slogans, he had made Carlisle the most famous Indian school of its day. Though there were always skeptics, as long as the government favored the boarding-school system Carlisle was safe. But Pratt and his approach were under siege in his last years before he retired as superintendent in 1904. Federal Indian education had become big business since its tentative beginnings in the 1870s. The $20,000 appropriated in 1876 had swollen to $2,638,390 by the end of the century when the government discontinued further financial support for the missionary "contract" schools.

By 1913 the supervisor of schools for the United States Indian Service could report that 78.3 percent of all Indian children were in school—5,109 in mission schools, 26,028 in public schools, and 27,584 in the government's 216 day schools, 74 reservation boarding schools, and 37 off-reservation boarding schools.[32] The off-reservation schools represented a revered tradition of getting the Indian away from retarding influences and among progressive ones, but they seemed a luxury at a time when the great task before the nation was not to establish experimentally the Indian's ability to learn, but to train the mass of young Indians for the challenging new world that the Dawes Act was opening up for them. There was another objection to the off-reservation schools. Despite the reams of contradictory evidence published by Carlisle,[33] folk wisdom still held that "back to the blanket" was the rule for the majority of returned students. The reservation schools were certainly more economical than their off-reservation counterparts, and perhaps more practical as well.

Leupp was the first commissioner to come out strongly against the off-reservation boarding schools. How, he asked, with characteristic bluntness, was it preparing the Indians for citizenship "to carry off the children indiscriminately, train them to despise practically all that their race stands for, and saturate them with the idea that, for whatever they wish, they have only to draw upon a rich and indulgent government?"[34] Far better to multiply the number of reservation day schools, the lowest level in the three-tier educational structure, and the one accessible to the great mass of Indian children. All students would acquire the rudiments in the day schools; some would continue on in the reservation boarding schools; and the able few would attend the off-reservation schools for a final polishing.

Leupp found the off-reservation schools more interested in self-aggrandizement than education. They were in hot competition with one another for students since funds were allocated on a per capita basis, and the result, Leupp charged, was "a regular system of traffic in . . . helpless little red people."[35] To end it, he issued a circular in 1908 prohibiting active student recruitment in the future. He also demanded that the off-reservation boarding schools justify themselves by offering "advanced training in the trades, in business and in domestic life."[36] His denials to the contrary notwithstanding, Leupp's policy of "trying to get rid of our boarding-schools" pointed the way to Carlisle's demise.[37]

Shortly after Leupp left office in 1909, only twenty of the twenty-six off-reservation boarding schools operating when he became commissioner were still in service. Pratt, feistier than ever in retirement, fumed over the destruction of a system he had helped create, and found behind Leupp's campaign to let the boarding schools "disintegrate by degrees"[38] the same selfish motive he always detected in the activities of the Indian Bureau: "Perpetual tribalism and the consequent endless control by the Indian System . . ."[39] In reply, Leupp wrote that "the whole subject pivots on the question whether we shall carry civilization to the Indian or carry the Indian to civilization, and the former seems to me infinitely the wiser plan."[40]

Leupp's views on Indian education were consistent with his opposition to all forms of instant civilization. They led him on the controversial question of the right "correlation of literary and industrial training for the Indian"[41] to side with those who thought that the Indians had much to learn from Booker T. Washington. Education should be practical. It should teach the Indian a skill that would enable him to be self-supporting. The average Indian would be a hewer of wood and a drawer of water, not a scholar. Off-reservation boarding schools produced a class of young Indians imbued with a sense of superiority, a smattering of useless knowledge, and an unwillingness to roll up their sleeves and get to work. As commissioner, Leupp laid his views on the line for a Carlisle graduating class. Each graduate, he stated, must "assume his full responsibilities in order that he might demand his fully privileges." The responsibilities should be accepted gladly, while the privileges would have to be earned. Very few would start at the top of the heap, and they might as well all accept that fact. So "take a cheerful view of life," he advised them, "be content to be a first-rate soldier in the ranks until you have earned your promotion to a higher place."[42]

This was vintage Booker T. Washington. But the situations of the Negro and the Indian were not really analogous. The one was earmarked for a segrated, menial existence, the other for full participation in white civilization. Leupp himself was a thoroughgoing amalgamationist who believed that the contrast between red and black was "as marked as that between shadow and sunshine."[43] There was no reason to provide for a permanent "mud sill" class or to think of Indian education in Tuskegee terms. Elaine Goodale Eastman, the veteran Indian educator and wife of a full-blood Sioux doctor, decried any attempt to impose an artificial ceiling on the Indian's ambitions. One professional Indian of her husband's caliber was "worth a thousand day-laborers as a practical demonstration of the equality of the races." Indians as a class were no more cut out to be menial laborers than white men. "Heaven forbid," she protested, "that these rising young Americans be taught to look upon themselves as an inferior class, set apart by Nature and heredity to be 'hewers of wood and drawers of water' for the 'superior' race!"[44] Industrial education designed to make the Indian permanently accept a lower station in life went against the grain of a people always considered too proud to be enslaved. It also went against the grain of the whole assimilation program.

As Commissioner of Indian Affairs, Leupp preached common sense rather than dogma and, according to a contemporary, approached the Indian problem as a human problem, seeking its solution "in the course of nature instead of [by] concocting artificial devices."[45] Much of what was to be done was mundane. The inheritance laws relating to allotments held in trust had to be rationalized, allotment sizes adjusted to meet environmental conditions, and the trust period made more flexible in order to accommodate both the competent and the less competent. An equitable distribution of the tribal funds had to be worked out. And always it had to be stressed that while the individualizing process was intrinsically good, there was no special virtue in rushing it. If, in the name of emancipating the Indians, allotment were so accelerated that it served only to liberate them from their lands and monies, then it would obviously prove counterproductive, throwing a pauperized people back onto the government rolls. If the trust period were indefinitely extended, of course, it would defeat its own purpose. Even if it were truly used as an "apprenticeship in civil responsibilities," it presented certain dangers.[46] Leasing was a case in point. Intended to offer the trustee a lesson in the wise management of his own land, leasing could just as easily transform the future farmer into an indolent landlord itching for the chance to get clear title, dispose of his property, and live on the proceeds, having learned nothing of the imperative of work.

"Our endeavor," Leupp wrote the year after leaving office, echoing the exact sentiments he had expressed on entering it, "ought to be to keep . . . [the Indian] moving steadily down the path which leads from his close domain of artificial restraints and protection toward the broad area of individual liberty enjoyed by the ordinary citizen. . . . If we can watch our body of dependent Indians shrink even by one member at a time, we may congratulate ourselves that the complete solution is only a question of patience."[47]

ACCELERATING THE ALLOTMENT PROCESS

Most assimilationists had no hesitation in assigning to the reservation the blame for the Indian's tardy progress. They so commonly likened it to a prison that the terms became synonyms in their vocabulary. "Imagine everything that is opposed to all that is American or modern in detail, and especially in principle, and you have an Indian reservation," one said.[48] The reservations, and the system of which they were a part, had perpetuated barbarism on American soil by offering it an environment closed to all progressive influences. "Is it any wonder twenty-five years of education have not solved the Indian problem," a critic wrote in 1903, "when tbe educated young men and women must choose to be either farmers, herders, or agency employees, and have to live under the blighting and deadening restraints and influences of the Reservation, the corrupting examples of immoral employees, and the despotism of the agent, where the corner-stone of free civilized society—government by law—has been omitted?"[49] The Indian was being forced to train for responsible American citizenship in a setting that was by definition un-American.

Talk about complications and the need for caution and a few palliatives in treating the Indian problem was just so much mumbo-jumbo. A radical cure could be prescribed with confidence. "Abolish it," a clergyman wrote of the reservation system in 1898. "All reservations in which the land is capable of allotment in severalty should be allotted as rapidly as the work of surveying and making out the warrants can be carried out."[50]

Successive presidential administrations did their best to speed up the allotment process. While Leupp personally counseled patience, he was in office during the years after 1906 when the Secretary of the Interior, with discretionary powers to shorten the twenty-five-year trust period, gradually accelerated the rate at which patents in fee were granted to "competent" Indians. The results were sobering. In the first three years after restrictions were eased, 60 percent of the Indians receiving patents were dispossessed of their lands and monies. Though the requirements for competency were quickly tightened again, the damage had been done. Yet pressures on the government to hurry the Indians along did not abate, and they found their champion in Cato Sells, a former Iowa lawyer and Texas farmer and stock raiser who served as Commissioner of Indian Affairs from 1913 to 1921.

In 1917, halfway through his administration, Sells began a drive to terminate the Indian question once and for all. Every able-bodied adult Indian of less than one-half native blood was to assume full control of his property as soon as the law would permit, while the Indian of one-half or more native blood who was found "after careful investigation" to be competent was to receive a fee patent at once. (One test was the completion of the full course of instruction in a government school with a signed certificate of competency from the teacher or principal.) Competent Indians were to have "unrestricted control" of their own money and, "as speedily as possible," a pro-rata share in tribal funds. Competency commissions were established to ensure that there would be no undue delays.[51]

No one could complain about bureaucratic foot-dragging under Sells. In the three-year period from 1917 to 1920, 10,956 fee patents were issued—1,062 more than had been granted in the preceding decade. Sells loved to cite these figures; they were, he insisted, concrete proof of "something definitely progressive and hopefully promising."[52] But only months after Sells left office his successor was urging caution in granting fee patents, for figures also showed that more than two-thirds of the Indians who had received clear title to their allotments had been partially or totally dispossessed.[53] The reports from the field were even more discouraging. Seventy-one of the eighty-seven field workers who responded to an official questionnaire reported that the Indians under their jurisdiction who had obtained fee patents were floundering.[54] Instead of land they owned Fords—and they would not own them for long. From bitter experience, the Coeur d'Alenes had arrived at their own definition of competency: "The only competent Indian was the one who refused to accept a fee patent."[55] It was time for retrenchment. The government would be "shirk[ing] its trust"[56] if it released the Indians from their reservation prisons before they were ready to cope with the outside world.

Sells's ill-fated speed-up policy had an ulterior motive. He was a firm believer in Indian citizenship, and allotment in severalty was the shortest path to that end. The Dawes Act had extended citizenship to all Indians who took out allotments. In 1906 the Burke Act, one of the most controversial measures of the assimilationist epoch, deferred citizenship until the expiration of the trust period. Leupp naturally thought the Burke Act a substantial improvement since it conformed to his gradualist philosophy by reserving the franchise to those legally competent to manage their own affairs.[57] To many assimilationists, however, the Burke Act represented in starkest terms the dangers of protecting the Indian from himself. Since 1887 the allotment policy had been needlessly complicated by "improvements" which, ostensibly designed to aid their passage from dependency to autonomy, effectively kept the Indians under the thumb of the Bureau of Indian Affairs. Thus Edgar B. Meritt, a law clerk in the bureau, described the deferment of citizenship under the Burke Act as "a mistake and a distinct step backward."[58]

In accelerating the issuance of patents in fee, then, Sells was simultaneously accelerating the granting of Indian citizenship. And when he mentioned that "about 225,000 allotments of land have been made . . . and during the last three years 10,956 fee simple patents have been issued," he was talking about new citizens, prospective and actual. After 1906 allotment in severalty was more than ever the means to an end, and Sells could boast with partial accuracy that "under my administration the Indian Bureau has made special effort to extend citizenship to the Indians and prepare them for its duties and responsibilities."[59] Through circumvention, policy had been returned to the path staked out for it thirty years before.

INDIAN CITIZENSHIP

Although the legislation modifying the Dawes Act at times threatened to swamp the allotment policy in the name of "benevolent caring,"[60] the idea of preparing the Indians for "the new physical, moral and political conditions" projected by the Indian Rights Association in 1886[61] guided the government through the first two decades of the twentieth century. Indians, it was often said, were not vanishing, but ascending the steps to civilization. "There is hope for the Indian," an editorial in the *Williamsport Grit* asserted in 1913.

The American red man is not going to die out. He is going to take his place in the world like the white man, and the day is not far distant when such a thing as an Indian problem will be history in the United States. To-day, the Indian is fast adopting the ways of the white man. He is proving himself industrious, independent, creative, and an all-round good American citizen.[62]

The issue of Indian citizenship was as old as the Republic. The Constitution passed over it by excluding "Indians not taxed" from the census count to establish the basis for apportioning representation and direct taxation among the states. However, since the ratification of the Fourteenth Amendment extending citizenship to the Negro in 1868, the question of granting the First American the same status had been heatedly debated. Those who supported Indian citizenship sometimes resorted to invidious racial comparisons, arguing, as one did, that since "descendants of the worst of all races are today worthy American citizens," the superior red man deserved equal treatment.[63] Opponents of Indian citizenship responded that the Negro's enfranchisement had proven a mistake that should never be repeated. A more benevolent view opposed general Indian citizenship on the grounds that it would expose the Indians to unscrupulous whites out to manipulate their vote and steal their land. A demonstration of competency should precede full citizenship. This position, embodied in the Burke Act, had derailed the movement toward Indian citizenship launched by the Dawes Act and accelerated in 1901 when citizenship was granted all members of the Five Civilized Nations in Indian Territory. Nevertheless, by 1906 some 166,000 Indians had become citizens, 65,000 through the allotment process and the rest as members of the Five Nations.[64]

Under Sells, in an intensely nationalistic period with the country at war, both Indian assimilation and the Americanization movement flourished. Back in 1889 the Commissioner of Indian Affairs had urged teachers to awaken "a fervent patriotism" in their Indian pupils by bombarding them with the symbols of United States citizenship—the Stars and Stripes, patriotic odes and anthems, the lives of the Founding Fathers—and by encouraging a selective amnesia. They "should hear little or nothing of the 'wrongs of the Indians,' and of the injustice of the white race," he ordered. "If their unhappy history is alluded to it should be to contrast it with the better future that is within their grasp."[65]

Rodman Wanamaker's 1913 "Expedition of Citizenship to the North American Indian"—discussed in the next chapter—was in this spirit; so was the ceremony whereby the government conferred citizenship on an Indian. The Secretary of the Interior called each applicant forward by his white name, asked him for his Indian name, handed him a bow, and instructed him to shoot an arrow. Addressing him by his Indian name, the secretary said: "You have shot your last arrow. That means that you are no longer to live the life of an Indian. You are from this day forward to live the life of the white man. But you may keep that arrow; it will be to you a symbol of your noble race and of the pride you feel that you come from the first of all Americans." Then the secretary, using the Indian's white name, told him to put his hand on the handle of a plow: "This act means that you have chosen to live the life of the white man—and the white man lives by work. From the earth we all must get our living, and the earth will not yield unless man pours upon it the sweat of his brow. Only by work do we gain a right to the land or to the enjoyment of life." The new citizen had to endure one final indignity: he was presented with a leather purse (to remind him that "the money you gain from your labor must be wisely kept"), a small flag ("the only flag you have ever had or ever will have"), and a gold-colored badge bearing the inscription "A Citizen of the United States."[66]

World War I was the turning point in the campaign for general Indian citizenship. At Carlisle, Captain Pratt, as an old army man, had put his students into uniforms and regimented their lives, teaching them the meaning of a straight line that they might march with heads erect into the full splendors of a civilized existence. The Indian police who patrolled the western reservations with the government's blessing after 1878 wore army uniforms that set them apart from the rest of their people as symbols of authority and as models of the rewards awaiting those who abandoned things Indian—dangling braids, beads, and feathers—and accommodated themselves to the new order. In World War I perhaps 17,000 Indians, 85 percent of them volunteers, donned the uniform of the United States to quell the Huns and win a lasting claim on the American sense of fair play. Ten Indians were awarded the Croix de Guerre; another 150 were decorated for valor, and inspirational stories about the self-sacrificing heroism of red soldiers on the battlefields of Europe circulated in the press. Indians subscribed for $25 million in Liberty bonds, and 10,000 joined the American Red Cross to support the war effort by knitting 100,000 garments and providing other aid to the fighting men.[67]

"If the red man can fight, why can't he vote?" one journal asked a month after the Armistice was signed. Red Fox Skiuhushu, a Blackfoot minister, wrote that the Indian's "grand and noble" contribution to the war "ought to cause every patriot to reciprocate . . . by urging a bill in Congress to have the Indian free, and bestow upon them full citizenship."[68]

Commissioner Sells agreed that the Indians' wartime performance indicated their readiness, and was quick to point out that
red soldiers, unlike the blacks, fought in integrated regiments,
"side by side with the white man, not as Indians, but as
Americans."[69] In 1919 Congress responded by granting citizenship to all Indian veterans who had received honorable
discharges. With their goal that much nearer, advocates of
general Indian citizenship renewed their efforts. "And shall
we bar the Red Man out?" the New England poet Edna Dean
Proctor asked:

> The Red Man was the primal lord
>   Of our magnificent domain,
> And craft, and crime, and wasting sword
>   Oft gained us mount and stream and plain.
> And shall we still add wrong to wrong?
> Is this the largess of the strong—
> His need to slight, his faith to doubt,
> And thus to bar the Red Man out,
>   Though welcoming all other men?
> Nay! let us nobly build him in,
> Nor rest till "ward" and "alien" win
>   The rightful name of citizen!
> Then will the "reservation" be
> Columbia's breadth from sea to sea,
> And Sioux, Apache, and Cheyenne
> Merge proudly in American![70]

Finally, on June 2, 1924, President Calvin Coolidge signed into
law an act making "all noncitizen Indians born within the
territorial limits of the United States" citizens thereof. Even
this act was a compromise of sorts. The Supreme Court in the
case of *United States* v. *Nice* (1916) had ruled that "citizenship
is not incompatible with tribal existence or continued guardianship, and so may be conferred without completely emancipating the Indians or placing them beyond the reach of congressional regulation adopted for their protection."[71] Thus
the Indian Citizenship Act did not resolve the legal complexities
of the red man's special status, nor did it substantially alter the
Bureau of Indian Affairs' jurisdictional authority over the

reservations. But a measure that had been so contentious and at times apparently so unattainable had won approval only a week after Congress passed the Quota Act restricting immigration into the United States. That alone was enough to make the Indian Citizenship Act a cause for celebration. It was the symbolic high point of the assimilationist era.

During the protracted struggle for passage of the allotment in severalty bill, Senator Henry L. Dawes had consistently maintained that the breaking up of the reservations would be "the beginning of the end of the Indian as an Indian."[72] Although Indians would disappear culturally and racially, they would survive individually. One could ask no more. But rhetoric aside, as Senator Henry M. Teller charged in 1881, the assimilationists were proposing to "utterly annihilate" a people in the name of benevolence.[73] Teller's was an isolated voice at the time, but the next half century confirmed his prophecy. In the process of exposing the fallacy of the Vanishing American by securing the Indian's future through allotment in severalty, the assimilationists had given new life to the old myth.

PART FIVE

AND THEN THERE WERE NONE
A Superseded Race

The field of research is speedily narrowing because of the rapid change in the Indian population now in progress; all habits, customs, and opinions are fading away; even languages are disappearing; and in a very few years it will be impossible to study our North American Indians in their primitive condition except from recorded history. For this reason ethnologic studies in America should be pushed with the utmost vigor.

—J. W. Powell, November 1, 1878, in "Surveys of the Territories. Letter from the Acting President of the National Academy of Sciences Transmitting a Report on the Survey of the Territories" (December 3, 1878), *House Misc. Doc. No. 5*, 45th Cong., 3rd sess., p. 26

A few decades hence Canonchet's, Pontiac's and Tecumseh's

race will be as dead as is the buffalo, and a hybrid will have taken its place.

The abolition of the Indian ethnologically as well as sociologically, was decreed by the laws under which he is being transformed into an American citizen.

—Charles M. Harvey, "The Indian of To-day and To-morrow," *American Monthly Review of Reviews,* Vol. XXXIII (June 1906), p. 697

CHAPTER THIRTEEN

WE HAVE COME TO THE DAY OF AUDIT:

The Vanishing American Returns

"Civilization," Francis Parkman had coldly reflected in 1852, "has a destroying as well as a creating power."[1] The railroad, that epitome of the crushing power of technological advance, had become a favorite American symbol for progress. Indians scattered in panic before its rush or contemplated it from afar with melancholy resignation in the allegorical art that graced the books and decorated the walls of the nation. The white man had prevailed, but, time proved, at a price. He had not eliminated the Indian; he had made him over in his own image, and the result, Parkman wrote in 1892 with a passion absent forty years earlier, was "an ugly caricature." Indians would survive by succumbing, like the West itself, to what Parkman pronounced "irresistible commonplace."[2]

The granting of general Indian citizenship in 1924 crowned the assimilationist epoch in Indian affairs. At the same time, it capped the popular revival of the Vanishing American under way since the passage of the Dawes Act. The passing of the frontier had turned the Wild West into a treasured memory, a mythical embodiment of the nation's youth. If the pioneer represented the forces of change that had transformed the West, the Indian naturally represented what had been lost. It was time to mourn and to remember. Vermillion war paint and eagle feathers, beaded moccasins and bear-claw necklaces, eagle-bone breastplates and brilliantly colored blankets, buf-falo-hide shields and bows and arrows—gaudy trappings of an obsolete barbarism—now reposed in museums, the objects of curiosity and respectful study, or were wrapped away in murky reservation cabins to be brought out only on special occasions, often to entertain the white man, who now seemed to love the brave display of native finery he had once labored to suppress. Now that dark cloth, shoe leather, and short hair were turning yesterday's warriors into immigrants in their own land, the white man had discovered that they possessed something precious, something basic to the nation's identity. The events of the 1890s directly shaped this perception of the Indian, and gave new life to the old idea of the Vanishing American.

THE 1890s MILIEU

In 1894 the Bureau of the Census issued an elaborately illustrated, oversized volume entitled *Report on Indians Taxed and Indians Not Taxed in the United States (Except Alaska) at the Eleventh Census: 1890*. It offered a statistical breakdown of the Indian enumeration and a discussion of previous population estimates that merely proved how little the census office had profited from Selden Clark's critique of the early figures. While the *Report* interjected an occasional note of skepticism, its neat tabulation of the variant tallies gave them authority. The census showed a total of 248,253 Indians living in the United States in 1890, a figure substantially lower than any previously re-corded. The successive census counts since 1850 had conclu-sively established the trend:

1850	400,764	1880	306,543
1860	339,421	1890	248,253
1870	313,712		

The impression created by this imposing column of figures was bolstered by the *Report*'s "Historic Review":

As the Indian felt the presence and weight of . . . civilization all of his past history and present life crowded upon him and he revolted, because he could see that his race was about to be covered with a cloud that would eventually engulf it. The white man's clutch was on his throat. With the advancing lines of white men it took no prophet to proclaim the Indian's doom. With clenched teeth, and club or gun in hand, he places his back to the rock and dies in resistance.[3]

The reference was to the battle of Wounded Knee, which, in the very year the census was taken, lent poignant substance to the statistical evidence.

Following the stunning Sioux victory on the Little Big Horn in 1876, Sitting Bull had emerged as the most notorious chieftain of them all, "savage, unmerciful."[4] But five years later he had surrendered to American authorities, ending a period of self-imposed exile in Canada and, for the foreseeable future, Indian resistance on the northern plains. In 1885, bored by the monotony of reservation life, he agreed to tour with Buffalo Bill Cody's Wild West show, an outdoor entertainment that brought the dime novel's heroics to life and gave permanent shape to the western myth. Hawking autographed pictures on the side, Sitting Bull was paraded about for four months as Custer's slayer. He did not tour again (the experience, his agent complained, instead of making him more docile had made him "very pompous and insolent").[5] Near daybreak on December 15, 1890, outside his cabin on Standing Rock Reservation, Sitting Bull was shot to death by Sioux policemen garbed in cavalry blue. As the guns went off, a circus horse presented to Sitting Bull at the conclusion of his tour with the Wild West responded to its cue, sitting down on its haunches and offering a hoof to "shake hands," an eerie counterpoint to tragedy.

Two weeks later a ragged band of Sioux who had fled into the Dakota Bad Lands after learning of the death of Sitting Bull were intercepted by four troops of Custer's old regiment, the Seventh Cavalry, and forced to surrender. Soldiers surrounded the Indian camp through the night. The next morning, December 29, during the testy process of disarmament, someone discharged a gun and furious fighting broke out. When it was done, the village on Wounded Knee Creek had been leveled and more than 150 Sioux lay dead on the ground. "We glory in the revenge of the Seventh," a Nebraska paper editorialized.[6] After a burial detail—contracted at the rate of two dollars per body—had pitched the frozen corpses of the slain Indians, nearly half of them women and children, into a mass grave and covered them over, it was time for more temperate reflection. Several popular histories wrung the last drop of blood from Wounded Knee, while friends of the Indian anxiously assessed its causes to see if they cast discredit on recent government policy. One fact was certain: the Indian wars were over. The "only comfort" that could be derived from Wounded Knee, a contemporary noted, "is that each such occurrence brings us a little nearer the inevitable end. Some day, our little army will not have to fight the Indians any more, because there will be no Indians left to fight."[7]

The ghost dance, or, as the press preferred to call it, the Messiah craze, fusing elements of native religion and Christianity in a dream of racial rejuvenation, had swept across the western reservations in 1890. It offered a compelling prophecy. The land was to be returned to the Indians, their dead restored to life. The great herds of buffalo were to reappear, and every vestige of the white man's presence was to be erased. A people whose culture had been shattered and whose present was as constricted as the shrinking boundaries of their reservations had sought escape by projecting their past into the future. For a moment the rebirth of Indian America had seemed as imminent as a man's next breath, as real as moccasined feet pounding the earth to the thump of drums. Then it was over. The apocalyptic vision of the ghost dance was buried on the battlefield at Wounded Knee. "A people's dream died there," an old Sioux holy man remembered sadly. "It was a beautiful dream."[8]

With the Indian wars enshrined in collective memory as the "winning of the West," another dream of cultural rejuvenation had also ended. The West had signified man's yearning for a better life in a better world, a future without limits on hope and growth and happiness. But by the 1890s the West had been stripped of its mythic potency, "'gone, gone with lost Atlantis,'" Theodore Roosevelt lamented, "gone to the isle of ghosts and of strange dead memories."[9] A Census Bureau *Bulletin* on the "Distribution of Population According to Density: 1890" reported matter-of-factly: "Up to and including 1880 the country had a frontier of settlement, but at present the unsettled area has been so broken into by isolated bodies of settlement that there can hardly be said to be a frontier line."[10]

This was cause for celebration—civilized progress had finally won the continent—but it was cause for sadness, too. The announcement of the frontier's demise stirred the imagination of a young professor at the University of Wisconsin who would profoundly alter the historical understanding of America's development. In "The Significance of the Frontier in American History," Frederick Jackson Turner argued that the frontier experience was the dynamic factor in molding a distinctive national character. Free land was the key. As long as it lasted, American society was perennially renewed, evolving from savagery to civilization and sloughing off European traits with each successive advance westward until the end product was essentially American.

Turner's ideas were first presented on a July evening in 1893, at a special meeting of the American Historical Association held in Chicago in conjunction with the spectacular World's Columbian Exposition. The session at which Turner spoke met in the Art Institute on the exposition grounds in the contrived beauty of the White City, republican splendor cast in plaster of Paris. The setting nicely complemented Turner's revisionist reading of the American past. Young, still raw, Chicago itself was an overgrown frontier town that mirrored Turner's theme and the fair's as well. Because his paper required polishing on the day it was to be delivered, Turner missed the chance to see a performance of Buffalo Bill's Wild West show with its calculated distillation of the frontier experience. Otherwise, he could have inspected the "death cabin" from which Sitting Bull was dragged the morning he was killed and could have seen a cavalryman ride by on the horse that performed its circus routine while the Sioux leader lay dying.[11] These mementos of recent western history belonged at an exposition commemorating the discovery of America.

On hand at the fair in Chicago was an aged Potawatomi chief, Simon Pokagon, who as a boy had often camped where the sprawling city stood. Officials had blundered in not inviting an Indian contingent to the exposition, and to make amends they gave Pokagon the honor of delivering the keynote address on Chicago Day. Educated, intelligent, and pious, Pokagon was an ideal choice. His essays, published in the popular magazines of the day, were humble, earnest, and, above all, progressive. A dense crowd gathered on the appointed morning to witness the ceremonies, as Pokagon stepped forward, dressed in navy blue with a cap and feathers on his head. Grasping a rope of red, white, and blue, he rang the new Liberty Bell to signal the opening of the fair, and, brushing aside tears, launched into his speech. "The question comes up to us again and again, 'What can be done for the best good of the remnant of our race?'" The answer to Pokagon was "plain and clear":

We *must* give up the pursuits of our fathers. . . . We must teach our children to give up the bow and arrow . . . and, in place of the gun, we must take the plow, and live as white men do. . . . Our children *must* learn that they owe no allegiance to any clan or power on earth except the United States. They must learn to love the Stars and Stripes, and, at all times to rejoice that they are American citizens.

He concluded with a sentiment that was to be inscribed on his monument: "The red man is your brother, and God is the Father of all."[12] After his death in 1899 there was a move to observe "Pokagon Day" in Chicago by setting aside one period for Indian study every autumn in the city's public schools.[13]

Pokagon was the white man's kind of Indian. But he most impressed fair-goers by parading as the representative of a vanishing race and selling copies of his address, printed on birch bark and titled *The Red Man's Greeting*. Described by one Chicago professor as "The Red Man's Book of Lamentations,"[14] Pokagon's *Greeting* was prefaced with a poem:

> Alas for us! our day is o'er,
> Our fires are out from shore to shore;
> No more for us the wild deer bounds;
> The plow is on our hunting grounds;
> The pale man's ax rings through our woods,
> The pale man's sails skim o'er our floods;
> Our pleasant springs are dry.
> Our children—look by power oppressed!—
> Beyond the mountains of the West,
> Our children go to die.[15]

The verse was not Pokagon's own, though some thought so, but a famous passage from Charles Sprague's "Ode, Pronounced at the Centennial Celebration of the Settlement of Boston, September, 1830." Pokagon, the "Longfellow of his race,"[16] had simply substituted "ours" for "theirs" throughout. Indeed, the poem's viewpoint clashed with Pokagon's progressive outlook, though his own ruminations had led him to the "almost certain" conclusion that the Indian would one day lose his identity by amalgamating with the white race. "Through intermarriage the blood of our people, like the waters that flow into the great ocean, will be forever lost in the dominant race; and generations yet unborn will read in history of the red men of the forest, and inquire, 'Where are they?'"[17] It was not what most of Sprague's generation had meant by the vanishing race, but in paraphrasing Sprague, Pokagon had suggestively linked the present with the past. Just as the Bostonians who listened to Sprague read his poem in 1830 could bask in the pathos of the red man's passing secure in the knowledge that they were safe from Indian attack, by 1893 Americans everywhere could afford the same sentimental detachment.

INDIANS ON EXHIBITION

Ever since the gala centennial birthday party in Philadelphia in 1876, Americans had been addicted to gargantuan fairs commemorating national progress. Expositions were designed to provide formal occasions for reflection on past glories and future prospects. As the beginning point in the American story, the Indian had a distinctive part to play. His decline was in reverse ratio to civilized advance. Consequently, as the fair mania spread westward from Chicago in the 1890s, the Vanishing American went with it.

In 1898 Omaha, Nebraska, was host to the Trans-Mississippi Exposition, a declaration of faith in the West's future in the face of drought and depression. More than half of the states participated, though there were few international exhibitors. One of the most popular features proved to be the Congress of American Indians. Involving from 400 to 550 representatives of twenty-three tribes (the great majority from the plains), the congress endeavored to show the public the old-time Indian camp life. Visitors saw men and women in traditional costume going about their domestic affairs: weaving, basket-making, arrow-shaping, dancing, storytelling, and playing games. The Indian Bureau, in authorizing this return to the primitive, had departed from its usual policy of discouraging all such anti-progressive activities because the exhibits had a serious educational purpose. James Mooney of the Bureau of Ethnology had taken pains to see that the Indian camp was authentic and would afford fair-goers what might well be their "last opportunity" to study "the red man in his primitive glory . . . under correct conditions of dwelling, costume, industry, and ceremonial,"[18] though twice-weekly sham battles and other crowd-pleasing entertainments eventually clouded the congress's original purpose and caused Captain Pratt of Carlisle to denounce it as "a Wild West show of the most degenerate sort."[19]

Although a knowledgeable student of native cultures like George Bird Grinnell found the multitribal village set up in a fair celebrating American progress to be "pathetic in contrast," he nevertheless observed that the congress "created interest in the Indians, stimulated inquiry, and awoke a desire to know more of them, their past and their present, and the outlook for their future."[20] He wrote a book to meet that demand. If Pratt had a point, it was that the congress stressed *only* the Indians' past, making it easy to ignore their present, deny them a future, and join with a journalist who thought it possible "There never will be again . . . such a gathering of the representatives of a fast-dying race, a uniting of six hundred Sioux, Omahas, Sacs, Foxes, Crows, Blackfeet, Cheyennes, Piutes, Apaches, Zuñis, Navajos, Moquis, Chippewas, Assinaboine, Arapahoes, Poncas, and Flatheads—wards of a nation that has conquered but not subdued them."[21] Tribal names still rolled off the tongue, rich, exotic, heavy with doom—just as they had for Jefferson a century before.

Such was the interest aroused by the Indian exhibition at Omaha that, Mooney predicted shortly after the fair closed, Americans could "expect to see ethnology a principal feature at future expositions so long as our aboriginal material holds out."[22] Despite Mooney's chilling qualifier, the "aboriginal material" was sufficient to send an Indian contingent to the

World's Fair at St. Louis in 1904—"The Last Race Rally of Indians," one journalist dubbed it[23]—and a delegation of "six full-blooded Blackfeet chiefs" to the Panama–Pacific International Exposition in San Francisco eleven years later, where they struck another journalist as the "most interesting and the most pathetic" figures at the fair. They had been sponsored by the Great Northern Railway as a means of promoting Glacier Park, but the writer chose to see them not as the harbingers of the twentieth-century tourist West they were, but only as "the door of yesterday."[24]

There was more than silly doom-mongering in all this. The Indian had become an established attraction at American expositions because the passage of time had made him "a curiosity in the land."[25] But he was also legitimately a native, and no celebration of national progress could properly ignore "the only people who can rightfully be called Americans." Schoolcraft had once asserted that the Indian and the white man were the alpha and omega of the ethnologoical chain, thereby suggesting that a vast cultural gulf separated the two. The same image was applied to the Indian display at the Omaha exposition, though with a different thrust. The Indian now was considered "the Alpha of the alphabet of American history," just as the exposition, "with its wealth of accumulated inventions, of art, science, and culture," was its omega, and Americans at the turn of the century were being invited to look with some tenderness on the few living remnants of their own beginnings.[26]

INDIAN VESTIGES

On August 29, 1911, at a slaughterhouse near Oroville, California, a small brown man, bewildered, ragged, and hungry, was found leaning against a barn, totally spent. Ishi, last of the Yahi Indians, had emerged from the wilderness to confront a different world, and in so doing had startled myth into life. Cooper's fiction had become fact, and though Ishi was no Uncas, in a country fascinated by every remnant of its frontier past, this strange, gentle man muttering in some unintelligible tongue was an instant curiosity. Ishi passed his first nights in civilization inside the Oroville jail, where he received offers to go on exhibition as "California's last wild Indian" or the "wild man of Oroville" before Alfred L. Kroeber of the University of California intervened and took him under the Museum of Anthropology's protective care. Thereafter, Ishi received all the attention that would be lavished on a dinosaur that happened to stumble into a paleontologists' convention. By the time of his death in 1916, he had provided an impressive body of otherwise unobtainable ethnological data on an extinct native culture, and, by personifying the Indian's racial destiny, had given an imposing concept intensely human form.[27]

While Kroeber was busy gleaning information from Ishi and compiling a words-and-picture record of the last Yahi, a photographer named Edward S. Curtis, fired by the realization that the habits and features of the old-time Indians were fast fading, pursued his mission of creating a comprehensive pictorial record of all the First Americans who still exhibited aboriginal traits. A modern George Catlin, Curtis explained his motivation in an extended anecdote. He was once asked by an educated Indian what he thought the future held and replied that though his questioner came from a relatively fortunate tribe, it was still decreasing "at the rate of three per cent a year." "Take this pencil and figure out your own solution," he said. After a few minutes of calculation, the Indian looked up with "a surprised, wondering expression" and exclaimed, "Why, if I live to be an old man there will be none of my people left." "Yes, my boy," Curtis responded, "there will be a few of your people left. It will be survival of a limited few of you who are best fitted to meet the changes which civilization is forcing upon you."[28]

Curtis went on to complete an enduring twenty-volume history, *The North American Indian* (1907–1930), embracing the western tribes from the plains to the Pacific Northwest, from the Southwest to California, and including even the Eskimos of Alaska. Each volume was accompanied by a supplementary folio of sepia-tinted plates that were equal to Curtis's artistry and secured his reputation as the most gifted photographer of the western natives. But the vision that informed the whole monumental work was compressed into a single picture copyrighted in 1904 showing a band of Navajos fading into the desert haze. Curtis titled it *The Vanishing Race* and placed it at the front of the first folio supplement. "The thought which this picture is meant to convey," he wrote, "is that the Indians as a race, already shorn of their tribal strength and stripped of their primitive dress, are passing into the darkness of an unknown future. Feeling that the picture expresses so much of the thought that inspired the entire work, the author has chosen it as the first of the series."[29]

No other Curtis photograph aroused more interest. Captivated by its mute pathos, a poet wrote:

> Into the shadows, whose illumined crest
>   Speaks of the world behind them where the sun
>   Still shines for us whose day is not yet done
> Those last dark ones go drifting. East or West,
> Or North or South—it matters not; their quest
>   Is towards the shadows whence it was begun:
>   Hope in it, Ah, my brothers, there is none:
> And yet—they only seek a place to rest.
>
> So mutely, uncomplainingly they go.
>   How shall it be with us when they are gone,
>   When they are but a mem'ry and a name?
> May not those mournful eyes to phantoms grow—
>   When, wronged and lonely, they have drifted on
>   Into the voiceless shadows whence they came?[30]

Contemporary reaction to *The North American Indian* generally echoed the vanishing-race theme and, accepting it at face value, praised Curtis for a contribution that could never be duplicated. "So long as books last and minds run toward faithful representation of actualities," a reviewer in the *American Anthropologist* predicted, "his pictures will form our most trustworthy graphic memorial of our passing aborigines."[31]

Zane Grey apparently had Curtis's photograph of the Navajos riding into the gloaming in mind when he wrote the melodramatic closing scenes of *The Vanishing American* (1925), a story of forbidden love between Nophaie, a Navajo youth, and Marian, a white girl, set among the mesas of the southwestern desert. Grey had resolved the affair in conventional fashion by disposing of the Navajo lover after allowing him a final soliloquy on the Indian's fate: "[His] deeds are done. His glory and dream are gone. His sun has set. Those . . . who survive the disease and drink and poverty . . . must inevitably be absorbed by the race that has destroyed him. Red blood into the white! It means the white race will gain and the Indian vanish." Not yet thirty, Nophaie already feels old, and desires only that "he too should vanish. . . . Death, sleep, rest, peace!" Since he opened his novel with a desert sunrise, Grey ends it with a fiery sunset. "It is—symbolic," Marian murmurs as she watches the Navajos ride off, and Grey drives home the point relentlessly:

"They are vanishing—vanishing. . . . Only a question of swiftly flying time! My Nophaie—the warrior—gone before them! . . ."
    At last only one Indian was left on the darkening horizon—the solitary Shoie—bent in his saddle, a melancholy figure, unreal and strange against that dying sunset—moving on, diminishing, fading, vanishing—vanishing.[32]

Such is the stuff on which motion pictures are made, and one year after Grey's novel was published, in 1926, Paramount released *The Vanishing American*. The advertising included a painting of a warrior astride his pony staring into the distance from the top of a high promontory. His head and torso have already faded into whiteness; beneath, a caption promises that the movie is "the final epic romance of the American Indian."[33] A second advertisement, patterned after Curtis's photograph, shows a party of Indians, heads bowed in dejection, passing into a narrow defile from which there would be no return. *The Vanishing American* was better than its ballyhoo, however. While the love story based on Grey's plot was predictably trite, the first third of the movie detailing the life of the ancient tribesmen of the Southwest and the arrival of the conquistadors was good enough for cinema historians to consider it "perhaps the best Hollywood motion picture about Indians ever made,"[34] and "one of the classics of the western."[35]

The Vanishing American rounded out a cinematic tradition that had flourished in the years before World War I, then tapered off as shoot-'em-up westerns began to monopolize the screen. In the early silent films the Indian was commonly stereotyped as a poetic noble savage squarely in the Hiawatha mold, courting a dusky maiden in a pristine forest or on the shore of a lake, whiling away the golden hours before the white man arrived to destroy his idyll. A good number of bloody savages also skulked through the movies of this period, searching for scalps. But prior to the 1920s the screen Indian had enjoyed a respect he would subsequently receive only infrequently until Hollywood again acquired racial consciousness in the late 1940s.

Popular interest in the Vanishing American reached a peak in the period just before World War I. In 1913 Joseph K. Dixon's book *The Vanishing Race* appeared, illustrated with portraits of impassive old warriors and a series of photographs of a group of Indians riding single file along a ridge, clopping off into the sunset, feathers trailing in the breeze as they resolutely advance to meet their fate. Lest the symbolism be too obscure, the captions were not: "Skirting the Sky-Line"; "The Final Trail"; "Down the Western Slope"; "Facing the Sunset"; "Vanishing Into the Mists"; "The Sunset of a Dying Race"; and "The Empty Saddle." "Listen for the heavy footfalls of departing greatness," Dixon told his readers. "Watch the grim faces, sternly set toward the western sky rim, heads still erect, eagle feathers, emblems of victory, moving proudly into the twilight, and a long, solitary peal of distant thunder joining the refrain of the soul—and it is night."[36]

Though the prose was Dixon's, and perhaps the pictures too, *The Vanishing Race* was the brainchild of Rodman Wanamaker, son of a Philadelphia dry goods tycoon and sponsor of three "expeditions" to the American Indian that were both commemorative and patriotic in purpose. Rodman's father, John, like many entrepreneurs of his time, had fused piety with profit-making through a long business career. In 1857, at the age of nineteen, the senior Wanamaker had read Longfellow's recently published *Hiawatha*, then taken a trip up "the great father of Rivers—the beautiful Mississippi." After viewing the surrounding countryside from some high bluffs near St. Paul, Minnesota, he had been been inspired to write his brother:

[I] looked upon the once happy hunting grounds and homes of the Red Men of the Forest. Sad was it to witness their desolation and listen to the story of their sufferings and wrongs—Oh! that their history could be blotted from the page of remembrance for alas! It is a bitter reflection upon the humanity and christianity of the White Man.[37]

Rodman, John's most artistic and sensitive offspring, inherited his father's sentimental regret about the Indian, and channeled a portion of the family's fortune into the work of preserving a photographic record of what he fondly called the vanishing race. Under his direction expeditions were sent West in 1908, 1909, and 1913; they brought back some 11,000 pictures and fifty miles of movie film.

The first expedition ("Rodman Wanamaker's Educational Expedition to the Indians") wandered through Yellowstone Park and wound up on the Crow reservation. Its chief accomplishment was a film play with a Crow couple playing the leads. The subject, not surprisingly, was Longfellow's *Hiawatha*, and the treatment, according to a promotional booklet issued by the Wanamakers, was properly reverent, stressing "the sweetness, power and stimulus of poetry," "a love of the beautiful," and "the mystery and magic surrounding the life of the Red man." Of course, the whole project gained added importance from the fact that time had almost run out for the Indian. "It is a long, long chapter, from the cordial welcome of the Red man when Columbus landed, to the fated end of the Red man over four hundred years later, but the end is almost here," the Wanamaker booklet insisted. "Our only hope, if we wish to keep the Indian, is to carve a statue of him in stone or mould his figure in bronze."[38]

The author of these sentiments, Joseph K. Dixon, director of the Wanamaker store's "Educational Bureau," the next year was in the Bighorn country leading the second Wanamaker expedition to the Indians. This time the purpose was to assemble representative "chiefs, scouts and warriors" from the western tribes for a "Last Great Indian Council." Their stories were to be taken down and a permanent photographic record made of the final gathering of the tribes. Soon the council fires would be snuffed out across the land, and the Indian lost to the world. Wanamaker, in short, was conducting the last rites for the First Americans, and the book that resulted—Dixon's

The Vanishing Race—was in effect a souvenir album of the occasion, dedicated TO THE MAN OF MYSTERY—THE EARTH HIS MOTHER—THE SUN HIS FATHER—A CHILD OF THE MOUNTAINS AND THE PLAINS—A FAITHFUL WORSHIPPER IN THE GREAT WORLD CATHE-DRAL—NOW A TRAGIC SOUL HAUNTING THE SHORES OF THE WESTERN OCEAN—MY BROTHER THE INDIAN.[39]

Dixon's text pounded home the title theme with an awesome persistence rarely matched in the annals of Vanishing American rhetoric, and his opening chapter was a peerless compendium of virtually every hallowed cliché on the subject. The Indian was steeped in a foreknowledge of his own doom: "There is a look in his face of bronze that frightens us." The Indian was unmalleable, and thus beyond the pale of civilization: "He had to give up all that was his and all that was dear to him—to make himself over or die. He would not yield. He died. He would not receive his salvation by surrender; rather would he choose oblivion, unknown darkness—the melting fires of ex-termination." The Indian was part of the wilderness he inhab-ited ("He lived and moved and had his being in the sanctuary of the hills, the high altar-stairs of the mountains, the sublime silences of the stately pines"), and thus the inevitable simile drawn from nature: "It is hard to think this virile, untamed creation has been swept like hurrying leaves by angry autumn gusts across the sunlit plains into a night without a star." Statistical proof was adduced: "Indisputable figures . . . place the decrease of Indian population in the United States, north of Mexico, since the coming of the white man, at 65 per cent." A "moral obligation" to study the Indian was asserted, as well as the need for haste "because all serious students of Indian life and lore are deeply convinced of the insistent fact that the Indian, as a race, is fast losing its typical characters and is soon destined to pass completely away." And the law of vices and virtues: "The character generally attributed to the Indian is that of a savage, but this blemish came upon him through contact with the white man. Their ingenuous and trustful nature quickly degenerated as they were enslaved, betrayed, and slain."[40]

In his last chapter, "The Farewell of the Chiefs," Dixon watched "these old heroes" as they passed out of the council tent, out "through the doorway that leads to a land without a horizon." Abjuring "the mockery of speech, they mounted their horses, and faced their final destiny." But they were not to exit silently. Only "a dull and vulgar rhetorician" would attempt "to parse the fathomless sorrow of their speech," Dixon wrote, before offering one chief's final incantation:

Brothers, the West, the West! We alone have the key to the West, and we must bravely unlock the portals; we can buy no lamp that will banish the night. We have always kept our time by the sun. When we pass through the gates of this dying day, we shall pass into a sunless land, and for us there shall be no more time, a forever-land of annihilating darkness.[41]

It was perhaps the most improbable speech in the annals of Indian literature, amply justifying the verdict of one veteran Indian agent that Dixon was a "hot air artist."[42]

Rodman Wanamaker's cherished object of Indian citizenship helps explain the odd juxtaposition in this period of Vanishing American rhetoric on one hand with plans for the Indian's assimilated future on the other. There was no contradiction here. Wanamaker's second expedition was intentionally commemorative. It waved farewell to the old generation of Indians in order to welcome the new. Thus his third and final expedition, the "Expedition of Citizenship to the North American Indian," was sent out in 1913 even as *The Vanishing Race* was being published. Once again Joseph Dixon was the leader, this time on a six-month trip scheduled to cover over 22,000 miles, 2,300 of them by stagecoach, and to visit 169 tribes and 89 reservations. The aim was to foster patriotism and a spirit of goodwill among the first Americans by unfurling the Stars and Stripes over their reservations. The flag to be used was the same one that had been hoisted at Fort Wadsworth, on Staten Island, on Washington's birthday earlier that year when President Taft and thirty-three full-blooded chiefs dedicated the National Memorial to the North American Indian—another grandiose Wanamaker project involving a neoclassical monument "to the memory of the North American Indian," that despite an initial flurry of publicity did not get off the ground.[43]

Once this hallowed flag had been raised over the reservation, tribal representatives were to sign a "Declaration of Allegiance to the United States Government," then the people were to sit back and listen to a recorded address by the new President, Woodrow Wilson, delivered, as he said, not to his red children, but to his red brothers. After presenting the tribe with an American flag of its own, the expedition would pack up and push on to the next reservation to repeat the same ceremony— 169 times in all.

In 1909, Wanamaker had bid the Indian adieu; four years later, he sponsored an expedition to "plant in the bosoms of these original Americans a love for the flag of the country that has adopted them," thereby preparing them for full citizenship.[44] The Indian was dead, but instead of a burial he was to be given a flag and the vote. The theory of assimilation could not have been defined more precisely.

THE END OF THE TRAIL: SCULPTORS AND THE INDIAN

Sculptors, with their penchant for the allegorical, traditionally create a nation's enduring symbolic art. In the United States, they were naturally attracted to the theme of the Vanishing American. At once time-honored and patriotic, it was also aesthetically agreeable since it afforded an opportunity to depict the human figure in the nude. Writers in the nineteenth century often compared the Indian to Greek statuary. Cooper's Uncas was likened to chiseled marble, such was his flawless, stony perfection, and George Catlin enthusiastically proclaimed the unspoiled Indians he encountered a match as physical specimens for the Greek athletes who inspired the classical sculptors. Even Francis Parkman, normally clear-eyed where noble savages were concerned, repeated the hoary anecdote about Benjamin West's first reaction on seeing the Belvedere Apollo in the Vatican: "By God, a Mohawk!"

In 1853 Thomas Crawford, the New York sculptor resident in Rome who subsequently ran afoul of Jefferson Davis over the headgear appropriate for an American Liberty, set to work on his first commission from the federal government, a bas-relief for the Senate pediment on the Capitol. Crawford took as his theme civilization's triumph over savagery. On either side of the central figure of America, standing between a rising sun and a proud eagle, he arranged smaller figures representative of the old order retreating in disarray before the new. To America's right are a soldier from the Revolutionary War period, a merchant, two sterling specimens of young manhood marching forward, a schoolmaster with a pupil, and a mechanic; to her left, a pioneer chopping down a tree, clearing away the wilderness while an Indian hunter looks back in dismay and an Indian mother cradles her baby in her arms. The most striking figure in the cluttered composition, one that Crawford favored as a separate piece, was that of a melancholy chief seated on a robe-covered outcropping, his elbow resting on his knee, propping up his weary head as he broods over the fate of his people. In him, Crawford wrote, "I have endeavored to concentrate all the despair and profound grief resulting from the conviction of the white man's triumph." Beside the Indians is an open grave, "emblematic of the extinction of the Indian race."[45]

Crawford's pediment figures were finished by the summer of 1856. His theme—civilization's progress in America—had been anticipated in another commissioned work erected at the east entrance to the Capitol in 1853, Horatio Greenough's *The Rescue*, depicting a towering frontiersman restraining a warrior from tomahawking a cringing white woman and her baby. But in the separate figure from the pediment, a statue known as *The Dying Chief Contemplating the Progress of Civilization*, Crawford had created the first important monument to the Vanishing American. "The attitude, air, and expression, the grand proportions, the aboriginal type of form and feature, the bowed head, the clenched hand, the stoical despair of this majestic figure," a critic wrote in 1870, "adequately and eloquently symbolize the destruction of a Race."[46]

When Augustus Saint-Gaudens, the doyen of American sculptors in the late nineteenth century, did his first large marble study in 1872 he chose as his theme Hiawatha. Later he pronounced Indian subjects "the youthful sin of every American artist."[47] Certainly following the World's Columbian Exposition at Chicago the Indian enjoyed an unprecedented vogue among sculptors. Even when the artist's intention was not primarily allegorical, his work was sure to be interpreted symbolically. Solon H. Borglum, a Nebraska rancher before he turned to sculpture, produced several Indian pieces including one, called *Desolation*, of a woman weeping at her husband's burial site. It seemed to a contemporary "to be invested with a something larger and more tragic than personal grief, and to symbolize rather the mourning of a dying race conscious of its doom. Its appeal is that of a sorrowing people rather than of an individual."[48]

More explicit were the works of Cyrus E. Dallin, a native of Utah, who studied sculpture in Boston and Paris, where, like others of his countrymen, he rediscovered America at a performance of Buffalo Bill's Wild West show. The result was an equestrian statue, *The Signal of Peace*, that secured his reputation when it won a medal at the Columbian Exposition. Dallin followed it up with three other equestrian subjects narrating the story of the white man's conquest of the Indian. *The Signal of Peace* depicts the initial friendly reception accorded the newcomers by the unsuspecting natives; *The Medicine Man* registers wariness and suspicion; *The Protest* shows the Indian in defiance, his fist clenched at the white intruders; and *The Appeal to the Great Spirit*, first exhibited in 1908, concludes the series as the Indian, dispossessed but never vanquished, pleads to his gods for some encouraging sign even as he accepts their decision with resignation. *The Appeal* received wide exposure through postcards and plaster replicas. Dallin thought it entitled him to favorable consideration as sculptor for the proposed Wanamaker memorial on Staten Island, where his work would have shared the spotlight with the Statue of Liberty—to which *The Appeal* was favorably compared as a popular masterpiece.[49] "More than a statue of a lone Indian," a typical plaudit went, "it is the story of a race."[50]

Adolph A. Weinman, a German-born sculptor educated in New York, executed an ambitious allegorical group for the 1904 Louisiana Purchase Exposition in St. Louis. Called *Destiny of the Red Man*, it included nine figures: the Great Spirit mounted on a buffalo, flanked on one side by a chief in full headdress, a hunter and his dog, and on the other by an Indian mother with her son, a backward-looking brave wrapped in a blanket, and a little child with his arm thrust up to the elbow through the eye socket of a buffalo skull. Behind the buffalo a medicine man sits expounding on better days to a rapt youth. Finally, there is an intrusive totem pole (these were Plains Indians) surmounted by a vulture that manages to destroy the sculpture's line with overstating the obvious. But Weinman never intended to be subtle. As he wrote years later, "In the composition of this group I have endeavored to symbolize the passing of an heroic race. . . . With the coming of the white man . . . it was but a matter of time for some of the many tribes, deprived of, or restrained in, their freedom loving way of life, to gradually become greatly reduced in numbers or completely extinct."[51] Weinman's sculpture, well received at the 1904 exposition, was not cast into bronze until 1947 and remained relatively unknown apart from the figure of the backward-glancing brave, which was reproduced separately.

Of all the sculptors, James Earle Fraser made the most distinctive contribution to the Vanishing American theme. Like Dallin, Fraser had grown up in the West as the colorful characters of frontier days were dying off. Trained in Minneapolis and Chicago, he worked in Paris for two years as an assistant to Saint-Gaudens (who was Weinman's mentor also) before returning to America in 1900. Dallin, Weinman, and Fraser all exhibited Indian subjects at St. Louis in 1904, and Fraser's most widely circulated work, the celebrated Indian-head–buffalo nickel first minted in 1913, was itself a symbolic tribute to the vanished West. It directly anticipated his masterpiece, *The End of the Trail*, which went on public display two years later at the Panama-Pacific International Exposition in San Francisco.

Fraser's immediate inspiration for *The End of the Trail* had come while viewing the western sculpture on exhibit at the Columbian Exposition. In 1894 he prepared the original small model, working it up on an epic scale (two and one-half times life size) for the 1915 fair, where it occupied a prominent place in front of the Court of Palms. "Before you," a guidebook informed exposition-goers, "is the end of the Indian race. The poor Indian, following his long trail, has at last come to the end. The worn horse and its rider tell a long, pathetic story."[52] Indeed, the statue of a forlorn warrior slumped forward on his pony, chin resting on his chest, his eagle plume drooping, his lance pointing to the ground, seemed the epitome of dejection and despair. Fittingly, at an exposition where Joseph Dixon lectured three times a day in the Palace of Education and sold photographs of the "Vanishing Race" to raise funds for the Wanamaker memorial, *The End of the Trail* won the gold medal for sculpture and the devotion of the public.

Small replicas of Fraser's statue were soon on sale everywhere. Bookends, ashtrays, postcards, advertisements, paperweights, trinkets, and even china and silverware featured it. Garish prints, in sepia and color, showing the horse and rider silhouetted against a dying sunset, eventually decorated many American walls.[53] Poets found in *The End of the Trail* a fresh source of inspiration. "Last of his race: the hour has come to die," one wrote:

> Silent, alone, his priest the sinking sun,
> All hope is dead, yet no despairful cry
> Escapes his mangled soul. The pit yawns nigh.
> Like ashes falling from a burnt-out sun,
> His plunge to bottomless oblivion.[54]

Fraser, as he himself modestly conceded, had clearly struck "a popular note of sympathy."[55]

As early as the 1820s William Cullen Bryant and other poets had imagined the day when the First American would be "driven into the western sea." Congressional orators had enlivened policy debate by weaving word-pictures of their own. "We have seen their most powerful nations dwindled down to poor wandering tribes, and their greatest kings reduced to beggarly chiefs," Oliver H. Smith told the House of Representatives in 1828:

We have seen them driven by the whites, from river to river, from State to State, from hill to hill, from mountain to mountain, and from forest to forest; the tide of white emigration still flowing West, and still pressing close upon them; and if we continue the present policy, the time cannot be very far distant, when the last sound of the Indian must die on the Pacific.[56]

The same idea appeared in art. John Mix Stanley, Catlin's contemporary, had executed an oil in 1857 showing a few

Indians huddled together on a narrow beach where the tossing waves and booming surf mark the close of their epoch. *The Last of Their Race,* he titled it. Others found humor in the situation. Frederick B. Opper, an illustrator renowned in the late nineteenth century for his comic sketches in *Puck* magazine, drew an unhappy brave standing on the edge of a cliff, rye bottle in hand, while civilization in the guise of a policeman prods him from behind with a billy club and orders him to "Move on, maroon brother, move on!"

Fraser's achievement was to convert this conventional image of the Vanishing American into stone. He regarded *The End of the Trail* not as allegory but as truth. As a small boy on the Dakota prairie he had heard old settlers say that one day the Indian would be forced off the continent. "This idea of a weaker race being steadily pushed to the wall by a stronger" infused his equestrian statue, and long after the exposition was over he dreamed of it cast in imperishable bronze commanding "some bold promontory" high above San Francisco Bay, with the breakers crashing below as nature rounded out his vision: "There they would stand forever looking out on the waste of waters—with nought save the precipice and the ocean before them—driven at last to the very edge of the continent. That would be, in very truth, 'The End of the Trail.'"[57]

Addressing a meeting of Friends of the Indian at Lake Mohonk, New York, in the autumn of 1916, Lawrence W. White, superintendent of the Lac du Flambeau Indian School, referred to Fraser's *End of the Trail*. "The subject was an Indian with everything to indicate that he was worn and weary and had abandoned all hope," White said. But speaking as a medical doctor, he reported that there *was* hope for the red man. Since disease was the primary cause of Indian decline, its containment should be the government's first priority. "We cannot solve the Indian problem without Indians," the Commissioner of Indian Affairs had stated. "We cannot educate their children unless they are kept alive." Improved medical care was working wonders on the reservations. "The Indian's constitution had been restored, his health conditions improved and death rate decreased wherever there are Indians to be found," White contended. Indian babies "come to stay, and are making statistics show to the world that the Indian is not a dying race." When Carlisle's student journal printed White's speech, however, it added a prefatory note pointing out that even if numerical decline had been checked, as "a distinct race, with racial ideals and characteristics," the Indian was still disappearing.[58] That was the crucial tenet of the new faith in the Vanishing American.

CHAPTER FOURTEEN

NOW OR NEVER IS THE TIME:
Cultural Extinction and the
Conservationist Impulse

The 1890s had marked a turning point in the American public's acceptance of the broad principle of conservation. Although westerners were inclined to see conservation much as they saw Indian policy—as just another ploy to deprive them of the same opportunities for exploitation and profit enjoyed by easterners of an earlier day—the necessity of wise-use resource management was winning powerful converts everywhere.

Turner's eulogy to the frontier expressed the general awareness that America's resources were finite. Poor farming methods and the exhaustion of the soil had to be acknowledged and remedied. Forests had to be protected if an adequate water supply was to be ensured for the future. The arid West required planned development if it was to be made agriculturally productive.

Beyond such utilitarian considerations, however, conservation satisfied aesthetic needs that often warred with a wise-use philosophy. The national park movement, tentatively launched in 1872 with the creation of Yellowstone, had gained momentum by the turn of the century. Wilderness values were in vogue. "Some at least of the forest reserves should afford perpetual protection to the native fauna and flora, safe havens of refuge to our rapidly diminishing wild animals of the larger kinds, and free camping grounds for the ever-increasing numbers of men and women who have learned to find rest, health, and recreation in the splended forests and flower-clad meadows of our mountains," Theodore Roosevelt advised Congress in 1901. Such reserves, he continued, "should be set apart forever for the use and benefit of our people as a whole and not sacrificed to the shortsighted greed of a few."[1] The park movement would attempt to fuse the wise-use with the aesthetic or preservationist impulse.

In the same period, American anthropology emerged as a profession with a mission. Looking back from the standpoint of 1899, James Mooney could perceive that the establishment of the Bureau of Ethnology twenty years earlier had "marked an era in the history of the science." Largely through the bureau's influence, "local research has been encouraged and organized society effort stimulated, chairs of anthropology have been established in our leading universities, ethnologic expeditions have been fitted out at private cost, and an intelligent public interest has been awakened which finds its reflex in congressional legislation."[2]

With the United States government committed to a policy of Indian assimilation, there would soon be no Indian cultures left to study. It followed that American anthropology's primary purpose would be the preservation of information about the vanishing cultures. Field work among the western tribes assumed the character of a desperate salvage operation that realized the immediate goals set out for the profession, and simultaneously stamped with the authority of science the assumption that the Indian was fated to disappear.

CONSERVING AMERICAN NATURE: BUFFALO, INDIANS, AND GEORGE BIRD GRINNELL

It was no coincidence that the conservation movement and the science of anthropology developed at approximately the same time in America. But the ties between conservation and anthropology were much older. In the earliest European representations of the New World, raw nature and the natives and animals inhabiting it constituted a single phenomenon—American wilderness.[3] To contemplate the parts was to contemplate the whole. As the forests fell under the axes of civilized man, for example, the Indians and the game they hunted retreated apace. By the late nineteenth century, the translation of this idea that had the most meaning for Americans connected the fate of the plains Indian warrior with that of the once-mighty buffalo.

Americans had long realized that the buffalo were in peril. In an official report made in 1829, William Clark and Lewis Cass warned that "a few years hence" the buffalo might "even be rare upon the immense plains which extend to the base of the Rocky Mountains."[4] When George Catlin embarked on his personal salvage operation among the western tribes in 1832— the year the federal government set aside Hot Springs, Arkansas, as the first "national reservation"—he recognized that the wilderness trinity of flora, fauna, and natural man was "under an equal doom." He wondered if by "some great protecting policy of government" they might be "preserved in their pristine beauty and wildness, in a *magnificent park*, where the world could see for ages to come, the native Indian in his classic attire, galloping his wild horse, with sinewy bow, and shield and lance, amid the fleeting herds of elks and buffaloes." But Catlin knew his dream was futile. "The buffalo's doom is sealed," he wrote, "and with their extinction must assuredly sink into real despair and starvation, the inhabitants of these vast plains."[5]

As American settlement advanced, the buffalo declined according to prediction. Its heavy winter robe had always been valued, but the real impetus to slaughter came in the 1870s when its summer hide began to serve as belting for the nation's machinery. The buffalo succumbed, another victim of industrial progress. While congressmen debated measures to curb the slaughter—and some high officials defended it as an efficient and inexpensive means of reducing the plains Indians to passive dependency—the destruction of the herds continued. Though exact dates differ, by the end of the 1870s there were no buffalo to speak of left on the southern plains. The hostility of the Indians gave the northern herds a temporary reprieve from the rifles of the hide hunters, but by 1884 the slaughter was virtually complete. William T. Hornaday, an authority on big-game conservation and author of the National Museum's pioneering report "The Extermination of the American Bison," believed that there were only eighty-five buffalo at large in the United States in 1889,[6] and four years later Theodore Roosevelt estimated "considerably less than half a hundred."[7]

When the full enormity of the deed sank in, the buffalo, like the Indian, became a common symbol for the vanished West. In the 1870s Colonel Richard I. Dodge had written of the first concerted onslaught on the southern herd that "the buffalo melted away like snow before a summer's sun"[8]—just as California's Indians had melted away before the western rifles in George Falconer Emmons's revealing phrase. A writer in 1893 expressed the opinion that "if one pities the poor Indian, he is also at liberty to pity the sad fate of the buffalo."[9] A poet wrote:

> On reservations now the blood grows cold
> In savage veins, where once 'twas fierce and bold.
> The Indian—proud—is destined soon to go,
> As in the Passing of the Buffalo.[10]

In lamentations laced with anger, writers urged that official action be taken to preserve the buffalo remnant. The American Bison Society was founded in 1905, and three years later President Roosevelt signed the bill creating the National Bison Range on the Flathead Reservation in Montana. American stamps, paper currency, and coinage all honored the buffalo between 1901 and 1923—and each had its plains Indian counterpart. Told that his buffalo–Indian-head nickel was the only coin "that is typically American—that would reveal to some later civilization its country of origin," James Earle Fraser commented: "I had not thought about it that way; all I tried to do was to express in these symbols—*America,* instead of merely copying some Greek temple or god."[11] After 1913, the buffalo and the Indian were in fact what they had long been in popular fancy, two sides of the same coin.

Of those who bemoaned the buffalo's disappearance in the late nineteenth century, none spoke out more emotionally than George Bird Grinnell, a pioneering conservationist as well as a student of the plains Indians. His 1892 article "The Last of the Buffalo" opened with a sentimental reverie:

On the floor, on either side of my fireplace, lie two buffalo skulls. They are white and weathered, the horns cracked and bleached by the snows and frosts, and the rains and heats of many winters and summers. Often, late at night, when the house is quiet, I sit before the fire, and muse and dream of the old days; and as I gaze at these relics of the past, they take life before my eyes.

Buffalo skulls that had eluded the bone-pickers could still be found here and there on the Great Plains, but "when these most enduring relics of a vanished race shall have passed away, there will be found, in all the limitless domain once darkened by their feeding herds, not one trace of the American buffalo."[12]

Grinnell was speaking as a scientist, trained in paleontology under the estimable O. C. Marsh of Yale, whom he had accompanied to Nebraska in 1870 in search of vertebrate fossils. Ten years later, at the age of thirty, Grinnell earned his doctorate. Meanwhile, he had participated in army exploratory expeditions out West in 1874 and 1875 as a naturalist, and had begun to publish occasionally in *Forest and Stream*, a weekly paper that he would edit from 1880 to 1911. Grinnell, who as a boy lived in the Audubon Park area of upper Manhattan and knew John James Audubon's widow, founded the first local Audubon Society in 1886. The next year he joined with Theodore Roosevelt in forming the Boone and Crockett Club, a sportsmen's association dedicated to game conservation. Between 1891 and 1910 he campaigned actively for the creation of Glacier National Park—a cause that introduced him to the Blackfoot Indians indigenous to the area. Grinnell's curiosity had already been pricked by the Pawnees he met in Nebraska. As time passed, he increasingly directed his talents and abundant energy to the study of Indian cultures—the Blackfoot, the Pawnee, and, especially, the Cheyenne.

Grinnell's transition from natural history to ethnology is revealing. "Like the wild bird and the beast, like the cloud and the forest tree, the primitive savage is a part of nature," he stated in 1895. "He is in it and of it."[13] There was no distinction to make. In many respects Grinnell was typical of nineteenth-century anthropologists, whose ethnological enthusiasms frequently grew out of their studies in natural history. Henry R. Schoolcraft, for example, began his career as a geologist and mineralogist, and "originally went to the west for the purpose of science."[14] Frustrated in his ambition to be appointed federal Superintendent of Mines of Missouri Territory, he settled for a position as Indian agent on the northwestern frontier and formed an enthusiasm for ethnology that dominated the rest of his life. Lewis Henry Morgan, the sometime lawyer from Rochester, discovered the Indian (partially through Schoolcraft's encouragement) before he went on to develop an abiding interest in natural history. Feeling "unambitious," and fascinated by the industrious activities of the beavers he had been observing over several summers, the "Father of American Anthropology" compressed his findings in 1868 into a monograph, *The American Beaver and His Works*. Based on his belief that animals share in man's moral attributes, Morgan reached the startling conclusion that "domestication or extermination is the alternative already offered not alone to species, but to families and orders of animals."[15] John Wesley Powell, first director of the Bureau of Ethnology, was a recognized geologist before he became an anthropologist in the Morgan tradition, while his assistant after 1894, W. J. McGee, began his career as a geologist and ended it as a hydrologist, sandwiching anthropological studies in between.[16]

Walter McClintock, a popular expert on the Blackfoot, first visited the tribe in 1896 as a member of a government expedition sent to recommend sites in the Northwest for national forest reserves. After McClintock informed the Blackfoot that he had come to protect their forests for future generations, a "strong and lasting friendship" resulted. Realizing that he had "an unusual opportunity" to study a people who must "soon lose their identity and disappear for ever," McClintock stayed among the Blackfoot for four years, gaining "as full a knowledge as possible of their characteristics and customs, their traditions and religion."[17] The conservationist impulse had transformed another naturalist into an anthropologist, though McClintock, while admiring the Blackfoot, viewed them as Stone Age men whose only hope for survival lay in early and complete assimilation.

Grinnell, like most of his contemporaries, believed that the Indians were in a state of retarded development—"grown-up children," as he customarily put it—and he regarded cultural change as a glacially slow process. "We are trying to force this wild creature, who once was free, into the hard, rigid mold of civilization, and we do not find him plastic." It was "asking much," Grinnell argued, to expect the Indian to become at once a civilized man.[18] Meanwhile, there was the Indian as Indian to be considered. Grinnell had a compelling message: "The Indian is a man, not very different from his white brother, except that he is undeveloped."[19] Years later Grinnell was still insisting that Indians "too often . . . have been studied merely as natural-history specimens, and described wholly from the outside. Their humanity has been forgotten."[20]

In time, Grinnell stopped referring to evolutionary categories as he grew more empathic. His personal experiences conditioned his viewpoint. He had known the old West, and had witnessed many of the changes that transformed it in the 1870s and 1880s. He could recall the exciting days when he and the West were young together, when the buffalo still ran and the Indians were free. Nostalgia cemented his emotional identification with the old-time plains Indian, and firmed his resolve to preserve a record of cultures rapidly being snuffed out on the reservations. "The whole fashion" of the Indians' lives had been altered, "and with the change came also a modification of custom and belief almost as great as that in their surroundings."[21] The need for immediate preservationist measures applied as much to the aboriginal cultures as to the forests and wild game. It was the recognition of this fact by individuals like Grinnell that linked the conservation movement and anthropological studies at the end of the nineteenth century. The one fed on the vanishing wilderness, the other on the Vanishing American, and a sense of great urgency was the common denominator.

ANTHROPOLOGY'S ETHNOGRAPHIC REORIENTATION

In the preface to *Ancient Society*, the culmination of his life's work, Lewis Henry Morgan drew back to assess the future needs of anthropology in the United States. What he called for was not more grand syntheses like his own, but ethnographic field work, methodical and exact, of the sort he had undertaken in the past. Moreover, writing in 1877, he struck what was to become a familiar note:

While fossil remains buried in the earth will keep for the future student, the remains of Indian art, languages and institutions will not. They are perishing daily, and have been perishing for upwards of three centuries. The ethnic life of the Indian tribes is declining under the influence of American civilization, their arts and languages are disappearing, and their institutions are dissolving. After a few more years, facts that may now be gathered with ease will become impossible of discovery. These circumstances appeal strongly to Americans to enter this great field and gather its abundant harvest.[22]

That same year, Daniel Wilson, a Scottish-born Canadian educator best known for his pioneering work on prehistoric man, delivered an address as chairman of the Permanent Subsection of Anthropology of the American Association for the Advancement of Science. He too concluded with a warning and an appeal. More facts, not more "startling hypotheses," were anthropology's first priority. "The work before you for years to come," he told his colleagues, "must be the accumulation of evidence, the cautious sifting of it in all its bearings, and the ascertaining what its teachings really are."[23]

Such strong declarations by two renowned anthropologists marked not only an awareness that research opportunities were vanishing with the primitive cultures, but also a conscious decision to reorder the priorities of American anthropology as it had developed since the Civil War in the thralls of evolutionary naturalism. In many ways, this change meant a sharp curtailment of expectations. Nurtured on Herbert Spencer, social scientists had been intent on defining the laws of social evolution that corresponded to the evolutionary laws in the natural sciences. Thus, for a man like John Wesley Powell, ethnological research in America was an endeavor worthy of government patronage because, in the short run, it would provide expert guidance to policymakers, and, in the long run, it promised to make a major contribution to the sum total of human knowledge. Those principles underlying social development throughout man's history could be correctly determined only by the close study of existing primitive cultures. Anthropology would be a "mirror for man"—modern man, who could see his own ancient past in the living survivals of the successive ethnic stages through which society evolved en route to civilization. In short, anthropology was programmed to reach socially useful conclusions, and to reach them promptly, since those conclusions were its ultimate justification. An apparently esoteric and even irrelevant study was, at bottom, eminently practical.

Impatient to discover the universal laws, evolutionary social scientists sometimes strained at the slow, plodding investigation that necessarily preceded their formulation. The temptation to curtail research and get on with defining the laws was enormous. Powell, who had himself done field work and recognized its fundamental importance to anthropology, had a penchant for sweeping generalizations that led him into the realm of philosophic synthesis and caused him to question whether the inductive methodology was the only pathway to scientific truth. In one essay, he defended deductive reasoning and argued that the primary categories or areas of human learning, the "irreducibles," might be derived from universal laws by substituting abstraction for analysis.[24] Powell's speculations served to draw a line between the old and the new traditions in turn-of-the-century American anthropology, between a sometimes inspired amateurism and an emergent academic professionalism.

Under the auspices of the American Social Science Association (1865), students of the separate branches of human activity formed their own organizations, which, along with university programs of study, encouraged a specialization that eventually militated against the wide-ranging curiosity, the concern with categorization of phenomena isolated from context, and the fondness for confident generalization that had characterized the founding fathers of the social sciences. Anthropology attained professional maturity within an intellectual climate skeptical of the nomothetic, or generalizing, tradition in the social and behavioral sciences. A pragmatic frame of mind encouraged a concentration on the particular—on phenomena—that clashed with the older preference for syntheses, and the phenomena themselves were recognized as immensely complex because they could be correctly understood only through a sensitive awareness of their interdependency.

Unilinear evolutionism of the sort espoused by Lewis Henry Morgan became a particular target for the new generation of university-trained scholars committed to an idiographic approach. Not "startling hypotheses," then, but, as Wilson had said, "the diligent accumulation of all the evidence on which a sound scientific induction can alone be based,"[25] had become the accepted end of the social sciences. In anthropology, this meant field work among primitive peoples. It meant, for American anthropologists, intensive investigations among the still-functioning Indian cultures. It meant a dominant concern with ethnography, the preservation of raw cultural data. It also meant that haste was essential, for science had discovered the desirability of procuring a detailed record of Indian cultures just when those cultures seemed perilously close to extinction.

FRANZ BOAS AND SALVAGE ETHNOGRAPHY

More than any other individual, Franz Boas represented the new order. Though he took his doctorate in physics at Kiel in 1881, he gravitated to geographical studies, then, following a stay among the Eskimos of Baffin Land in 1883, anthropology. His commitment was firm by 1886. Boas left his native Germany that year on the first of what proved to be several field trips to the Pacific Northwest coast. Over the next decade, having decided to remain in the United States and become an American citizen, he filled a succession of posts, including a stint from 1889 to 1892 at Clark University, where he directed the first American doctorate awarded in anthropology. After serving as assistant chief of the Department of Anthropology with the World Columbian Exposition in Chicago and as curator of the newly established Chicago Field Museum, Boas secured a permanent position with the American Museum of Natural History as assistant curator of ethnology and somatology in 1896, and assumed a lectureship in physical anthropology at Columbia University. Three years later he was appointed professor of anthropology, a title he held until his retirement in 1936. From these two centers of learning, the Museum of Natural History and Columbia, Boas's influence spread; by 1905, when he resigned his position at the museum, his exacting standards and concern with a rigorously empirical methodology were already woven into the fabric of professional anthropology as it emerged in the United States.[26]

For all his legendary objectivity and caution, Boas had never been immune to the fear that Indian cultural disappearance was imminent, and he was committed to the task of preserving an ethnographic record of the western tribes. Sent to British Columbia by the British Association for the Advancement of Science to conduct an ethnological survey of the coastal tribes, he submitted a preliminary report in 1888 accompanied by "a few remarks" on future research in the region. Only in limited areas could the customs of the coastal natives still be studied "uninfluenced by the whites," and it was but a matter of time before they too would be altered. The Indians' physical features had already been blurred through intermarriage, and even their languages were "decaying." "An early study of the ethnology of the province must be considered a necessity," Boas summed up. "A few years hence it will be impossible to obtain a great part of the information that may now be gathered at a comparatively slight expense."[27]

In 1906, in Quebec City, Boas, addressing the International Congress of Americanists on "Ethnological Problems in Canada," said, "Day by day the Indians and their cultures are disappearing more and more before the encroachments of modern civilization, and fifty years hence nothing will remain to be learned in regard to this interesting and important subject."[28] Three years later, "prompted by its urgency," he reiterated this warning at a meeting of the British Association for the Advancement of Science:

With the energetic economic progress of Canada, primitive life is disappearing with ever-increasing rapidity; and, unless work is taken up at once and thoroughly, information on the earliest history of this country, which has at the same time a most important bearing upon the general problems of anthropology, will never be obtained.[29]

These pleas, echoed by others, helped determine the course of anthropological research in North America for a generation.

The emotive language of decay and death set a tone in perfect harmony with popular opinion. Like Catlin before them, Boas and his scientific contemporaries used it with a deliberateness that attested to their dependence for financial support on parsimonious governments and impoverished scientific bodies, as well as to their limited interest in the contemporary Indian. Relatively pure primitive cultures were everything; completed cultures had virtually no anthropological value. European anthropologists had to be satisfied with the secondary evidence of archeological and linguistic remnants. Americans could study the real thing, functioning aboriginal cultures approximating those of ancient man in the Old World. It was a glorious, a not-to-be-missed opportunity whose attractiveness to the student of human social development was suggested by the French ethnologist Claude Lévi-Strauss in 1960 when he remarked wistfully on the meaning of the death of Alfred Kroeber to the science of anthropology and to him personally: "He is the last of the North American ethnologists to have known the Indians"—Ishi, that is. "No untamed Red Skins—certainly they are no longer—rather those who had been so in their youth. . . . With Kroeber it is truly the America before Christopher Columbus which has died completely."[30] Implicit in Lévi-Strauss's reflection is justification for the fervor with which the first generation of professional anthroplogists pursued their investigations of the Indian cultures. "Now or never is the time in which to collect from the natives what is still available for study," one of Boas's protégés insisted in 1911. "What is lost now will never be recovered again."[31]

Under the auspices of the Museum of Natural History, anthropologists fanned out over the northern plains in the early years of the twentieth century. Their task was basic: not in-depth study of a single tribe, but the accumulation of as large a body of ethnographic data on as many Indian cultures as possible in the shortest span of time. On the plains, many of the first professionally trained anthropologists gained their field experience. Franz Boas until 1905 and Clark Wissler thereafter directed the salvage operation. Both had earned their own credentials in the field and under duress. Boas back in the 1880s had chafed under the restrictions imposed on his

West Coast ethnological survey by the British Association for the Advancement of Science, which stipulated that he devote himself to a "general 'synopsis'" of the whole province rather than concentrate on "local details" as he preferred to do.[32] Wissler, in turn, had gone to the homes of the Blackfoot, the Dakota Sioux, and others—a total of ten reservations—between "the dawn of the present century" and 1905.[33] Kroeber went to the Arapaho, the Gros Ventre, and, briefly, the Ute, the Shoshone, and the Bannock; Paul Radin to the Winnebago; and Robert H. Lowie to the Northern Shoshone, the Blackfoot, the Chippewa, the Assiniboine, the Hidatsa, and the Crow. In his memoirs Lowie vividly recalled the sense of extreme urgency that had him hopping from tribe to tribe between 1906 and 1908, unable to gain mastery over the data of any one group or enjoy the luxury of "intensive linguistic study."[34]

The need to record as much information as possible before the native cultures vanished took precedence over everything else. While Americans were reading *The Virginian* and admiring the paintings of Frederic Remington and Charles M. Russell, while Buffalo Bill's Wild West show was still touring the country in a losing battle for popularity against the moving pictures that were already bringing the old West to the screen for countless thousands, while the national park movement and the conservationist ethic flourished under a President who loved to recall his personal experiences out in Dakota, American anthropologists were earning their professional credentials on western reservations among cultures they perceived as on the verge of extinction.

The devoted accumulation of ethnographic data—Boasian historical particularism or phenomenalism—has seemed to some modern critics to border on anthropological antiquarianism. Exhibiting that "cold enthusiasm for truth" that he so admired,[35] Boas between 1886 and 1900 had made eight field trips to the Northwest coast, compiling a vast fund of information on tribal life, particularly mythology, language, and art, with a concentration on the Kwakiutl. He published an estimated 10,000 pages of ethnographic materials in which he let the facts speak for themselves; no artificial order could be imposed on them without doing damage to the delicate tissue of a human culture whose diversity mirrored that of nature, and whose ultimate "meaning" resided in that very diversity. The data were culturally conditioned, of course, but nonetheless "true." The only question of accuracy that might legitimately be raised was whether they faithfully reflected the perceptions of an individual informant. Put differently, a culture is what it is perceived to be by those who are part of it. Working from this premise in his own studies, Boas had encouraged an open-ended ethnographic investigation among the native cultures that would be terminated only with their demise.[36]

The harshest judgments today on Boas's contribution to anthropology turn on the charge that the necessary corrective to freewheeling evolutionary theorization became in time a retarding factor. Boas was a born critic—"one whose works rest essentially in an unfeeling criticism of his own work and that of others," he conceded with a measure of scientific pride.[37] But salutary caution eventually became a picky and counterproductive negativism, the argument goes, while the insistence on a rigorous standard of evidence became a radical empiricism aggressively hostile to science's ultimate aim, the statement of general principles. "From the very earliest period," Marvin Harris has written, "the Boasian program suffered the embarrassment of a virtue which was at the same time its chief vice. It was inductive to the point of self-destruction."[38] But, as Harris goes on to say, this failure arose from the circumstances. The Indian cultures were disappearing; precious data were vanishing daily; field work consequently was the first order of business. General laws could be formulated later, when all the evidence was in and there was ample time to pore over it.

Even for Boas, the data ultimately were the means to an end, the scientific solution of theoretical problems. "Forcing phenomena into the strait-jacket of a theory is opposed to the inductive process by which the actual relations of definite phenomena may be derived," he had argued in 1896, but he believed that "certain laws exist which govern the growth of human culture, and it is our endeavor to discover these laws." However, the crucial thing was to recognize that "the solid work is still all before us."[39] Ethnography was the anthropological equivalent of wilderness preservation. It drew upon the belief in the Vanishing American and substantially reinforced it.

JAMES MOONEY ON INDIAN NUMBERS

Most anthropologists did not mean to endorse the impression that the Indian was, strictly speaking, vanishing. Their concern was with "pure" primitive cultures, which were relatively perishable and seemed to have no chance of survival. But the problem of Indian numbers—the traditional basis for the theory of the Vanishing American—was another matter. Ever since Selden Clark and Garrick Mallery challenged the accepted aboriginal population estimates in the 1870s and pronounced them wildly inflated, authorities had maintained that Indian decline was more apparent than real. In the first number of the *American Anthropologist* for 1905, in an article titled "Popular Fallacies Respecting the Indians," Henry W. Henshaw of the Bureau of American Ethnology echoed Mallery in refuting the old notion that the Indians had experienced a sharp numerical decrease since the advent of the Europeans.[40] When the second volume of the bureau's long-awaited *Handbook of American Indians North of Mexico* appeared in 1910, Henshaw's article was reprinted under the heading "Popular Fallacies" with one major deletion: his discussion of "Indian Population." That topic was covered in a separate entry written by another bureau ethnologist, James Mooney.[41] Like Henshaw, he too would expose fallacies on the subject of Indian numbers—but his particular targets would be Mallery and the revisionists.

Born in 1861, Mooney had been attracted to things Indian from childhood. At the age of twelve he began to compile a list of all the tribes in the Western Hemisphere, organized on geographical principles. Under Powell, one of the Bureau of Ethnology's pet projects would be a definitive synonymy of the North American tribes intended to alleviate the confusion caused by variant designations. Classification would be along linguistic lines, all tribes being grouped into stocks or families. This work, Powell believed, "to a great extent underlies and is the foundation for every field of ethnologic investigation among Indians."[42] The synonymy was considered of such importance that, beginning in 1885 under Henshaw's direction, it became the bureau's first priority, taking precedence over the individual research of the staff members. That same year, Powell, who was impressed with the work Mooney had already accomplished toward a comprehensive tribal listing, brought him into the bureau to assist Garrick Mallery with the synonymy for the Iroquoian and Algonquian families.

The synonymy languished. Henshaw's time was increasingly taken up with administrative duties, while Mallery turned his full attention back to Indian sign language and pictographic writing. Mooney, who had an abiding interest in the eastern remnants of once powerful tribes, concentrated on the North Carolina Cherokees and their medicinal lore. By the spring of 1889 he was sending out circulars requesting information on place names, antiquities, and survivors for a proposed monograph on the Indians of the Middle Atlantic slope, and the next year was engaged in preliminary research for an aboriginal map of old Cherokee country. His work was interrupted late in 1890 when he was sent to Indian Territory at his own request to investigate the ghost-dance phenomenon among the Southern Cheyenne, Arapaho, Kiowa, Comanche, Apache, Caddo, and Wichita. Subsequently, he enlarged his study to include the Sioux, Northern Cheyenne, Northern Arapaho, Shoshone, and Paiute, among whom the movement originated. With the completion of his field work near the end of 1893— and the publication of his monograph on the ghost dance three years later—Mooney became the bureau's resident expert on the plains tribes and a specialist on the Kiowa, though he never lost his interest in the Eastern Cherokees, and this interest may have drawn him into a consideration of the thorny question of aboriginal numbers.[43]

At the annual meeting of the American Anthropological Association in December 1906, Mooney read a paper on "The Decrease of the Indian Population."[44] The bureau's report for 1907–1908 indicates that Mooney had begun an intensive investigation of Indian numbers, and it would remain his principal concern until 1914. He hoped to prepare a book-length monograph on aboriginal population to be included in the bureau's bulletin series, as the definitive word on the subject. Mooney's methodology was straightforward. He divided the map of North America into fifteen zones, then twenty-five, and, working from east to west, tried to trace "the wasting fortunes of each tribe and tribal remnant under change of name and habitat, further subdivision, or new combination, to the end."[45] His ambitious project was to embrace all related matters, including the causes of Indian decline—for it was his conviction that there had indeed been a decline of from two-thirds to three-quarters of the total native population present at the time of discovery.

Though Mooney's work was endorsed by successive bureau chiefs as an "important foundation study of American ethnology,"[46] and though its early appearance was forecast annually, in the end it yielded little. The one exception was Mooney's brief article on Indian population in the *Handbook of American Indians North of Mexico* (whose publication, incidentally, represented the realization of Powell's goal a quarter of a century after he committed the bureau to the preparation of a synonymy of Indian tribes).

Formerly, the bureau had championed the position taken by Mallery on aboriginal population. Henshaw and Powell himself assumed that the Indians of North America never numbered more than about 500,000, and this had become the bureau's official line. But Mooney advanced a contrary view, and since it found its way into the *Handbook*, intended by the bureau to be the authoritative compendium on the Indians north of Mexico, it meant that the bureau had changed its stance. Mooney dismissed as "untenable" the contention that Indian numbers had been more or les stable throughout history, given "the patent fact that the aboriginal population of whole regions has completely disappeared." Some well-meaning individuals had even been fooled into assuming an *increase* in Indian population by including in their estimates mixed bloods, who for all practical purposes were white. Once mixed bloods were excluded, the "Indian of the discovery period," the true full blood, was seen to have suffered a drastic numerical decrease. In explanation, Mooney adduced the usual list of causes—

disease, liquor, wars—and added one of his own: "low vitality due to mental depression under misfortune." Following Clark and Mallery's lead, authorities had slashed the traditional estimate of the North American aboriginal population by half, to the 500,000 figure. Mooney simply restored the older total by suggesting a native population in pre-Columbian times of "nearly 1,150,000 Indians, which is believed to be within 10 per cent of the actual number."[47]

In the same year that the second volume of the *Handbook* appeared, 1910, Mooney presented a case study at a meeting of the Mississippi Valley Historical Association. It bore the telltale title "The Passing of the Delaware Nation." This time Mooney pulled no punches. Mallery, he charged, was directly responsible for popularizing the fallacy of the non-vanishing Indian. "In spite of the looseness of argument plainly evident on examination" of Mallery's paper, and the fact that "scores of tribes have disappeared without a survivor within the historic period," Mooney wrote, "the doctrine has found acceptance with philanthropists, missionaries, and officials who, being unacquainted with the Indian past, are loathe to believe that the efforts of so many years have produced so little result in the preservation of the race." After citing his own in-progress study, which would conclusively document the fact *and* extent of Indian atrophy, Mooney echoed the conclusion reached in his *Handbook* entry, and "believed to be within ten per cent of correctness," that a "decrease of approximately two-thirds" of the original North American Indian population had occurred since 1492. The Delawares, whose very name conjured up Cooper's *The Last of the Mohicans* and all the sunset imagery of the Vanishing American tradition, served Mooney as "a typical illustration of the shifting fortunes and steady decline of our native tribes."[48]

As late as 1915 Mooney was still addressing learned societies on "The Passing of the Indian," and advising his audiences to read his work on "the past and present Indian population" for corroboration.[49] But by then, having plugged away at his population study for seven years, he was losing his enthusiasm, and evidently abandoned it entirely around this time to return to his earlier, more manageable concern with Cherokee sacred formulas. Perhaps Mooney realized that his investigation of aboriginal numbers was only leading him into an endless labyrinth of contradiction and imprecision.

When Mooney died in 1921, the *Handbook* entry on Indian population and a few scattered papers were all that marked his years of labor. A long essay, *The Aboriginal Population of America North of Mexico*, was published posthumously, in 1928, but itself stands as a testament to frustration. In the Preface, John R. Swanton noted that after Mooney completed his examination of New England and the Mid-Atlantic states he "seems to have been interrupted and all that remains of the other sections of the more comprehensive undertaking is contained in loose notes, with which practically nothing can be done." The fact that the "Summary of Results" at the end of the paper placed the aboriginal population of North America at 1,152,950 would indicate that Mooney prepared it as early as 1908 for the bureau's *Handbook* and, despite his subsequent researches, had never got around to revising it. "In justice to the author," Swanton cautioned, "it must be remembered that . . . [this paper] represents the advance results of a more extensive but never completed enterprise."[50] An obituary in a professional journal paid fitting tribute to Mooney: "When he once reached a conclusion he maintained it with unfaltering courage and clung to it with a tenacity which not infrequently seemed to his friends to be carried to extremes, but of the honesty of his intentions there could be no doubt."[51]

The significance of Mooney's work is difficult to judge. Like most of his contemporaries, he had no patience with nice distinctions between absorption and extinction. The Natchez, he wrote, were "not exterminated, but rather extirpated, which after all is but another word for the same process."[52] The Delawares and the Powhatan Confederacy were the types of their race in his mind, and his population study fizzled out about where his personal interest did, leaving an account of the New England and Mid-Atlantic-slope tribes that corroborated the most pessimistic conclusions about Indian decline. Mooney's one deviation from his eastern preoccupation, his investigation of the ghost-dance movement among the western tribes with its inherent pathos, could only have confirmed him in his conviction that the Indian was truly a vanishing race.

Because the *Handbook* was long the standard source on the North American Indians, Mooney's views influenced anthropologists and historians alike. As eminent an expert as Kroeber used Mooney's estimates, though he scaled the 1,150,000 figure down to 900,000.[53] Today, when estimates as high as 10 million are bandied about in discussions of the aboriginal population north of Mexico, it would seem that Mooney's error was in not going far enough in the right direction. The key point for our purposes is that his heresy became orthodoxy, and the Vanishing American, in its most literal sense, an accepted historical fact.

As Parkman had reminded his countrymen in the 1850s, destruction was the price of civilized progress. Through the nineteenth century Americans had been willing to pay it, chewing up an enormous chunk of the continent in fewer than a hundred years and threatening to devour the rest, leaving nothing for posterity. Conservation was in the nature of a public accounting. Wise use of resources could ensure a perpetual supply of timber and the like, but it could not preserve the wilderness for those who regarded nature as a reflector of the divine mind and a precious repository of aesthetic values. Either wilderness areas were set aside and protected or else future generations would never know the wonder of a mighty land before it was tamed. There was no compromising on the issue.

The Indians' way of life was doomed by the same forces that had destroyed the wilderness in such short order. Their cultures, cut off from the conditions that had nurtured them, could not survive into the twentieth century. Indians would change to accommodate themselves to American civilization, and in changing, disappear. The anthropological conservationists accepted what they considered inevitable and conducted a cultural salvage operation intended not to salvage cultures but a paper record of them. *The Craftsman* in 1906 placed their activities in context:

We are just waking up here in America to appreciating the big interests of our own country and to a sense of cherishing our original greatness. We are painting our plains, protecting our forests, creating game preserves, and at last—not saving the existence of the North

American Indian, the most picturesque roving people on earth, but making and preserving records of them from an historical, scientific and artistic point of view.[54]

Not only were the Indian cultures vanishing; in the same period informed opinion held that the race also was fading away through amalgamation with the whites.

CHAPTER FIFTEEN

THERE WILL BE NO "LATER" FOR THE INDIAN:

Amalgamation and the Vanishing Race

Writing in 1823, Edward Everett methodically analyzed the logic behind a policy of Indian assimilation. We lament that they have vanished, he noted, and "we would take measures to preserve the present stock. But what is it we would preserve?" Not their languages, apparently, since the friends of the Indian were eager to replace these with English. "Is it their mode of life, tenure of property in common, their manners—that which makes them in all externals to be what they are:—is it these, which we deplore as lost, and would fix and perpetuate where they still exist?" The answer, of course, was no. Those who championed the Indians would gather them into "convenient settlements, wean them from the chace, teach them individually to hold a farm in fee, and plough and dig it." Nor did the civilized man admire the native religions and traditions. "Is there anything left then that we wish in fact to preserve?" Everett demanded. "Nothing, in the last analysis, but the copper color; and why a civilized, christianized person, speaking our language, subsisting by regular labor, is any the better for being copper colored, we cannot see." Indeed, those who like Thomas Jefferson advocated racial amalgamation would eliminate even the distinction of color. "All this may be well," Everett continued,

but what becomes meantime of the Indians? The very efficacy of this course is to hasten their disappearance. This the shrewder natives

243

themselves understand. They know that their identity consists in their manners, languages, mode of life, and religion. They know that to change these, to make them speak English, live on farms, and practice the civilized arts would be most directly to annihilate them as Indians![1]

Assimilation would effect the same end as extermination and more insidiously and more surely because it would annihilate without raising a sword or a murmur of protest. The allotment of land was, Theodore Roosevelt declared, "a mighty pulverizing engine to break up the tribal mass,"[2] and some of its proponents contemplated a second stage in which the individualized Indian would be racially absorbed as well. Fittingly, a focal point in the assimilationist campaign became the last stronghold of red power in North America: Indian Territory.

THE END OF INDIAN TERRITORY

Under their own governments out West following removal in the 1830s, the Five Civilized Tribes had opposed every attempt to extend allotment in severalty to their domain, and in 1887 appeared to win a substantial victory when they were exempted from the Dawes Act's provisions. But their special prerogatives had been steadily eroding since the Civil War, when the "treason" of some tribesmen in allying with the Confederacy and fighting for another lost cause left all of the Five Nations vulnerable to the charge that they had forfeited their treaty rights.[3] Pressures mounted to open Indian Territory to white settlement as railroad schemers, farmers, disappointed claimants to tribal membership, and ambitious politicians advanced their separate causes. They converged on one demand: allotment in severalty leading to complete assimilation.

C. J. Hillyer, attorney for the Atlantic and Pacific Railroad, presented his company's case for a right of way through three hundred miles of Indian Territory by trotting out the arguments that had justified removal and isolation nearly half a century before. As always, the best interests of red and white were deemed identical, though the means recommended to attain them were the opposite of those employed in the 1830s. Hillyer began his argument for the right of way by asserting a crisis in the affairs of the Five Nations that required drastic remedy. White civilization was pushing against the borders of Indian Territory on three sides, Hillyer insisted, and it could not be indefinitely stayed. While some of the Indian citizens were reasonably advanced, many of the 66,000 who inhabited the territory were "blanket Indians." Their numbers were declining at a rate of "not less than two percent" annually. Characteristically indolent, few "long hairs" farmed, and the proportion of lands in the territory "actually utilized" for agriculture was "exceedingly small." Thus the Indians could be charged with gross misuse of the soil, as well as a failure to become actively engaged in business and commerce.

Even the much-touted systems of tribal government were of "an inferior quality," Hillyer argued. All told, Indian Territory was an impediment to regional and national progress, and the issue now boiled down to a question—as it always had where Indian rights were concerned—of whose claims would be judged superior. Should some seventy thousand square miles of "fertile country, in the center of the republic"—an area greater than that of the six New England states combined, nearly twice as large as the state of Ohio—be left in the hands of a "semi-civilized, non-producing, and indolent" people so demonstrably unfit to develop it? The answer was self-evident, but Hillyer was not about to leave anything to chance. "The law of settlement and development has been uniform," he asserted. "The restless advance of an industrial civilization," on reaching the boundaries of any given Indian country, "has recognized in them an obstacle to its progress, and in obedience to a law which knows no exception, has removed them from its path." Allotment would now do the work of removal. Indian Territory had been created in obedience to the theory that civilization destroys; it was to be extinguished in obedience to the theory that "civilization comes from *contact*, and not from isolation."[4]

Railroad schemes constituted one kind of pressure on the integrity of Indian Territory. There were many others. The old dream of an all-Indian state had gradually faded and by 1878 was moribund—unmourned for the most part by the Five Civilized Tribes, who preferred their own forms of nationhood. But the persistent demand that Indian Territory be formally organized as a conventional territory and legally opened to white settlement grew shriller. By the 1890s, in a period of national depression, farmers were anxiously looking around for new land and new opportunities, and many cast a covetous eye on "this fair Indian Eden."[5] White interlopers outnumbered the Indian citizens by at least four to one, and friction between the races was growing. "The remedy for this threatening aspect of affairs is plainly the substitution of a territorial government by all inhabitants for the present tribal governments of the Indian minority," a federal official concluded in 1896.[6]

As in the 1830s, internal dissension wracked the Five Nations, undercutting their ability to mount a unified resistance against outside pressures. Disgruntled claimants to tribal membership worked against the existing governments. W. J. Watts, president of the Cherokee Indian Citizenship Association, supported allotment as the best means of ridding Indian Territory of its "wide-spread monopolisitic evil" whereby political power and property accrued to the few, and of its "fossilized missionaries" out to protect their vested interests. The existing situation, Watts wrote, retarded progress and delayed the day when the American Indian would become an Indian American. "Hurrah for Statehood!" one of Watts's adherents whooped as he broke into verse:

> Hurrah for allotment!—Statehood!
>   For Progress and Enterprise,
> Advancement and manufacturies,
>   Progress, and growth, likewise.
> Then will this country prosper,
>   Develop, and be great!
> The favored few will "take a walk"
>   When the Territory becomes a State.[7]

In 1889 homesteaders occupied an area on the western border of Indian Territory known as the Oklahoma District. The next year it was formally organized as Oklahoma Territory, and an invitation issued to the Five Civilized Tribes to amalgamate. Subsequent rushes, notably into the Cherokee Outlet in 1893, further reduced the Indian domain. Beginning in 1898, after five years of intensive negotiations between tribal leaders and a commission headed by Senator Dawes, the provisions of the General Allotment Act were gradually extended over Indian Territory. The Curtis Act, passed that year, gave broad powers to the Dawes Commission to wrap up its business by completing the rolls of citizens of the Five Nations for the purpose of allotting their lands in severalty and terminating their governmental autonomy, irrespective of their wishes on the matter. The job was scheduled to be completed in 1906 and the tribal governments dissolved on March 4, though in fact they functioned until statehood the next year. Then Indian Territory, the "shrunken residue" of the millions of acres that once constituted Indian country, was wiped from the map.[8] The last of the autonomous Indian nations with which the United States government had negotiated solemn treaties were no more.

The symbolic importance of these events was not lost on the general public. In 1903 Thomas F. Millard wrote that "the American Indian now finds himself face to face with the always inevitable, but long deferred, absorption by the white race. The hour of his elimination is at hand." The Five Civilized Tribes, the "tangible remnant of the aborigines of North America," were becoming "plain, every-day" citizens, and it was "practically certain" that another year would see the Indian's "final disappearance from among the nations of the world, his identity forever lost under the broad mantle of United States citizenship."[9] Three years later a fellow journalist pronounced Millard's prediction accurate, for the dissolution of the political organization of the Cherokees, Choctaws, Creeks, Chickasaws, and Seminoles marked "the final chapter in the Indian's annals as a distinct race."[10]

THE CASE FOR INDIAN AMALGAMATION

During the land scrambles that accompanied the opening of Indian Territory, discussion frequently turned to the large numbers of white men who had taken Indian wives and thus qualified for a share in tribal holdings. *The Taylor-Trotwood*

Magazine, published in Tennessee and editorially devoted to the segregation of black and white, carried a glowing article about Oklahoma, "The Newest American State," that concluded on a curious, teasing note:

You look for the Indian in the Indian Territory. . . . Instead of a squaw as pictured in the books your Minnehaha is a human butterfly, with eyes like jet and hair the hue of the raven; she sings like the oriole of her native woods. She is a thing of beauty and a joy for ever, and she and each of her sisters has a great big farm.[11]

Several years before, another writer had flatly asserted that "the harmonious blending of the two races" was "the great solution of the Indian question as regards the five civilized tribes,"[12] and by the turn of the century this opinion, applied to the Indian problem generally, was widely accepted.

Though assimilation did not necessarily imply anything more than one popular definition of the American melting pot as a mold in which foreign (that is, other than white Anglo-Saxon Protestant) elements were to be recast into proper American form, Indian assimilation traditionally implied more than acculturation. The native population was small—just an infinitesimal fraction of the whole American population—and while a massive infusion of Indian blood might pollute the national type, the limited amount available could do no harm and might even do some good. Anyway, the process of red-white amalgamation was irreversible. "When three more generations have passed, it may not be possible to find a drop of pure Indian or negro blood on this continent," John Wesley Powell prophesied in 1885. "Civilization overwhelms Savagery, not so much by spilling blood as by mixing blood, but whether spilled or mixed, a greater homogeneity is secured."[13] The wisdom of the ethnologist was corroborated three years later by scientific evidence when a medical doctor reported the results of a breathing test designed to distinguish full-blood Indians from mixed bloods. His premise was that aboriginal and civilized man breathe differently, the one in the abdomen, the other in the chest. Since only thirty-three of the eighty-two Indian girls tested conformed to the aboriginal model, obviously "a rapid amalgamation" was taking place, and it was "quite evident that the day will not be far distant when the remnant of the once proud American Indian will be incorporated into the white race."[14] Moreover, anthropometric measurements indicated that the product of intermixture was a type more fertile than and physically superior to either parent stock.[15]

In the government's painstaking compilation from the thirteenth census, *Indian Population in the United States and Alaska, 1910*, tables, graphs, and maps bolstered a conclusion that the text made explicit:

The results of the studies on sterility, on fecundity, and on vitality all point toward one conclusion, and that is that the increase of the mixed-blood Indians is much greater than that of the full-blood Indians, and that unless the tendencies now at work undergo a decided change the full-bloods are destined to form a decreasing proportion of the total Indian population and ultimately to disappear altogether.

While 56.5 percent of the Indians enumerated were full bloods, 35.2 percent of those reported were mixed bloods. Of the mixed-blood population, 20.6 percent were less than half white, 27.7 percent were exactly half and half, and 49.9 percent were more than half white, indicating an unmistakable trend among mixed bloods toward ever greater whiteness. Further evidence for this trend appeared in a table illustrating fecundity among Indian women of childbearing age married for at least one year. An average of 8.6 percent of those falling into this category had produced no children; but the sterility rate of marriages between full bloods (10.7 percent) was markedly higher than that between Indian and white partners (6.7 percent). "Thus sterility is considerably less common in cases of miscegenation than in cases of marriage between full-bloods. Furthermore, the proportion of issueless marriages decreases directly as the amount of white blood in the married couple increases."[16] In short, the 1910 census provided a formidable battery of evidence to support the contention that the Indian was being absorbed.

Francis E. Leupp, who as Commissioner of Indian Affairs under Theodore Roosevelt had the honor of presiding over one stage of this vast amalgamation, allowed that "for persons very sensitively organized, so close a union as marriage with those of widely different ancestry, associations and mental habits is always a hazardous experiment." But Leupp allayed fears by projecting as the offspring of the red-white union a veritable superman:

With his Indian blood he inherits keenness of observation, stoicism under suffering, love of freedom, a contempt for the petty things which lay so heavy a burden on our convention-bound civilization; with his white blood the competitive instinct, individual initiative, resourcefulness in the face of novel obstacles, and a constitution hardened to the drafts made upon its strength by the artificialities of modern life.[17]

The marriage of red and white was apparently one of those rare matches made in heaven; even Roosevelt is said to have regretted that he did not have "a strain of Indian blood" in his veins.[18]

AMALGAMATION IN CONTEXT: SEGREGATION, IMPERIALISM, AND IMMIGRATION RESTRICTION

To understand how great this deviation was from accepted racial practices, and how suggestively it speaks of the Indian's unique position in American thought, one need only remember that red-white amalgamation was being proposed in a context of racial segregation in the South, imperialism abroad, and nativism at home, all entailing deep distrust, fear, suspicion, and loathing of darker, "inferior" peoples.

In 1910, at a time when Commissioner Leupp was giving his blessing to red-white intermarriage, commingling between white and black was taboo in the United States. Rarely mentioned apart from lurid images of rape and debasement, it was seen as contrary to an "instinct" in the white race and damned as "mongrelization" when it did occur. Few contemporary issues aroused more emotion, and one writer captured popular feelings on the subject when he observed:

Tell the average American that he is descended from Pocahontas, that his blood may be traced to Confucius, or that his daughter has secretly married one of Madame Blavatsky's mythical Indian Mahatmas, and the chances are that he will be flattered and gratified. You stumble over no "ethical principle"; you encounter no fatal racial prejudice. Tell him that his great-great-grandfather was probably a powerful potentate from the Congo or the Niger, and you touch the acme of insult. It would be safer to accuse him of highway robbery.[19]

Segregation in the South rested on the assumption of permanent black inferiority. Thus any blurring of racial lines endangered the structure of society. Every demand for black political and civil rights translated into a threat to white womanhood that had to be savagely suppressed lest the southern social order be brought down in ruins. Poor whites, beset with economic anxieties and most vulnerable to racist fearmongers, were constantly reminded that it was their daughters the black man would want to marry unless discouraged by the law and other, extralegal measures.

Lynching—"the color line in crimson," according to a southern lawyer[20]—provided a means of maintaining white supremacy in the name of racial purity. A survey published in 1919 by the National Association for the Advancement of Colored People came up with the staggering total of 2,522 blacks lynched between 1889 and 1918, most of them in the South.[21] In the face of federal indifference and a judiciary disinclined to uphold the spirit of the Fourteenth and Fifteenth Amendments, the Negro found the pathway to political, social, and economic opportunity blocked by segregationist legislation. A resurgent back-to-Africa movement was one symptom of a despair not matched since the bleak days of the mid-1850s.

White disparagement of blacks went so far as to proclaim them a doomed race. They had been steadily degenerating since emancipation, just as pro-slavery apologists had predicted, and their end was now fast approaching. The theory of the "vanishing Negro" had gained prominence in the early years of Reconstruction when southern journalists warned that radicals and carpetbaggers were endangering the black man's continued existence by elevating him to an unnatural position of equality that might precipitate a race war and would certainly work to his detriment. The census of 1870 did reveal a dramatic slowdown in the normal rate of black increase, and despite the statistics ten years later indicating a leap in black numbers, vestiges of the theory of Negro degeneracy survived well into the twentieth century.

In 1900, for example, John Roach Straton of Mercer University in Macon, Georgia, on the basis of actuarial data collected a few years before, maintained that the black population was declining throughout the South. Straton argued that history supports "the principle that a weak race, which is unassimilable in its nature, when brought suddenly into contact with the higher civilization of a strong race, unconsciously destroys itself." A rising crime rate, a more pronounced susceptibility to disease, a shorter life span—these traced the Negro's downward path to extinction. What had been true for the Cherokee seventy years before was true for the black man in 1900:

> If the present relationship between the whites and blacks points to the permanent degeneracy and ultimate racial death of the negroes, it will become our duty to save this simpleminded and in many respects worthy people, who are not here through any choice of their own. . . . If racial contact is seen to prove disastrous to the weaker, then segregation must be enforced. . . . No plan for picking up the negro race *en masse* and moving them from the country, or to some isolated portion of it, is practicable. But by establishing conditions elsewhere which would invite the negro there, and then assisting him to go, the problem might be solved.[22]

While the only acceptable long-range solution for blacks was permanent isolation, segregation would do for the time being. It would prevent close contact between the races and afford the Negro a respite from the crushing pressures of direct competition. Segregated, he would have the opportunity to advance at his own pace within his limited capabilities. But after all—and here the Vanishing American of an earlier day stirred back to life—it was unlikely that the black man could ever improve sufficiently to survive. Several prominent supporters of removal in the 1830s had harbored doubts that the policy they advocated would be enough to save the Indians. Since then, however, evolutionary theory had intervened, and for all its racist bias it did assume a progressive principle. No race as such could be doomed. Yet some racial theorists insisted that the Negro was the exception. Over an enormous span of time he had evolved into a "permanent variety" or even an "incipient species," and no longer shared in normal human potential.[23]

Despite the convenience of the argument that the black man was an "outcast from evolution," the Vanishing Negro did not convince most racial conservatives, let alone racial moderates. For one thing, blacks had earned grudging respect for their military service in the Civil War, and since then, had demonstrated fighting abilities that discredited the image of servility. For another, the fact of a large and growing Negro population was too obvious to be ignored. It remained a popular axiom that the Negro was a pliable or "plastic" race, in contrast to the "petrified" or granite Indian. The black could improve, albeit slowly, because of his imitative nature and his willingness to learn from the white. The Indian, for all of his storied virtues, disdained to work—"if you make him work he dies"—and as a consequence, incapable of progress, was fated to disappear.[24] One ex-slave, falling into the same trap as Henry Highland Garnet and Frederick Douglass half a century before, rebutted John Straton's case for the Vanishing Negro on all too familiar grounds:

. . . comparison between the negro and the Indian is odious. The two are as dissimilar in character as races can well be. The Indian has almost absolutely refused the white man's civilization. He has fought for his inalienable rights always, and preferred extinction rather than accept the white man's religion; and though fed from the public crib and housed and educated by the government, he has not kept pace with the progress of the negro. The conditions of the two races are in no way analogous.[25]

The last sentence agreed with conventional wisdom, and given the dominant white stereotypes of red and black, the Negro rather than the Indian *was* the logical candidate for full inclusion in American life. But emotion outbalances logic in the realm of racial thought, and it was the Indian who was invited to join in the affairs of the nation, even to intermarry with the white race, while the black was consistently shunned.

The controversy engendered by American imperialism in the 1890s provided a second forum for the airing of racial views that would make the acceptance granted red-white amalgamation all the more remarkable. Anti-imperialists included in their ranks several southerners who were not about to acquiesce quietly in the annexation of the Philippines with its nonwhite population. Just as racism played a role in checking the "all Mexico" enthusiasm of the 1840s and in the opposition to slavery expansion, so it united with humanitarianism and democratic precepts in the 1890s to resist American expansion abroad. Imperialists countered with a humanitarian rationale of their own. Everyone knew that the rapid spread of civilization was imperiling primitive peoples around the globe, so it had become the "white man's burden" to raise the darker races through a gradual exposure to civilized practices before it was too late. In the evolutionist's defense of imperialistic morality, then, the stark law of the survival of the fittest had been supplanted by a life-giving mission on the part of the strong toward the weak, the white toward the colored. If anti-imperialism was high principle tainted with racial prejudice, imperialism was power made respectable by racial benevolence.

Majority opinion in 1899 held that God had made manifest His will and none could resist it. Anyway, there was precedent for colonial rule in the United States' long relationship with the Indians.[26] A few skeptics fretted over the practical problem of administering another nonwhite race. What in the nation's history of dealings with the red and the black gave hope of success where the yellow race was concerned? But here too the imperialists had an answer. "Because we have failed to keep alive and uplift a race of untamable savages," one minister reasoned, "it does by no means follow that we should be powerless to uplift another race of inferior folk who possess a more plastic character and a more enduring vitality."[27] Another imperialist took a different tack, suggesting that red and black men should be offered the chance to advance themselves by serving as a military force in the Philippines. Negro troops would be ideal since "they are perfectly at home under the scorching suns and in the torrential rains of the tropics," while, like the British, "we have our own Sikhs and Goorkhas in our Sioux and Apaches; an aboriginal military caste." Perhaps after the fighting was over, some of these troops might even be induced to stay permanently in the Philippines.[28]

As for the Filipinos, their destiny within the American union was murky. That they were of an inferior race was generally acknowledged. But what precisely was the white American's mission to them? How were they to be artificially elevated, given the inflexible laws of evolutionary development? The question was an old one; only the people involved were new. An army doctor writing in a professional journal in 1905, Major Charles E. Woodruff, despaired of extending American institutions directly to the Malays because they were "children scientifically," in a condition of "arrested brain evolution." The enlargement in cerebral capacity necessary to bring them up to a civilized level would take thousands of years. Until then, "Malays will still be Malays, and white men will still be white men." The only qualifications Woodruff would admit related to racial intermixture. "The half-breeds, quarter-breeds, etc., may be of any grade of intelligence, according to that of their white parents."[29] Miscegenation apparently was the sole means of bursting free from evolutionary thralldom.

Imperialism created a racial climate seemingly unpropitious for any policy of immediate Indian assimilation; but there was more. By the 1890s American Anglo-Saxonism was in full-throated cry against the contamination of Aryan purity, cultural and racial. New immigrants—southern European, neither Protestant nor English-speaking, uneducated in the ways of American democracy—were crowding into the port cities and threatening Anglo-Saxon predominance in the United States. Instead of being transformed by America, they were transforming America. In the vanguard of the doom-mongers—Boston-centered and patrician for the most part—was Francis A. Walker, still poring over census figures and reading in them dire lessons for his countrymen. After studying the 1890 returns, which showed that 5,250,000 immigrants had arrived in the previous decade, he was forced to conclude that the law of survival of the fittest had played an unexpected trick on Americans. Instead of surviving the influx of immigrants by meeting them head-on, Anglo-Americans had adopted a defensive posture. Faced with wage-cutting because of the growing pool of unskilled immigrant labor, they had chosen to maintain their standard of living by voluntarily reducing family size. In that direction, Walker warned, lay racial suicide, for the immigrants, instead of augmenting the existing American population, were actually supplanting it.[30]

New England, once a hotbed for humanitarian causes like

abolitionism and Indian policy reform, now led the way in demanding limits on immigration. The Immigration Restriction League was founded in Boston in 1894, and a Harvard professor, Robert DeC. Ward, was foremost among those urging the passage of immigration laws that would be based on "a proper eugenic selection of the incoming alien millions."[31] Madison Grant, a New Yorker who took his first degree at Yale, in 1916 published a glum biological-historical treatise with the memorable title *The Passing of the Great Race*, which lamented the almost irreversible deterioration of the Nordic type worldwide. Four years later, Lothrop Stoddard, a Harvard Ph.D., extended the discussion into the realm of post–World War I geopolitics in the first of his several popular volumes, *The Rising Tide of Color Against White World-Supremacy*. It carried an introduction by Madison Grant that expressed the racial outlook of the restrictionists in a few sentences:

Democratic ideals among an homogeneous population of Nordic blood, as in England or America, is one thing, but it is quite another for the white man to share his blood with, or intrust his ideals to, brown, yellow, black, or red men.

This is suicide pure and simple, and the first victim of this amazing folly will be the white man himself.[32]

The perspective of the Wards, Grants, and Stoddards was that of an embattled soldier, surrounded on all sides but still stoutly resisting the foe. The question was how much longer he could hold out, and the answer would be determined by how fast the government acted to provide relief in the form of legislation restricting immigration.

The Ku Klux Klan, moribund since the 1870s, was revived in 1915 and lumped Jews and Catholics with Negroes among its primary targets, winning a ready response not only in the South but in the Midwest and Pacific Northwest as well. The 1920s witnessed a retreat from global mission, and the resulting isolationism was conducive to nativism. As the nation turned in on itself, it rediscovered the Indian and found him different. He was not an alien, but the First American, and so Francis Leupp could sanguinely predict:

There will be no "later" for the Indian. He is losing his identity hour by hour, competing with whites in the labor market, mingling with white communities and absorbing white pioneers into his own, sending his children to the same schools with white children, intermarrying with whites and rearing an offspring which combines the traits of both lines of ancestry. In the light of this new day which is now so near its noon, he need not be an inspired seer to discern the approaching end of his pure aboriginal type and the upgrowth of another which will claim the name "American" by a double title as solid as the hills on his horizon.[33]

In striking counterpoint to the immigration quotas set in 1924, Congress that same year made all Indians full-fledged citizens. At a time when the embattled Anglo-Saxon could see in other ethnic types only a threat, nativism welcomed the native into the fold.

AMBIVALENCE ABOUT AMALGAMATION: WHITE WOMEN, SQUAWMEN, HALF-BREEDS

It would be misleading to overstate the case for red-white amalgamation. It was never generally condoned. Acceptance was almost always conditional on circumstances and the pairings involved. But even ambivalence set it apart from the issue of black-white intermixing, since it meant that there were positives as well as negatives to be pondered.

On the negative side lay the conviction that all race mixing was contrary to God's intentions, unnatural, and wrong. In His wisdom He created the white, yellow, brown, red, and black, and it was not man's place to blur His colors. From this perspective, red-white unions were to be condemned, and judgment was implicit in three stereotypes: the "squawman," a white man who cohabited with an Indian woman; the "squaw" he lived with; and their offspring, the "half-breed." As for red *men* and white *women*, propriety held that only the lower order of females would voluntarily choose an Indian paramour. Thus when an ultra-respectable woman like Elaine Goodale, the first field superintendent of Indian schools, chose to marry the part-Santee medical doctor Charles A. Eastman in 1891, she had to explain her decision to, as she put it, "make the gift of myself to a Sioux." "It followed almost inevitably upon my passionate preoccupation with the welfare of those whom I already looked upon as my adopted people," she recalled, and she made it "with a thrilling sense of twofold consecration": to be a good wife and mother, and to be of lifelong service to her husband's race.[34] Such service aside, it was assumed that the white woman would ordinarily be the unwilling victim in a union consummated through force—that is, as the captive ravished by her Indian captor, her body defiled, her spirit still pure.

This frontier tradition of "a fate worse than death" was enshrined in the hundreds of captivity narratives that constituted one of America's oldest literary genres. Whenever Indians attacked, the tradition goes, women were grimly admonished to "save the last bullet for yourself." Suicide was preferable to dishonor—a view embedded in postbellum southern fiction whose white heroines were given to jumping off cliffs to end the burning shame of rape by a Negro. Rape, in turn, justified whatever revenge the white man took on the rapist—which meant, by the logic of racism, the entire race of the rapist. Future Mississippi governor James K. Vardaman in 1897 declared that "we would be justified in slaughtering every Ethiop on the earth to preserve unsullied the honor of one Caucasian home."[35] He might have been echoing the sentiments of Ella Wheeler Wilcox, a genteel poet of wide popularity, who wrote of the Indians just the year before:

Their cause was right, their methods all were wrong.
Pity and censure both to them belong.
Their woes were many, but their crimes were more.
The soulless Satan holds not in his store
Such awful tortures as the Indians' wrath
Keeps for the hapless victim in his path.
And if the last lone remnants of that race
Were by the white man swept from off the earth's fair face,

Were every red man slaughtered in a day,
Still would that sacrifice but poorly pay
For one insulted woman captive's woes.[36]

The white obsession with interracial rape was a durable one; it assumed that the darker races spent most of their time lusting after white women—so desirable, yet so unattainable. Racism fed on this kind of sexual ethnocentrism—and sexual insecurity. Since white men felt free to interbreed with the women of other races, interracial rape was their self-exculpatory fantasy.

In the wake of Indian wars like the Minnesota Sioux uprising of 1862, reclaimed women captives told shattering tales of sexual abuse. But on the whole the Indian rapist never made the impact on the white imagination that his black counterpart did. Perhaps the eighteenth-century European theorists who had described the Indian male as a near-hermaphrodite lacking in virility to a degree dangerous to his racial survival contributed to the opinion that, unlike the Negro, he presented no serious sexual threat to white womanhood. In the prudish popular fiction of the nineteenth century, the issue of red-white sex was usually passed by with averted eyes and general agreement that the Indian man, for reasons of innate nobility or whatever, rarely violated white women.[37] Even the captivity narratives were not one-dimensional in their presentation of native character, and long before Benjamin Franklin and the Frenchman Crèvecoeur apotheosized the wood-smoke and buckskin allure of camp life it was something of a truism that whites taken captive by the Indians at a tender age frequently formed a lasting attachment.

The "white Indian" was a figure outside the usual racial categories. In preferring the red man to his own kind—that is, in opting for savagery over civilization—he offered a troubling commentary on the supposed superiority of European culture, and lent dramatic credence to the theory of the Noble Savage or Child of Nature. Returned white captives who had grown accustomed to life in the forest were irresistibly drawn back, taking "the first opportunity of escaping again into the woods, from whence there is no redeeming them" Franklin wrote.[38] This "phenomenon of transculturation," as an anthropologist has called it,[39] represented a male-oriented escapist fantasy, fully elaborated in the romantic tale of Pocahontas's rescue of Captain John Smith. According to Smith's own account, Powhatan's executioners were about to beat out his brains when Pocahontas, "the king's dearest daughter . . . got his head in her arms and laid her own upon his to save him from death."[40] Pocahontas established the convention of the alluring Indian princess,[41] and, through her later marriage to John Rolfe, made red-white amalgamation relatively acceptable.

The Pocahontas-Smith-Rolfe tradition maintained its hold on the colonial imagination, particularly in the South, despite periodic Indian wars. Several prominent southerners in the eighteenth century proclaimed intermarriage the solution to the Indian problem. In 1784 the Virginia legislature debated a bill providing bounties to the white partners in red-white unions and additional awards for each child born to them. As President, Jefferson freely predicted that the copper race would eventually be absorbed into the white one. "You will mix with us by marriage," he told a delegation of Delawares in 1808. "Your blood will run in our veins and will spread with us over this great island."[42] Red-white amalgamation was seen as a marriage of common types because the native's fabled independence and love of freedom were in line with core American values.

The squawman and the half-breed were the pivotal figures in the whitening of the red race. The squawman is a ubiquitous presence in western history. He and his Indian mate had a valuable economic role in the fur trade, securing fur monopolies through family ties.[43] He often filled the important office of interpreter during negotiations. And in the early reservation period he provided a role model for his in-laws. While he was regarded with unmasked contempt by many white Americans who saw him as a lazy, debauched wretch living off his wife's annuity pittance—the very kind of role model the Indian did not need—others perceived him as a necessary catalyst in the assimilation process.[44] With the passage of time, the squaw-man took on a certain romantic aura as the bridge over that "impassable gulf" that Parkman thought must forever separate the races. In an atmosphere heavy with smug ethnocentrism, he offered a refreshing breath of cultural relativism. "The Indians liked to hear of the strange ways of the white people," Thomas Leforge remarked in his rollicking memoirs of life as a "white Crow Indian." "They wondered at these peculiarities, the same as white people wonder at the customs prevailing exclusively among Indians."[45]

When the frontier passed, however, the interracial couple

was left stranded, and a relationship once as natural as it was convenient became for some an acute embarrassment. Granville Stuart, a prominent Montana cattleman, cold-bloodedly assessed his own marital situation in an 1873 letter to his brother James, who had just separated from his Indian wife. Granville had been married to an Indian woman for eleven years and she had borne him seven children, but he had begun casting about for an opportunity "to reconstruct my social basis & close out my present family arrangements":

... I shudder with horror when I contemplate getting old in my present fix, or ever to get poor would be awful, it does very well while one is young, but it dont last, & my repugnance to my present mode of life increases daily—you are now free of all incumberances and for heavens sakes James do keep so, just think of having to go anywhere with such an outfit as mine. on the cars for instance & then to settle in a strange place & live in defiance of public opinion as we have always done. it wont do when one begins to get old & besides I dont want to live always in this cold climate it dont agree with me, & with my present outfit I can never go anywhere else—I remember your saying that you or I could never marry any respectable or high toned or rich woman after our conduct. Now dont entertain any such idea ... outside of this particular vicinity, we could marry almost who we pleased regardless of their station or wealth.

Granville repeated his advice—"Again James I entreat you to keep clear of any entangling 'liason' [*sic*] for you will bitterly regret it if you dont"—and closed his letter with a stunningly inappropriate "All send best love."[46]

Granville Stuart's warning could have served as the text for the many novels, poems, stage plays, and motion pictures about red-white love (or lust) that made their appearance in the first quarter of the present century. They offered the thrill of illicit sex without violating the taboo against black-white dalliance. Moreover, they were relentlessly moralistic, committed with few exceptions to the proposition that "fate frowns upon miscegenation."[47] Tragedy hovered over all red-white affairs. One of the partners either terminated it in obedience to the inexorable law of color consciousness, or else made the ultimate sacrifice, surrendering up life itself.

The offspring of red-white unions, the mixed blood or half-breed, represented the midpoint in the Indian's biological absorption. In the past, the half-breed was depicted as the embodiment of the vices-and-virtues theory, combining the worst of both races. "Amalgamation deteriorates us without improving them," the fur trader Alexander Ross wrote in the 1850s.[48] Yet another view maintained that white blood could uplift the native races. During the removal controversy those anxious to discredit the notion that the Cherokees were semi-civilized routinely argued that any progress the tribe had made was due to its mixed-blood component. "Like their brethren of the red race everywhere else," the House Committee on Indian Affairs reported in 1830, the pure Cherokees exhibited "the same characteristic traits of unconquerable indolence, improvidence, and an inordinate love of ardent spirits."[49] Even as balanced a scholar as Lewis Henry Morgan flirted with the "important idea" whether or not it was "in virtue of the white blood already taken up and distributed among the emigrant nations [in Indian Territory] the improvement we see among them has come to pass."[50] Years later, the National Intelligence Tests showed that mixed bloods on the average scored higher than full bloods, a finding that was cast into doubt when it was pointed out that the tests measured degree of acculturation as much as native ability.[51]

Many Americans disdained the mixed blood. Others perceived him as a tragic figure, a marginal person caught between two cultures and often rejected by both. Such "highly stimulated savages," one anthropologist declared in 1881 in reference to mixed bloods and educated Indians, "either perish miserably or become lazaroni among their own people or the dominant race."[52] Others saw the half-breed as the harbinger of an integrated society. "The intermingling of the white and Indian races in social, political, and commercial relations in the United States will bring about to a considerable extent an amalgamation in the course of the years," Thomas Moffett, a historian of the Protestant missions to the Indian, observed in 1914. "The mixed breeds, in whom the strains of blood of the two races have mingled, are generally a superior type, with the better traits of both races accentuated."[53] Confronted by the reality of amalgamation, the primary white response was ambivalence.

INDIAN PROGRESSIVES

The values integral to the Dawes Act—veneration of private property, individual initiative, and self-sufficiency—as well as white attitudes about everything from cleanliness to standards of beauty, left a deep impression on an entire generation of Indians. "Progressives" on and off the reservation eagerly prepared themselves for the "new day" by identifying fully with whites. Prominent among them were graduates from Carlisle and similar institutions.

Captain Pratt, in his zeal to improve the Indian, undoubtedly fostered a self-loathing in his more receptive students. Impressionable young people exposed to the philosophy of "kill the Indian and save the man" concluded that their own people were vile and wretched because they were Indian. An educator in the Pratt tradition, Andrew S. Draper, called for fewer Indian day schools and more boarding schools on the grounds that "you have to get rid of the parents in some way."[54] From this perspective, Indian customs and beliefs were totally expendable. A Hampton graduate remarked: "What does the Indian of today care about his art? or about some ancient tool that a scientist might uncover? That time is past, and should be kept there. Personally, I wouldn't give up the experiences I have had for all the old-time ceremonies and 'Indian culture.'"[55] But in denying their culture, the young Indians were also denying their racial identity.

Luther Standing Bear, a member of Carlisle's first Sioux Indian class, took Pratt's teachings to heart. When he returned to the Standing Rock Reservation in South Dakota, he did not go "back to the blanket" but clung to his newly acquired civilization. Industrious, puritanical, and proud of his attainments (including a skin lightened by lack of exposure to the prairie sun), Standing Bear was obsessed above all else with cleanliness. He rejected one Indian maiden as a prospective bride because her underskirt was "far from clean," and married a half-breed girl who bore him a daughter (named Lily, in honor of her fair skin) and then a dark-skinned son (who was "a very fine baby, nevertheless").[56] In 1933, five years after he published these words in his autobiography, and at a time when it was more in vogue to be Indian, Standing Bear was less certain about the Carlisle experience. It had touched him only on the outside—inwardly, he had remained a Sioux: "Who can say that the white man's way is better for the Indian?"[57]

Carlos Montezuma, an Apache boy captured by the Pimas in a bloody raid about 1871 and sold to an itinerant photographer named Carlos Gentile, was raised in white society and educated at the University of Illinois. He earned his medical degree at Chicago Medical College in 1889. A stint as a reservation doctor made him an intransigent foe of the Bureau of Indian Affairs, which he blamed for retarding Indian progress. Montezuma found a natural ally in Pratt, served three years as resident physician at Carlisle, then established a private practice in a fashionable district of Chicago. He became a success as a society doctor and as a prominent crusader for Indian citizenship and for abolishment of the bureau. From 1916 until his death in 1923 he published an outspoken monthly magazine, *Wassaja*, dedicated to the familiar Prattian proposition that "the best way to get the Indians out of the control of the Indian Bureau is to get them out of the control of the Indian Bureau."

Montezuma "knows nothing of his native Apache language, nor is there a trace of Indian superstition or habit to be found in him," a contemporary approvingly noted.[58] He was an active Mason, a member of the First Baptist Church, and an attractive bachelor popular with white women, one of whom he married in 1913. But late in life, worn out by illness and his long struggle for Indian rights, he abandoned his Chicago practice, left his wife behind, and returned to the McDowell Reservation in Arizona to die in a humble wickiup far from the hospitals and medical care that had been his chosen work. It was a puzzling, immensely provocative gesture, but its significance was lost in a full-blown Masonic funeral and a eulogy delivered by a Phoenix pastor:

His life links together in a marvelous way the past and the present of our country—its oldest savagery with its newest civilization.

His life becomes a twofold lesson to us today. To the Indians he is an example of what any Indian may become. . . . To the American (the newer American) he is a reminder of what capacity the Indian possesses.[59]

Charles A. Eastman, a part-Santee Sioux descended on his mother's side from the soldier-artist Seth Eastman, spent his boyhood training as a warrior. He had been raised in the belief that his father was one of those hanged after the suppression of the Minnesota Sioux uprising of 1862, and he grew to young manhood with a single purpose in life, to avenge his father's death. One can imagine the shock he suffered when, in 1873, his father, not only alive but a Christian convert, arrived at the Santee camp in Manitoba to reclaim his son and take him back to the States to attend the white man's school. Eastman was fifteen years old at the time and his disorientation was total: "I felt as if I were dead and traveling to the Spirit Land; for now all my old ideas were to give place to new ones, and my life was to be entirely different from that of the past." Though he took a degree in medicine, married a white woman (the self-sacrificing Elaine Goodale), and became a devout Christian and a popular lecturer on the Chautauqua circuit, Eastman's writings reflect a sense of loss. His prose became animated when he recalled his childhood. "What boy," he asked, "would not be an Indian for a while when he thinks of the freest life in the world? This life was mine."[60] No such passion enlivened his account of his later career, which was studded with pious platitudes like "Happily, I had missed the demoralizing influences of reservation life [by going directly into school], and had been mainly thrown with the best class of Christian white people."[61]

Some educated Indians never vacillated. Jacob Morgan, who would become the Navajo tribal chairman (1938–1942), was trained at Hampton and permanently transformed by the experience.[62] He remained an inveterate opponent of romantic whites and reactionary Indians alike, and exemplified in purest form the generation of "red progressives" who, committed to assimilation and the self-help gospel, fluent in English, middle-class in values, and adept at propaganda, emerged in the second decade of the twentieth century to lead their less enlightened brethren into the melting pot. In 1911 they founded an organization of their own, the Society of American Indians. Foremost among the goals outlined in its constitution was "to promote and cooperate with all efforts looking to the advancement of the Indian in enlightenment which leave him free, as a man, to develop according to the natural laws of social evolution."[63]

Favorably publicized when it was launched, the society attracted a distinguished membership—"educators, clergymen, authors, playwrights, professional men of various callings, mechanics, farmers and students," but "no blanket Indians."[64] Drs. Eastman and Montezuma were early and active members, as was Arthur C. Parker, a one-fourth Seneca anthropologist who devoted himself to promoting the society's causes and served as editor of its *Quarterly Journal.* The society proposed to speak "for the weak and helpless, for the discouraged and hopeless of our race scattered over this broad land."[65] Instead, urban based and professionally oriented, it was badly out of touch with the vast majority of Indians living on the reservations, which it constantly condemned as an unmitigated evil. Dr. Montezuma called them prisons, and insisted that the society was not concerned with the "insides of our prison walls or the persecutions of the Indians," but with "how to beat down those walls, to destroy them all."[66] In the end, despite its lofty pretensions, the society was not broadly based enough to be effective, but it does stand as a compelling testament to the power of the assimilationist doctrine.

The attitude of the Indian progressives toward red-white amalgamation was ambiguous, and they rarely raised the subject in their several periodicals: Carlisle's *The Indian Craftsman* (1909–1910) and *The Red Man* (1910–1919); the Society of American Indians' *Quarterly Journal* (1913–1915) and *American Indian Magazine* (1915–1920); Carlos Montezuma's *Wassaja* (1916–1923); and Red Fox Skiuhushu's *American Indian Tepee* (1919–1924). But one magazine, *The American Indian,* published from 1926 to 1931 in Tulsa, Oklahoma, did offer a revealing insight into the progressive Indian's relationship to white culture. Initially described as "The Official Publication of the Society of Oklahoma Indians," *The American Indian* eventually broadened its scope to reflect the "true character" of the whole race. Yet it remained very much an Oklahoma journal, devoted to Indian pride, but given over to distinctly middle-class American concerns. It featured glamorous portraits of stylish

Five Nations women, social news about prominent Indian families, reports on the fortunes of the Indian schools' football teams, and canned historical pieces and biographies of successful Indians. The magazine's political awareness was never high, and it took no consistent editorial position on current Indian affairs. Perhaps most expressive of its acceptance of white values were its scattered, demeaning references to Negroes.

Stories about the Indian's valiant service in World War I managed to reflect discredit on the Negro soldier—mostly because he, unlike the Indian, had to serve in segregated regiments.[67] *The American Indian* asserted the red man's right to mix on an equal footing with white people, but denied the same privilege to blacks. It expressed resentment that "rabid abolitionist" pressure had forced the inclusion of former Five Nations black slaves on the tribal rolls after the Civil War. As a consequence of this pressure, red-black intermixing, an established fact of southeastern Indian life, had continued out West to the detriment of the Indian's social standing.[68] Census takers in 1910 found their efforts to determine the number of Negro and Indian mixed bloods stymied by a "disinclination" on the part of Indians to admit to such a mixture,[69] and it remained a popular truism that while "red" and "white" blood blended "easily and quickly," both resisted fusion with "black" blood.[70]

Refuting a news story about the death of a black graduate of Carlisle, *The American Indian* contended that "this was a glowing error. Negroes were not admitted at Carlisle. In fact, the Indian has never recognized the equality of the negro in the class room, or in any endeavor, anywhere, at any time."[71] The statement rings with disdain at such an unseemly assumption, but it was false. One of Carlisle's best-known graduates, Chief Buffalo Child Long Lance as he styled himself, was actually Sylvester Long, the son of a part-Negro school janitor and a Croatan (red, white, and black) woman. Admitted to Carlisle as an Eastern Cherokee, Long Lance later claimed to be a Blackfoot and achieved fame as an athlete, war hero, newspaper reporter, popular writer, movie actor, and the author of a fanciful 1928 autobiography about his wandering boyhood on the plains. In it occurs a passage as sad as it is ironic: "In the civilization in which we live, a man may be one thing and appear to be another. But this is not possible in the social structure of the Indian, because an Indian's name tells the world what he is: a coward, a liar, a thief, or a brave."[72] Trapped in his own web of lies, Long Lance killed himself in 1932. The newspapers attributed his suicide to an extended drinking spree—a fitting end for an Indian, as they saw it, and an unintended tribute to his successful masquerade. But Buffalo Child Long Lance was more than just a clever poseur. A fusion of America's three major races, he was a martyr to prejudice.

The Indian Council Fire of Chicago, with a red and white membership, sponsored a bill before congress in the mid-1930s making it a crime punishable by fine or imprisonment for anyone "other than an Indian to represent himself as an Indian." "We draw the color line very sharply," the Council Fire's secretary said. "We do not admit to membership any Indian who is mixed with Negro blood. . . . The white race does not class mulattoes as white. Why should the Indian?"[73]

But racism was always a treacherous ally. While whites might accord the Indian more respect than the Negro, this never meant that the Indian was their equal. Writing in 1929, the Secretary of the Interior asserted that "the Indian stock is of excellent quality. It can readily merge with that of the Nation."[74] However, acceptance could be withdrawn as casually as it was offered, as the Reverend Dr. Barnabas, Ph.D., complained in a letter addressed to Vice-President Charles Curtis in 1931 and published in *The American Indian*. Barnabas, of Indian background, had discovered that the Improved Order of Red Men admitted "only white American citizens" to membership—an "un-American" policy, he protested to the part-Indian Curtis, for a fraternal organization "founded on the manners, customs and tradition" of the native American and dedicated to the tortuous proposition that "good Red Men make good white men, and good citizens, husbands and fathers."[75]

Writing in 1957, Evon Z. Vogt, a student of Indian acculturation, remarked on the "incredibly" slow pace of assimilation, given earlier expectations. The rate of Indian-white amalgamation nationally, and particularly in areas with a heavy concentration of Indians, was "astonishingly low," and this was a major factor retarding assimilation. There was no "large mixed Indian-white population . . . to provide cultural models and reference groups along the continuum of acculturation for the conservative nuclei still living in the native-oriented Indian communities." To other explanations for the failure of assimilationist hopes, Vogt added his own: "persisting Anglo-American 'racial' attitudes . . . which strongly devaluate other physical types bearing different cultural traditions."[76] The amalgamationists had exempted the Indian from racial prejudice in making their case for inclusion; it awaited a social scientist working in the race-conscious 1950s to point out that prejudice knew no favorites.

Amalgamation was the assimilation program at its most literal, and it made perfectly good sense within the tradition of the Vanishing American. The distinction between cultural absorption and racial absorption was always a fine one, and that between racial absorption and racial extinction even finer. Writing in 1902 about the last generation of full-blood Indian babies the world would ever know, William R. Draper observed that the frontier hatred for the Indian had abated, and with it the belief that his race was "destined to extinction." "The Indian race is becoming absorbed and amalgamated rather than exterminated," Draper assured his readers. But his title, "The Last of the Red Race," carried more conviction.[77]

PART SIX

CHOICE
Indian Policy Through World War II

Fundamentally, the Reorganization Act is a declaration by the Government that the Indian as a race shall have the opportunity to live on; that the Indian civilization, as an element of human culture, shall live on. It means also that the life of the Indian shall not be a segregated or artificially protected existence, but shall be part and parcel of those cultures and interests which, in their aggregate, constitute the United States.

—Harold L. Ickes, Foreword to "Reorganization Number," *Indians at Work*, July 31, 1936, p. 3

Instead of trying to reduce all groups to the same pattern, we are now beginning to see the value of encouraging within one strong nation many different races and customs. Rather than a melting pot, America might be thought of as a great pageant of peoples. In

271

such a pageant, the Indian in the future, as he has in the past, may play a brilliant and colorful role.

—Edwin R. Embree, *Indians of the Americas: Historical Pageant* (Boston: Houghton Mifflin, 1939), p. 249

CHAPTER SIXTEEN

TO EACH AGE ITS OWN INDIAN:
The 1920s and the Changing Indian

In 1921, in his first annual report as Commissioner of Indian Affairs, Charles H. Burke concisely outlined the government's Indian policy: "The general course of treaties, agreements, and legislation has been in line with the purpose of reserving definite areas of land as tribal estates and of allotting therefrom as rapidly as possible freeholds in severalty, with the aim of inducing by this transfer of tribal to individual holdings a departure from old communal traits and customs to self-dependent conditions and to a democratic conception of the civilization with which the Indian must be assimilated if he is to survive."[1] For all that had intervened since the passage of the Dawes Act, Burke's words could as easily have been written in 1887 as in 1921. Consistency had been the paramount feature of federal Indian policy for three and a half decades. Seven administrations had come and gone, Democratic as well as Republican, since the General Allotment Act became law, and the government was still faithfully adhering to its main principles.

But in 1921 the United States was on the eve of a reform movement that would revolutionize Indian policy. In the decades following the Dawes Act, attitudes toward the Indian had been marked by two pronounced and contradictory tendencies. One school of thought, romantic, backward-looking, and nostalgic, saw the Indian as a vanishing race and lamented his demise; the other, pragmatic, forward-looking, and unsentimental, saw the American Indian becoming the Indian American and hailed his transformation. Both were convinced the Indian was amalgamating and his culture deteriorating. But what the one regretted, the other—the dominant view before 1920—applauded.

Because the minority view was persistent and often eloquent, it gradually shook the general complacency. Perhaps the Indians could only be saved through assimilation, as official policy would have it. But something irreplaceable—"a precious heritage of enjoyment . . . superior to anything the rest of the world has to offer," according to Mary Austin[2]—was being lost in the process. Moreover, it was a heritage that *could* be preserved. The government had set out to eradicate native culture, and cultural decline had followed. The same government, if it chose to do so, could reverse the process, or at least arrest it where it was.

"To each age its own Indian," Erna Fergusson remarked in 1936,[3] and in her age it was the "Changing Indian" instead of the Vanishing American. As attitudes made an about-face, so did policy. In the 1930s, in the depths of the Depression, the Indian came into his own, for the first time allowed a substantial choice on the question of segregation or integration, of maintaining tribal relations under a modern corporate structure or abandoning them completely to join the white world outside the borders of the reservation. Such would be the "New Deal" offered the Indians in the 1930s. It was the culmination of more than a decade of dedicated work by reformers who had found an emotional, galvanizing issue in 1922 among the Pueblos of the southwestern desert—as well as their models for the Changing Indian.[4]

THE BURSUM BILL CONTROVERSY

On July 20, 1922, H. O. Bursum, a New Mexico Republican, introduced a bill in the Senate to settle the claims of non-Indians resident on Pueblo lands in New Mexico. The Bursum bill, as it came to be known, was reported out of the Committee on Public Lands and Surveys with the endorsement of Albert B. Fall, Secretary of the Interior and a former Republican senator from New Mexico, who claimed that it had the support of all parties concerned, including the Commissioner of Indian Affairs, and was virtually "an administrative measure." The Senate passed the bill without debate, but its momentum petered out in a storm of denunciation. By January 1923 the *New York Times* declared it, "happily, dead or moribund."[5]

The Pueblos, a sedentary, agrarian people, had occupied their adobe villages through the centuries, each pueblo enjoying title in communal fee simple to the lands cultivated by its members. Over the years non-Indians had drifted onto portions of the Pueblo lands and occupied them with or without color of title. Designed to resolve the conflicting titles resulting from the overlapping Spanish, Mexican, and United States grants, the Bursum bill effectively confirmed the claims of non-Indians with color of title as well as those without so long as the claimants had enjoyed "peaceable possession" since 1900. Trespassers on the Pueblo lands whose claims to occupancy did not go back twenty-three years were still entitled to a "special finding" in court and, if the judgment was in their favor and the Secretary of the Interior concurred, were to be allowed to purchase their holdings at the assessed value exclusive of improvements. Only possession was open to contest; the extent of a claim was not.

In all this, the Pueblos had no voice, and thus no means of defending the land base that for them was survival. Approximately 60,000 of 340,000 acres of Pueblo lands were in dispute, and the Bursum bill meant that the interests of some 3,000 non-Indian claimants (who, with their families, numbered about 12,000) would take precedence over those of 8,000 to 9,000 Indians living in twenty pueblos. The bill also struck a decisive blow at Pueblo cultural integrity by providing that internal disputes be adjudicated in the federal courts, where the individual Indian would be released from the tribal clutch. The Bursum bill, its opponents charged, was tantamount to a death sentence for the Pueblos.

So obnoxious was the bill that it effected a spontaneous alliance among the factious friends of the Indian, and stimulated a general awakening of public concern. The president of the conservative Indian Rights Association remarked that in the organization's forty years' experience there had "never been anything to equal the splendid publicity" that the Pueblos' cause attracted.[6]

Stella M. Atwood, chairman of the Indian Welfare Committee of the General Federation of Women's Clubs, was in the forefront of the opposition to the Bursum bill. She was, moreover, instrumental in involving John Collier as "research agent" on behalf of the federation. A "keen-faced, quick, highly jittery" man who peered out at the world from behind "gleaming glasses,"[7] Collier was the model reform agitator, steeped in progressive ideology and committed to "constructive democracy" and collective action. He had cut his teeth as a community organizer with the People's Institute in New York City before moving to California and a post as director of social science training at the State Teachers College in San Francisco. Collier discovered the Pueblos late in 1920 as a guest of Mabel Dodge Luhan at Taos, New Mexico. Their cause became his all-consuming passion. Intensely serious, idealistic, and dedicated, he demanded involvement as a moral duty.

Collier combined the realism of a social worker with a poetic, visionary streak that permitted him to pass effortlessly from the mundane to the ethereal in his tireless effort to see justice done to the First American. His enormous knowledge was organized by a consistent world view that swept less disciplined opponents away like so much jetsam in the flow of life. There was rarely an earlier Collier to quote against the later one. He became in short order the most dominant figure in the area of Indian affairs, and remained so until his retirement in 1945 as commissioner of the bureau he had relentlessly assailed throughout the 1920s. Indeed, until his death in 1968 Collier never relaxed and never gave up. He was always on hand to point out government abuses with the scorn of a mystic who recognized that in the end the Indian would prevail and his timeless communal wisdom would transform the so-called civilized world—either that, or else there would be no world left to transform.[8]

The Pueblos, at Collier's behest, came together in 1922 for a historic all-pueblos council that issued "An appeal to the People of the United States." "We have reached a point where we must either live or die," it warned. The Bursum bill "will complete our destruction."[9] Mary Austin, Zane Grey, Carl Sandburg, Stewart Edward White, Hamlin Garland, and even D. H. Lawrence—who, within two months of arriving at Taos, had heard about the Bursum bill till he was "sick of it"[10]—lent their names and often their pens to the Pueblo cause. The prestigious American Association for the Advancement of Science and the American Anthropological Association joined in the opposition. White speakers and Pueblo dignitaries exhorted the crowds at meetings in Chicago, New York, and Washington, D.C., pleading for justice and contributions to the Pueblo Indian Defense Fund. Standing on the edge of the platform, one old Zuñi likened his position there to the predicament of his people: neither could advance one step "without perishing."[11] It was like a return to 1879 when the Poncas riveted eastern attention to the plight of the Indian. New Indian rights organizations sprang up—most notably the American Indian Defense Association, with Collier its executive secretary—while stories circulated in the press reminiscent of those bootless efforts of the 1830s to forestall removal by picturing the Cherokees as super-Indians, a civilized and exceptional people staring doom in the face. The Pueblos, once described as "the Indian who is not poor,"[12] were portrayed as an ancient people, peaceable cultivators, paragons of domestic virtue, deeply religious, hospitable, and patriotic. They constituted perhaps "the oldest democracies on the face of the earth," and were artistically advanced, Christianized, and, all told, "unlike in every way any other Indians."[13]

As reformers lauded the Pueblos—at some cost to the overall Indian cause since they so persuasively differentiated them from the others—they castigated the federal bureaucracy for its failures. The Pueblos were suffering from trachoma and syphilis and dying off from tuberculosis. Hunger oppressed them. The government was too busy to care—too busy rubber-stamping land theft and depriving the Pueblos of their water rights, a life-or-death consideration in the arid Southwest. A callous guardian was shamefully neglecting its wards and mismanaging their patrimony by "protecting them with a feather while it attacked them with a club," Collier charged.[14] The criticism was well deserved, but in one respect unfair. It put the government in an impossible double bind, requiring it to remedy all that ailed the Pueblos without disturbing traditional customs or the authority of the tribal governments.

Smarting from the reformers' attacks, federal officials struck back. Bursum insisted that he was "just as good a friend of the Pueblos as any man," and would be "quick to resent any effort to deal unfairly with them."[15] Clearly the opposition to his bill was politically motivated, he charged. A calculated campaign of innuendoes and lies, designed to discredit the government and to cast aspersions on the integrity of those who supported the measure, was responsible. Secretary Fall, who had announced his resignation because of the pressure of "private business interests," added that he only wanted a "square deal" for the Indians.[16]

As a result of the popular agitation, the Senate recalled the Bursum bill. Hearings were held in both Houses to consider alternative proposals. Denied the opportunity at one point to testify before the House Committee on Indian Affairs, Collier found willing outlets in the press and took his case directly to the public in a barrage of articles mixing panegyrics to the Pueblos with attacks on the executive branch of the government and "certain land-grabbing interests" who were working hand in glove to effect the "extermination of Pueblo life." The Indians' only option was to "disperse or die"—unless the conscience of the American people could be roused.[17]

Senior officials from the Bureau of Indian Affairs denounced such reformer propaganda. "It has attempted to undermine the bureau, estrange the Government from its wards and blacken the character of men," the assistant commissioner said. "It deserves the strongest rebuke this committee can administer."[18] The rebuke was forthcoming. The House committee report of February 27, 1923, included a blistering indictment of the propaganda against the Bursum bill:

Nothing to compare with it has heretofore been seen in connection with Indian legislation pending before Congress. This propaganda has been insidious, untruthful, and malicious and will result in great harm to the Indians of this country if it is permitted to be continued. Some of this propaganda is nothing more nor less than criminal libel. . . . Those responsible for this propaganda deserve the strongest condemnation from all fair-minded people.[19]

For all its bluster, the report signaled defeat for the Bursum bill. That "monster,"[20] that "special piece of villany,"[21] that "thoroughly vicious measure,"[22] had been stopped cold, though the Pueblo lands question, as events subsequently confirmed, was far from resolved. Henceforth, however, there would always be skeptical observers on hand monitoring the government's actions. And in 1924 a plateau was attained with the passage of a compromise measure creating a three-man Pueblo Lands Board to adjudicate claims without preempting the Indians' right to take counteraction in court against adverse decisions.

THE CONSERVATIVE-PROGRESSIVE CLASH

With the obnoxious Bursum bill defeated, the old rifts in the ranks of the Indians' friends opened up again. The Indian Rights Association, still preaching a doctrine of assimilation, soon grew disenchanted with "the Collier organization's" stridency and its commitment to "a continuation of the old order of things among the Pueblos."[23] Collier, in turn, professed himself baffled by the association's "inveterate hostility" toward tribal life "strangely accompanying devoted service" to the Indian cause in other areas.[24]

The divisive question was whether the Indian should be programmed for a future within white civilization, or whether white civilization should learn to coexist with him. In December 1923, a few months before Congress passed the Indian Citizenship Act, Secretary of the Interior Hubert Work convened a select "committee of one hundred" citizens—the National Advisory Committee on Indian Affairs—to ponder existing policy and plan for the future. The sixty to seventy-five individuals who actually assembled in Washington represented a cross-section of opinion, though they divided roughly into two camps, "the conservatives and the progressives," as *The Nation* called them.[25] Arthur C. Parker, secretary of the Society of American Indians and a prominent advocate of assimilation, served as chairman. Considered a "red progressive" a few years before, he was now labeled a conservative, thus testifying to the changing attitudes that had forced Secretary Work to convene the advisory committee in the first place. The choice of Parker as chairman alienated the liberal faction, and one participant found it "amusing" to observe how the two groups drifted apart, the conservatives to the right of the hall, the progressives to the left.[26] One issue that sharply polarized opinion was the right of American Indians to practice their traditional ceremonial dances.

For years, friends of the Indian had disapproved of everything that perpetuated Indianness and retarded assimilation. But Indian religions could be assailed directly only by ignoring First Amendment rights. Consequently, the assimilationists attacked the related ceremonies instead, charging that they were "obscene," "superstitious," "immoral," and "degrading." The "dance evil" was a favorite target.[27] Francis E. Leupp, who as commissioner had been unusually open-minded about Indian culture, nevertheless advanced a typical case against the dances. Among the "strongest influences for race demoralization," they were no longer genuinely religious in intention but had become primarily recreational.[28] As such, Leupp argued, they were subject to bureau regulations.

The Commissioner of Indian Affairs brought the matter to a head in February 1923 when he endorsed a series of recommendations passed by a conference of missionaries to limit dances to one a month, of one-day duration, with none at all permitted during the planting and harvesting season from March through August. No Indian under the age of fifty could attend, and the bureau would undertake "careful propaganda . . . to educate public opinion against the dance." The Indians had a year to comply with the commissioner's regulations before "more arbitrary methods" would be employed.[29] The Secretary of the Interior hinted darkly at Pueblo rites "which are against the laws of nature."[30] Others mentioned the unmentionable—phallic rituals, sodomy, and the "vicious maltreatment" of women and children[31]—while everyone deplored the dictatorial control exerted by a few evil caciques or priests over the minds and bodies of devotees.

The Indian's religion "is really, not merely theoretically, one piece and substance with his life," *The Survey* editorialized in response. "It expresses with great beauty and intensity his unity with God and the forces of nature, and in so doing involves the whole cluster of esthetic and moral reactions which we call a culture. Poetry, song and music, decoration, costume and symbolism, all are interconnected with these Indian ceremonies."[32] In other words, Indian religion and culture were one and the same and thus both should find shelter under the umbrella of the First Amendment.

Secretary Work, in his annual report for 1924, praised the National Advisory Committee on Indian Affairs for its desire to "bring the Indian into the fullness of Caucasian civilization."[33] The committee had, in fact, split over exactly this issue. War had badly shaken the complacent faith in civilization's moral authority that underlay the assimilation policy. An intellectual shift toward cultural relativism had blurred distinctions and softened judgments previously rendered with ethnocentric arrogance. The poet Witter Bynner wrote, "We need not be so cock-sure of our own ways as to interfere heavy-handedly with an Indian's ways."[34] "Let us try to adjust ourselves again to the Indian outlook, to take up an old dark thread from their vision, and see again as they see, without forgetting we are ourselves," D. H. Lawrence urged.[35] Mary Austin contended that the remaining residue of native culture should be viewed as "a National Asset, having something the same valuation as the big trees of California and the geysers and buffaloes of Yellowstone."[36]

Cultural relativism was to provide the philosophical basis for an enlightened Indian policy. The crucial question was not whether the Indian would civilize or die, then, but whether diverse cultures could live together in fruitful harmony or were fated to "poison and devour each other."[37]

FRANZ BOAS AND CULTURAL RELATIVISM

Cultural relativism required reevaluation of the Lockean premise of the *tabula rasa*, which in stressing individual equality at birth devalued the external factors that shaped subsequent development. Cultural and racial distinctions were necessarily secondary, not fundamental. Certainly reformers had read Locke this way. But social scientists in the early twentieth century were increasingly convinced that culture did play a decisive role in shaping the individual. Their view reflected a new interest in ethnicity and the influence of the community upon its members, which in turn led to a reassessment of the merits of cultural diversity. Assimilationists had simply assumed that minorities could be incorporated into white American civilization without suffering any loss. The new appreciation of cultural determinants undercut this assumption, encouraging a greater respect for variety.[38]

If cultural relativism mirrored intellectual disenchantment with contemporary society, it also represented dissatisfaction in academic circles with unilinear evolution as a master explanation for social development. Since evolutionary theory posited distinct gradations of culture—and of worth—on a scale ranging from savagery to civilization, value judgments were built into it. The turn of the century questioning of evolution thus served to clear the way for a less ethnocentric, more relative approach to other cultures.

Franz Boas was a leader among those anthropologists who attacked evolutionary doctrine where it was most vulnerable, on the problem of cultural similarities among widely dispersed peoples. Some of these similarities could be accounted for by independent development; others, by diffusion or borrowing. No single explanation was tenable. The precise ethnical periods Morgan had described, predicated as they were on universal parallel development, had to be modified by examining the historical connections between cultures and the resultant spread of forms and ideas through contact, not independent discovery. "It would seem," Boas observed in 1909, "that an acceptable general theory of the development of civilization must meet the demand that the historical happenings in any particular region conform to it."[39] Evolutionary theories were no exception, and the value judgments based on them were, by extension, as suspect as the theories themselves.

Boas's critique of evolutionary ethnology also challenged the orthodox belief that culture, defined as the end product of human creativity, could be subdivided into stages signifying levels of attainment and of racial aptitude. Only the white race had demonstrated a capacity for civilization, the argument went, a short step to the conclusion that only the white race *had* a capacity for civilization. Boas recognized that such a self-flattering conceit was merely racism masquerading as science. In an address on "Human Faculty as Determined by Race" delivered in 1894, he first disarmed his audience by conceding that white racism was quite understandable. "Proud of his wonderful achievements, civilized man looks down upon the humbler members of mankind," he said, and "other conditions being equal, a race is always described as lower the more fundamentally it differs from the white race." In judging his attainments greater than those of others, however, civilized man had concluded that his "aptitude for civilization" was also greater. Consequently, "the achievement and the aptitude for an achievement have been confounded." Investigations into the physical and psychological characteristics of the races had disclosed no innate differences in capacity, and no racial basis for cultural attainment. In pointed rebuttal to Morgan's theory of barbaric brains and inviolate ethnical periods, Boas flatly stated that there was no "proof of cumulative increase of faculty caused by civilization."[40]

Boas most fully elaborated his ideas on race in 1911 in *The Mind of Primitive Man*, a book described by one of his students as "a Magna Carta of race equality."[41] He intended it to persuade a large general audience, but his devotion to the canons of a strictly inductive methodology and his graceless prose style did not equip him as a popularizer, though *The Mind of Primitive Man* stands as an anthropological classic. In his 1938 revision, which was indicative of his lifelong concern with the subject, Boas put the book's central proposition succinctly: "If . . . we can show that the mental processes among primitives and civilized are essentially the same, the view cannot be maintained that the present races of man stand on different stages of the evolutionary series and that civilized man has attained a higher place in mental organization than the primitive man." Everywhere, he argued, the human mind is fundamentally the same. Apparent differences in levels of performance are culturally, not genetically, determined. "Race,"

Boas wrote, "is entirely subordinate to cultural setting."[42] All humans enjoy equal "racial" capacity, then, and hence there is no ceiling on any one race's potential. Since the human species is one and the same in mental endowments, "mongrelization" is a meaningless phobia and racial superiority—like the doctrine of racial purity—a logical fallacy. There was no ultimate correlation between race and culture, and there was no reason to assume that one culture was "better" than another.

Cultural relativism did not suddenly win over the American public in the 1920s, a decade notorious for bigotry, a scientific flirtation with eugenics, and a popular adherence to the doctrine of Aryanism. Nor did cultural relativism eliminate the ethnocentric value judgments inherent in older evolutionary theories. But twentieth-century social scientists were increasingly willing to accept the power of cultural determinants over individual behavior, and this effected a theoretical revolution whose main tenet Boas had anticipated back in 1883 while relaxing in an Eskimo igloo in Baffin Land. "As a thinking person," he had jotted in a letter diary, "for me the most important result of this trip lies in the strengthening of my point of view that the idea of a 'cultured' individual is merely relative and that a person's worth should be judged by his *Herzenbildung*."[43]

THE SOUTHWEST AND THE NON-VANISHING AMERICAN

Boas personally did not follow through on the practical applications of his ideas. He remained the objective and detached scientist. His field work among what he perceived as disintegrating cultures on the Northwest Coast did not result in a close, emotional empathy with the Indians he was studying. Indeed, students of most of the northern and western tribes approached their work with an ingrained fatalism. But a different impression of Indian cultural vitality was emerging from the field work of anthropologists in the Southwest. They had found not decay and despair, but ancient ways of life still thriving in a remote corner of the United States. They had found an Indian people with a future.

Frank Hamilton Cushing was the pathbreaker. A protégé of

John Wesley Powell, Cushing was persuaded to undertake a
study of the Zuñi for the Bureau of Ethnology. He fastened
onto the novel idea of becoming, as a colleague put it, "an
Indian among Indians."[44] He lived with the Zuñi for five years,
from 1879 to 1884, adopting their mode of dress and becoming
fluent in their tongue. He was initiated into the most "esoteric"
secret society, the Priesthood of the Bow, and held one of the
highest offices in the pueblo. By 1882 Cushing was writing
about Zuñi life from the vantage point of a privileged insider.[45]
The ethnographic quality of his work on Zuñi mythology is
debatable since he was more adept at conveying a feeling for
myth than recording it with scientific precision. But he was a
superb popularizer, and one of his peers regarded him as "the
ideal student of ethnology,"[46] the white man who had finally
penetrated the mystery of the Indian mind and an alien way
of life. Indiscreet and insensitive in publishing secret lore—a
breach of trust that left the Pueblos suspicious of his anthropological successors—Cushing did perform the service of
bringing a living native culture into the consciousness of white
America. Others after him also discovered the desert peoples,
and the image that they promulgated of a flourishing native
populace served as a convincing rebuttal to the tradition of the
Vanishing American.

Edward S. Curtis's haunting photograph of a band of Indians
riding into the desert twilight (*The Vanishing Race*) and Zane
Grey's novel of an ill-fated red-white romance (*The Vanishing
American*) both used the Navajo to make their didactic point.
This amused Walter Stanley Campbell, who, writing under the
pen name Stanley Vestal, was a widely read expert on plains
culture. The Navajos, he observed, "are numerous, they are
rich, they are industrious, and self-supporting, and they are
gaining in numbers and wealth. Vanishing, indeed!"[47] In fact,
as the situation sorted itself out, plains Indians, whose old-time
culture was in shambles, came to represent the vanishing race,
and Navajos and Pueblos the revolutionary idea of Indian
continuity and survival. Frederick Monsen, a photographer
who in 1889 went to live among the Hopis, a Pueblo people
sequestered inside the huge Navajo reservation in northeastern
Arizona, elaborated upon the distinction:

A nomadic tribe gathers few traditions, and its very mode of life prevents a continuance of the elaborate and often beautiful religious observances which form so large a part of the life of the Hopi. . . . Nothing can be done to bring back to these wandering tribes their old-time freedom and supremacy. In the majority of instances this already has ceased. . . . Their buffalo has passed together with their former freedom; their hunting grounds are gone and their liberty has been taken away; their entire environment is changed, and in consequence they have lost all the individuality which made vital their art and customs and so made them worth preserving. But with the Hopi all this is different. Their isolation and conservative habits of mind have prevented the possibility of the white man's civilization taking any real root among them, and they have so far escaped "development" along civilized lines. Their environment remains the same as it was hundreds of years ago. . . .[48]

While he personally found the Hopis "incomparably less attractive" than the plains Indians among whom he did his principal field work, Robert Lowie admitted the validity of Monsen's description. The Hopis whom he visited in 1915 and 1916 had "not only far and away the most complex culture of all the tribes known to me," he wrote, "but also had preserved relatively much more of it."[49]

An explanation was not hard to find. The Hopis had preserved their traditional economic base, and it had supported their culture substantially unchanged through the years. In contrast, the advent of the reservation era had abruptly terminated the customary existence of the free-roaming buffalo hunters and warriors of the plains. Cherished religious ceremonials like the sun dance had been banned. Their children were forbidden to speak their own language in the schools they were forced to attend. A culture based on the hunt and the raid lay in ruins. Whenever old plains Indians told their life stories, they sounded the same sad refrain: "When the buffalo went away the hearts of my people fell to the ground, and they could not lift them up again. After this nothing happened."[50] The plains warriors who lived on into the twentieth century— truly a lost generation—could salvage what was dearest to them only in memory.

In isolated areas of Arizona and New Mexico, the sedentary Pueblos and the wandering Navajos followed their old ways, hoeing their gardens, tending their flocks, weaving their blankets, fashioning their silver and turquoise jewelry, going to "sings," and practicing ancient rites much as they had always done. White farmers did not covet their desert domain, and their very isolation sheltered them from the outside world. The Navajos had once enjoyed a considerable reputation as horseback warriors, in contrast to the Pueblos, a "gentle folk,"[51] a "quiet race,"[52] who were seen as having "the habits, intelligence, and enterprise of a semi-civilized people."[53] But with their defeat in the 1860s, the Navajos had adjusted to life on a vast reservation. They "are now practically a pastoral people," one investigator reported in 1883, adding as a cautionary note that they had not yet lost their "martial spirit and capacity."[54]

Visitors to the Pueblos and Navajos usually commented on how Indian they were, and Oscar Lipps in 1909 thought it "safe to assume" that the Navajo would "always remain an INDIAN. He shows no disposition to amalgamate with any other race."[55] James Mooney, otherwise so consistent in his conviction that Indian numbers everywhere had declined since the arrival of the white man, conceded that the Navajos were an exception, and offered in explanation that the tribe continued to "live in its old habitat upon its own accustomed food resources, with its blood unpoisoned and without continual disturbances from the outside."[56] Certainly the 1910 census supported Mooney. On one map showing degrees of racial intermixture, Navajo country appeared as a bastion of red purity, while the graph establishing the "proportion of full-blood and mixed-blood Indians, and of Indians of full-tribal blood, in each principal tribe" put only the Hopi before the Navajo in racial homogeneity.[57]

The cohesiveness and purity of Pueblo and Navajo life attracted a wide range of Americans, none more influential in promoting a positive image of the southwestern cultures than the painters who began congregating in Taos and Santa Fe late in the nineteenth century. Indian subjects were enjoying an artistic vogue. The Wild West school, led into prominence by the most successful illustrator of his day, Frederic Remington, relished violent action and made the clash between red and white an enduring theme in American art. Though Montana's "cowboy artist" Charles M. Russell was often linked with

Remington, he saw the Indian as "the nobleman of the plains" and chose to enshrine him in pre-reservation vigor still resisting civilized progress. This empathy put Russell in the company of painters like George de Forest Brush, Edwin W. Deming, and N. C. Wyeth, who portrayed the Indians outside historical context as masters of the forests and the marshes, kings of the awesome wilderness that was once America. Their most characteristic works on Indians were poetic, tranquil, and allegorical, and a writer in the New York *Post* shrewdly distinguished them from the Wild West artists: "One might say that Mr. Remington has seen the story of the hard-pressed native along the sights of a rifle, and Mr. Deming wrapped in one of their own blankets."[58]

The painters who flocked to Taos and Santa Fe were wrapped in blankets too, but they borrowed theirs from a living people. A critic writing in 1921 about one of them noted that the Indian he pictured was neither "the rampant warrior nor the crushed and apologetic being who is sometimes visualized as the true type of this 'vanishing race.'" Instead, he depicted a "sturdy primitive people . . . who are refusing to vanish with the timorous and apathetic haste which tradition has assigned to them."[59] That was the keynote of the southwestern school of Indian painting. Taos seemed timeless, its Indian culture a permanent entity. When Joseph Sharp, a gifted portraitist and painter of the red man's domestic life, left Taos to set up quarters on the Crow reservation in Montana, he said, explaining his apparent defection, "I went north because I realized that Taos would last longer."[60]

Other portraitists like DeCost Smith, E. A. Burbank, Winold Reiss, and W. Langdon Kihn, to name the best known, set out in the period from the 1890s through the 1920s to preserve a pictorial record of what they fancied to be a "disappearing race."[61] For them, Indians were "spoiled" once they had donned whites' clothing; Reiss and Kihn posed their models in native finery long after it had been abandoned in daily wear. The picturesqueness of the Pueblos and the Navajos, in contrast, was entirely natural. Ernest L. Blumenschein, a founder of the Taos artists' colony, approvingly noted that the local Indians made rules "to counteract all the outside influence that

might destroy their traditions. . . . The monthly dances are
thanks to their great god above for the corn and the beans; the
Pueblo blood is not mixed with white; and more to our
particular point, the Indian of Taos wears the clothes of an
Indian."[62] Consequently, the Southwest was a magnet for
painters seeking colorful, authentically American material in
a setting of astonishing natural beauty.

In *Patterns of Culture*, a celebrated 1934 study of cultural
configurations—and a landmark in the case for cultural relativism—Ruth Benedict opened her discussion of the Pueblos
with what was by then an orthodox tribute:

The Pueblo Indians . . . are one of the most widely known primitive
peoples in Western civilization. They live in the midst of America,
within easy reach of any transcontinental traveller. And they are
living after the old native fashion. Their culture has not disintegrated
like that of all the Indian communities outside of Arizona and New
Mexico. Month by month and year by year, the old dances of the
gods are danced in their stone villages, life follows essentially the old
routines, and what they have taken from our civilization they have
remodelled and subordinated to their own attitudes.[63]

In reporting the phenomenon of southwestern cultural survival
and exposing the public to a counterimage of the Vanishing
American, anthropologists, writers, and painters stimulated a
surge of interest in all Indians. The Non-vanishing American
was, events would prove, a concept of enormous consequence.
It caught white Americans in an unusually receptive mood and
helped reshape Indian policy.

THE VOGUE OF THE DESERT

The publicity surrounding the Bursum bill, particularly the
rhapsodic portrayal of Pueblo culture by the bill's opponents,
alerted the nation to the endangered Indian societies in the
Southwest. Americans searching in the aftermath of World
War I for alternatives to a materialistic civilization that seemed
to place scant premium on human values, that moved to the
rhythm of factory whistle and machinery instead of seasons
and sun, looked to the Southwest. "What a relief to turn from
the War and its drives to softly mellowed pueblos where grown

men raised what they ate in peace," a contemporary wrote in retrospect. "From feminism, free love, and flaming books to a sanely humorous people who took sex as simply as weather. From anguished searchings for something to replace religions proven sterile, to sunlit ceremonies worshipping nature with both beauty and intensity."[64]

And so they came—painters, writers, and a host of the merely curious. "To your tents, O America. Listen to your own, don't listen to Europe," D. H. Lawrence advised in 1920,[65] and when Walter Lippmann dismissed him as "plainly in the Noble Savage phase,"[66] Mary Austin tartly replied that there was already "a lusty art movement in America which is feeding itself from that top-soil of human experience deposited here by the aboriginal."[67] The desert was abloom with life and renewed hope. What brings the artists here? a Taos resident asked, and answered that "above all" it was "the very air vibrating with 'the creative urge,' the sense of the undiscovered, the time to think, to work on uninterruptedly, the time to give one's soul a chance and the time to dream!"[68]

Taos and indeed the whole desert Southwest had become an escape, a domestic outlet for the expatriate urge that made postwar Paris a literary mecca. Primitivism was a fad in a decade that had learned from Freud that civilized man repressed healthy, natural drives to his psychological detriment. In *The Torrents of Spring: A Romantic Novel in Honor of the Passing of a Great Race* (1926), Ernest Hemingway mocked the period's twin intellectual enthusiasms, the uninhibited, spontaneous Negro and the poetic, noble Indian. He set one scene in a speakeasy for Indian veterans where the patrons imbibed under the framed, autographed portraits of such friends of the Indian as D. H. Lawrence, Stewart Edward White, Mary Austin, and Mabel Dodge Luhan, and were served by a Negro bartender whose "dark haunting" laughter floated out the club's window into the night.[69]

To seekers of the exotic in the 1920s, Harlem was the American Congo. It was a one-night stand, "a white man's holiday" according to the *New York Times*, replete with bootleg liquor, cocaine, ebony chorus lines, and the "joyous rhythms" of jazz.[70] For white "slumming parties," Harlem was the place to shed a few inhibitions and enjoy life on a more sensuous plane before returning to the other side of town. The Harlem Renaissance, a major artistic movement and an assertion of black pride, was the substantial base on which the aesthetic of the "New Negro" rested in the 1920s. But white Americans were interested in escape. "Love, sex, passion . . . hate"—that was the Harlem of mass fantasy captured in Carl Van Vechten's best-selling novel *Nigger Heaven* (1926).[71]

The Southwest was something else again, still relatively inaccessible, "a land whose beauty takes the breath like pain."[72] It offered a reprieve from the concrete confinement of the city, and lured a generation convinced of the tonic effects of wilderness:

> Dear earth, it almost seems a sacrilege
>   After the patterned ways my feet have trod
> On cobblestones and pavements beaten hard,
>   To set my sandaled feet upon your sod.
> Oh shoes, tread lightly on the tender breast
>   Of earth. It breathes so near the heart of God.[73]

The Santa Fe Railroad offered its own seductive appeals. "Gee! We are going to see real, live Indians," one advertisement showing three beaming children proclaimed. Another, beneath a color reproduction of an E. I. Couse painting of a Taos father and son, asked, "Why not, this summer? Gratify the urge of the wanderlust—go—see Far West scenic regions."[74] Out there in the desert was an alternative to the work ethic. Out there was "the land of poco tiempo,"[75] "The Country That God Remembers,"[76] the land where time has "stood still."[77] Out there, perhaps, was happiness.

"It was there the last rays of the setting sun found us," a visitor to the Hopis wrote in 1915:

On a house top, watching the little panorama in the street below us, of the youths sitting in the shadows, idly smoking and watching through indolent eyes, the girls in brilliantly colored shawls and hair wound high over each ear, playing among themselves. Then to look over the fields and see the Indian farmers leaving the tilling of the soil and slowly climbing the trail towards home, to hear the bleating of sheep, and finally seeing them in a hazy dust cloud with the old shepherd behind them with his dog. Young married women, their sleeping children tied on their backs in shawls, glanced up at us and smiled a greeting as they hurry on to the evening service at the mission.[78]

This twilight pastoral seems right out of Gray's "Elegy"; but life, not death, was the message. Within the United States there lived a class of native peasants, their folkways intact, their outlook defiantly unmodern. They offered a model of timeless serenity, of permanence and contentment enough to make the Southwest the "land of journey's ending."

LAWRENCE, LA FARGE, AND COLLIER

D. H. Lawrence, "willed" to Taos by Mabel Dodge Luhan in 1922, confessed to a long-standing fascination with "the Indian, the Aztec, old Mexico. . . . *There* is glamour and magic for me." But he also expressed uneasiness about what he might find at Taos because he feared the presence there of "a colony of rather dreadful sub-arty people," and wondered if the Indians were "dying out, and is it rather sad?"[79] Conscious of the irony, he sat draped in a red Navajo blanket to watch Indians in white cotton sheets perform a sacred dance whose mystery he could not penetrate, respond though he might to "the subtle incessant insistent rhythm of the drum, which is pulsated like the heart, and soulless, and unescapable."[80] He sensed a dark, immemorial tribal knowledge that bordered on "unconscious animosity" toward whites and confirmed just how far they had grown from their primal roots.[81]

This was Lawrence's primary conclusion; civilized man could not go back. The visionary who in 1920 had urged Americans to their tents now admitted, "I can't cluster at the drum any more,"[82] and castigated those do-gooders who came to help the Indians. "You can't 'save' them," he admonished Mabel Luhan, "and politics, no matter *what* politics, will only destroy them."[83] Fashionable neoprimitivism repelled him, and he sneered at the American desire to be "an *intellectual* savage":

White Americans do try hard to intellectualize themselves. Especially white women Americans. And the latest stunt is this "savage" stunt again.
    White savages, with motor-cars, telephones, incomes and ideals! Savages fast inside the machine; yet savage enough, ye gods![84]

At his most caustic, Lawrence reduced the 1920s romance with the desert tribes to a tourist show with "lots of sand, and painted savages jabbering, and snakes and all that. Come on, boys! Lots of fun! The great Southwest, the national circus-ground."[85] It all struck him, he wrote elsewhere, "like comic opera played with solemn intensity."[86] But Lawrence, as a self-confessed escapist, like those he mocked, intellectualized the Indian, making of him an exotic primitive possessed of a blood knowledge denied the more cerebral white man; he too bent the Indian to his own myth of the native.

In inviting Lawrence to Taos, Mabel Luhan had an ulterior motive. She had recognized in his writing a soul mate and had hoped that he, with his intuitive grasp of the unconscious, would be *the* recorder of the Taos experience. In short, she hoped to enlist his pen on the Indian's behalf. But Lawrence resisted her and fled to Mexico to find inspiration and the time to write the great novel that eventually came from his stays in the Southwest, *The Plumed Serpent* (1926). In it, he at last partially achieved the fusion between red and white ways of knowing that he thought would one day make America truly a *New* World. One cryptic sentence expressed what he had learned in New Mexico about the Indian's mystical relationship with nature and eternity: *"Thou shalt acknowledge the wonder."*[87]

In the end, it did not matter that Lawrence failed to meet expectations. For others too had experienced the tug of the primitive, and received through the Indians an intimation of the truths underlying existence. The vogue of the desert tribes in the 1920s resulted in novels as varied as Elizabeth Pickett's *Redskin* (1929), a potboiler about an educated Navajo's dilemma that even managed to work the artists' colony at Taos ("an Athens of the West") into its plot, and Oliver La Farge's lyrical Navajo love story, *Laughing Boy*, which won the Pulitzer Prize for literature in 1929.

Laughing Boy's plot turns on a contrast between the almost idyllic quality of pure Navajo life and the shoddy, corrupting influence of white civilization on it. Laughing Boy and Slim Girl symbolize the two extremes: he is an untainted produce of his people, delighting in horse-racing, jewelry-making, and the simple manly pleasures; she is a marginal woman, educated in white schools where "they tried to make us not be Indians," worldly-wise and cynical.[88] She has become a prostitute out of contempt for the white man's teachings, but now desires to reclaim her heritage by marrying a "long hair" Indian, a role Laughing Boy unwittingly fills. The couple reside in a town on the edge of the reservation. Laughing Boy is drawn to the shallow, easy life of the white man (i.e., liquor), while Slim Girl struggles to recover the traditional skills she has lost (i.e., weaving). In the end, after Slim Girl's double life as devoted wife and white man's whore has been exposed and atoned for, the shadow of deceit over the couple's happiness is lifted, Indianness asserts itself, and the two flee into the interior of the reservation, only to find tragedy. Slim Girl is struck down, and Laughing Boy, a wiser, soberer man, continues on alone, vowing never again to stray from the Beauty Path of his people.

La Farge had fashioned an Indian romance attuned to the emotions of the 1920s—even Laughing Boy's return to the sanctuary of the Navajo reservation was but another variation on the escape to the desert. A neophyte anthropologist, La Farge considered the Indian way of life "inexorably doomed," for the law of vices and virtues was still at work in the twentieth century and contact with white civilization, which every year was penetrating deeper into Navajo country, "meant conflict and disaster." "I put this idea into the book," La Farge remembered, ". . . and then I let myself out by sending my hero, after the final tragedy, back into my own dreamland, the untouched, undisturbed Navajo country where the white man was not a factor and would not become one within my time." In the Indians, La Farge wrote, "my whole urge to flight found its direction."[89] *Laughing Boy* was popular in part because La Farge's escapism tapped a need in the public, and his book offered a chance to participate vicariously in the southwestern dreamland.

For a few, the encounter with the desert peoples proved a shattering conversion. By temperament a romantic, John Collier habitually sought escape from the pressures of urban life in the out-of-doors. He arrived in Taos from Los Angeles with his family in late December 1920, witnessed the various festivals associated with Christmas, and was profoundly moved by the Red Deer Dance. It was a "forthgiving religious (as we white people know it) and cosmical (as we white people do not know) ceremony" which transported participants and spectators "into a region of existence where thousands of years bloomed coldly in the hearts and brains of simple, hardworking, present-day humans." Thirty-nine years later Collier could still remember the excitement that gripped him at Taos as the full meaning of what he was experiencing struck home. The Pueblo dances, he wrote, "entered into myself and each one of my family as a new direction of life—a new, even wildly new, hope for the Race of Man."[90]

This was why the controversy over the Pueblo lands and religious practices mattered so much. The implications of assimilation through allotment, "the sacred fetish of America's Indian policy for a generation now," had achieved clearest definition among the Pueblos because they, more than any other group, represented what mankind stood to lose with the elimination of the Indian cultures. Writing in 1923, less than a year after becoming actively involved in Indian affairs, Collier said the Pueblos, "with their self-government, their world-old democracy, their institutions for causing the human spirit to bloom into love and splendor, must be permitted to live their own lives, forward into their own future, not apart from the White man's world but coöperating with it as the Pueblos, of all Indians, are the most willing and able to coöperate."[91]

Throughout the 1920s the Pueblos and subsequently the Navajos were the cynosures of reformist concern. According to *The Survey*, they constituted the "two chief Romances of the American Indian—two future romances among others less complete—which may partly retrieve the hundred Lost Romances, wasted or killed."[92] It was presumptuous to write off thousands of other Indians because their tribal relations were less intact, their cultures and bloodlines less pure, their settings less exotic. The noble savage, wild, free-spirited the antithesis of societal restraint, had now become the model member of an organic community, the perfect tribalized being. Those who did not fit this mold, like the settlement Indians of the past, were somehow less Indian.

But the Pueblos and the Navajos were a start. They embodied

a potent new idea: the Indian was destined to last as long as the mesas and the sky under which he flourished, altering externals but not essentials. This theory of the Changing Indian would guide federal policy through the next decade and beyond.

CHAPTER SEVENTEEN

TO PLOW UP THE INDIAN SOUL:
The Indian Reorganization Act

Writing in 1925 about the sentimentalism of those who looked to the red man's "beautiful vanished past" and longed to restore it, Flora Warren Seymour, a member of the Board of Indian Commissioners established in 1869 as a cornerstone of President Grant's Peace Policy, complained that Americans meet the Indian's problems "not with intelligence, but with incoherent emotion. . . . We are swept along by continued waves of popular sentiment," she said. "To-day we ride on the crest of a great wave of feeling; to-morrow we collapse feebly into the trough of indifference."[1]

Seymour's tacit assumption, that by 1925 the champions of the Pueblos had exhausted their energies and their concern, proved wildly premature. Pressure for substantial policy reform continued to build. In 1929, Hugh L. Scott, a soldier who had campaigned against the plains tribes back in the 1870s and since become a respected figure in Indian affairs, declared that "today is the accepted time, the psychological moment. Reform is in the air. People want it."[2]

PRECURSORS TO THE INDIAN NEW DEAL

Certainly John Collier and the American Indian Defense Association had never let up. Collier publicized instances of government abuse whenever he encountered them: the Osage oil scandals in Oklahoma; the apparently endless Pueblo land question and the religious rights controversy; the Flathead hydroelectric power dispute in Montana; and the myriad problems of the Navajo, from oil rights to bridges. Reservation Indians were "red slaves." "Spiritual and physical doom" hung over them.[3] They were almost "vanquished,"[4] and it was a "miracle"—indeed, a testimonial to their resilience and vitality—that the "Indian body and soul have endured so long."[5] If in the 1880s George Manypenny blamed the army and Helen Hunt Jackson congressional inaction for America's "century of dishonor," forty-odd years later Collier singled out the Bureau of Indian Affairs. When he wrote that the Indians were "hammering at the prison door," the prison he meant was bureau control, not the reservation. He focused his attention on that nineteenth-century carryover of the assimilation policy, the Indian boarding-school system. It was an open scandal: terrified children "snatched" from the bosom of their families to feed "the maw of the boarding schools," "swept into trucks, loaded like sheep, and away"[6]—away to a misery of loneliness and disease for healthy outdoor bodies suddenly confined, subjected to institutional regimentation and discipline, underfed, even starved, beaten and brutalized in the government's unrelenting campaign to efface "Indianhood and Indian family life."[7]

Nettled by critics like Collier and desirous of rectifying wrongs, Secretary of the Interior Hubert Work in June 1926 ordered an independent body, the Institute for Government Research, to prepare a report on conditions among the Indians, with recommendations for improvements in the Indian Service. A staff assembled under Lewis Meriam submitted its report to the secretary in February 1928. Published as *The Problem of Indian Administration* and known as the Meriam Report, it consisted of almost nine hundred pages of evidence and recommendations, all carefully phrased to avoid the emotionalism of the Bureau of Indian Affairs' detractors.

The report set out not to judge the bureau or dwell on the past, but to make constructive suggestions for the future. Nevertheless, it told a distressing story of a people pauperized by those who professed to be acting in their best interests. Clearly, past policy *had* been misguided. Allotment in severalty, unaccompanied by a dedicated effort to train the Indians as farmers, was bound to fail from the outset. Apparently the government "assumed that some magic in individual ownership of property would in itself prove an educational civilizing factor, but unfortunately this policy has for the most part operated in the opposite direction," the report observed. Individuals had been systematically dispossessed; the Indians' land base had been gobbled up. Education, too, had been a failure. The boarding-school system rested on the outmoded theory that the Indian child had to be removed "as far as possible from his home environment; whereas the modern point of view in education and social work lays stress on upbringing in the natural setting of home and family life." The government's assimilation program with its twin goals of absorption and cultural extinction could only be seen as a tragic blunder.[8]

The Meriam Report's recommendations were in keeping with this judgment. The allotment policy should be pursued with "extreme conservatism" in the future. Indian education should abandon the boarding schools in favor of reservation day schools or, better yet, the integration of Indian children into the public schools. Both recommendations were predictable, but the Meriam Report did break new ground in its stance on the ultimate goals of Indian policy:

The fundamental requirement is that . . . [the Indian Service] be made an efficient educational agency, devoting its main energies to the social and economic advancement of the Indians, so that they may be absorbed into the prevailing civilization or be fitted to live in the presence of that civilization at least in accordance with a minimum standard of health and decency. . . .

. . . The effort to substitute educational leadership for the more dictatorial methods now used in some places will necessitate more understanding of and sympathy for the Indian point of view. Leadership will recognize the good in the educational and social life of the Indians in their religion and ethics, and will seek to develop it and build on it rather than to crush out all that is Indian. The Indians have much to contribute to the dominant civilization. . . .

The ideas contained in this passage, tinged with the theory of cultural relativism, were in themselves a departure from official orthodoxy. But the report's most innovative proposal was the

option of either assimilation *or* separatism—a long overdue
acknowledgment that Indians were in fact citizens as well as
wards.[9]

Everyone understood what it meant for the Indian to "merge
into the social and economic life of the prevailing civilization,"
but the second option required elaboration. Some Indians did
not want to become white men, strange as this might seem.
They wanted to remain Indian, to "preserve what they have
inherited from their fathers, and insofar as possible to escape
from the ever increasing contact with and pressure from the
white civilization." They were entitled to do so, as many of
their white supporters had been insisting. The Meriam Report
even expressed sympathy for the sentimental desire to enclose
the Indians in a "glass case" and preserve them as "museum
specimens for future generations to study and enjoy." But
having gone this far—and having shackled the champions of
Indian cultural autonomy to its own exaggerated metaphor—
the report proceeded to argue that "the Indians cannot be set
apart from contacts with the whites. The glass case policy is
impracticable." Even among the Pueblos civilization had permanently transformed traditional life-styles. Individual Indians
wanted to change with the times, try new jobs, live in houses
with the latest conveniences, dress in whites' clothing, be treated
by trained physicians in fully equipped hospitals, and have
their children attend schools where they would be educated to
survive in the modern world. Individuals must not be abandoned in an effort to preserve tribes, nor must those Indians
who chose the tribal option be written off. Their health and
sanitary conditions would have to be brought up to civilized
standards too, or else the government would be guilty of
abetting their decline through an unconscionable, even criminal
neglect. One conclusion was unavoidable: the government
would have a role to play for another thirty or forty years
before the Indians would be "capable and efficient citizens
. . . able to take care of themselves and to contribute to the
nation from the best of their own original American culture."[10]

On the whole, the Meriam Report met with a warm reception.
More than eighty friends of the Indian, gathered in Atlantic
City, endorsed its recommendations in January 1929. The

president of the American Indian Defense Association was not satisfied, however, and pursuing the line already laid down by Collier, charged that the report was too timid in assigning blame to the bureau.[11] Collier, though, recognized that the report's conciliatory tone was its chief virtue, giving it credibility among those who automatically turned a deaf ear to shriller critics like himself. Moreover, the report was a compendium of hard documentary evidence. Thus Collier could conclude that for all its shortcomings no publication in Indian affairs since Helen Hunt Jackson's *A Century of Dishonor* was as "important, and none . . . as challenging, humiliating and horrifying."[12]

But the Meriam Report by itself was not enough to placate the bureau's detractors, and even as it was being submitted to the Secretary of the Interior, the Senate in February 1928 ordered an investigation of its own. Despite bureau opposition and the charge of redundancy, a subcommittee of the Senate Committee on Indian Affairs was taking testimony by November. Before the hearings were finally completed in August 1943, Congress had accumulated a mammoth fund of information bearing on the First American's situation in his native land. The Senate investigation had an official bite that delighted reformers, and as the "sworn record" of "blasting testimony" swelled into "a long exhibition of horrors," the answer to a pressing question—"Who, or what, has created this situation?"—became self-evident: "The Indian Bureau, and it alone."[13] Of course, the bureau was people, and under the direction of Charles H. Burke since 1921 it had resisted fundamental change. Burke simply dismissed most criticism as ill-founded and counterproductive. A change of personnel was mandatory, *The Nation* maintained, since the Senate investigation had revealed the Burke administration to be "faithless."[14] In the spring of 1929, the new President, Herbert Hoover, decided to give the bureau a "thorough house-cleaning"[15] and persuaded a fellow Quaker, Charles J. Rhoads, a prominent Philadelphia banker and president of the Indian Rights Association, to succeed Burke as commissioner.

Historians commonly date the beginning of the Indian New Deal with the appointment of Rhoads and his assistant com-

missioner, another Quaker named J. Henry Scattergood. Secretary of the Interior Ray Lyman Wilbur set the tone of the
new administration by announcing a "weaning" policy for the
Indian, which was greeted with cautious optimism despite
the fact that it leaned toward the sink-or-swim philosophy of
traditional assimilationists.[16] Promising "a new deal for the
young Indian and a square deal for the old Indian," Wilbur
committed the bureau to the goal of making the red man "a
self-supporting and self-respecting citizen" within twenty-five
years. He did add that where cultures had "the means of
subsistence and the vigor to survive, as demonstrated in some
areas in the Southwest," they would be preserved, and that
concession seemed enough to reassure the reformers.[17] The
major contribution of Wilbur's program was its recognition of
an idea whose time had finally come: the incorporation of
tribes along modern business lines, each empowered to operate
its own tribal estate. This would be a way of at last resolving
the anomaly of tribal governments within the United States, as
well as the ancient problem of Indian title. Collier, for one,
defended Wilbur's weaning policy on the grounds that its
"individualization statements" were properly balanced with "a
clear, forceful statement of a program of tribal incorporation."[18]

But the spirit of cooperation between administrators and
reformers was short-lived. By the spring of 1930 the bureau's
critics were again in full chorus. Rhoads and Scattergood were
men of personal integrity and goodwill, no doubt, but they
had failed to "clean house"[19] and, one senator charged, "the
same old policies are pursued, the same ruts are followed, and
the same disappointing results obtained."[20] To prevent the
continuing erosion of the Indian land base, they had suggested,
lands left intestate on the death of an Indian allottee with more
than one heir should revert to the tribal estate. Tribal incorporation should be explored. An Indian claims court should
be established to ease a contentious problem that was a continuing source of unhappiness. But nothing definite was done
about any of these proposals, and as the panic that seized the
country in 1929 deepened into the Depression, the bureau
retreated from broad, searching reform. A petition from the
representatives of forty-nine tribes, alleging that Wilbur, Rhoads,

and Scattergood had reneged on all their "wonderful promises," was read in the Senate in March 1932:

We assert that they have forsaken their programs. They have broken their promises. They have set up new evils of far-reaching kinds—evils which their predecessors did not sponsor.... We solemnly affirm that conditions among the Indians today ... are more deplorable than they have been at any time since the United States became guardian over the Indians.[21]

A stinging indictment, the petition brought an angry retort from Wilbur,[22] who complained in his annual report that the Indian's progress "will always be hampered by a vociferous and emotional fringe of white people who encourage his grievances. The Indian suffers alike from enemies who exploit his property and friends who exploit his grievances."[23]

The mutual disenchantment stemmed in part from an official cautiousness that the bureau saw as prudence and its critics as timidity. They contended that Wilbur, Rhoads, and Scattergood had been given a mandate for reform, then frittered it away. In education, for example, many changes were made, but the most pressing issue—that of the boarding schools—went unresolved. Rhoads personally favored channeling Indian students into reservation day schools or local public schools. But practical considerations weighed heavily on his mind. Monies had to be carefully administered. The boarding-school facilities already existed. It was imperative that they be used for the time being. Thus, rather than trying to eliminate boarding schools, Rhoads thought it more important to make them "as effective educationally as it is possible to make them."[24] Indeed, because of the Depression, he wrote, Indian families were demanding that their children be admitted into the boarding schools, where they would be fed and clothed, and the bureau was "engaged in a serious effort to prevent these schools from being badly overcrowded."[25]

Wilbur insisted that the Department of the Interior's overriding priority in the midst of the Depression was continental conservation—not "the hoarding of natural resources for a hazy, indefinite future," but "intelligent and thoughtful planning for every resource."[26] By conservation Wilbur meant wise use, not preservation, and he took the same approach to the

Indian. For all his flirtation with the modish notion of cultural pluralism, he was at bottom an old-fashioned assimilationist: "The reservation develops a sense of retreat and of defeat in the mind of the Indian. . . . The sooner the Indian grasps the fact that his present success means his amalgamation with the general population the better the results are bound to be."[27]

The reformers could only shake their heads. In 1929, Collier wrote, Wilbur and Rhoads stood "on a great divide. They knew the facts and the truth, and proclaimed them. They marked out and publicly espoused a program of general direction and of detail—a program of reorientation, reconstruction, and, for the Indians, salvation."[28] But, knowing what they knew, they chose not to act. Thus the system of 1929 was the system still, and Wilbur and Rhoads were the new Work and Burke. They too would have to go before meaningful change could take place.

After Franklin D. Roosevelt's overwhelming victory at the polls in November 1932, he received an urgent document, signed by more than six hundred educators, social workers, and concerned citizens, drawing his attention to the "extreme, even tragic" situation of the natives. "We do not believe we are exaggerating when we suggest that your administration represents almost a last chance for the Indians."[29] By the time Roosevelt took office in March 1933, 15 million Americans were unemployed and morale was low. But the very desperation of the situation created an opportunity for reform and change that made the previously unthinkable thinkable. On April 20, despite the initial opposition of several senators, John Collier was confirmed without objection as Commissioner of Indian Affairs.

A CLIMATE FOR REFORM: THE 1930s

President Roosevelt's appointment of Collier has often been cited as one of his more courageous. Certainly Collier was a controversial figure. For more than a decade he had badgered the bureau; now he was to head it. He had been the ideal reformer, self-assured, passionately moralistic, intolerant of error or excuse; now he was an administrator, a bureaucrat. At forty-nine, he was to have his chance on the other side of the commissioner's desk. The switch in roles might have chastened someone else, but Collier had faith in his policies and in his own abilities. Indeed, though he would imply that the office sought him out, he in fact campaigned for it, confident that he could handle administrative duties ably. Oliver La Farge, who opposed Collier's nomination because he was appalled by his sanctimonious attacks on others, in time came to regard him as "beyond all comparison the best Commissioner we have ever had."[30] La Farge's judgment has stood up remarkably well.

Collier was the right man in a unique situation. In the 1930s a huge number of dazed Americans were sharing in the predicament of "the other Americans." The poor, chronically unemployed and underfed, and customarily viewed as the losers in a necessary struggle for survival, no longer seemed so reprehensible or so alien. Nor, by the same token, did those minority groups struggling for cultural survival. A sociologist writing in 1932 stated a conclusion that hard times corroborated: "No culture is so perfect that it will not bear improvement by borrowing from almost any other culture."[31] Cultural relativism had been an intellectual abstraction in the 1920s; in the 1930s it took on a simple logic. Collier's views, once so iconoclastic, were now attuned to the mood of mingled hope and despair. "We—I mean our white world in this century—are a shattered race—psychically, religiously, socially and esthetically shattered, dismembered, directionless," he told an audience in 1934. Since civilization had proven itself a failure, he said,

let us examine with a wondering and tender concern, and with some awe, these Indian communities which by virtue of historical accidents and of their own unyielding wills are even today the expressions, even today the harborers, of a great age of integrated, inwardly-seeking life and art. What seed are they keeping, for the soil and climate of a future age of our own which may become a possible soil and climate for them?

"We may," Collier concluded, "be helped through knowing them, and even through trying to help them, in their desperately unequal struggle for continued existence."[32]

The old intellectual fancy that the Indian offered an alternative to America's destructive pioneering heritage had gained topical urgency as winds blew away the soil and turned the interior of the continent into a dust bowl. Disaster forcefully brought home the reality of limits and encouraged a new respect for the native peoples, who, according to informed opinion in the 1930s, had lived in harmony with their environment for perhaps two hundred centuries. As an alternative to the creed of rugged individualism, the Changing Indian was never more compelling nor more relevant.[33]

Back in 1913 a senator from Colorado had baited Gifford Pinchot, the most respected conservationist of his day, with the suggestion that he wanted to "keep everything petrified and stagnant." To Pinchot, the senator sarcastically declared, the American Indian was "the ideal conservationist."[34] By the 1930s the Indian as "the ideal conservationist" seemed infinitely wiser than his civilized counterpart. Nathanael West, in a furious assault on the Horatio Alger success myth, *A Cool Million; or, The Dismantling of Lemuel Pitkin* (1934), conjured up an Indian rebellion led by Harvard-educated Israel Satinpenny, who unleashed his forces on the white world with a soul-stirring speech:

We accepted the white man's civilization, syphilis and the radio, tuberculosis and the cinema. We accepted his civilization because he himself believed in it. But now that he has begun to doubt, why should we continue to accept? His final gift to us is doubt, a soul-corroding doubt. He rotted this land in the name of progress, and now it is he himself who is rotting. The stench of his fear stinks in the nostrils of the great god Manitou.

Americans, Satinpenny continued, had filled up "all the secret places of the earth" with manufactured articles until "even the Grand Canyon will no longer hold razor blades."[35] Two years later, Ernest Thompson Seton, a popular nature writer who had influenced John Collier's thinking, offered his version of "The Redman's Message":

The Civilization of the Whiteman is a failure; it is visibly crumbling around us. It has failed at every crucial test. . . .
Our system has broken down. . . . Wherever pushed to a logical conclusion, it makes one millionaire and a million paupers. . . .
We offer you the Message of the Redman, the Creed of Manhood. We advocate his culture as an improvement on our own, if perchance by belated repentance, remorse, restitution, and justification, we may save ourselves from Divine vengeance and total destruction . . . so

that we may have a chance to begin again with a better, higher thought.[36]

These were, of course, messages for the times. Besides holding up the Indian as a conservationist model, however, they implied that he, in turn, must be conserved.

Conservation was a New Deal code word; to the Department of the Interior it was gospel. It meant saving and restoring the land through that "imaginative and purposeful" planning that Roosevelt had promised the American people.[37] It meant a careful shepherding of precious resources in the public interest, as well as bold programs to reverse the damage already inflicted on the environment. It also meant reclaiming the native cultures—preserving them not merely on paper, but in life. George Catlin's dream of a "magnificent park" where Indians and buffalo might race forever free across the open plains would never be realized. But the government would try to translate the heart of his reverie, the preservation of Indianness within the borders of the United States, into workable policy. Hard times had produced "an atmosphere that tolerated experiments" and the limited cultural relativism necessary to pass what Oliver La Farge called "the most important general piece of Indian legislation since the Allotment Acts," the Indian Reorganization Act of 1934.[38]

RESTORING THE INDIAN DOMAIN

Looking back on the Indian New Deal, John Collier outlined its three main objectives in this order:

Economic rehabilitation of the Indians, principally on the land. Organization of the Indian tribes for managing their own affairs. Civil and cultural freedom and opportunity for the Indians.[39]

Land was foremost. To Indians, it was life itself, Senator William H. King asserted in 1933, and its loss under the allotment policy "a racial catastrophe."[40] King, a Democrat from Utah, became involved in Indian affairs in the early 1920s and later served as one of Collier's mouthpieces in Congress. He harangued his restive colleagues with lengthy speeches (prepared by Collier) on the evils of the Indian

Bureau, and linked the congressional preoccupation with reduction in bureau personnel and expenditures to the spoliation of Indian resources and the exhaustion of tribal funds by a faithless, even callous guardian. The bureau, through its allotment policy, was perpetuating itself at the Indians' expense. Allotment had opened the way for annual raids by the bureau on the tribal funds accrued largely through the sale of "surplus" reservation lands. Thus even as Indian land holdings were shrinking—having been reduced by some 65 percent since 1887—the monies acquired as compensation were being consumed by a voracious bureaucracy. "No system," King fumed in a characteristic speech in 1932, "could be more cynically devised to strip the helpless wards of the Government of their property under the shadowy form of law than the allotment system which Congress and the executive agencies have continued to maintain and enforce through successive decades." King personally worried more about the economic than the social implications of the allotment policy, but he did pause occasionally to warn that "unless fundamental changes are instituted at once, the Indians are a doomed race."[41]

Collier, of course, had been saying this for a decade, and as commissioner he was not about to back down on his contention that the "Carl Schurz dogma" ("the Indian cannot be managed or civilized save by destroying his tribal and community life and wiping out his race memory")[42] was the single greatest misfortune to befall the First Americans. Its principal tool, allotment in severalty, had facilitated Indian spiritual and material decline. The result, Collier wrote in 1934, was poverty bordering on starvation in many areas, a 30 percent illiteracy rate, a death rate twice that of the white population, and the loss of more than 90 million acres of Indian land. But the dispossession of the Indians had always to be understood within the larger policy of "whitening" the red man. "Bewildered, demoralized and discouraged" by what was happening to them, the Indians had not so much changed colors as sunk into a lassitude that matched their impoverishment. What was called for was "an exact reversal of historic Indian policy on every point."[43] Previously, policy had served the white demand for Indian land; now policy would have to serve the Indian demand for land.

Four months after taking office, Collier could report that efforts were under way to preserve the existing Indian land base. Twelve thousand two hundred Indians had been employed by what would become the Civilian Conservation Corps' Indian Division on reservation reclamation projects chosen by the tribes themselves. Before the corps was terminated in 1942, 85,000 Indians had served in it and more than seventy reservations had benefited.[44] Equally imperative was the need to check any further land loss. Collier accomplished this by issuing an order in August 1933 that "no more trust or restricted Indian lands, allotted or inherited, shall be offered for sale, nor certificates of competency, patents in fee, or removal of restrictions be submitted to the Indian Office for approval." In effect, the Dawes Act and its various amendments had been indefinitely suspended. Now the government that had "made the Indian a landless man . . . must restore the land to him," Collier insisted, and he began seeking federal funds to begin the reversal.[45] A bemused critic thought it paradoxical that Collier should demand the restoration of land to the Indians in order to make them self-sufficient at a time when those Indians already on the land—in South Dakota, for instance— were plagued by locusts and drought and dependent on cash doles for survival.[46]

But land was just part of a comprehensive program of revitalization that would serve as the foundation for an Indian New Deal. By February 1934—still less than a year after Collier took office—the necessary legislation was before Congress, and the gauntlet had been flung by a latter-day Helen Hunt Jackson, Robert Gessner, who dedicated his 1931 exposé, *Massacre: A Survey of Today's American Indian*, to "the First Congress that will eradicate what Lincoln seventy years ago called 'an accursed system.'"[47]

INDIAN REORGANIZATION ACT

Forty-eight pages long in its printed version, the Wheeler-Howard Indian Rights bill (named after the chairmen of the Senate and House Indian Affairs Committees, Democrats Burton K. Wheeler of Montana and Edgar Howard of Nebraska) envisioned a sweeping reform in Indian policy. Title

I, "Indian Self-Government," proposed to grant Indians under federal control "the freedom to organize for the purposes of local self-government and economic enterprise, to the end that civil liberty, political responsibility, and economic independence shall be achieved among the Indian peoples." Specifically, the federal government's authority over the reservations was to be phased out and the Indians, on petition by one-fourth of the adults affected, were to receive charters granting them the same governmental powers as incorporated entities. The charters, subject to a three-fifths ratification vote, would define the territorial limits of the Indian community, criteria for membership in it, and the form of government it would adopt. They would also guarantee the civil liberties of member Indians in accordance with the American Constitution and provide for "the gradual elimination of administrative supervision as the Indian community shows progress in the effective utilization of its resources and the prudent disposal of its assets."

The Secretary of the Interior was authorized to grant the chartered Indian communities any of a wide range of options and powers, including the right to organize as federal municipal corporations, to establish community courts, to acquire "the tribal, corporate, or community interests" of individuals who chose to leave, and to veto the assignment of Indian Bureau employees deemed unacceptable. Communities were entitled to a fair measure of control over the expenditure of congressional funds earmarked for their use and complete control over the expenditure of tribal funds. They reserved the right to request the transferral of "any separable function or service" from the federal government to themselves. Most controversially, a chartered community could "regulate the use and disposition of property" by its members, "condemn and take title to any lands or properties" necessary for the purposes authorized by its charter, and "acquire, manage, and dispose of property, subject to applicable laws restricting the alienation of Indian lands and the dissipation of Indian resources." This meant that chartered communities would have enormous discretionary powers over the land within their jurisdiction short of the right to dissipate what must be a perpetual estate. The bill's "home rule" section, however, gave the Secretary of the

Interior and the Commissioner of Indian Affairs a veto power to protect the rights of minorities in the chartered communities and to enforce provisions for the conservation of the communities' resources.

Title II dealt with special educational privileges for Indians and a more Indian-oriented curriculum in the government schools, Title III with the ending of allotment and the conserving and developing of Indian lands as "a permanent basis of self-support" for the tribes, and Title IV with another controversial proposal, the establishment of the Court of Indian Affairs.[48]

The Wheeler-Howard Indian Rights bill was John Collier's brainchild, the purest expression of his reform vision. He tub-thumped for it, holding ten Indian "congresses" between March 2 and April 24 and doing his best to woo the public and the tribes. But the United States Congress was unimpressed, and just a week after the bill was introduced in the House, Collier was forced to issue a defensive "memorandum of explanation." It focused first and most emotionally on Title III, "Indian Lands," and dealt in a summary fashion with the other sections. Over and over Collier was at pains to allay fears aroused by the bill and to correct "persistent misconceptions." The bill would not take land away from individual Indians or affect heirship rights; it was not a scheme to give land to the landless; nor did it introduce "any socialistic or communistic idea or device." It was firmly based on the principle of business incorporation, and was not intended to segregate the Indians from white society or force their return to tribal ways. Finally, Collier assured Congress, the bill did not "arrogate to the Indian Office or to the Interior Department added power."[49]

But these arguments fell on unreceptive ears. The dream of a rejuvenated, autonomous Indian presence in the United States had proven too radical in its pristine form. The ten Indian congresses Collier had convened to demonstrate support for his bill instead demonstrated substantial opposition not just to its particulars but to the philosophical assumptions behind it. Collier's dream, it turned out, was not every Indian's dream, and though the congresses were a testament to his ability to win over hostile crowds through persuasion, sincerity, and sheer force of personality, he could not delude himself or Congress into divining strong grass-roots support for the measure. But Collier shared the reformer's usual blind spot of *knowing* that his program was in the best interests of those it proposed to help, whether they knew it or not. He had never been a man to mince words—one senator described him as "frankness personified."[50] The more adamantly the Indian Rights bill ordered that this or that be done to give the Indian a "New Deal," the more it aroused suspicions that it was a traditional bureau dictate extending controls over every facet of Indian life. It was a long, complicated piece of legislation full of disturbing provisions that could be easily misunderstood.[51]

Collier's denials to the contrary notwithstanding, the Indian Rights bill *did* envision a tribal future for the red man. Still under the spell of the Southwest, Collier assumed that inside every Indian, no matter how assimilated, there lurked a Pueblo waiting to be freed, a communal being eager to shuck off the trappings of individualistic, materialistic white civilization in order to recapture a long-lost communal past. It was the assimilationist's error in reverse. J. C. Morgan, the Navajo leader, and Arthur C. Parker, the Seneca anthropologist, deplored the Indian Rights bill's separatist bias.[52] Naturally, those individuals and groups who were the most assimilated were the most upset. The bill was a "radical, communistic" measure intended to reimpose bureau dictatorship over American Indian citizens, the president of the New York Senecas charged.[53] In the name of a decrepit tribalism, it proposed to strip the individual Indian of his property rights. One organization representing the Five Civilized Tribes fretted over the measure's segregationist implications. Amalgamation was already far advanced in Oklahoma, and white and red got along famously. The Indian Rights bill would only drive a wedge between the races, precipitating a "prejudice which will imperil our social and economic status."[54] The bill, an Oklahoma Cherokee congressman declared, would turn "the hands of Indian civilization back for a century."[55] The metaphor was confused, but its meaning was not. The Wheeler-Howard Indian Rights bill was a retrogressive, coercive, subversive measure designed to wipe out fifty years of Indian progress under the Dawes Act. And its author, John Collier, a native of Georgia, was out to secure a slick, updated form of segregation without removal.

The critics of the Wheeler-Howard bill were disarmed and partially mollified by the bureau's substantially amended draft and the substitute measures eventually hammered out in the Senate and House committees. Collier would always insist that they preserved the "main essentials of the original bill"[56] (about three-fourths, he told one writer),[57] but in fact only Title III came through relatively unscathed. Both Wheeler, who had never been very enthusiastic about Collier's bill, and Howard were quick to dissociate the committee versions from the discredited prototype that bore their names but had originated in the Indian Bureau. Howard, for example, said of the compromise measure that eventually passed Congress, "The original bill would not recognize this as its own child."[58] It was an understandable exaggeration, designed to quiet the controversy whipped up by the first version which had severely qualified the prospects for any reform. President Roosevelt came to the rescue with a strongly worded endorsement of the bill as "a measure of justice that is long overdue." "Indians throughout the country have been stirred to a new hope," he wrote. "They say they stand at the end of the old trail. Certainly the figures of impoverishment and disease point to their impending extinction as a race unless basic changes in their conditions of life are effected."[59] It was a calculated appeal, responsive to the uneasy tradition of the Vanishing American, and in the months that followed it was often cited to maintain the crisis atmosphere that would facilitate passage.

"The continued application of the allotment laws . . . must be terminated," Roosevelt had insisted,[60] and Howard, in defending the first section of the modified House bill prohibiting further allotments, stated flatly that he did not "anticipate any voice will be raised against this provision." Nothing could indicate more clearly how much ideas had changed in a decade. Allotment in severalty, the vital core of Indian policy for almost half a century, now was curtly dismissed as "a costly tragedy both to the Indians and to the Government."[61] Only Clarence C. Dill, a feisty senator from the state of Washington who was not about to concede that the average Indian was the average white man's equal, managed to modify an important provision in the sections of the Senate bill dismantling the allotment policy. The bill had "directed" the Secretary of the Interior to restore to tribal ownership the unsold "surplus" lands on allotted reservations. Now the secretary was merely authorized to restore such lands "if he shall find it to be in the public interest." Senator Dill gave the bill an unintentional compliment when he described it as "the most backward step, so far as the opening of the western country is concerned," that he had faced in his twenty years in government. Wheeler's reply was blunt. The Dawes Act's sponsors "apparently assumed" that after 1887 "no more children would be born to Indians," and thus had made no provision for the land needs of later generations. "As far as I am concerned," the Montana senator stormed, ". . . I do not care if every white man in my State wants to rob the Indians; I am not going to stand on the floor of the Senate and be a party to it."[62] While principle in this instance did not win out, the bill emerged from open debate substantially intact, and was passed on June 12 with only minor amendments.

In the House, Howard took the initiative by outlining in uncompromising terms the record of "ruthless spoliation of defenseless wards" that had followed the passage of the Dawes Act. In 1887, there were fewer than 5,000 landless Indians; in 1934, more than 100,000. Indian trust funds, amounting to $29 million in 1887 and augmented by another $500 million during the intervening years, had shrunk to only $13.5 million by 1934. Far from making the Indians self-supporting citizens, the Dawes Act had made half of them "virtual paupers" living on total family incomes of $48 a year. In 1887, the annual Indian death rate was something like eighteen per thousand; in 1934, twenty-six per thousand—twice that of the general population. But the statistics relating to land loss under allotment were always the most disturbing:

In 1887 our Indian wards numbered 243,000. They owned 137,000,000 acres of land, more than one-third good farming land and a considerable portion of valuable timberlands. Today they number about 200,000. Their land holding has shrunk to a mere 47,000,000 acres.

Of this remnant only 3,500,000 acres may be classed as farming lands, 8,000,000 acres as timberlands of any value, 16,000,000 acres as good grazing lands, and 19,000,000 acres, almost one-half the Indian land remaining, as desert or semiarid lands of limited use or value.[63]

The facts spoke for themselves, providing the single strongest argument for terminating allotment.

Because allotment in severalty had always been a means to assimilate the Indian, its repudiation implied that assimilation would no longer be the major goal of federal Indian policy. Howard admitted as much, noting that the Indian Rights bill would "strike a body blow at the twin evils of economic and social disintegration of the Indians":

[Our] formula for civilizing the Indians has always been the policy of intolerance and suppression combined with a forcible religious and educational proselytism designed to compel the Indian to give up his own beliefs and views of life, his languages and arts and customs, and accept those of the white man.

In permitting and encouraging the destruction of everything that was uniquely Indian, whether art or language or social custom, mythology or religion, or tribal and clan organization, the Government has not only destroyed a heritage that would make a colorful and priceless contribution to our own civilization, but it has hampered and delayed the adaptation of the Indian to white civilization.[64]

Cultural relativism had at last found a place in policy. On June 15 the House passed an amended version of the Senate bill by the comfortable margin of 95 to 30.

Since the House amendment—in effect, everything but the bill's title—was unacceptable to the Senate, the bill went to a committee of conference from which it reemerged in its final form, a melding together of the two versions that changed many particulars but nothing substantial. The Senate gave its consent with minimal comment; the House heard a prepared statement outlining the compromise measure's pertinent features, and after being reassured by Roy Ayers of Montana that little of the original, "vicious" Wheeler-Howard bill had been retained, agreed to the revision.[65]

The Wheeler-Howard Act—variously called the Indian Reorganization Act and the Indian New Deal—stands today as an enormous legislative achievement despite the alterations it underwent during passage. A much simpler measure than that originally proposed, the act consisted of nineteen sections, the first eight of which concerned Indian lands. Allotment in severalty was halted on all reservations, and the trust period was indefinitely extended for allottees who did not already have clear title, though those with holdings on the public domain were exempted from this and other provisions. The Secretary of the Interior was given discretionary power to restore to tribal ownership remaining "surplus" lands on reservations previously opened, as well as to acquire additional territory to augment the Indian land base. Congress agreed to appropriate up to $2 million per year for this purpose.

Although Collier's "Indian Self-Government" scheme was dismantled, parts reappeared. Section 16 provided that any tribe or tribes residing on the same reservation had the right to organize for the common welfare, and could adopt an "appropriate" constitution and bylaws which would become effective when ratified by a majority vote at a special election called by the Secretary of the Interior. The tribal government under its constitution could employ legal counsel with the secretary's approval, and had the power to control land sales and leases and to negotiate with federal, state, and local governments. Too, it would be advised ahead of time of congressional appropriations affecting tribal interests. Under Section 17 the secretary could, upon petition by one-third of the adult Indians, issue a charter of incorporation to a duly constituted tribe which, when ratified by a majority of the adults on the reservation, would entitle it to "own, hold, manage, operate, and dispose of property of every description, real and personal," just as any business corporation could, though the incorporated tribe was not permitted to "sell, mortgage, or lease for a period exceeding ten years any of the land included in the limits of the reservation." Up to $250,000 annually was provided to defray the expense of organizing the Indian chartered corporations and tribal governments, and a $10 million revolving fund was set up from which the secretary could make loans to promote the economic development of the chartered corporations and their individual members.

Other sections gave preference to Indian applicants for positions in the bureau and authorized a substantial sum for loans to Indian students seeking a postprimary education. For the purposes of the Reorganization Act, Indians were defined as all persons of Indian descent who were members of recognized tribes under federal jurisdiction and "all other persons of one-half or more Indian blood." The Oklahoma tribes were specifically exempted from the act's self-government provisions, and, by Section 18, every Indian group was entitled to opt out if it so desired. "This Act," the critical clause read, "shall not apply to any reservation wherein a majority of the adult Indians, voting at a special election duly called by the secretary of the interior, shall vote against its application." The secretary had one year in which to arrange for the elections.[66]

CHOICE AND TRIBALISM

Ironically, the Indian Reorganization Act's most innovative feature—apart from its reversal of the usual pattern of Indian land loss—was not originally John Collier's doing. Collier had always meant to consult with the Indians about his legislative program, and never intended the provisions of the Indian Rights bill to be mandatory; the ten congresses he had assembled to ponder (and, he hoped, approve) the bill were in themselves precedent-setting. But the opt out clause included in the Reorganization Act was the work of the bill's critics. For the first time in the history of federal Indian affairs, the Indians themselves would have "the unusual privilege" of accepting or rejecting a government policy initiative by referendum.[67]

The choice was not coercion-free. Since only incorporated tribes could take advantage of the revolving loan fund, the Indian Rights Association pointed out, there was "pressure upon all Indian groups and individuals to accept the prescribed plan of organization."[68] And Section 18 was interpreted as meaning that a majority of all adult Indians *eligible* to vote— not simply a majority of those who chose to vote—had to reject the act to avoid coming under its provisions.

But Section 18 went far beyond anything offered the Indian

since the abrogation of the treaty system, and certainly beyond anything contained in previous policy statements. The Removal Act of 1830 had included an option provision, but it was an option so loaded against not removing, so coercive in intent and application, that it was no option at all. The General Allotment Act, in turn, unlike the earlier versions of it that Congress had debated in the 1880s, made no concession to Indian wishes. The power of decision-making rested with white officials exclusively. Thomas A. Bland and his National Indian Defense Association had mystified the act's supporters by urging not only that treaties and Indian title be honored, but also that the Indians have the right by vote to reject the allotment policy on their reservation if they opposed it. Such a veto, the Indian Rights Association had replied, would create "an insuperable obstacle" blocking "the Indian's pathway to civilization."[69] The guardian must decide, not the ward. In the Indian Reorganization Act the government had at last abandoned this position and stipulated that Indians be involved in deciding their own future.

Wheeler and Howard both noted that all the objectionable compulsory features of Collier's Indian Rights bill had been eliminated in committee. "In the original bill," Congressman Ayers maintained, "everything was mandatory—the Indian Department could crack its whip . . . and the Indian had to 'root, hog, or die.'" Instead of being a self-government bill, Ayers claimed, "it was the most autocratic, dictatorial program ever heard of." Now, everything was "optional with the Indians."[70]

Collier naturally remained convinced that his bill had been misconstrued and was superior to the watered-down version passed by Congress. Nevertheless, he could only attribute the fact that seventy-eight of the 252 bands and tribes eligible to vote—including, most disappointingly, the Navajos—rejected the Reorganization Act to "energetic campaigns of misrepresentation" and the lack of sufficient time (though the year originally provided was extended to two) in which to fully acquaint the Indians with the benefits they would derive from participation.[71] There were offsetting victories, however. By special acts the "essential principles" of Indian reorganization were extended to the natives of Alaska and Oklahoma in 1936, and eventually 110 tribes completed the process of constitution-making and ratification and eighty-four of them became chartered corporations. But organized opposition persisted through the 1930s and the Reorganization Act experienced an almost immediate backlash, including reduced congressional appropriations and moves in both Houses to repeal it outright. Its enemies never rested, and while Collier was willing to chalk up some criticism to "an apparently incurable confusion of mind," he believed that selfishness and greed accounted for the persistent efforts to derail the Indian Reorganization Act before it had a fair chance to prove itself.[72]

Historians in the last few years have questioned the radical credentials of the Reorganization Act, arguing that it was in many ways a piece of legislation designed to freeze the Indian's situation where it was. While Collier called it a "first step" and one of his opponents called it a "backward step," a recent student has called it "no step at all."[73] But Collier endeavored to make it in fact what it was not on paper, a fulfillment of his original intentions. Consequently, many Indians, stranded between changing official philosophies, were understandably bewildered by the new policy. For, profess as he might that assimilation in the long run was inevitable and only its coerciveness under the Dawes Act objectionable, Collier was vulnerable to the charge leveled by Elaine Goodale Eastman that his objective was "clearly not to assimilate but to perpetuate Indians and Indianism."[74] He was attempting to turn back the tide, the Indian Rights Association maintained, but "whether we wish it to be so or not, whether we encourage or discourage it, the amalgamation of the Indian with the white race in the United States is in process."[75]

Collier's contemporaries, in short, perceived his program as revolutionary, and he chafed under their criticisms not only because they were unfair—after all, the Indian New Deal proposed to *do* something to improve the living conditions of the average Indian in the here and now—but also because they were right. The end goal of his policy was suspect once one looked beyond the notion of preserving Indianness in the present as a basis for future progress. Progress in what direc-

tion? What ultimately was to become of the Indian and, for
that matter, the Indian Bureau? Was the reservation system to
be permanent? Or would the bureau's powers gradually be
transferred to the constituted and chartered Indian bodies?
Either way, in what sense would the Indian assimilate?

The concept of cultural pluralism, of course, answered many
of these questions. It was neither necessary nor desirable that
all Americans be the same. But in practical rather than theoretical terms, cultural pluralism implied differentiation and
segregation, and neither coincided with what most Americans
understood by assimilation. Collier personally had long since
made a commitment to the lasting value of the native cultures
and the importance of a continuing Indian presence in American life. Over and over, then, he was skewered by the simplistic
but effective charge that he was holding the Indians hostage
to the past and forcing them into a "segregated serfdom."[76]
The phrase "red slavery" had returned to haunt the expert
propagandist who coined it, and who now, as commissioner,
was left to dismiss similar slogans as the work of irresponsible
propagandists.[77]

Whatever else is said, the fact remains that Collier *was*
steering Indians toward the kind of reservation retrenchment
that, he believed, could alone preserve their culture and race
through the twentieth century. It is ironic, then, that along the
way he felt compelled to becloud his purpose to the extent that
a policy damned in its time for thwarting Indian assimilation
is today commonly damned by red-power spokesmen as an
insidious "part of a long range plan to terminate indigenous
nations."[78]

Ray Lyman Wilbur, who as Secretary of the Interior had
endured his full share of Collier's barbs, took pleasure in the
Indian New Deal's problems and relished his old critic's dis-
comfiture. "Collier put the Indians back under the blanket—
and then took the blanket away!" he observed with smug
satisfaction in 1947.[79]

But Collier had already framed his rebuttal. His policy was
"to recognize and respect the Indian as he is," he told an
interviewer in 1935. "It is objected that we are proposing to

make a 'blanket Indian' of him again. That is nonsense. But if he happens to be a blanket Indian we think he should not be ashamed of it."[80] The choice must be given Indians, individually and as a group, whether to preserve tribal relations within the relatively secluded reservation setting or to merge with society at large. Since the choice did not exist after 1887, it had been necessary to create through legislation the conditions that would permit it. This was where the Indian Reorganization Act came in. It was an instrument, however clumsy, to facilitate choice. Past policy had adequately provided opportunities for those who chose to assimilate; now provision had to be made for those who wanted to enjoy a "functioning self-government."[81] That was the Reorganization Act's purpose. If it was biased in favor of reservation segregation, so be it; it was not as biased as the Dawes Act had been in forcing assimilation. For Indians who did not like it, there was the opt out clause, and thus a choice. "Perhaps the most drastic innovation of the last two years has been our effort not only to encourage the Indians to think about their own problems but even to induce them to," Collier told his interviewer. "Our design is to plow up the Indian soul, to make the Indian again the master of his own mind. If this fails, everything fails; if it succeeds, we believe the Indian will do the rest."[82]

CHAPTER EIGHTEEN

IT IS ONLY WELL BEGUN:
The New Deal Legacy

"Is the Indian task finished?" John Collier asked an audience in 1939. "Are all the problems of the Indian solved? Very far from it. We have only commenced."[1]

Despite the criticism it generated, Collier's program, with the Indian Reorganization Act at its core, had held up well through the 1930s. But 1941 brought war, and the Indian was shoved far into the background of national concerns. The bureau's quarters in Washington were given over to the war effort, and all but Collier and a few office personnel relocated in Chicago. Reform initiative petered out; consolidation and retrenchment were the order of the day. Collier, however, never relinquished his sense of the Indian's importance: "The sunken stream can flow again, the ravaged desert can bloom, the great past is not killed. The Indian experience tells us this." Even as he found himself vexed by the frustrations of administrative office, his vision of Indianness expanded to encompass the Western Hemisphere and every portion of the globe where men were fighting the good fight against the "totalitarian horror" and colonialism in all its guises.[2] In time Collier came to the conclusion that the Indian with his "passion and reverence for human personality and for the web of life and the earth" was mankind's "*long* hope," indeed his "only long hope." These were convictions that would be best expressed as a private citizen, and with the war all but won, Collier tendered his resignation as Commissioner of Indian Affairs. On March 15, 1945, President Roosevelt accepted it with sincere regret.[3]

322

Collier had been commissioner longer and had left a deeper impression on the office than any other man. His influence on Indian affairs is still being felt. Despite all that has passed since 1934, including an all-out onslaught against tribalism in the 1950s, the President of the United States in 1968 could remark that the Indian Reorganization Act "laid the groundwork for democratic self-government on Indian reservations," and his Secretary of the Interior could give as "the whole philosophy" behind his Indian policy the New Deal principle that "in a diverse society such as ours, the Indian ought to have a choice."[4]

This was the spiritual legacy from the 1930s. But the Indian New Deal also essayed solutions to a succession of problems that preoccupied officials at the time, and continue to preoccupy them today. A review of the New Deal record in the areas of education, religious and cultural liberty, social science principles in administration, Indian law, land claims, reservation conservation, and political rights thus offers a selective but revealing introduction to contemporary Indian affairs.

INDIAN EDUCATION

With the publication of the Meriam Report in 1928, a thoroughgoing reform of Indian education, particularly the-boarding-school system, became mandatory. The Rhoads-Scattergood administration made its greatest progress in the area of education; the Collier administration, with its more radical philosophy buoyed up by the flow of New Deal money, then accelerated change. If Indians were to have a meaningful New Deal in their homeland and take advantage of the choices offered by the Reorganization Act, it was essential that they be equipped with a modern education.

W. Carson Ryan, a prominent educator and the major contributor to the Meriam Report's education section, became Director of Indian Education in August 1930. So high was the esteem in which reformers held him that he weathered the criticism directed at the Rhoads-Scattergood administration to continue on in office under Collier until 1935. Ryan's program was predicated on the development of a community-based on-reservation school system, a formal liaison between federal and state governments to permit Indian students to attend the public schools, and the gradual phasing out of the boarding schools as well as the improvement of those still in service. It was Collier's particular hope that day schools would multiply and become "real centers for Indian community life" involving adults as well as children.[5] (The practical difficulties of such an innovative approach were apparent on the Navajo reservation, where the forty-one new day schools failed to serve the needs of a mobile population scattered over a vast area.) The educational goals posited by Ryan were also pursued by his successor, Willard Beatty, who served as director until 1952. Both Ryan and Beatty were progressive educators, and the philosophical continuity in their leadership over twenty-two years brought improvements in Indian education ranging from a more humanistic and personalized curriculum to an overall upgrading in faculty and facilities.[6]

The 1930s, in particular, were a time of dynamic change. The vexing boarding school question made for good publicity as bureau spokesmen cited statistics proving that closures were at last eradicating not just an antiquated educational system, but the crash assimilation ideology it had served since the 1870s. Assimilation was not entirely disavowed; but it would have to occur slowly, through normalized contact. Under the Johnson-O'Malley Act, passed in 1934, the Indian Bureau could contract with individual states for the education of Indian children in the public schools. This seemed a hopeful new direction, but Beatty became increasingly convinced that the states took the federal money without providing the same creative approach to the special needs of Indian pupils that the reformed government schools were offering. Staff in the state schools was often inferior, and the learning of English actually retarded. As time passed, Beatty developed a real fondness for the much-maligned boarding schools, pointing out that with new facilities and a new administrative outlook they were, for children from deprived families, "a haven of affection and security" and "a home away from home."[7]

A study that appeared the year after Collier left office concluded that substantial progress had been made in Indian education. In 1928, only 8 percent of the children were at or ahead of grade, and 27 percent were more than five years behind; by 1946, 38 percent of the children were at or above grade, and only 4 percent were more than five years behind. Indian students were going on to college in unprecedented numbers.[8] Obviously, there was still much room for improvement, but in 1946 the momentum for that improvement appeared irresistible.

Education in the past had been a tool for assimilation; Collier wanted it made over into a tool for cultural revitalization. Instead of effacing native culture, schools could encourage it. In the original Indian Rights bill, a section under "Special Education for Indians" declared it "to be the purpose and policy of Congress to promote the study of Indian civilization and preserve and develop the special cultural contributions and achievements of such civilization, including Indian arts, crafts, skills, and traditions."[9] While this provision fell by the wayside, its spirit permeated the New Deal as the rhetoric of cultural pluralism was turned into policy.

RELIGIOUS AND CULTURAL RIGHTS

A veteran fighter for Indian religious freedom, Collier as commissioner was naturally committed to a policy of ending "the political identification of the mission bodies with the Indian Bureau."[10] Accordingly, in January 1934, he issued a circular forbidding interference with native religious and ceremonial activities. He remained steadfast in his conviction that Indian worship should be protected. "The prayer of the Navajos is as sweet and fine as anything in the Bible," he remarked in 1935.[11] But the religious freedom issue was complex. What if it was Indian discriminating against Indian, a religious minority being persecuted by the tribal majority? Should this be tolerated? The Native American Church, with its controversial peyote ritual, was a case in point, and Collier vacillated. On the theory that "Indian tribes ought to be permitted to make their own mistakes," he allowed the Navajo tribal council to prohibit the peyote ceremonies, but reversed his position when it came to the Taos Pueblos.[12]

Back in the 1920s the assimilationists had presented an easy target. Their argument that the real religious liberty issue on the reservations was the right of Christian Indians to worship without tribal interference smacked of sophistry, given the blatant oppression of native dances and ceremonials by white officials. The situation then seemed clear-cut, and the champions of native rights had no trouble choosing sides: the tribe or community should be free to guide the religious life of its members. But the peyote question was something else. A 1965 study sponsored by the Board of National Missions of the United Presbyterian Church concluded that since the 1930s there had been "little interference with Indian faiths" except where the Native American Church was concerned. Moreover, it was not the missionary bodies or the federal and state governments that were leading the attack on peyote and thus on the church members' constitutional right to worship freely. It was the tribal governments that were the intolerant defenders of religious orthodoxy—and it was a Presbyterian missionary body that had singled out the peyote controversy as "the major civil rights problem" in the area of Indian religious freedom.[13]

Collier's January 1934 circular on the native religions also forbade the repression of Indian languages in the schools, a government policy since the 1880s. "Anything less than to let Indian culture live on would be a crime against the earth itself," Collier maintained,[14] and as part of its program of cultural revitalization the bureau undertook not only to permit but to actively encourage Indian arts and crafts.

Through the 1920s the promotion of native arts had been an effective means of arousing interest in the Indian cause and enlisting support for the reform movement. The result was an "almost bewildering efflorescence" of native creativity that helped restore racial pride while supplementing the meager earnings possible on the reservation.[15] With the creation of the Indian Arts and Crafts Board in 1935, the government formally involved itself in the problems of production and marketing, variant quality, and regulation of the "spurious imitations" that were flooding the market for genuine Indian handicrafts: Navajo rugs and jewelry, Pueblo pottery, Pima and Apache basketry, and plains Indian leather goods and beadwork, ranging in artistic merit from collector's items to tourist curios.[16] Painting in watercolors and oils was a new art form that appealed to Indians and white patrons alike. It flourished among the Kiowas and Pueblos, and eventually found a place in the school curriculum, proving that the ancient and the modern could mesh to the mutual benefit of red and white. Indian art, Mary Austin observed, has the "power to make of the world a more spacious place in which to live. By its vitality, its effect of consistent change, like the subtle alterations of a growing plant, the art of the Indian links the observer with a past and a future in true genetic relationships."[17]

Like other New Deal initiatives, the Indian arts and crafts revival suffered a decline through the 1950s, then experienced a resurgence in the next decade. A 1962 estimate reported that between $7 and $8 million worth of Navajo handicrafts were sold out of Gallup, New Mexico, each year—up from an estimated $80,000 in sales in 1939–1940. As for less tangible considerations, the Commission on the Rights, Liberties, and Responsibilities of the American Indian reported in 1966 that Indian arts and crafts provided "a cultural anchor for the tribesmen," a more sensitive appreciation of Indian history for the white man, and "a genuine aesthetic contribution to our civilization."[18]

APPLIED ANTHROPOLOGY AND INDIAN POLICY

The Meriam Report was a model of what could be done by drawing on the expertise of trained social scientists. Collier's social-work background and deep respect for the ideas of Lester Frank Ward had convinced him that "in the ethnic field research can be made a tool of action essential to all the other tools, indeed, that it ought to be the master tool,"[19] and he believed that anthropologists should be invited to play a continuing role in policy formulation and implementation.

At a meeting of the American Association for the Advancement of Science in Pittsburgh in 1934, the Indian Bureau won a pledge of support from the assembled scholars. Discussion centered on how anthropologists could facilitate the work of organizing and chartering Indian communities with a minimum of damage to traditional life ways. The prospect of an ongoing role for anthropology in the training of Indian Service personnel generated enthusiasm, and it was proposed that a census of interested anthropologists be compiled that would list areas of expertise and expedite the process of getting the right person for the right job. It was further suggested that a consulting anthropologist be assigned to the Indian Bureau staff with the responsibility of coordinating anthropological research for the government.[20]

In the past, Collier's faith in anthropology as part of an applied science of Indian affairs had been sorely tested. Only Alfred Kroeber, Robert Lowie, and a few others had willingly supported the Indian Reporganization Act. Franz Boas, having abandoned his canon of scientific detachment to oppose Collier's nomination as commissioner, had since stayed aloof from policy debate. Eventually he, along with a dozen other prominent anthropologists, endorsed the Indian New Deal. But Collier thereafter was insistent that the purposes and "various implementations" of his program were not their work, despite opinion to the contrary.[21]

The problem, as Collier saw it, was that American anthropologists were still burdened by a belief in the Vanishing American.[22] They were committed to the study of "pure" aboriginal societies to the exclusion of partially integrated— or, in their view, disintegrated—groups. Though cultural relativism had effected a theoretical revolution, American anthropology's objectives were not generally reoriented until the early 1930s, when the study of the acculturation process among peoples "whose modes of life are undergoing, or have undergone, extensive change as a result of ascertainable historic contacts with alien cultures" became an "outstanding development" in the science of man.[23] A Boas student like Margaret Mead, accustomed to field work among the relatively untainted societies of Melanesia, despaired of studying the Omaha of Nebraska, whose culture she perceived to be a devastated ruin devoid of ethnological interest.[24] But Mead's monograph on the Omaha, *The Changing Culture of an Indian Tribe* (1932), proved of practical value despite her pessimism, since its analysis of the cultural wreckage caused by allotment convincingly documented the case for intelligent reform.

If reservations could no longer be seen as temporary havens of vanishing aboriginal cultures, they could be seen as living social-science laboratories, of as much interest to the student of the acculturation process as a newly discovered tribe would be to the ethnographer of olden times. Because anthropology had updated its interests, Collier was prepared to enter into a partnership that would strive to accommodate federal policy to existing Indian cultures rather than bureaucratic convenience.

The heady enthusiasm whipped up in Pittsburgh in 1934 led the following year to the establishment of the Applied Anthropology Unit, which operated in the Indian Bureau until budgetary considerations (and colliding scientific and administrative values) closed it down in 1937. The unit's "most important single task," field workers were told, was to study the social structure of the tribes and communities that chose to take advantage of the Reorganization Act "so that the constitutions drawn up will be based on the actual social life of the group."[25]

Looking back in 1944 on his experiences as second director of the Applied Anthropology Unit, Scudder Mekeel had a number of criticisms to make. The process of drawing up tribal constitutions had been much too hurried, he pointed out, and in many instances a document had been adopted that actually clashed with the group's social and economic value system. In some cases the Reorganization Act's elective features had undermined the tribe's political structure by ousting established leaders, depreciating the wisdom of elders, and exacerbating divisions along the lines of age (old versus young), purity of blood (full versus mixed), and education. In-service training was still needed to acquaint old-line bureau employees and new personnel with the cultural traditions of the people with whom they were working. These and other problems suggested to Mekeel that the time had come for a thorough, objective evaluation of the Indian Reorganization Act's "social and economic effects on the various American Indian societies."[26]

Collier, in reply, concurred with the last recommendation, but pointed out that Mekeel's appraisal was badly out of date. The termination of the Applied Anthropology Unit had in no way ended anthropological involvement in government policy, and since 1940 specialists had been making an "exhaustive and even profound review" of how the Indian New Deal was functioning in practice.[27]

There would be no retreat from the ideal of a scientific management of Indian affairs. A 1941 conference sponsored by the American Association on Indian Affairs made this abundantly clear. Designed to bring a wide range of expertise to bear on the Indian's situation, the symposium attracted administrators and academics from several disciplines. Working in conjunction, it was hoped, they could shed light on "a problem of applied science."[28] This interdisciplinary approach to Indian affairs represented what Collier would call the second epoch in the partnership between anthropology and the New Deal. Initially, anthropologists had been assigned to specific research projects with narrowly defined objectives—a written form for the Navajo language or organizational studies preparatory to the adoption of tribal constitutions, for example. Such piecework reflected the assumption that a people's culture consisted of interrelated but essentially discrete components that could be isolated and "fixed" without reference to the whole.

By 1941 the government had shifted its philosophy. The Indian groups were organic units, and anthropological techniques would have to respect this fact. Every culture constituted a functioning whole, and all the parts were subordinate to its total pattern or configuration. If the pattern were correctly apprehended, then policy objectives could be shaped to harmonize with the intrinsic character of the whole society. The new ideal, then, was a thorough, interdisciplinary study of each tribal group as a sociocultural unit.

In 1941 Collier helped launch the immensely ambitious Indian Education Project set up to study personality development among Indian children and the implications for bureau administration. Things were kept manageable by limiting the project to the Hopi, Navajo, Zuñi, Papago, and Sioux. Anthropologists, physicians, educators, psychologists, economists, sociologists, psychiatrists, and agronomists formed research teams, met in seminars with the bureau personnel and the Indians concerned, and interpreted the data as it accumulated in light of practical applications. An overriding consideration was how the bureau "should and could adjust" to meet the Indians' needs.[29]

It was a promising start, aborted by Collier's departure from the bureau in 1945. His successors were not about to continue an apparently interminable project which, were its findings ever implemented, would shatter the centralized, even monolithic management of Indian affairs and plunge them into an administrative morass. Moreover, the Hopi study had produced harsh words on the federal government's performance, and the post-Collier bureau was not prepared to bankroll criticism. Cut free from government participation in 1947, the project yielded up its monographs and faded out as a potentially dynamic experiment in applied social science.[30]

Many of the uses to which anthropologists were put in the New Deal's first epoch subsequently appeared unwise or ineffective—Collier could cite the attempt to advise the Hopi on drafting a constitution, and the study done by Scudder Mekeel among the Pine Ridge Sioux. In turn, the comprehensive interdisciplinary research projects of the second epoch were "stopped dead in their tracks" as *applied* science once Collier left office.[31] Anthropologists did contribute extensively to the in-service training of bureau teachers, and thus to the advances made in Indian education in this period. The study of anthropology was affected, too. Clyde Kluckhohn, for one, found that his collaboration with the bureau clarified his understanding of covert and overt culture and the corresponding distinction between a culture's configuration and its pattern.[32]

Covert culture, in particular, was a deceptive factor in evaluating the extent of Indian acculturation and, for that matter, in dealing with Indians on a day-to-day basis. "Out of the investigations have emerged a field theory of culture and a crossdiscipline methodology for the multidimensional study of the acculturation process, not only in its technological and sociological manifestations, but also at the psychological and symbolic levels," the Indian Education Project's coordinator wrote in 1950.[33] But, to the question raised by Collier in his foreword to the project's first published report—"Will we administrators, who include all the field forces of Indian

Service, use the light?"[34]—the answer in the years that followed would have to be an almost unqualified no.

INDIAN LAW AND LAND CLAIMS

In one area where expertise was sorely needed—that of Indian law, especially law relating to land title— the New Deal scored a solid victory. Others before Collier, including Francis Leupp, had urged the establishment of an Indian claims commission to adjudicate land disputes. Title IV of the original Wheeler-Howard bill provided for the creation of the Court of Indian Affairs with jurisdiction over land claims, and between 1934 and 1945 at least eighteen bills were introduced in Congress proposing to settle the Indian claims. One after another they fell victim to the visions of untold billions in future settlements that danced, not entirely without justification, in congressmen's heads. But there was a first, economical step that could be taken: the codification of Indian law.

"Based upon more than 4,000 treaties and statutes and upon thousands of judicial decisions and administrative rulings,"[35] Indian law was the despair of Indians, administrators, and lawyers alike. In 1942, under the direction of a gifted lawyer in the Interior Department, Felix S. Cohen, the first *Handbook of Federal Indian Law* was published. An oversized volume suffused with the New Deal philosophy, its purpose, according to the Secretary of the Interior, was to "give to Indians useful weapons in the continual struggle that every minority must wage to maintain its liberty," and it admirably fulfilled its author's commitment to legal functionalism—the belief, as he put it, "that understanding of the law, in Indian fields as elsewhere, requires more than textual exegesis, requires appreciation of history and understanding of economic, political, social, and moral problems."[36] Cohen considered the *Handbook* to be a product of the American mind in the 1930s, a piece of practical scholarship, and it proved exactly that.

With the creation of the Indian Claims Commission in 1946, the year after Collier left office, several anthropologists and ethnohistorians became applied scientists of necessity, as expert witnesses for both the government and the tribes in the litigation over land title that continues to this day. The *Handbook* had brought order and a crusading fervor to Indian law; it was a device begging to be used. The Claims Commission promised the settlement of long-standing Indian grievances, especially those relating to land claims based on everything from specific treaty to aboriginal title. The act establishing the commission allowed five years from passage for all claims to be filed, and was due to expire in 1956. The termination date was extended four times, to 1978, when the period allotted proved insufficient to handle the 852 claims filed.

The *Handbook* had opened up a Pandora's box as far as officials in the 1950s were concerned. When it was reissued in a new edition in 1958, stripped of its New Deal embellishments and substantially gutted, the rule was advanced that "legal answers to questions of Federal Indian law will be found predominantly in the latest statutory law and judicial determination of justiciable issues." In addition, the hope was expressed that the new edition would foreclose "further uncritical use of the earlier edition by judges, lawyers, and laymen."[37] Given the explicit purpose behind Cohen's *Handbook*, this could only be regarded as a tribute to its success.

RESERVATION CONSERVATION AND LIVESTOCK REDUCTION

Land was "the most critical substantive problem of the Indian New Deal," according to John Collier.[38] Without an adequate land base there could be no tribal future. Indian land claims settlements had an incalculable potential, but there was a need for immediate action. Ending the allotment policy turned out to be easy enough. Harder by far was the job of conserving what remained of the Indian domain and actually augmenting it to accommodate a growing population. In the first instance, the Indians themselves were sometimes at odds with the government; in the second, treasury watchdogs in Congress and local white populations usually opposed reservation expansion.

The reduction of Navajo livestock holdings, the single most traumatic conservation issue of the Collier years, boiled down to a matter of priorities and pitted scientific expertise against tribal wisdom. From the perspective of the administrator the problem was simple: the Navajos owned far more animals than their land base could support. For years the government had urged a pastoral economy on them, and for years their reservation had been badly overgrazed. From its creation in 1868 it was too small, although additions tripled its size from 4 to more than 12 million acres by 1911. In the same period the Navajo population grew from 8,000 to 30,000. While the land base remained virtually constant through the 1920s, the population continued its rapid increase. By 1933 there were more than 45,000 Navajos living on a reservation that, according to scientific calculations, should sustain 1.3 million sheep units but whose capacity, with the wind and rain erosion concomitant to overgrazing, had fallen to under 600,000 sheep units. Moreover, the Navajo livestock holdings were sharply increasing in the face of a declining market that would normally have absorbed some of the surplus. Ecologically speaking, the reservation was swarming, with 1,152,000 sheep and goats and another 50,000 horses and cattle (equivalent to 200,000 sheep units). Efforts had been made to curtail the number of animals, particularly the number of horses, but by 1933 the situation had reached crisis proportions. Drastic reductions of more than 50 percent of all Navajo livestock were mandatory if what was still usable of the inadequate range were to be saved.[39]

Collier and other bureau officials first presented these "implacable facts" to the Navajo tribal council in July 1933, thereby initiating what Collier later described as "a social, economic and political struggle and effort well-nigh as intense and as dubious of outcome as any to be witnessed among men."[40] After much persuasion and no little arm-twisting, the tribal council, created at the government's behest in 1923, relented and agreed to back the stock reduction program. Over the next decade it persevered in an immensely unpopular policy that deprived its people of "meat, milk, wool and transportation" and struck at the heart of cherished Navajo values ranging from family tradition to the individual's sense of self-worth.[41]

Stock reduction was a bitter experience. The Navajos were forced to stand by and watch their sheep and goats sold off or, in an incident that entrenched itself in tribal lore, slaughtered by sometimes callous officials. A few who resisted an order to reduce their horse herds were jailed. The mood was ugly, and violence threatened. The Indian Rights Association branded John Collier a "dictator"[42] and accused him of conducting "a near reign of terror" on the Navajo reservation.[43] He became an object of "burning hatred"[44] among the very people whose problems so preoccupied him that one plains Indian sarcastically suggested that the bureau he headed be renamed the Bureau of Navajo Affairs.[45]

Collier never retreated from the position that "exigent overall requirements" had to take precedence over Navajo wishes on the matter of stock reduction.[46] His only regret was that the attempt to win the Navajo people over to the program had been bungled by the bureaucracies involved—the Indian Bureau, the Soil Conservation Service, and the tribal council. Because it was a centralized body like itself, the bureau preferred to operate through the tribal council, and had ignored the two hundred "local land-use, mutual-aid, man-and-woman guided community groups" that were the real seats of Navajo life and decision-making.[47] Perhaps, as one historian has argued, this failure was symptomatic of a basic fault in the Indian New Deal, an obsession with restoring tribalism at the expense of the kind of community organization that might have aroused broad-based, grass-roots support for Indian self-determination.[48]

If most historians have accepted the necessity of the stock reduction program while challenging the way in which it was administered, the Navajos have shown no such equanimity. "Regardless of the need for the action, fundamental human rights were violated in the rush to reduce the livestock," a recent tribal history contends. "The Navajos have not forgotten the experience!"[49]

The Navajo livestock reduction program was a low spot in the Indian New Deal. It permanently alienated the commissioner and the largest Indian nation in the country. It showed Collier to be capable of the same high-handed paternalism he had deplored in his predecessors, and partially vindicated D. H. Lawrence's savage judgment that it was "his saviour's will to set the claws of his own White egoistic *benevolent* volition" into the Indians.[50] But also it showed the Navajos to be something less than the selfless conservationists of sentimental tradition. In the long run, stock reduction had some beneficial side effects. It united the Navajos as never before behind their tribal council and stiffened their resolve to act independently of the bureau. And it improved the quality of the Navajo stock, with the result that fewer sheep produced more and better wool.

In contrast to the livestock reduction program, the bureau's efforts at land acquisition were commended even by the critical Indian Rights Association.[51] After eight years in office, Collier claimed that almost 4 million acres had been added to the tribal estates.[52] Then funds dried up as the acquisition program fell victim to a more cautious administrative perspective on New Deal expenditures, a declining enthusiasm for the collectivist experiments of the early 1930s, the opposition of western representatives on the House appropriations committees, and flaws in the Reorganization Act itself. Only the tribal funds were left available for land purchase, and these were woefully inadequate to the task. The bureau estimated that a minimum of $60 million was needed for land acquisitions to bring the Indians up to a subsistence level and another $70 million to achieve an acceptable standard of living. All told, Congress appropriated only $5,075,000 for land purchase before World War II brought an end to further expenditures.[53]

THE TERMINATIONIST CHALLENGE TO
SELF-DETERMINATION

In the postwar period, during the Red scare that brought Senator Joseph McCarthy to power, the Indian policy shaped in the 1930s was nearly reversed. The appointment of Dillon S. Myer as Commissioner of Indian Affairs in May 1950 set the rollback into motion. To his critics, Myer was upright and sincere, but a cold, efficient automaton keen for power. He had come into prominence as director of the War Relocation Authority, which was responsible for the removal from the West Coast and internment inland of Japanese-Americans during World War II. In his official capacity he had taken a bleak view of the possibilities for humanizing the detention centers, looking to their termination at war's end as the best means of alleviating a disagreeable necessity.

Myer had carried this viewpoint over into Indian affairs, and was convinced that the reservations were concentration camps because he administered them, as he had the Japanese internment centers, as though they were. Thus the Indians had to be "freed" from the prisons Myer erected around them in his mind. This scenario, constructed and popularized by John Collier,[54] who had crossed swords with Myer in the early 1940s when the Indian Bureau was briefly involved in administering the Japanese internment camp at Poston, Arizona, was overdrawn, but it contained a kernel of truth, as the record of erosion of Indian rights under Myer confirmed. Harold Ickes, doubtless feeling responsible for having brought Myer into the Interior Department and recommending him for commissioner, castigated his former protégé as "a blundering and dictatorial tin-Hitler." He had surrounded himself with "underling third-raters," Ickes charged, and had set out to make the bureau "a puppet show, with him pulling the strings."[55] But Myer's managerial approach to Indian affairs, unrelieved by idealism or any special affection for Indians, was in tune with the times, and set the tempo for policy developments in the early 1950s.

Congress was receptive to the Myer philosophy. Espousing a motive as laudable as it was illusive—to free the Indians from bureau paternalism and make them equal citizens of the United States—both Houses flirted with measures that would have repealed the Indian Reorganization Act outright before settling in 1953 on a remarkable concurrent resolution. Back in 1924, Collier had warned that "all our national crimes toward . . . [the] tribes were sanctioned in our own thinking by the fact that we were going to make these Indians 'free.'"[56] Nearly thirty years later, in the name of emancipating the Indians by ending their status as wards and granting them "the rights and prerogatives" of citizenship, Congress proposed, "as rapidly as possible," to free "from Federal supervision and control and from all disabilities and limitations specially applicable to Indians" five tribes (the Flathead, Menominee, Klamath, Potawatomie, and Chippewa) as well as all the Indian bands located in California, Florida, New York, and Texas, and to terminate the regional offices of the Bureau of Indian Affairs in these states.[57]

Termination, as the program came to be known, had a long history. Almost from the moment the bureau was formally organized in 1834, Congress periodically set out to close it. At some point, the reasoning went, drawing freely on the tradition of the Vanishing American, the Indian problem would be solved and the government's responsibilities would end. Termination also fed on the fact that everyone loved to hate the bureau—the Indians themselves, as well as their white friends and foes.

Phasing out the bureau and turning whatever services remained to be performed over to state and local authorities was one of the few consistent ends of Indian policy. For example, the impetus of the Meriam Report had been to encourage a wide range of expertise in Indian affairs at the expense of centralized bureau control. Collier was in wholehearted agreement. His administration had sought to encourage a natural termination by having the organized tribes take over certain governmental functions as soon as they felt able. Gradualism had been the keynote. The Indian Claims Commission, with its mandate to settle outstanding claims against the government, implied eventual termination of the Indian-government relationship; certainly many congressmen interpreted it that way. Similarly, when the Public Health Service, which had been active in the campaign to improve the deplorable state of Indian health since the 1920s, assumed total jurisdiction in this area in 1955, no one seemed upset.

Other forms of termination, however, aroused immediate opposition. Without Indian consent, Congress in 1953 granted the states the right to assume civil and criminal jurisdiction over the Indian reservations, an action that violated the integrity of Indian country, raised shades of the Georgia-Cherokee controversy of the 1820s, and exposed the overall shape of Indian policy as it was emerging in the 1950s.

Termination under President Eisenhower meant the end of the Bureau of Indian Affairs, the reservations, and Indian distinctiveness. In conjunction with a "relocation" program intended to get the Indians off the reservations and into jobs in the cities, it meant the ultimate integration of the tribes into white society. Most of all, termination meant a direct repudiation of the New Deal's reservation-based program of tribal revitalization and the principle of choice.

The reaction to the 1953 House Concurrent Resolution and the termination bills that followed built up slowly and then began to snowball. Predictably, old New Dealers like Collier and, in his independent way, Oliver La Farge were on hand with their denunciations. Felix Cohen, who died in 1953, left as a legal weapon in this latest struggle for Indian rights the argument that schemes to liberate Indian wards and make them citizens were based on a semantic fallacy. The Indians *were* citizens and, moreover, were not, nor ever had been, wards in the strict sense of that term. The government was their trustee, not their guardian. "Guardianship is a relation that limits the personal rights of a ward," Cohen explained. "Trusteeship is a relation that limits the property rights of a trustee and makes the trustee the servant of the trust beneficiary."[58] The Concurrent Resolution's rhetorical bombast could not conceal its true intention. As Cohen had earlier observed:

Governmental taking of land from white men is called "expropriation"; taking of land from Indians is called "freeing the Indian from the reservation" or "abolishing the reservation system." If a government repudiates its obligations to a white man we speak of "governmental bankruptcy"; if a government repudiates its obligations to an Indian, this is commonly referred to as "emancipating the Indian."[59]

Indian rights groups and Christian bodies also decried the haste with which termination was being pushed ahead, though the General Board of the National Council of Churches saw no need to insist on the principle of Indian consent, urging only "consultation" as a moral responsibility on the government's part.[60] Some critics detected in termination and relocation a covert land grab by the same western interests that had so profitably backed the allotment policy in 1887. Politicized by their New Deal involvements and the vogue of applied science, anthropologists also rallied to the defense of the Indians' right to self-determination, becoming for the first time an active voice in policy debate.

There was an accompanying flurry of public interest in the Indian. The guest editors of a special "Indian affairs" issue of one prestigious journal were led to remark in 1957 that "white Americans seem continually to be rediscovering the Indians."[61] A repentant Hollywood, vilified for propounding the "bloody savage" image in countless westerns, reeled out a string of sympathetic movies with the unvarying message that historic Indian-white conflicts were the result neither of red savagery nor white ill will, but rather of the activities of a handful of heartless whiskey traders, mercenary gunrunners, glory-hunting army officers, corrupt Indian agents, and malfeasant politicians—all white men, but representative of private vices, not public ones.

The Indians themselves, somewhat fatalistic about their chances of influencing decision-making where white interests were at stake, had acquired enough organizational and lobbying skill in two decades to mount a stiff resistance to termination. The National Congress of American Indians, established in 1944 and representing more than one-third of the nation's tribes, called for a unified stand in "this emergency"[62] and in 1955 issued the Indian Nine Point Program, which restated many New Deal precepts and underlined the necessity of preserving the reservations and protecting the Indian domain. A joint letter from several native groups flatly asserted that "the reservation land base . . . is vital to the future of our people,"[63] and the National Congress consistently fought for this position throughout the 1950s. Nor were Indian leaders about to stand by and let the Bureau of Indian Affairs be dismantled by congressional fiat. For though it was a favorite scapegoat, the bureau was also, paradoxically, a guarantor of tribal and cultural survival. It was the administrative embodiment of the Indian's special status and of those legal rights, based not on kindness or generosity but binding agreements made in exchange for land, that constituted an enduring claim on the American conscience.

The issue underlying the entire termination controversy was whether or not the government should continue to offer the Indians the New Deal option of living in distinct communities on their reservations. That the question of assimilation should recur was not surprising; that it should recur so soon and in such a reactionary form was surprising. Senator Arthur V. Watkins, a Utah Republican and one of the prime movers behind termination, in 1948 opposed any attempt to educate Navajo children in their own language. They needed to be with white children in order to prepare for a future away from the reservation. Representative Wesley D'Ewart of Montana, another prominent terminationist, agreed, adding that it was best to "break the ties" while Indian children were young in order to "get them assimilated with the white race."[64] Commissioner Myer also rejected cultural pluralism and the Indian right to remain different. Speaking of the natives of South Dakota, he said in 1951 that they were "at a point where they should be mingling more and more with the non-Indian population instead of living as a tight, close-knit group within the mental and physical confines of the reservation."[65]

When Collier charged that Myer was ignoring the bilateral decision-making process in his drive "to atomize and suffocate the group life of the tribes,"[66] it must have seemed to him as though the previous thirty years had never happened, as though Secretary Fall and Commissioner Burke were still in power and the "sentimental reformers" were just starting out to win recognition for Indian rights.

Of course, things had changed. A conference of anthropologists meeting in Chicago in 1954 concluded that predictions about the inevitability of Indian assimilation were "unwarranted" and that the Indian groups would survive, adjusting, adapting, but never disappearing.[67] There would be no "last of the Mohicans or anything like that," one of their number observed in a public radio broadcast.[68] By extension, termination was based on a false premise, a point that anthropologist Edward Spicer made when he noted that the operative assumption in Indian policy had always been not so much that assimilation was inevitable as that it was *desirable*. It was this assumption that needed to be "publicly argued, so that its inconsistency with other basic American assumptions, such as freedom of religion, would become clear and explicit in public policy."[69]

Opinion had turned against cultural pluralism in the 1950s,

and termination was a symptom of that fact. Collier, reacting to the "one-hundred per cent Americanism" of the right, deplored the belief that "human, social, and ethnic 'different-ness'—anything that holds itself out from the fiction of the American melting-pot—is anti-American, un-Christian, out-moded, and perhaps disloyal or barbarous."[70] But equally inimical to pluralism in the 1950s was a crusading liberalism determined to abolish what it regarded as artificial barriers blocking the way to a fully integrated society. Assimilation had reappeared under a new name. Integration meant an end to the Indian's separate community existence. It meant desegre-gation without the legalistic connotations of that term when applied, as it usually was, to the black civil rights movement in the South. What was clear was that segregation was "wrong," even for a people who might *choose* to be segregated. The right to a unique cultural destiny was decidedly secondary to what one anthropologist called "the sad truth that anything that serves to perpetuate the Indians' distinctiveness from the rest of the American community may serve also to perpetuate their second-class status in that community." From the liberal per-spective, "the struggle for American Indians should no longer be concentrated on an impractical enclave or ghetto survival."[71]

The 1960s brought their own rebuttal as the civil rights movement was complicated by the struggle for black power and by a racial consciousness, particularly among college youth, that seemed to reject the white cultural mainstream. Those Indians still resisting the latest pressures to integrate them suddenly found themselves joined by a rainbow spectrum of ethnic groups who claimed they were proud to be different. Termination had fizzled out as a major program by 1960, but not before two tribes were terminated—the Menominee and the Klamath—and not before many Indians had become suspicious enough of government intentions to jealously guard their rights in the future.

President Eisenhower's successors pledged themselves to a reactivated New Deal rooted in freedom of choice and the notion of a partnership between the Indians and the govern-ment. "I propose a new goal for our Indian programs," Lyndon Johnson declared in 1968, "a goal that ends the old debate

about 'termination' of Indian programs and stresses self-determination; a goal that erases old attitudes of paternalism and
promotes partnership self-help."[72] Two years later Richard
Nixon pronounced forced termination "wrong" and promised
"a new era in which the Indian future is determined by Indian
acts and Indian decisions."[73] It was not the first "new dawn"
or "new day" or "new deal" or "new goal" or "new era" that
the Indians had been promised. But it did reaffirm the
importance of the one really *new* element in Indian policy, the
Indian himself.

The record shows that the Indian New Deal did not constitute
the "brief golden age" that Harold E. Fey imagined in 1955,[74]
however brightly it shone in contrast to the ominous trends
then developing. Fey and his co-author were nearer the truth
when they later wrote of the "years of faltering accomplishment" under John Collier.[75] Clearly, some New Deal reforms
did not prove desirable, while other, apparently sound programs quickly unraveled once Collier resigned. For example,
in Indian education, where the New Deal had hoped for so
much, the gains triumphantly proclaimed in 1946 did not last.
In a blistering report issued in 1969, the Senate Committee on
Labor and Public Welfare's special subcommittee on Indian
education charged that the nation's policies and programs for
educating the Indians were "a national tragedy" constituting
a "failure of major proportions."[76]

Indeed, for a while it seemed as though the whole Indian
New Deal would prove short-lived. Only eleven years after
Collier left office, a historian of the Five Civilized Tribes
warned that it was her "considered judgment" that "only twice
before—during the forced removals of the 1830s and the
liquidation of tribes that followed the General Allotment Act
of 1887—have the Indians been so seriously menaced." Not
only was the country in massive retreat from the idealism of
the New Deal years, but the great reforms in Indian policy in
the 1930s had been "set in reverse."[77]

Yet, three Presidents after Eisenhower affirmed their commitment to freedom of choice, or self-determination, as the
fundamental tenet of Indian policy. Besides the principle of

choice—a choice that made the Indian at last an integral factor in Indian affairs—the Collier New Deal also left both a legal and philosophical legacy to future policy. Because of the Reorganization Act, more than three-quarters of the tribes today have constitutions of their own guaranteeing them certain rights within the American political structure that cannot easily be set aside. "With the exception of the period from 1954 to 1961," Vine Deloria has commented, " . . . the policy of the government has been supportive of tribal sovereignty and self-government."[78] As for the Indian New Deal's philosophical legacy, Maury Maverick of Texas described it best during a congressional debate. "The Indian Reorganization Act has reversed the historic policy of our Government toward Indians," Maverick remarked:

That historic policy was the Indian property must pass to whites; that Indian organization must be repressed or prevented; that Indian family life must be dismembered through land allotment and through compulsory confinement of Indian children in institutions remote from their homes. The historic policy has taken it for granted and has decreed that the Indians as a race must die. The new policy, which is embodied in the Indian Reorganization Act, seeks exactly the opposite results. The new policy says that Indian property shall not pass to whites; that Indian organizations must be encouraged and assisted; that Indian family life must be respected and strengthened; and that the Indian as a race must not die but shall be allowed to live and to increase.[79]

Such was the lasting legacy of the Indian New Deal.

EPILOGUE
We Live Again

Nothing seemed to give John Collier more satisfaction than the thought that his administration has been responsible for reversing the process of Indian decline. "It is my part only to voice what is sure and momentous—that the Indian lives now in spirit as in flesh, one of the great races, with his own future and his potencies for our whole world," he proudly boasted in 1942.[1] Throughout the 1920s Collier and his associates had anguished over the imminent death of the Indian spirit.[2] The occasional reformer had invoked the Vanishing American on its most literal level. William S. Hart, cowboy hero of the silver screen, estimated in 1923 that the Indians were losing numbers at the rate of 2,000 each year[3]; in 1927, an editorialist claimed general agreement that the Indian death rate was "shockingly high."

The Bureau of Indian Affairs conceded that between 1920 and 1925 Indians averaged 22.8 deaths per 1,000 persons each year—double the rate for the white population. This increase of forty-eight percent in the Indian death rate pointed to the extinction of the entire Indian population in another quarter century, the American Indian Defense Association argued.[4] Propaganda aside, the Indian death rate was abnormally high, the result of tuberculosis (which was killing Indians at seven and a half times the rate it was killing white men), an excessive infant mortality rate (two and five-sevenths times the white rate under the age of one, and even higher between the ages of

345

one and three), other diseases, unsanitary home conditions, lack of medical facilities, and unfamiliarity with hygiene.[5]

The appalling mortality figures became most useful for reform purposes in the 1920s when it could be shown that the Indian's situation had measurably worsened since the implementation of the General Allotment Act. Between 1887 and 1926 there had been an actual decline in the Indian birth over death rate (from 1.116 percent births over deaths to .6 percent deaths over births).[6] One hardly needed additional proof that the assimilation policy should be abandoned forthwith and tribalism given a chance to rescue the Indian race spiritually and physically. Read in succession, John Collier's annual reports as commissioner of Indian affairs constitute a great moral drama full of hope and promise. In 1933, the total number of estimated and enumerated Indians stood at 320,454—an increase over the previous year's figures of 3,220 or one percent.[7] It was not much, but the *New York Times* and others published the news.[8] The next year Collier reported a total of 327,958 Indians, an increase of 7,504 or 2.3 percent, though one-half of the jump was explained by the addition of 4,483 California Indians to the bureau's count. Collier cautioned that Indian population figures should be regarded as estimates since the bureau defined as an Indian "any person of Indian blood who through wardship, treaty, or inheritance has acquired certain rights," while the Census Bureau used as a rule of thumb a degree of Indian blood sufficient for the person to be recognized in his community as an Indian.[9] No agreement between the census and the bureau's statistics could be expected. The data had to be accepted as more or less unreliable. This, naturally, did not discourage Collier from keeping tabs. In 1935 he reported 330,861 Indians, an increase of 2,903, of whom 690 came from one agency that had not been included previously. Thus the natural increase was 2,213 or .7 percent over the previous nine months.[10] In 1936, the enumeration stood at 334,013, an increase of 3,152, or one percent,[11] and by the next year the total had risen to 337,366.[12] Although aware of the limitations on his evidence, in January 1938, Collier reported an Indian population of 342,497—up 5,131 from the previous year—and an overall trend for the preceding eight years that showed the Indian population increasing by about 1.2 percent annually, while the population at large was gaining at only .7 percent. Collier opened his 1938 report with a triumphant declaration, printed in bold face type: "THE INDIANS ARE NO LONGER A DYING RACE."[13]

There was one rather somber note, however, given Collier's dedication to Indian racial survival: full-blood Indians *were* on the decline, and "while this vital race of people has more than held its own in numbers, it is gradually losing its racial identity and slowly but surely is blending with the surrounding population."[14] By the next year, even this seemingly irreversible process had been checked, and Collier could report the happy news that "the Indian race is no longer vanishing. It is neither dying out nor is it rapidly merging into the white society. Indians as Indians will apparently continue as a part of American life for many years." This unexpected turn of events was explained by the fact that mixed-bloods on certain reservations had begun to "marry back into the Indian group rather than to marry whites." A relatively balanced white male-female ratio in Indian country was responsible; white men could now marry within their own race. Some western states had passed antimiscegenation laws. As a consequence, both mixed- and full-blood Indians were forming "a more and more definitely self-conscious racial minority group," a trend that confirmed critics of the Indian New Deal in their fears but pleased Collier enormously. He found the Indian's future "brighter today than at any time since the advent of the white man."[15]

The Indians were not vanishing numerically, biologically (through absorption) or culturally. With that fact established, one great drama was over. After 1937 Collier no longer bothered with detailed tabular statements of Indian population trends, resting content in the knowledge that "improved and expanded clinical and preventive work, reinforced by better food . . . and by a new spirit of hope . . . have reversed the life-tide of the Indian race."[16] Others echoed Collier's optimism. Clark Wissler, curator-in-chief of anthropology at the American Museum of Natural History, in 1934 in an article on "the rebirth of the 'Vanishing American,'" argued that for more than forty years Indian numbers had been on the upswing.

Despite persistent, gloomy predictions of Indian decline, the Indian birth rate was actually the highest in the nation.

Wissler would later undertake a thorough investigation of the changing population profile of the northern plains tribes. His 1934 essay, however, was based on a superficial examination of familiar estimates. Assuming that James Mooney's figures were generous and that the population of North America in 1492 was closer to 750,000 than 1,000,000, then the Indian population of Canada and the United States in the 1930s (443,365), Wissler wrote, would suggest a decrease of about forty percent. Assuming also that the Indian population was stable almost to the end of the eighteenth century, and that it then dropped sharply as a consequence of disease and Indian-white warfare, it followed that most of this decrease had occurred before the Indians were confined to reservations. If one accepted the estimate of 294,574 Indians living in the United States in 1865, there was evidently a further erosion in Indian numbers until the nadir of 1891—246,834 souls, a decline doubtless owing to the temporary stresses of adjusting to new, reduced circumstances. Since 1891 Indian numbers had steadily increased until in 1933 they stood at Collier's 320,454. By Wissler's arithmetic, the Vanishing American had been a dead issue for forty years.[17] His conclusions were necessarily as suspect as the data on which they were based, but they seemed authoritative. Illustrating his article was a vivid graph of the trend of plains Indian population since 1780 in which the figure of a feathered warrior shrank to diminutive proportions by 1895 before sprouting up again until in the 1930s it had regained the stature of a century before—a "spectacular comeback," as one journal said.[18] By 1936 the Indian birth rate had climbed to 48 per thousand, "probably the highest in the world" according to the New York Times.[19] Meanwhile, the Indian death rate between 1928 and 1939 dropped from 27 per thousand to 13 per thousand.[20] Clearly, Indians, far from vanishing, were increasing at a phenomenal rate.

Some wary veterans of the Indian numbers game were unimpressed. The evidence, Collier's argument to the contrary notwithstanding, pointed unmistakably to the continuing dilution of Indian blood and thus the progressive whitening of the red race. One of Wissler's colleagues at the American Museum of Natural History, H. L. Shapiro, believed that the growing percentage of mixed-bloods in the Indian population counts—35.2 percent in 1910 and 42.45 percent in 1930— *underrepresented* the actual mixed-blood component. Even accepting the official figures, during this twenty-year span mixed-bloods had multiplied by 51.03 percent, full-bloods by only 2.59 percent. "Thus the increase in the number of Indians which has recently been attracting some notice appears to be largely the consequence of a growth among the acknowledged mixed-bloods, since the full-bloods are merely holding their own in actual numbers," Shapiro maintained. Moreover, the mixed-blood population on the average was younger than the full-blood population, which implied a more rapid future increase. Statistics also showed that mixed-blood women were having more children than their full-blood counterparts, and more of them were surviving. "At this rate," Shapiro concluded, "the future Indian population will become proportionately more and more a mixed one." As a consequence, Collier's policy was somewhat unrealistic. "Instead of assisting the biologically assimilated to become sociologically assimilated, we are artificially and deliberately impeding such a desirable consummation," Shapiro charged. "Let us by all means continue the essential labor of protecting the Indian in his way of life. . . . But let us also cease to preserve as Indians those who have biologically lost any claim to that status."[21]

The implication was clear that, entranced by the relatively intact communal and cultural life of the Pueblos and Navajo, Collier had based his Indian New Deal on overwhelmingly pure-blood and thus utterly unrepresentative native populations. One Northern Indian, who deplored the Collier administration's efforts to "win undue credit for stopping the vanishing of 'THE VANISHING AMERICAN,'" insisted that "the only *important* example of population increase must be Collier's favorite and standard Indians, which he uses as type for race— the Navajos." Almost all others were speedily amalgamating, and the Indian "race," in truth, was vanishing.[22]

Arguments over the actual rate of Indian-white amalgamation served mainly to show that the Vanishing American was still a factor in policy discussion and projections about the Indians' future. A more serious complaint was that Collier's rosy picture of Indian progress hid the dismal truth. Indian health, although a bureau priority since 1921, had only marginally improved. In the middle 1950s the chief of the Division of Indian Health, U.S. Public Health Service, could still cite grim statistics. The Indian tuberculosis rate was from five to twenty-eight times that of the total population. Indian infants died at a rate two to seven times that of the surrounding non-Indian population, and diseases like pneumonia, influenza, infant diarrhea, and enteritis still accounted for half of all Indian deaths. The average white male American in 1950 lived sixty-one years, the average Indian male thirty-six. A Navajo man had a life expectancy of twenty, a Papago, seventeen.[23] Inadequate housing, inadequate health care, inadequate food, inadequate sanitary facilities, inadequate income, along with a chilling suicide rate and a heavy incidence of alcoholism— these, not sentimental clichés, represented Indian reality. "The spiritual richness of the much Indian life is real," a student of the Papago wrote, "but it does not wipe away the tragic cost of economic poverty."[24] The New Deal's vision of Indian rebirth had been altogether too sanguine.

The denial of the Vanishing American in the 1930s was not the end to a hoary tradition, which survives often as a strawman to be demolished with the statistics of Indian increase. In 1960 Oliver La Farge updated his image of the "changing Indian" in an article on "The Enduring Indian." "Americans of European descent have always believed that the original Americans would somehow vanish," the lead-in stated. "But despite slaughter, assimilation, disease and dislocation, Indians continue to maintain their identity."[25] Such prose became commonplace with the national rediscovery of the Indian a few years later. In December 1967, *Life* magazine proclaimed the "Return of the Red Man,"[26] and in short order most of the major periodicals had followed suit. Soon books about Indians were rolling off the presses, United States history texts were being revised to give the First American his due, Red Studies courses were popping up in college catalogues, movies and television shows were vying to present the Indian view and turquoise jewelery was high fashion. But the sentimental myth of an extinct race had not yet disappeared. As an Indian spokesman wryly asked in 1968, "What can you do when society tells you that you should be nonexistent?"[27]

The myth of the Vanishing American lives on, sustained by literary and artistic tradition older than the Republic. It is entrenched in the documents of Indian affairs. The psychological imperative of cultural guilt periodically infuses it with new vigor. Felix S. Cohen, a shrewd observer of the myth, linked concept to cause. "Deep in the American conscience is a sense of having wronged the original possessors of our continent," he wrote in 1948:

This twinge of national conscience may show itself in appropriations for aid to the starving Navajo, or in other humanitarian efforts. But most deeply it shows itself in a desire to believe that the Indian is, either physically or culturally, a dying race, unable to utilize white man's civilization, and therefore an obstacle in the road to progress. And so we think of the Indian, head bowed on a drooping horse at "the end of the trail."[28]

Today the modish word "genocide" carries the burden of the Vanishing American.[29] It implies a deliberate program of extermination and a devastating moral judgment, but it too ignores the native *fact* today. The presence of those who were wronged seems unbearable. Avoidance and denial become the most reassuring responses, and the Vanishing American conveniently encapsulates them in a tradition reeking of inevitability. What the white man did was terrible. It was wrong. It could not be helped. It cannot be remedied.

The obvious rebuttal to the Vanishing American is the Indian himself. When "red power" became a byword in the press, it suggested something more substantial than love beads, headbands, and anthologies of Indian oratory. It was a counterimage to the tradition of stoic decline as forceful as black power's clenched fist upraised in defiance. Red militancy— bumperstickers, slogans, hard demands, and violent confrontations aside—drove home a simple point: the Indians will not vanish. They are not going to make it easy for everyone else by fading away to some happy hunting-ground. Nor will they allow the public the convenient escape of remorse over past wrongs. They are not "returning" from anywhere; they have been here all the time, and they will be here tomorrow. More than anything else, red power is an assertion of that fact: "WE LIVE AGAIN WE LIVE AGAIN WE LIVE AGAIN WE LIVE AGAIN WE LIVE."[30]

Almost fifty years have passed since John Collier launched the Indian New Deal, and if policy continues to move in the fifty-year cycles that have marked its course since the founding of the Republic, the 1980s could well be comparable in importance in American Indian affairs to the decades of the 1830s, 1880s, and 1930s. In 1975 Congress established the American Indian Policy Review Commission to undertake an ambitious investigation into federal–Indian relations and to set down guidelines for "a policy for the future." Five of the eleven members appointed by Congress were Indian; so were almost half of the commission's staff and most of its task force members and specialists, "a precedent of great importance." The commission was at pains "to listen attentively to the Indians . . . , to recognize realistically their own points of view, . . . and to heed their voices for the righting of wrongs, the ending of frustrations and despair, and the attainment of their needs and aspirations as Indians and as free and proud Americans." Submitted in 1977, the commission's final report self-consciously aspired to be a Meriam Report for our times. Predictably, its 206 recommendations rested on the principle of Indian self-determination. It defined the tribes as "sovereign political bodies" and their relationship with the government as "a special trust" requiring good will and good faith. The report's thrust was summed up in a question: "From the misdirected present, can the United States Government redirect its relations with the American Indians to enable them to determine their own lives now, and in the future?"[31]

Reports are not policies, of course, and that of the American Indian Policy Review Commission has been condemned by some Indian spokesmen as meaningless, if well-intentioned.[32] Time and congressional action alone will tell. But the precedents for Indian participation in decision-making are beginning to add up to a rule of law.

The present vogue of the Indian will pass as such vogues have passed before. White friends will again lapse into silence. But Indian voices will continue to be heard, speaking out on their own behalf. "No one else on the Mother Earth has the right to attempt to define us or our existence," participants in The Longest Walk, from California to the nation's capital, declared in their position paper in July 1978.[33] That year, the Indian Claims Commission's mandate finally expired. But the lands claims issue goes on before the courts, and successful suits have been brought by the Penobscots and Passamaquoddies of Maine and the Narragansetts of Rhode Island—peoples declared extinct two centuries ago, their names long synonymous with the Vanishing American. Besides cash bonanzas and a permanent land base, they have won tribal recognition which brings with it access to federal grant monies. The danger of a revitalized tribalism resting on government recognition has not been lost on the Indians; but they are willing to use white tools for their own purposes.[34] Even the Vanishing American has been turned to Indian ends: the United Native Americans, a San Franciso-based red power group in the 1960s, patterned its symbol after the familiar silhouette of James E. Fraser's *End of the Trail*. But the message now is Indian resurgence as the warrior, his spear pointed skyward, leans back to restrain his snorting pony. Eager for the fray, the native American will enter the twenty-first century unsubdued, unassimilated—and unmistakably alive.

NOTES

Preface

1. John Collier, "Office of Ind. Affairs," *Ann. Rep., Secy. Interior, 1938* (Washington, D.C., 1938), p. 209.
2. "The Angry American Indian: Starting Down the Protest Trail," *Time,* XCV (Feb. 9, 1970), 15.
3. Joseph Story, "Discourse, Pronounced at the Request of the Essex Historical Society, September 18, 1828, in Commemoration of the First Settlement of Salem, Mass.," *The Miscellaneous Writings, Literary, Critical, Juridical, of Joseph Story, LL.D.* (Boston, 1835), p. 80.
4. Ruth Miller Elson, *Guardians of Tradition: American Schoolbooks of the Nineteenth Century* (Lincoln, Neb., 1964), pp. 71–81.

A Note on Numbers

1. Bryce Nelson, "Non-whites Increase Hold on American Population," Victoria, B.C., *Times-Colonist,* Feb. 25, 1981, p. 51; and U.S. Bureau of the Census, *Statistical Abstract of the United States: 1974,* 95th Ed. (Washington, D.C., 1974), p. 30, Table 33.
2. Robert L. Faherty, "The American Indian: An Overview," *Current Hist.,* LXVII (Dec. 1974), 243.
3. Wilbur R. Jacobs, "The Tip of an Iceberg: Pre-Columbian Indian Demography and Some Implications for Revisionism," *W&MQ,* 3rd ser., XXXI (Jan. 1974), 123.
4. Henry F. Dobyns, *Native American Historical Demography: A Critical Bibliography* (Bloomington, Ind., 1976), pp. 45–48, and "Brief Perspective on a Scholarly Transformation: Widowing the 'Virgin' Land," *Ethnohistory,* XXIII (Spring 1976), 101, survey the literature regarding the creation of the "New American Race," as it is now being called.
5. Henry F. Dobyns, "Estimating Aboriginal American Population, 1: An Appraisal of Techniques with a New Hemispheric Estimate," *Current Anthro.,* VII (Oct. 1966), 395–416.
6. Francis Jennings, *The Invasion of America: Indians, Colonialism, and the Cant of Conquest* (Chapel Hill, N.C., 1975), chap. 2.
7. For anthropological reactions to Dobyns's essay, see "Comments," *Current Anthro.,* VII (Oct. 1966), 425–40 (and, for Dobyns's "Reply," 440–44); Harold E. Driver, "On the Population Nadir of Indians in the United States," *Current Anthro.,* IX (Oct. 1968), 330, which uses BIA figures to arrive at a lower nadir—250,000 instead of 332,000—than Dobyns, but fails to take into account the obvious limitations on bureau computations; and Driver,

Indians of North America (Chicago, rev. ed., 1969), 63–65, which scales Dobyns's estimate for the area of the United States exclusive of Alaska down to 2.5 million. Indications of growing support for the estimates of Dobyns and others, particularly in regard to disease as a catastrophic depopulating factor, can be found in *Ethnohistory*, XXIII (Spring 1976), notably Virginia P. Miller, "Aboriginal Micmac Population: A Review of the Evidence." The growing sophistication of the debate over Indian numbers is apparent in William M. Denevan, ed., *The Native Population of the Americas in 1492* (Madison, Wisc., 1976).

Chapter One: Their Power Has Been Broken

1. Philip Freneau, "The Indian Burying Ground" (1787), in Fred Lewis Pattee, ed., *The Poems of Philip Freneau, Poet of the American Revolution*, 3 vols. (Princeton, N.J., 1902–1907), II, 369–70.

2. John Adams to Thomas Jefferson, June 28, 1812, in Lester J. Cappon, ed., *The Adams-Jefferson Letters: The Complete Correspondence between Thomas Jefferson and Abigail and John Adams*, 2 vols. (Chapel Hill, N.C., 1959), II, 310–11.

3. Benjamin Smith Barton, *New Views of the Origins of the Tribes and Nations of America* (1798), quoted in Daniel J. Boorstin, *The Lost World of Thomas Jefferson* (New York, 1948), p. 88.

4. Thomas Jefferson to Benjamin Hawkins, Feb. 18, 1803, in Paul Leicester Ford, ed., *The Writings of Thomas Jefferson*, 10 vols. (New York, 1892–99), VIII, 21.

5. James D. Richardson, *A Compilation of the Messages and Papers of the Presidents, 1789–1902*, 10 vols. (Washington, D.C., 1903), I, 503–4.

6. Samuel Purchas (1625) quoted in Francis Jennings, "Virgin Land and Savage People," *Am. Q.*, XXIII (Oct. 1971), 521.

7. Edward Waterhouse (1622) quoted in Gary B. Nash, *Red, White and Black: The Peoples of Early America* (Englewood Cliffs, N.J., 1974), pp. 62, 126.

8. Richardson, *Messages and Papers*, I, 475, 493, 525, 563, 576.

9. [Washington Irving], "Traits of Indian Character," *Analectic Mag.*, III (Feb. 1814), 145, 154–56.

10. Message from the British to the American ministers, Sept. 4, 1814, and the American reply, Sept. 9, 1814, in *Am. State Papers, Class I: Foreign Relations*, 6 vols. (Washington, D.C., 1832–59), III, 715–16.

11. John C. Calhoun, Report to the House of Reps., Dec. 5, 1818, in W. Edwin Hemphill, ed., *The Papers of John C. Calhoun*, 14 vols. to date (Columbia, S.C., 1959–81), III, 342, 350.

12. Henry Clay, Jan. 20, 1819, in *Annals of Cong.*, 15th Cong., 2nd sess., p. 639.

13. William Clark to James Barbour, Mar. 1, 1826, in "Civilization of the Indians" (Mar. 9, 1826), *House Doc. No. 124*, 19th Cong., 1st sess., p. 4.

14. The congressional debate in January and February of 1819, over Andrew Jackson's activities in Florida during the Seminole war, produced several such expressions: Richard M. Johnson, Ky., Jan. 20; James Barbour, Va., Jan. 25; Felix Walker, N.C., Jan. 27; John Rhea, Tenn., Jan. 27; John Floyd, Va., Feb. 8, in *Annals of Cong.*, 15th Cong., 2nd sess., pp. 659; 780; 851, 854; 855–62; 1106–7, 1115–16.

15. "Congressional Report," *Niles'*, XXVI (Apr. 10, 1824), 92.

16. Robert F. Berkhofer, Jr., *Salvation and the Savage: An Analysis of Protestant Missions and American Indian Response, 1787–1862* (Lexington, Ky., 1965), pp. 5–6.

17. Roy Harvey Pearce, *The Savages of America: A Study of the Indian and the Idea of Civilization* (Baltimore, rev. ed., 1965 [1953]), p. 33.

18. "Indian Language and Condition," *Am. Q. Rev.*, III (June 1828), 417–18.

19. *The Removal of the Indians. An Article from the American Monthly Magazine: An Examination of an Article in the North American Review; and an Exhibition of the Southern Tribes, in Civilization and Christianity* (Boston, 1830), pp. 58, 72.

20. "Indians Removing Westward" (Jan. 7, 1828), *House Rep. No. 56*, 20th Cong., 1st sess., p. 2.

21. [Nathan Hale], "Heckewelder's Indian History," *NAR*, IX (June 1819), 170.

Chapter Two: The Anatomy of the Vanishing American

1. George F. Holmes, quoted in "The American Indians," *Commercial Review*, V (Mar. 1848), 272.

2. Jefferson to William Ludlow, Sept. 6, 1824, in Andrew A. Lipscomb, ed., *The Writings of Thomas Jefferson: Library Edition*, 20 vols. (Washington, D.C., 1903), XVI, 75.

3. E. G. House, Introduction to Henry Trumbull, *History of the Indian Wars* . . . (Boston, new ed., 1846), p. 1.

4. "The North American Indians," *Q. Rev.* (London), XXXI (Apr. 1824), 108.

5. [Nathan Hale], "Heckewelder's Indian History," *NAR*, IX (June 1819), 156.

6. John Elliott, Feb. 22, 1825, *Register of Debates in Cong.*, 18th Cong., 2nd sess., p. 640.

7. Eliza Lee, *Naomi; or, Boston Two Hundred Years Ago* (1847), quoted in G. Harrison Orians, *The Cult of the Vanishing American: A Century View, 1834–1934* (Toledo, 1934), p. 6.

8. William Tudor, Jr., "An Address Delivered to the Phi Beta Kappa Society . . . ," *NAR*, II (Nov. 1815), 19–20.

9. William Cullen Bryant, "An Indian at the Burying-place of His Fathers," *Miscellaneous Poems Selected from the United States Literary Gazette* (Boston, 1826), p. 17.

10. I. McLellan, Jr., "Hymn of the Cherokee Indian," in *The American Common-place Book of Poetry, with Occasional Notes* (Philadelphia, 1839), pp. 397–98.

11. G. W. Cutter, "The Death of Osceola," *Buena Vista: and Other Poems* (Cincinnati, 1848), p. 37.

12. Charles Sprague, "American Independence: An Oration Pronounced before the Inhabitants of Boston, July 4, 1825," *The Poetical and Prose Writings of Charles Sprague* (Boston, 1851), pp. 150–53.

13. George Falconer Emmons, "Replies to Inquiries Respecting the Indian Tribes of Oregon and California" (May 20, 1852), in Henry R. Schoolcraft, *Information Respecting the History, Condition and Prospects of the Indian Tribes of the United States*, 6 vols. (Philadelphia, 1851–57), III, 210, 225.

14. John Adams to Thomas Jefferson, June 11, 1813, in Lester J. Cappon, ed., *The Adams-Jefferson Letters: The Complete Correspondence between Thomas Jefferson and Abigail and John Adams*, 2 vols. (Chapel Hill, N.C., 1959), II, 328.

15. [Edward and John Everett], "Letters on the Eastern States," *NAR*, XI (July 1820), 96–97.

16. Henry R. Schoolcraft, *An Address, Delivered before the Was-ah Ho-de-no-son-ne, or New Confederacy of the Iroquois, August 14, 1846* (Rochester, N.Y., 1846), pp. 5–6.

17. Daniel Webster, quoted in George Catlin, *Last Rambles amongst the Indians of the Rocky Mountains and the Andes* (London, 1868), pp. 46–49.

18. [Timothy Flint], "Indian Mounds," *Western Mag. and Rev.*, I (July 1827), 143.

19. "American Antiquities," *Western Monthly Rev.*, I (Mar. 1828), 656.

20. "Black Hawk," *Am. Q. Rev.*, XV (June 1834), 427.

21. [Timothy Flint], "Sketches of the Character of the North American Savages," *Western Mag. and Rev.*, I (July 1827), 141.

22. Philip Freneau, "On the Civilization of the Western Aboriginal Country" (1822), in Lewis Leary, ed., *The Last Poems of Philip Freneau* (New Brunswick, N.J., 1945), pp. 69, 71.

23. *Ibid.*, p. 69.

24. Tudor, "Address Delivered to the Phi Beta Kappa Society," p. 31.

25. Orians, *The Cult of the Vanishing American*. The only other novel of this genre that still attracts a reading audience is William Gilmore Simms's *The Yemassee: A Romance of Carolina* (1835).

26. James Fenimore Cooper, *The Last of the Mohicans* (New York, Signet, 1962), pp. 38, 361, 367, 414–15.

27. [William H. Gardiner], "Cooper's Novels," *NAR*, XXIII (July, 1826), 166–68.

28. Joseph C. Hart, *Miriam Coffin* (1834), quoted in Louise K. Barnett, *The Ignoble Savage: American Literary Racism, 1790–1890* (Westport, Conn., 1975), pp. 55–56.

29. Elémire Zolla, trans. by Raymond Rosenthal, *The Writer and the Shaman: A Morphology of the American Indian* (New York, 1973), pp. 3, 180.

30. "Publisher's Adv." prefacing Mary H. Eastman, *The Romance of Indian Life* (Philadelphia, 1853).

31. Cooper, *Last of the Mohicans*, pp. 332, 119–20.

32. "The American Aborigines," *Niles'*, XV (Nov. 14, 1818), 185.

33. "Catlin's North American Indians," *U.S. Mag., and Democratic Rev.*, XI (July 1842), 44.

34. Catlin to Daniel Webster, Apr. 4, 1852, in Marjorie Catlin Roehm, *The Letters of George Catlin and His Family: A Chronicle of the American West* (Berkeley, Calif., 1966), p. 442 (also, p. 452).

35. George Catlin, *Letters and Notes on the Manners, Customs, and Condition of the North American Indians*, 2 vols. (New York, 1841), I, 2–9.

36. *A Descriptive Catalogue of Catlin's Indian Gallery* . . . (London, n.d. [1840]), p. 3.

37. Catlin, *Letters*, I, 8–9, 123.

38. James Barbour, Secretary of War, Feb. 16, 1826, in "Preservation of the Indians," *Niles'*, XXX (June 10, 1826), Supp., 275.

39. Catlin, *Letters*, I, 16.

40. Putnam Catlin to Francis Catlin, Mar. 18, 1838, in Roehm, *Letters of George Catlin*, p. 127.

41. *Catalogue of CATLIN'S INDIAN GALLERY of Portraits, Landscapes, Manners and Customs, Costumes, &c. &c....* (New York, 1838), pp. 34–35, No. 492.

42. Catlin, *Letters*, II, 256, 266.

43. *Ibid.*, I, 10, 61; II, 156–58.

44. [Jared Sparks], "History of the Indians," *NAR*, XIX (Oct. 1824), 464.

45. [Edward Everett], "Politics of Ancient Greece," *NAR*, XVIII (Apr. 1824), 398–99.

46. [Edward Everett], "On the State of the Indians," *NAR*, XVI (Jan., 1823), 33–34, 36–39.

47. Everett, "Letters on the Eastern States," p. 95.

48. Edward Everett, "The Battle of Bloody Brook" (1835), *Orations and Speeches on Various Occasions*, 4 vols. (Boston, 1850–68), I, 636, 640.

Chapter Three: The Pathology of the Vanishing American

1. John Heckewelder, *History, Manners, and Customs of the Indian Nations Who Once Inhabited Pennsylvania and the Neighbouring States* (Philadelphia, rev. ed., 1876 [1818]), p. 93.

2. Edward Waldo Emerson and Waldo Emerson Forbes, eds., *Journals of Ralph Waldo Emerson*, 10 vols. (Boston, 1909–14), VII, 23.

3. Thomas Jefferson, *Notes on the State of Virginia* (New York, Torchbooks, 1964), pp. 91–92.

4. Henry R. Schoolcraft, *Information Respecting the History, Condition and Prospects of the Indian Tribes of the United States*, 6 vols. (Philadelphia, 1851–57), I, 191.

5. Jefferson, *Notes*, pp. 92, 98–102.

6. "Indian Language and Condition," *Am. Q. Rev.*, III (June 1828), 416.

7. D. H. Lawrence, *Studies in Classic American Literature* (New York, 1923), pp. 15, 35. Lawrence was referring to a passage in *The Autobiography of Benjamin Franklin*: "If it be the design of Providence to extirpate these savages in order to make room for cultivators of the earth, it seems not improbable that rum may be the appointed means. It has already annihilated all the tribes who formerly inhabited the sea-coast."

8. John C. Parish, "Liquor and the Indians," *Palimpsest*, III (July 1922), 201. See George F. G. Stanley, "The Indians and the Brandy Trade during the Ancien Régime," *Revue d'historie de l'Amérique Française*, VI (Mar. 1953), 489–91; and R. C. Dailey, "The Role of Alcohol among North American Indian Tribes as Reported in The Jesuit Relations," *Anthropologica*, N.S., X (1968), 45–59.

9. "A Metabolic Clue to Indian Endurance and Intolerance for Alcohol," *Psych. Today*, VI (July 1972), 16.

10. Jerry McLeod and Stanley Clark, "It's in the Blood," *Canadian Welfare*, L (Sept.-Oct. 1974), 16–20.

11. Nancy Oestreich Lurie, "The World's Oldest On-going Protest Demonstration: North American Indian Drinking Patterns," *Pac. Hist. Rev.*, XL (Aug. 1971), 311–32.

12. [Lewis Cass], "Service of Indians in Civilized Warfare," *NAR*, XXIV (Apr. 1827), 404.

13. Lewis Cass to George Catlin, Dec. 8, 1841, in *Catlin's Notes of Eight Years' Travels and Residence in Europe, with His North American Indian Collection*, 2 vols. (London, 3rd ed., 1848), I, 59, 252.

14. Cass, "Service of Indians in Civilized Warfare," pp. 404–5.

15. Lewis Cass, Feb. 1, 1855, *Cong. Globe*, 33rd Cong., 2nd sess., p. 513.

16. Cass, "Service of Indians in Civilized Warfare," p. 405.

17. Henry R. Schoolcraft, *Personal Memoirs of a Residence of Thirty Years with the Indian Tribes on the American Frontiers* ... (Philadelphia, 1851), p. 326 (diary entry for July 14, 1829).

18. Cass, "Service of Indians in Civilized Warfare," p. 405.

19. H. J. Spinden, "The Population of Ancient America," *Ann. Rep., Smithsonian, 1929* (Washington, D.C., 1930), pp. 470–71.

20. Henry F. Dobyns, "Estimating Aboriginal American Population, 1: An Appraisal of Techniques with a New Hemispheric Estimate," *Current Anthro.*, VII (Oct. 1966), 411, 415.

21. William Bradford, *Of Plymouth Plantation, 1620–1647*, edited by Samuel Eliot Morrison (New York, 1952), p. 72.

22. Report, datelined New Orleans, June 6, 1838, in E. Wagner Stearn and Allen E. Stearn, *The Effects of Smallpox on the Destiny of the Amerindian* (Boston, 1945), p. 89.

23. See Lewis Cass, Secretary of War, "Small Pox among the Indians" (Mar. 30, 1832), *House Exec. Doc. No. 190*, 22nd Cong., 1st sess., pp. 1–3. Congress provided for the vaccination of the Indian population by act of May 5, 1832.

24. George Catlin, *Letters and Notes on the Manners, Customs, and Condition of the North American Indians*, 2 vols. (New York, 1841), I, 94–95; II, 257–59.

25. Schoolcraft, *Information*, I, 257–58. A recent study, while confessing imprecision, notes a drop in the Mandan population in 1837 of from 1,600–1,800 to 125–150. (Martin Ira Glassner, "Population Figures for Mandan Indians," *Ind. Historian*, VII [Spring 1974], 41, 45.)

26. Catlin, *Letters*, II, 258–59.

27. Don Russell, "How Many Indians Were Killed?" *Am. West*, X (July 1973), 62.

28. Sherburne F. Cook, "Interracial Warfare and Population Decline among the New England Indians," *Ethnohistory*, XX (Winter 1973), 1–24.

29. [Lewis Cass], "Indians of North America" *NAR*, XXII (Jan. 1826), 111–12.

30. Lewis Cass, in "Removal of Indians Westward" (Feb. 16, 1832), *House Doc. No. 116*, 22nd Cong., 1st sess., pp. 14–15.

31. Samuel Stanhope Smith, *An Essay on the Causes of the Variety of Complexion and Figure in the Human Species* (1810, 2nd ed.), quoted in Bernard W. Sheehan, *Seeds of Extinction: Jeffersonian Philanthropy and the American Indian* (Chapel Hill, N.C., 1973), p. 195.

32. A Military Gentleman Attached to the Yellowstone Expedition in 1819, "Notes on the Missouri River, and Some of the Native Tribes in Its Neighbourhood," *Analectic Mag.*, N.S., I (Apr. 1820), 301.

33. [Edward Everett], "On the State of the Indians," *NAR*, XVI (Jan. 1823), 34–35.

34. See Douglas Edward Leach, *Flintlock and Tomahawk: New England in*

King Philip's War (New York, 1958), pp. 22–23, 152–54; and Howard H. Peckham, "Indian Relations in the United States," in John Francis Mc-Dermott, ed., *Research Opportunities in American Cultural History* (Lexington, Ky., 1961), pp. 36–38.

35. See Wilcomb E. Washburn, "The Moral and Legal Justifications for Dispossessing the Indians," in James Morton Smith, ed., *Seventeenth-Century America: Essays in Colonial History* (Chapel Hill, N.C., 1959), pp. 15–32; and Washburn, *Red Man's Land/White Man's Law: A Study of the Past and Present Status of the American Indian* (New York, 1971), pt. I.

36. Albert Gallatin, *A Synopsis of the Indian Tribes within the United States East of the Rocky Mountains, and in the British and Russian Possessions in North America* (New York, 1973 [1836]), pp. 154–55, 159.

37. [Nathan Hale], "Heckewelder's Indian History," *NAR*, IX (June 1819), 167–70.

38. Everett, "On the State of the Indians," p. 33.

39. [Washington Irving], "Traits of Indian Character," *Analectic Mag.*, III (Feb. 1814), 146.

40. Peter Wraxall, quoted in Walter H. Mohr, *Federal Indian Relations, 1774–1788* (Philadelphia, 1933), p. 178.

41. Cass, "Indians of North America," p. 110.

42. Benjamin Franklin, "Observations Concerning the Increase of Mankind and Peopling of Countries" (1751), in John Bigelow, ed., *The Works of Benjamin Franklin (Federal Edition)*, 12 vols. (New York, 1904), II, 345.

43. "Reflections on the Institutions of the Cherokee Indians, from Observations Made during a Recent Visit to that Tribe: In a Letter from a Gentleman of Virginia, to Robert Walsh, Jan.–June 1st, 1817," *Analectic Mag.*, XII (July 1818), 46, 54–55.

44. [Lewis Cass], "Removal of the Indians," *NAR*, XXX (Jan. 1830), 69, 72–73.

Chapter Four: Isolation

1. Henry Knox, Report of the Secretary of War to Congress, July 10, 1787, in Clarence Edwin Carter, ed., *The Territorial Papers of the United States*, vol. II (Washington, D.C., 1934), 31.

2. Luke Lea, "Rep., Com. Ind. Affairs" (Nov. 27, 1851), in *Sen. Exec. Doc. No. 1*, 32nd Cong., 1st sess., pp. 273–74.

3. James Monroe, Second Ann. Message, Nov. 16, 1818, and Special Message, Mar. 30, 1824, in James D. Richardson, *A Compilation of the Messages and Papers of the Presidents, 1789–1902*, 10 vols. (Washington, D.C., 1903), II, 46, 235–36.

4. Henry R. Schoolcraft, *Personal Memoirs of a Residence of Thirty Years with the Indian Tribes on the American Frontiers* (Philadelphia, 1851), pp. 319, 629 (diary entries for Nov. 7, 1828, and Dec. 31, 1838).

5. For policy in this period, see Walter H. Mohr, *Federal Indian Relations, 1774–1788* (Philadelphia, 1933); and Francis Paul Prucha, *American Indian Policy in the Formative Years: The Indian Trade and Intercourse Acts, 1790–1834* (Cambridge, Mass., 1964), chap. 1.

6. *Am. State Papers, Class I: Foreign Relations*, 6 vols. (Washington, D.C., 1832–59), III, 705–24.

7. See Annie Heloise Abel, "Proposals for an Indian State, 1778–1878," *Ann. Rep., Am. Hist. Assn., 1907*, 2 vols. (Washington, D.C., 1908), I, 87–104; and Ronald N. Satz, *American Indian Policy in the Jacksonian Era* (Lincoln, Neb., 1975), chap. 5.

8. See Prucha, *American Indian Policy in the Formative Years*, for a thorough study of the Trade and Intercourse Acts.

9. H. Knox, Secy. War, "Instructions to Brigadier General Rufus Putnam," May 22, 1792, in *Am. State Papers, Class II: Indian Affairs*, 2 vols. (Washington, D.C., 1832–59), I, 235.

10. "On the Causes of the Depopulation of the American Indians," *Analectic Mag., and Naval Chronicle*, VII (Apr. 1816), 328.

11. See Robert F. Berkhofer, Jr., Introduction to Isaac McCoy, *History of Baptist Indian Missions* (New York, 1970), pp. v–xxvii; and George A. Schultz, *An Indian Canaan: Isaac McCoy and the Vision of an Indian State* (Norman, Okla., 1972).

12. See Robert F. Berkhofer, Jr., "Model Zions for the American Indian," *Am. Q.*, XV (Summer 1963), 176–90.

13. *Annals of Cong.*, 15th Cong., 2nd sess. (Dec. 23, 1818), p. 426.

14. "Amelioration of the Indians," *Niles'*, XV (Jan. 30, 1819), 420–23.

15. Richardson, *Messages and Papers*, II, 46.

16. Richard Peters, ed., *The Public Statutes at Large of the United States . . . to March 3, 1845* (Boston, 1846), III, 516–17. The regulations governing participation in the Indian civilization program were circulated on Sept. 3, 1819, and Feb. 29, 1820, and, along with a progress report on the act (Jan. 15, 1820), can be found conveniently in W. Edwin Hemphill, ed., *The Papers of John C. Calhoun*, 5 vols. (Columbia, S.C., 1959–71), IV, 295–96, 575–77, 697–98.

17. Jedidiah Morse to John C. Calhoun, Oct. 16, 1820, and Calhoun to Morse, Feb. 7, 1820, in Hemphill, ed., *Papers of John C. Calhoun*, V, 399; IV, 648.

18. Jedidiah Morse, *A Report to the Secretary of War of the United States, on Indian Affairs* (New Haven, 1822), p. 66.

19. For expressions of this view, see [Nathan Hale], "Heckewelder's Indian History," *NAR*, IX (June 1819), 168–70; [Edward and John Everett], "Letters on the Eastern States," *NAR*, XI (July 1820), 95; [Edward Everett], "On the State of the Indians," *NAR*, XVI (Jan. 1823), 39–45; "Indian Language and Condition," *Am. Q. Rev.*, III (June 1828), 410–11, 417–22; and "The Indians," *Niles'*, XXXVIII (Mar. 20, 1830), 67.

20. Thomas L. McKenney, *On the Origin, History, Character, and the Wrongs and Rights of the Indians* (New York, 1846), pp. 48–49.

21. Thomas Jefferson to Meriwether Lewis, June 20, 1803, in Donald Jackson, ed., *Letters of the Lewis and Clark Expedition, with Related Documents, 1783–1854* (Urbana, Ill., 1962), p. 64.

22. Benjamin Franklin to Mr. Parker, Mar. 20, 1751, in John Bigelow, ed., *The Works of Benjamin Franklin (Federal Edition)*, 12 vols. (New York, 1904), II, 336.

23. See Ora Brooks Peake, *A History of the United States Indian Factory System, 1795–1822* (Denver, 1954).

24. Thomas Jefferson, confidential message to Congress, January 18, 1803, in Jackson, ed., *Letters of the Lewis and Clark Expedition*, p. 11.

25. See W. Sheridan Warrick, "The American Indian Policy in the Upper Old Northwest Following the War of 1812," *Ethnohistory*, III (Spring 1956), 112–13; and R. S. Cotterill, "Federal Indian Management in the South," *MVHR*, XX (Dec. 1933), 348.

26. Report, Committee on Indian Affairs, Mar. 23, 1824, in "Congressional Report," *Niles'*, XXVI (Apr. 10, 1824), 91–93.

27. James Monroe, Special Message, Mar. 30, 1824, in Richardson, *Messages and Papers*, II, 235–36.

Chapter Five: A Magnanimous Act of Interposition

1. Paul Leicester Ford, ed., *The Writings of Thomas Jefferson*, 10 vols. (New York, 1892–99), VIII, 243–44.

2. Meriwether Lewis to Jefferson, Dec. 28, 1803, in Donald Jackson, ed., *Letters of the Lewis and Clark Expedition, with Related Documents, 1783–1854* (Urbana, Ill., 1962), p. 148.

3. Thomas Jefferson to Gen. Horatio Gates, July 11, 1803, in Richard Skolnik, *1803: Jefferson's Decision—The United States Purchases Louisiana* (New York, 1969), p. 155.

4. William G. McLoughlin, "Thomas Jefferson and the Beginning of Cherokee Nationalism, 1806 to 1809," *W&MQ*, 3rd ser., XXXII (Oct. 1975), 548.

5. Visitors to the southern tribes generally saw what they were predisposed to see. If they favored removal, then they were sure to find that the tribes exhibited the spectacle of a few educated half-breeds living in relative luxury and prosperity while the mass of their tribesmen lived in poverty and ignorance (for example [Lewis Cass], "Removal of the Indians," *NAR*, XXX [Jan. 1830], 71; Rep., Senate Committee on Indian Affairs, Feb. 22, 1830, in *Register of Debates in Cong.*, 21st Cong., 1st sess., app., pp. 93–94; the report of the House Committee on Indian Affairs, "Removal of Indians" [Feb. 24, 1830], *House Rep. No. 227*, 21st Cong., 1st sess., pp. 19–24; and speech of Sen. John Forsyth, Ga., Apr. 15, 1830, *Register of Debates in Cong.*, 21st Cong., 1st sess., pp. 328, 339). If they opposed removal, then the southern Indians were industrious tillers of the soil, evincing remarkable advancement in all aspects of their lives (for example, speeches of Sen. Theodore Frelinghuysen, N.J., Apr. 9, 1830, and Sen. Asher Robbins, R.I., Apr. 21, 1830, *Register of Debates in Cong.*, 21st Cong., 1st sess., pp. 319, 377; "The Choctaw Indians," *Niles'*, XXXVIII [July 3, 1830], 345; and "The Cherokee Indians," *Niles'*, XXXVIII [July 24, 1830], 394–95).

6. First Ann. Message, Dec. 2, 1817, Special Message, Mar. 30, 1824, Eighth Ann. Message, Dec. 7, 1824, in James D. Richardson, *A Compilation of the Messages and Papers of the Presidents, 1789–1902*, 10 vols. (Washington, D.C., 1903), II, 16, 235, 261.

7. Rep. Samuel F. Vinton, Ohio, Feb. 20, 1828, in *Register of Debates in Cong.*, 20th Cong., 1st sess., p. 1570.

8. Lynn Hudson Parsons, "'A Perpetual Harrow upon My Feelings': John Quincy Adams and the American Indian," *New Eng. Q.*, XLVI (Sept. 1973), 339–62.

9. "The Creek Indians," *Niles'*, XXXVI (June 13, 1829), 257–59.

10. First Ann. Message, Dec. 8, 1829, in Richardson, *Messages and Papers*, II, 458–59.

11. *Ibid.*

12. Michael Paul Rogin, *Fathers and Children: Andrew Jackson and the Subjugation of the American Indian* (New York, 1975), chaps. 6–7.

13. First Ann. Message, Dec. 8, 1829, in Richardson, *Messages and Papers*, II, 457–58.

14. Alfred Balch to Jackson, Jan. 8, 1830, in John Spencer Bassett, ed., *Correspondence of Andrew Jackson*, 7 vols. (Washington, D.C., 1926–35), IV, 116.

15. Special Message, Jan. 27, 1825, in Richardson, *Messages and Papers*, II, 281–82.

16. Second Ann. Message, Dec. 6, 1830, in Richardson, *Messages and Papers*, II, 521–23.

17. [Lewis Cass], "Indians of North America," *NAR*, XXII (Jan. 1826), 119.

18. Samuel F. Vinton, Ohio, Feb. 20, 1828, in *Register of Debates in Cong.*, 20th Cong., 1st sess., p. 1581.

19. Cass, "Removal of the Indians," pp. 66–67, 109, 115.

20. Charles Francis Adams, ed., *Memoirs of John Quincy Adams, Comprising Portions of His Diary from 1795 to 1848*, 12 vols. (Philadelphia, 1874–77), VII, 89–90.

21. James Barbour, Jan. 25, 1819, in *Annals of Cong.*, 15th Cong., 2nd sess., p. 765.

22. "Preservation and Civilization of the Indians" (Feb. 21, 1826), *House Doc. No. 102*, 19th Cong., 1st sess., pp. 5–12.

23. William McLean, Ohio, Feb. 19, 1828, in *Register of Debates in Cong.*, 20th Cong., 1st sess., p. 1560.

24. Thomas L. McKenney to Samuel Worcester, Corresponding Secy., Am. Board of Commissioners for Foreign Missions, Oct. 30, 1817, in "American Indians," *Portico*, V (Apr., May, June 1818), 441. See Herman J. Viola, *Thomas L. McKenney, Architect of America's Early Indian Policy: 1816–1830* (Chicago, 1974).

25. Thomas L. McKenney to James Barbour, Secretary of War, Dec. 13, 1825, in "Preservation and Civilization of the Indians" (Feb. 21, 1826), p. 16.

26. Thomas L. McKenney to John H. Eaton, Secretary of War, Mar. 22, 1830, in *Sen. Doc. No. 110* (Mar. 25, 1830), 21st Cong., 1st sess., p. 3.

27. Thomas L. McKenney, Rep., Office of Ind. Affairs, Nov. 1, 1828, in *House Exec. Doc. No. 2*, 20th Cong., 2nd sess., p. 80.

28. Thomas L. McKenney, "Address" (1829), in his *Memoirs, Official and Personal* (New York, 1846), pp. 240–41. And see Francis Paul Prucha, "Thomas L. McKenney and the New York Indian Board," *MVHR*, XLVIII (Mar. 1962), 635–55.

29. Edward Everett, Mass., May 19, 1830, in *Register of Debates in Cong.*, 21st Cong., 1st sess., p. 1074.

30. See "Indians Removed Westward," *Niles'*, XXXVI (July 25, 1829), 357. Though Francis Paul Prucha, "Indian Removal and The Great American Desert," *Indiana Mag. of Hist.*, LIX (Dec. 1963), 298–322, rebuts the notion that the region in which the Indians were to be colonized was popularly

regarded as the Great American Desert, the fact remains that the region *was* considered to be barren and unattractive, bordering on the "desert" itself.

31. "William Penn" [Jeremiah Evarts], *Essays on the Present Crisis in the Condition of the American Indians* (Boston, 1829), p. 100.

32. [Jeremiah Evarts], "Removal of the Indians," *NAR*, XXXI (Oct. 1830), 439.

33. James C. Mitchell, Dec. 18, 1827, in *Register of Debates in Cong.*, 20th Cong., 1st sess., p. 821.

34. Peleg Sprague, Apr. 17, 1830, in *Register of Debates in Cong.*, 21st Cong., 1st sess., p. 357.

35. Elbert Herring, "Rep., Ind. Bureau" (Nov. 19, 1831), in *House Exec. Doc. No.* 2, 22nd Cong., 1st sess., p. 172.

36. Lewis Cass, "Rep., Secy. of War" (Nov. 21, 1831), in *House Exec. Doc. No.* 2, 22nd Cong., 1st sess., pp. 172, 30.

37. See *Register of Debates in Cong.*, 21st Cong., 1st sess., pp. 309, 318, 357, 381–83.

38. Richard Peters, ed., *The Public Statutes at Large of the United States . . . to March 3, 1845* (Boston, 1846), IV, 411–13. For the hard line on Indians who declined to remove, see Thomas L. McKenney to Hugh Montgomery, Cherokee Agent, June 6, 1830, in "Removal of the Cherokees," *Niles'*, XXXVIII (Aug. 21, 1830), 457; and Elbert Herring, "Rep., Office of Ind. Affairs" (Nov. 28, 1833), in *Sen. Doc. No. 1*, 23rd Cong., 1st sess., p. 184.

39. Felix S. Cohen, "The Erosion of Indian Rights, 1950–1953: A Case Study in Bureaucracy," *Yale Law Jour.*, LXII (Feb. 1953), 352.

40. Thomas L. McKenney, *On the Origin, History, Character, and the Wrongs and Rights of the Indians* (New York, 1846), pp. 106, 132–33.

41. Jared Sparks to Lewis Cass, Oct. 28, 1829, in Herbert B. Adams, ed., *The Life and Writings of Jared Sparks, Comprising Selections from His Journal and Correspondence*, 2 vols. (Freeport, N.Y., 1970 [1893]), I, 282.

42. Peters, *Statutes at Large*, IV, 412. The act establishing the position of Commissioner of Indian Affairs also provided for the phasing out of various personnel ("agents, subagents, interpreters, and mechanics") as may, "from time to time, become unnecessary, in consequence of the emigration of the Indians, or other causes." (*Ibid.*, p. 564.)

43. Alexis de Tocqueville, *Democracy in America*, edited by Phillips Bradley, 2 vols. (New York, Vintage, 1945), I, 369.

44. William Lumpkin, Feb. 20, 1828, in *Register of Debates in Cong.*, 20th Cong., 1st sess., p. 1587.

45. Joseph M. White, Feb. 20, 1828, in *ibid.*, p. 1589.

46. "The Cherokees," *Niles'*, XXXVI (Mar. 14, 1829), 41 (repr. from the *Cherokee Phoenix*, Jan. 28, 1829).

47. Daniel J. Boorstin, *The Americans: The National Experience* (New York, 1965), pt. 5. For isolation and Jacksonian reform, see David J. Rothman, *The Discovery of the Asylum: Social Order and Disorder in the New Republic* (Boston, 1971).

48. Thomas Hart Benton, Mar. 1, 1825, in *Register of Debates in Cong.*, 18th Cong., 2nd sess., p. 712.

49. "The American Aborigines," *Niles'*, XV (Nov. 14, 1818), 187.

50. George Catlin, *Letters and Notes on the Manners, Customs, and Condition of the North American Indians*, 2 vols. (New York, 1841), I, 18, 258–64.

51. W. Medill, "Rep., Com. Ind. Affairs" (Nov. 30, 1846), in *House Exec. Doc. No. 4*, 29th Cong., 2nd sess., p. 225.

52. Jefferson Davis, Mar. 3, 1849, in *Cong. Globe*, 30th Cong., 2nd sess., p. 678.

53. [James L. Orr], "Terms of Treaties Hereafter to Be Made with Certain Tribes of Indians," *House Rep. No. 133* (Apr. 7, 1854), 33rd Cong., 1st sess., p. 6.

54. George Minot, ed., *The Statutes at Large* . . . (Boston, 1851), IX, 204.

55. Memorial, N.Y., Nov. 30, 1846, in "Statistics, Etc., of the Indian Tribes" (Feb. 9, 1847), *House Rep. No. 53*, 29th Cong., 2nd sess., p. 2.

56. Henry R. Schoolcraft, *Information Respecting the History, Condition and Prospects of the Indian Tribes of the United States*, 6 vols. (Philadelphia, 1851–57), IV, 484–86; VI, xxvi.

57. L. Lea, "Rep., Com. Ind. Affairs" (Nov. 27, 1851), in *Sen. Exec. Doc. No. 1*, 32nd Cong., 1st sess., p. 274.

58. D. Lowry, "Moral Questions Relative to Practical Plans for Educating and Civilizing the Aborigines," in Schoolcraft, *Information*, II, 529–30; and D. Lowry, "Education, Christianity, and the Arts," in *ibid.*, III, 478–79.

59. Alexander H. H. Stuart, "Rep., Secy. Interior" (Nov. 29, 1851), in *Sen. Exec. Doc. No. 1*, 32nd Cong., 1st sess., p. 502.

60. Orlando Brown, "Rep., Com. Ind. Affairs" (Nov. 30, 1849), in *Sen. Exec. Doc. No. 1, Pt. 3*, 31st Cong., 1st sess., p. 946. For the view that the reservations "probably saved the Indian from virtual extinction," see Alban W. Hoopes, *Indian Affairs and Their Administration, with Special Reference to the Far West, 1849–1860* (Philadelphia, 1932), p. 238; William T. Hagan, "Indian Policy after the Civil War: The Reservation Experience," in *Indiana Historical Society Lectures, 1970–1971: American Indian Policy* (Indianapolis, 1971), p. 22; and Robert A. Trennert, Jr., *Alternative to Extinction: Federal Indian Policy and the Beginnings of the Reservation System, 1846–51* (Philadelphia, 1975).

61. William P. Dole, "Rep., Com. Ind. Affairs" (Oct. 31, 1863), *House Exec. Doc. No. 1*, 38th Cong., 1st sess., pp. 129–30.

62. Jackson, First Ann. Message, Dec. 8, 1829, in Richardson, *Messages and Papers*, II, 457–58.

63. "An Address Delivered to the Colonization Society of Kentucky, at Frankfort, December 17, 1829, by the Hon. Henry Clay . . . ," *African Repository, and Colonial Jour.*, VI (Mar. 1830), 18–19.

64. Arthur Schlesinger, Jr., "The Causes of the Civil War: A Note on Historical Sentimentalism," *Partisan Rev.*, XVI (Oct. 1949), 980.

Chapter Six: Red, White, and Black

1. David Donald, "Toward a Reconsideration of Abolitionists," *Lincoln Reconsidered: Essays on the Civil War Era* (New York, 1956), pp. 19–36.

2. See James M. McPherson, *The Struggle for Equality: Abolitionists and the Negro in the Civil War and Reconstruction* (Princeton, N.J., 1964).

3. *National Anti-Slavery Standard* (Boston), May 1, 1869, quoted in Linda K. Kerber, "The Abolitionist Perception of the Indian," *Jour. of Am. Hist.*, LXII (Sept. 1975), 271.

4. Open letter from Wendell Phillips to Gen. William T. Sherman, July 17, 1876, in "The Indian Question," *Charleston Jour. of Commerce*, July 22,

1876. For the links between abolitionism and Indian reform, see Robert W. Mardock, "The Anti-slavery Humanitarians and Indian Policy Reform," *Western Humanities Rev.*, VII (Spring 1958), 131–46, and *The Reformers and the American Indian* (Columbia, Mo., 1971), esp. chaps. 1, 3.

5. Robert T. Lewit, "Indian Missions and Antislavery Sentiment: A Conflict of Evangelical and Humanitarian Ideals," *MVHR*, L (June 1963), 48.

6. See William Stanton, *The Leopard's Spots: Scientific Attitudes toward Race in America, 1815–59* (Chicago, 1960), pp. 52–53; and George M. Fredrickson, *The Black Image in the White Mind: The Debate on Afro-American Character and Destiny* (New York, 1971), chap. 3.

7. J. C. Nott and George R. Gliddon, *Types of Mankind; or, Ethnological Researches, Based upon the Ancient Monuments, Paintings, Sculptures, and Crania of Races, and upon Their Natural, Geographical, Philological, and Biblical History* ... (Philadelphia, 1854), pp. 69, 77.

8. Oliver Wendell Holmes, "Oration" (1855), in Cephas and Eveline Warner Brainerd, eds., *The New England Society Orations: Addresses, Sermons and Poems Delivered Before The New England Society in the City of New York, 1820–1885*, 2 vols. (New York, 1901), II, 298. For the American School and the Indian, see Reginald Horsman, "Scientific Racism and the American Indian in the Mid-Nineteenth Century," *Am. Q.*, XXVII (May 1975), 152–68.

9. Francis Parkman to Henry Stevens, Mar. 28, Oct. 29, 1846, in John Buechler, ed., "The Correspondence of Francis Parkman and Henry Stevens, 1845–1885," *Transactions, Am. Phil. Soc.*, N.S., LVII, pt. 6 (1967), 16.

10. Francis Parkman, *The Oregon Trail* (New York, Signet, 1950 [1849]), pp. 148–49, 179, 198, 114, 105, 123, 116, 178, 201–2, 205–6.

11. See, for example, Francis Parkman, *The Conspiracy of Pontiac and the Indian War After the Conquest of Canada*, 2 vols. (Boston 1910 [1851]), I, 48; "Indian Antiquities in North America," *Christian Examiner and Religious Misc.*, L (May 1851), 418; "James Fenimore Cooper," *NAR*, LXXIV (Jan. 1852), 151; *Vassall Morton* (Boston, 1856), p. 244; and "Manners and Customs of Primitive Indian Tribes," *NAR*, CI (July 1865), 51, 63.

12. Fredrickson, *Black Image*, p. 101.

13. Samuel George Morton, *Crania Americana; or, A Comparative View of the Skulls of Various Aboriginal Nations of North and South America: To Which Is Prefixed an Essay on the Varieties of the Human Species* (Philadelphia, 1839), p. 75.

14. "The Indian Tribes of the United States," *De Bow's Rev.*, XVII (July 1854), 76.

15. Alexis de Tocqueville, *Democracy in America*, edited by Phillips Bradley, 2 vols. (New York, Vintage, 1945), I, 347.

16. Alexis de Tocqueville, *Journey to America*, edited by J. P. Mayer, translated by George Lawrence (Garden City, N.Y., Anchor, rev. ed., 1971), p. 119 (entry for July 4, 1831).

17. James Garfield to Jacob D. Cox, July 26, 1865, in Fredrickson, *Black Image*, p. 185.

18. Henry Highland Garnet (1843), in Arthur Zilversmit, "The Abolitionists: From Patience to Militance," in James C. Curtis and Lewis L. Gould, eds., *The Black Experience in America: Selected Essays* (Austin, Tex., 1970), p. 63.

19. Frederick Douglass, "The Claims of the Negro Ethnologically Consid-

ered" (1854), in Philip S. Foner, ed., *The Life and Writings of Frederick Douglass*, 2 vols. (New York, 1950), II, 308.

20. Henry Highland Garnet, *The Past and Present Condition and the Destiny, of the Colored Race: A Discourse Delivered at the Fifteenth Anniversary of the Female Benevolent Society of Troy, N.Y., Feb. 14, 1848* (Miami, Fla., 1969), p. 25.

21. A black speaker at a New York meeting in 1831 used the Cherokees as an example of that "intelligence and refinement" to which the Indian could aspire, and as a "practical refutation of the vain assertion" that it was "impossible to civilize the red man": "It is too late now to brand with inferiority any one of the races of mankind. We ask for proof." (*Liberator*, Feb. 12, 1831.) When Douglass came up with the idea of Negro superiority to the Indian at the 1869 meeting of the American Anti-Slavery Society, he was roundly berated by another participant for committing "the same sin that the nation has been committing against his own color." (Kerber, "Abolitionist Perception of the Indian," p. 294.)

22. See Benjamin Quarles, *Black Abolitionists* (New York, 1969), pp. 215–22; and Eric Foner, *Free Soil, Free Labor, Free Men: The Ideology of the Republican Party before the Civil War* (New York, 1970), pp. 274–75.

23. Morton Cronin, "Currier and Ives: A Content Analysis," *Am. Q.*, IV (Winter 1952), 328–29.

24. E. C. Matthews, *How to Draw Funny Pictures: A Complete Course in Cartooning* (New York, 1928), pp. 64, 142.

25. *Madisonian*, July 1876, quoted in Rex C. Myers, "Montana Editors and the Custer Battle," *Montana*, XXVI (Spring 1976), 30.

26. Harry T. Peters, *Currier & Ives: Printmakers to the American People* (Garden City, N.Y., 1942), p. 16, plates 22 and 23.

27. Hinton Rowan Helper, *Nojoque; A Question for a Continent* (New York, 1867), pp. 216, 214.

28. George M. Weston, *The Progress of Slavery in the United States* (New York, 1969 [1857]), p. 244.

29. Thomas Wentworth Higginson, "The Ordeal by Battle," *Atlantic Monthly* (July 1861), quoted in Fredrickson, *Black Image*, p. 119.

30. Elias Boudinot, *A Star in the West; or, A Humble Attempt to Discover the Long Lost Ten Tribes of Israel . . .* (Freeport, N.Y., 1970 [1816]), p. 160.

31. Caption on a 1505 engraving, quoted in Lewis Hanke, *Aristotle and the American Indians: A Study in Race Prejudice in the Modern World* (Bloomington, Ind., 1959), p. 5.

32. See James Harvey Young, *The Toadstool Millionaires: A Social History of Patent Medicines in America before Federal Regulation* (Princeton, N.J., 1961), pp. 176–79, 192–93; Arrell M. Gibson, "Medicine Show," *Am. West*, IV (Feb. 1967), 34–39, 74–79; and John G. Cawelti, "The Frontier and the Native American," in Joshua C. Taylor, *America as Art* (Washington, D.C., 1976), pp. 154–55.

33. See E. McClung Fleming, "From Indian Princess to Greek Goddess: The American Image, 1783–1815," *Winterthur Portfolio*, III (1967), esp. 39–46; and "Symbols of the United States: From Indian Queen to Uncle Sam," in Ray B. Browne, Richard H. Crowder, Virgil L. Lokke, and William T. Stafford, eds., *Frontiers of American Culture* (Lafayette, Ind., 1968), pp. 1–24.

34. The 1776 quotation is in Felix S. Cohen, "Americanizing the White

Man," in Lucy Kramer Cohen, ed., *The Legal Conscience: Selected Papers of Felix S. Cohen* (New Haven, 1960), p. 318. See Leroy V. Eid, "Liberty: The Indian Contribution to the American Revolution," *Midwest Q.*, XXII (Spring 1981), 279–98.

35. Montgomery C. Meigs to Thomas Crawford, Apr. 26, 1854, in Robert L. Gale, *Thomas Crawford: American Sculptor* (Pittsburgh, 1964), p. 124.

36. Jefferson Davis to Meigs, Jan. 15, 1856, in Charles E. Fairman, *Art and Artists of the Capitol of the United States of America* (1927), *Sen. Doc. No. 95*, 69th Cong., 1st sess., p. 169.

37. Meigs to Crawford, Apr. 26, 1854, and Crawford to Meigs, Mar. 19, 1856, in Gale, *Thomas Crawford*, pp. 124, 156.

38. Edward Ball, Ohio, May 26, 1856, in *Cong. Globe*, 34th Cong., 1st sess., app., p. 623.

39. See Louise Hall Tharp, *Saint-Gaudens and the Gilded Era* (Boston, 1969), pp. 352, 357–58; and Ted Schwarz, *A History of United States Coinage* (San Diego, 1980), pp. 230–36.

40. L[ouis] A[gassiz], "The Diversity of Origin of the Human Races," *Christian Examiner and Religious Misc.*, XLIX (July 1850), 144.

41. William P. Ewing, "Lay of the Last Indian," in George Johnson, ed., *The Poets and Poetry of Cecil County, Maryland* (Elkton, Md., 1887), pp. 183–84.

42. Benson J. Lossing, "Our Barbarian Brethren," *Harper's M.*, XL (May 1870), 811.

43. Robert Patterson, "Our Indian Policy," *Overland Monthly*, XI (Sept. 1873), 213–14.

44. "Lo! The Poor Indian," *Harper's W.*, XV (Apr. 22, 1871), 363 (cartoon is on p. 361).

45. Thomas Nast, "Give the Natives a Chance, Mr. Carl [Schurz]," *Harper's W.*, XXIV (Mar. 13, 1880), 173.

46. J. Q. Smith, "Rep., Com. Ind. Affairs" (Oct. 30, 1876), in *House Exec. Doc. No. 1, Pt. 5*, 44th Cong., 2nd sess., p. 389.

Chapter Seven: Can He Be Saved?

1. George Ainslie, "The Indian Question," *Presbyterian Q. and Princeton Rev.*, N.S. 3, IV (July 1875), 438.

2. Thomas L. McKenney and James Hall, *The Indian Tribes of North America; with Biographical Sketches and Anecdotes of the Principal Chiefs*, 3 vols. (Edinburgh, 1933–34 [1836–44]), III, 160–84.

3. [Christopher C. Andrews], "The Condition and Needs of the Indian Tribes," *NAR*, XC (Jan. 1860), 69, 70.

4. H. V. R., "A Plea for the Indian," *Catholic World*, XLII (Mar. 1886), 850.

5. George Catlin, *Letters and Notes on the Manners, Customs, and Condition of the North American Indians*, 2 vols. (New York, 1841), I, 184.

6. Ainslie, "The Indian Question," p. 438.

7. Robert Patterson, "Our Indian Policy," *Overland Monthly*, XI (Sept. 1873), 211.

8. George E. Ellis, *The Red Man and the White Man in North America* (Boston, 1882), pp. 232–33.

9. J. D. Cox, "The Indian Question," *International Rev.*, VI (June 1879), 627.

10. Patterson, "Our Indian Policy," p. 207.
11. See Helen Marie Bannan, "Reformers and the 'Indian Problem,' 1878–1887 and 1922–1934" (unpub. Ph.D. diss., Syracuse University, 1976), chaps. 3–5, esp. pp. 152–57, 215–20, 240–54, and "The Idea of Civilization and American Indian Policy Reformers in the 1880s," *Jour. Am. Culture*, I (Winter 1978), 787–99; and Michael C. Coleman, "Not Race, but Grace: Presbyterian Missionaries and American Indians, 1837–1893," *Jour. of Am. Hist.*, LXVII (June 1980), 41–60.
12. Samuel B. Maxey, Feb. 19, 1886, *Cong. Record*, 49th Cong., 1st sess., p. 1632.
13. Benson J. Lossing, "Our Barbarian Brethren," *Harper's M.*, XL (May 1870), 796.
14. Hubert Howe Bancroft, *The Works of Hubert Howe Bancroft*, 39 vols. (San Francisco, 1886–90), XXXIX: Literary Industries, p. 305.
15. *Ibid.*, p. 345.
16. Bancroft, *Works*, I: *Native Races, I: The Wild Tribes*, pp. 4–16.
17. Bancroft, *Works*, II: *Native Races, II: Civilized Nations*, pp. 1, 4, 28.
18. *Ibid.*, pp. 31, 33, 41, 82.
19. *Ibid.*, pp. 41, 51.
20. Bancroft's theory and practice were not always consistent. He suffered from a severe case of negrophobia, and viewed the influx of non-Anglo immigrants into the United States sourly. See the selection from his *Retrospection* (1912), reprinted in I. A. Newby, ed., *The Development of Segregationist Thought* (Homewood, Ill., 1968), pp. 79–83.
21. For Morgan's strong influence on his generation, see J. W. Powell, "Sketch of Lewis H. Morgan, president of the American Association for the Advancement of Science," *Pop. Science Monthly*, XVIII (Nov. 1880), 117, 119–21; Bernhard J. Stern, *Lewis Henry Morgan: Social Evolutionist* (Chicago, 1931), chap. 6, esp. pp. 192–95; and Carl Resek, *Lewis Henry Morgan: American Scholar* (Chicago, 1960), pp. 142, 150.
22. Lewis Henry Morgan, *Ancient Society; or, Researches in the Lines of Human Progress from Savagery through Barbarism to Civilization*, edited by Eleanor Burke Leacock (Cleveland, Meridian Books, 1963 [1877]), pp. 3, 13. Morgan presented a paper on "Ethnical Periods" at the AAAS meeting in 1875 which departed most noticeably from the corresponding chapter in *Ancient Society* in not subdividing savagery. See *Proc., A.A.A.S., Twenty-fourth Meeting, held at Detroit, Michigan, August, 1875* (Salem, Mass., 1876), pp. 266–74.
23. Morgan, *Ancient Society*, pp. 8–9, 36, 562, 541.
24. *Ibid.*, Preface, pp. 515, 37–38.
25. See "Views of the Minority" in "Lands in Severalty to Indians" (May 28, 1880), *House Rep. No. 1576*, 46th Cong., 2nd sess., pp. 8–9.
26. Morgan, *Ancient Society*, pp. 506–7.
27. *Ibid.*, p. 562.
28. See Bannan, "Reformers and the 'Indian Problem,'" pp. 185–92, and Dwight W. Hoover, *The Red and the Black* (Chicago, 1976), pp. 151–62.

Chapter Eight: He Can Be Saved

1. Second Ann. Message, Dec. 5, 1870, in James D. Richardson, *A Compilation of the Messages and Papers of the Presidents, 1789–1902*, 10 vols. (Washington, D.C., 1903), VII, 112.

2. See Chester E. Eisinger, "The Freehold Concept in Eighteenth-Century American Letters," *W&MQ*, 3rd ser., IV (Jan. 1947), 42–59, which discusses the pervasiveness of the "Jeffersonian myth" or, as he prefers, "freehold concept" in the eighteenth century; Richard Bridgman, "Jefferson's Farmer before Jefferson," *Am. Q.*, XIV (Winter 1962), 567–77, for a rebuttal of sorts that argues for an aristocratic planter myth and against a democratic yeoman myth until after the Revolution; Henry Nash Smith, *Virgin Land: The American West as Symbol and Myth* (Cambridge, Mass., 1950), Book 3, for the agrarian myth as a dynamic factor in American western expansion; and Richard Hofstadter's compressed discussion of the yeoman and the agrarian myth in *The Age of Reform: From Bryan to F.D.R.* (New York, 1955), chap. 1.

3. J. D. C. Atkins, "Rep., Com. Ind. Affairs" (Oct. 5, 1885), in *House Exec. Doc. No. 1, Pt. 5*, 49th Cong., 1st sess., p. 5.

4. Henry L. Dawes, in *Proc., Fifth Ann. Meeting, Lake Mohonk Conf.* (1887), reprinted in Francis Paul Prucha, ed., *Americanizing the American Indians: Writings by the "Friends of the Indian" 1880–1900* (Cambridge, Mass., 1973), p. 109.

5. "The American Aborigines," *Niles'*, XV (Nov. 14, 1818), 186.

6. Henry S. Pancoast, *Impressions of the Sioux Tribes in 1882, with Some First Principles in the Indian Question* (Philadelphia, 1883), p. 9.

7. Henry R. Schoolcraft, *Information Respecting the History, Condition and Prospects of the Indian Tribes of the United States*, 6 vols. (Philadelphia, 1851–57), I, 433 (later substantially modified, to 8,000 acres per hunter, V, 485); and "The Indians of the United States—Their Past, Their Present, and Their Future," *De Bow's Rev.*, XVI (Feb. 1854), 144.

8. T. Hartley Crawford, "Rep., Com. Ind. Affairs" (Nov. 25, 1838), in *Sen. Doc. No. 1*, 25th Cong., 3rd sess., p. 454.

9. George E. Ellis, *The Red Man and the White Man in North America* (Boston, 1882), p. 585. For the best short expression of this theme, see Alexander H. H. Stuart, "Rep., Secy. Interior" (Nov. 29, 1851), *Sen Exec. Doc. No. 1*, 32nd Cong., 1st sess., p. 503. Also, William T. Hagan, "Private Property, the Indian's Door to Civilization," *Ethnohistory*, XV (Spring 1956), 126–37; and Helen Marie Bannan, "Reformers and the 'Indian Problem,' 1878–1887 and 1922–1934" (unpub. Ph.D. diss., Syracuse University, 1976), 271–76, 280–83.

10. Lewis Henry Morgan, *Ancient Society; or, Researches in the Lines of Human Progress from Savagery through Barbarism to Civilization*, edited by Eleanor Burke Leacock (Cleveland, Meridian Books, 1963 [1877]), pp. 511–12, 554–6.

11. *Ibid.*, pp. 561–62.

12. Francis Parkman, "The Native Races of the Pacific States," *NAR*, CXX (Jan. 1875), 34.

13. John C. Lowrie, "Our Indian Affairs," *Presbyterian Q. and Princeton Rev.*, N.S. 3, III (Jan. 1874), 13.

14. Byron Cutcheon, Mar. 10, 1886, *Cong. Record*, 49th Cong., 1st sess., p. 2273.

15. J. C. Calhoun, Secretary of War, circular, Sept. 3, 1819, in Appendix to Jedidiah Morse, *A Report to the Secretary of War of the United States, on Indian Affairs* (New Haven, 1822), p. 290.

16. H. B. Peairs, "United States Indian Schools," *Red Man*, VI (June 1914), 415.

17. Draft of Instructions to Puyallup Employees, Oct. 1, 1879, in Robert

H. Keller, Jr., "American Indian Education: An Historical Context," *Jour. of the West*, XIII (Apr. 1974), 78.

18. Frederic Remington, "Artist Wanderings among the Cheyennes," *Century*, XXXVIII (Aug. 1889), 540.

19. *General George Crook: His Autobiography*, edited by Martin F. Schmitt (Norman, Okla., new ed., 1960), pp. 169–73. In his memoirs, Howard did leave the impression that he, "thanks to Divine help, which I love to recognize and acknowledge," successfully extended Grant's Peace Policy over the Southwest, thereby effecting an unprecedented—if brief—period of peace throughout Indian country. (*My Life and Experience among Our Hostile Indians* [Hartford, Conn., 1907], pp. 11, 121.)

20. Elaine Goodale Eastman, *Pratt: The Red Man's Moses* (Norman, Okla., 1935).

21. Helen W. Ludlow, *Captain Pratt and His Work for Indian Education* (Philadelphia, 1886), pt. 1, p. 4.

22. Richard Henry Pratt, *Battlefield and Classroom: Four Decades with the American Indian, 1867–1904*, edited by Robert M. Utley (New Haven, 1964), pp. 7–8. The same theme is developed at greater length in chap. 23. Pratt began his memoirs in 1909 and completed them in 1923, the year before he died.

23. Pratt to Pres. Rutherford B. Hayes, Mar. 9, 1880, in *ibid.*, p. 251.

24. Helen W. Ludlow, "Indian Education at Hampton and Carlisle," *Harper's M.*, LXII (Apr. 1881), 669.

25. Helen W. Ludlow, *Ten Years' Work for Indians at the Hampton Normal and Agricultural Institute, at Hampton, Virginia* (Hampton, Va., 1888), p. 14.

26. Anna C. Brackett, "Indian and Negro," *Harper's M.*, LXI (Sept. 1880), 627–30.

27. Ludlow, "Indian Education at Hampton and Carlisle," p. 660.

28. S. C. Armstrong, Preface to Ludlow, *Ten Years' Work*, p. 5. Also, August Meier, "The Beginning of Industrial Education in Negro Schools," *Midwest Jour.*, VII (Spring 1955), 36–39; and David Wallace Adams, "Education in Hues: Red and Black at Hampton Institute, 1878–1893," *South Atlantic Q.*, LXXVI (Spring 1977), 159–76.

29. See R. H. Pratt, "American Indians; Chained and Unchained: Being an Account of How the Carlisle Indian School Was Born and Grew in Its First 25 Years," *Red Man*, VI (June 1914), 398–401, which deals directly with the clash of opinion between Pratt and Armstrong over the merits of assimilation versus segregation in race education.

30. Pratt, *Battlefield and Classroom*, pp. 214–16.

31. Richard H. Pratt, "Violated Principles the Cause of Failure in Indian Civilization," *Jour. Mil. Serv. Inst. U.S.*, VII (Mar. 1886), 59.

32. "A Way Out," in *Proc., Ninth Ann. Meeting, Lake Mohonk Conf.* (1891), reprinted in Prucha, ed., *Americanizing the American Indians*, pp. 272–76.

33. Pratt, *Battlefield and Classroom*, p. 311.

34. See Pratt "Violated Principles," p. 48; "The Advantages of Mingling Indians with Whites," in *The Indian Policy: Papers read at the Nineteenth Annual Conference of Charities and Correction, held at Denver, 1892* (N.p., 1892), pp. 45, 50–51; *Indian Schools: An Exposure. Address Before the Ladies Missionary Societies of the Calvary M. E. Church, Washington, D.C., April 6* (Washington, D.C., ca. 1915), p. 5; and *Battlefield and Classroom*, pp. 214, 312.

35. Brackett, "Indian and Negro," p. 627.

36. James C. Welling, "Race Education," *NAR*, CXXXVI (Apr. 1883), 363.

37. Pratt to Rep. Thaddeus C. Pound, Jan. 13, 1881, in *Battlefield and Classroom*, p. 259.

38. Carl Schurz, "Present Aspects of the Indian Problem," *NAR*, CXXXII (July 1881), 15–16.

39. Pratt, "Advantages of Mingling Indians with Whites," p. 56.

40. J. Evarts Greene, "Our Dealings with the Indians," *Proc., Am. Antiq. Soc.*, N.S. XI (Apr. 1896–Apr. 1897), 40.

41. *Transactions, Anthro. Soc. Washington*, I (1882), pp. 45–46.

42. Pratt, *Battlefield and Classroom*, p. 305; also, "Education of Indians," *Public Opinion*, XVIII (June 27, 1895), 730; and *The Indian Industrial School, Carlisle, Pennsylvania: Its Origins, Purposes, Progress and the Difficulties Surmounted* (Carlisle, 1979 [1908]), pp. 35, 52–53, 55.

43. Pratt, *Battlefield and Classroom*, pp. 31, 83, 270–71, 303–7, 312, 336; and *The Indian Industrial School, Carlisle, Pennsylvania*, pp. 28–29, 32–33, 35–36, 51.

44. Pratt to Rep. Pound, Jan. 13, 1881, in *Battlefield and Classroom*, p. 259.

45. George S. Wilson, "How Shall the American Savage Be Civilized?" *Atlantic Monthly*, L (Nov. 1882), 606.

46. Elaine Goodale, *Captain Pratt and His Work for Indian Education*, pt. 2, p. 8.

47. Elaine Goodale, "Plain Words on the Indian Question," *New Eng. Mag.*, N.S., II (Apr. 1890), 148.

48. "Monument Erected to Brig. Gen. R. H. Pratt by Carlisle Students and Other Indians," *Am. Ind.*, I (Dec. 1926), 6.

49. Herbert Welsh, "The Indian Question Past and Present," *New Eng. Mag.*, N.S. III (Oct. 1890), 263.

50. [H. B. Whipple], "The Indian System," *NAR*, XCIX (Oct. 1864), 459.

51. Grover Cleveland, Fourth Ann. Message, Dec. 3, 1888, in Richardson, *Messages and Papers*, VIII, 796.

52. Byron Cutcheon, Mar. 10, 1886, *Cong. Record*, 49th Cong., lst sess., p. 2272.

Chapter Nine: The Convenient Extinction Doctrine

1. Henry Knox, July 7, 1789, quoted in Walter H. Mohr, *Federal Indian Relations, 1774–1788* (Philadelphia, 1933), p. 172.

2. William Hobart Hare, *Reminiscences. An Address* (Philadelphia, 1888), p. 11.

3. Benson J. Lossing, "Our Barbarian Brethren," *Harper's M.*, XL (May 1870), 796.

4. "Our Indian Tribes," *Boston Rev.*, II (Sept. 1862), 517–23.

5. Charles Lowe, "The President's New Indian Policy," *Old and New*, III (Apr. 1871), 498–99.

6. F. A. Walker, "The Indian Question," *NAR*, CXVI (Apr. 1873), 386–87.

7. [Selden N. Clark, comp.], *Are the Indians Dying Out?: Preliminary Observations Relating to Indian Civilization and Education* (Washington, D.C., Nov. 24, 1877), pp. 4–11.

8. *Ibid.*, p. 12, also pp. 4, 21.

9. *Ibid.*, pp. 18, 20.

10. *Ibid.*, pp. 40, 42. Also see Alice C. Fletcher, *Indian Education and Civilization* (1888), *Sen. Exec. Doc. No. 95*, 48th Cong., 2nd sess., pp. 152–53, which summarizes the Clark report findings and updates the Indian population counts to 1886.

11. See H. H. [Helen Hunt Jackson], *A Century of Dishonor: A Sketch of the United States Government's Dealings with Some of the Indian Tribes* (New York, 1881), p. 338; and S. C. Armstrong, *Report of a Trip Made in Behalf of the Indian Rights Association, to Some Indian Reservations of the Southwest* (Philadelphia, 1884), p. 27.

12. Garrick Mallery, "The Former and Present Number of Our Indians," *Proc., A.A.A.S., Twenty-sixth Meeting, held at Nashville, Tenn., August, 1877* (Salem, Mass., 1878), pp. 340–41, 345. Also, Mallery, "Some Common Errors Respecting the North American Indians," *Bulletin, Phil. Soc. Washington*, II (Oct. 10, 1874–Nov. 2, 1878), 175–81, which combines two papers presented by Mallery, one at the November 24 meeting, the other on December 8. Since the second one was already scheduled for publishing in the AAAS *Proc.*, it is only summarized here.

13. Mallery, "Former and Present Number of Our Indians," pp. 350–53.

14. *Ibid.*, pp. 356, 362, 364. Mallery's penchant for evolutionary logic is also evident in his review, "Otis's Indian Question," *Nation*, XXVII (July 4, 1878), 14, which does provide for the possibility of accelerated progress through environmental change.

15. Mallery, "Former and Present Number of Our Indians," pp. 365–66.

16. Edward Howland, "Our Indian Brothers," *Harper's M.*, LVI (Apr. 1878), 775.

17. George W. Manypenny, *Our Indian Wards* (Cincinnati, 1880), pp. xxi–xxiii.

18. J. W. Powell, "Report," *First Ann. Rep., Bur. Ethn., 1879–'80* (Washington, D.C., 1881), pp. xxviii–xxix; "Indian Linguistic Families of America North of Mexico," *Seventh Ann. Rep., Bur. Ethn., 1885–'86* (Washington, D.C., 1891), p. 33; and "Are Our Indians Becoming Extinct?" *Forum*, XV (May 1893), 346, 354.

19. "The North American Indians," *Littell's Living Age*, CXXXIX (Nov. 16, 1878), 434, 436 (reprinted from the *Times* [London]). Also, Elwell, S. Otis *The Indian Question* (New York, 1878), chap. 1; *Twelfth Ann. Rep., Board of Ind. Commissioners* (1880), reprinted in Francis Paul Prucha, ed., *Americanizing the American Indians: Writings by the "Friends of the Indian" 1880–1900* (Cambridge, Mass., 1973), p. 193; James E. Rhoads, *The Indian Question in the Concrete* (Philadelphia, 1886), pp. 3–4; E. G. D., "Is the Indian Dying Out/Figures that Seem to Point the Other Way," *New York Times*, Feb. 14, 1887, p. 2; and J. Worden Pope, "The North American Indian—The Disappearance of the Race a Popular Fallacy," *Arena*, XVI (Nov. 1896), 945–59.

20. "Decrease of the Indians," *New York Times*, June 24, 1878, p. 4.

21. George E. Ellis, *The Red Man and the White Man in North America* (Boston, 1882), pp. 94–97, 594–95.

22. James H. Carleton, July 25, 1865, in [J. R. Doolittle], *Condition of the Indian Tribes* (1867), *Sen. Rep. No. 156*, 39th Cong., 2nd sess., app., pp. 432–33. For more army opinion on the Vanishing Indian, see DeB. Randolph

Keim, *Sheridan's Troopers on the Borders: A Winter Campaign on the Plains* (Philadelphia, 1885 [1870]), p. 3; G. A. Custer, *My Life on the Plains; or, Personal Experiences with Indians* (New York, 1874), pp. 15, 17; Henry B. Carrington, *The Indian Question. An Address* [BAAS, 1875] (Boston, 1909), pp. 13–14; and Richard Irving Dodge, *The Plains of the Great West and Their Inhabitants* (New York, 1959 [1877]), pp. 261, 273, 416. On military ambivalence toward the Indian, see William B. Skelton, "Army Officers' Attitudes toward Indians, 1830–1860," *Pac. Northwest Q.*, LXVII (July 1976), 113–24; and Thomas C. Leonard, "Red, White and the Army Blue: Empathy and Anger in the American West," *Am. Q.*, XXVI (May 1974), 176–90 (which, slightly revised, appears in Leonard, *Above the Battle: War-Making in America from Appomattox to Versailles* [New York, 1978], chap. 3).

23. John Gibbon, "Our Indian Question," *Jour. Mil. Serv. Inst. U.S.*, II (1881), 102, 106–7.

24. C. E. S. Wood, "Our Indian Question," *Jour. Mil. Serv. Inst. U.S.*, II (1881), 133–34, 180–81.

25. Governor Sir William Berkeley, 1671, quoted in Wilcomb E. Washburn, *The Governor and the Rebel: A History of Bacon's Rebellion in Virginia* (Chapel Hill, N.C., 1957), p. 20.

26. *Bismarck* (D.T.) *Tribune*, June 17, 1874, reprinted in Herbert Krause and Gary D. Olson, *Prelude to Glory: A Newspaper Accounting of Custer's 1874 Expedition to the Black Hills* (Sioux Falls, S.D., 1974), p. 11.

27. J. W. Powell, "An Overland Trip to the Grand Cañon," *Scribner's*, X (Oct. 1875), 677.

28. "Our Indian Tribes" (1862), p. 517.

29. D. C. Poole, *Among the Sioux of Dakota: Eighteen Months Experience as an Indian Agent* (New York, 1881), p. 152.

30. I. Edwards Clarke, "By Rail to the Rocky Mountains," *Galaxy*, VI (Nov. 1868), 672.

31. Mark Twain, "The Noble Red Man," *Galaxy*, X (Sept. 1870), 427.

32. "Mark Twain on the Indians," *Home and Farm* (Louisville, Ky.), Aug. 1, 1876, p. 6.

33. Bill Nye, *Bill Nye and Boomerang; or, The Tale of a Meek-eyed Mule, and Some Other Literary Gems* (Chicago, 1881), pp. 161, 249.

34. Brander Matthews, "The Centenary of Fenimore Cooper," *Century*, XXXVIII (Sept. 1889), 797.

35. John Esten Cooke, "Cooper's Indians," *Appleton's*, XII (Aug. 29, 1874), 264–67.

36. Twain, "Noble Red Man," p. 428.

37. James Fenimore Cooper, *The Last of the Mohicans* (New York, Signet, 1962 [1826]), p. 336.

38. Ambrose Bierce, *The Englarged Devil's Dictionary*, edited by Ernest Jerome Hopkins (Garden City, N.Y., 1967), p. 4.

39. John E. Maxwell, Mar. 20, 1875, in the *Faribault* (Minn.) *Republican*, Apr. 7, 1875, reprinted in Arthur J. Larsen, ed., "The Black Hills Gold Rush: Letters from Men Who Participated," *N.D.H.Q.*, VI (July 1932), 305.

40. *Cheyenne* (Wyo.) *Daily Leader*, Mar. 3, 1870, reprinted in Dee Brown, *Bury My Heart at Wounded Knee: An Indian History of the American West* (New York, 1971), p. 189.

41. George Hoar, *Cong. Record*, 47th Cong., 1st sess., pp. 2414, 2417–18.

42. Preston Plumb, in *ibid.*, pp. 2418–20.
43. Preston Plumb, quoted in Elmer Ellis, *Henry Moore Teller: Defender of the West* (Caldwell, Idaho, 1941), p. 109.
44. Wood, "Our Indian Question," p. 134; Gibbon, too, arrived at this point in his discussion ("Our Indian Question," pp. 109–10).
45. "A Curious Indian Relic," *Americana*, VII (Feb. 1912), 130.
46. "Indians in the United States," *Americana*, VII (Nov. 1912), 1091–92. The correspondent was Thomas Waterman, University of California.
47. George Ainslie, "The Indian Question," *Presbyterian Q. and Princeton Rev.*, N.S. 3, IV (July 1875), 438–39.

Chapter Ten: In Search of the One True Answer

1. Second Ann. Message, Dec. 6, 1886, in James D. Richardson, *A Compilation of the Messages and Papers of the Presidents, 1789–1902*, 10 vols. (Washington, D.C., 1903), VIII, 519.
2. DeB. Randolph Keim, *Sheridan's Troopers on the Borders: A Winter Campaign on the Plains* (Philadelphia, 1885 [1870]), p. 295.
3. Wm. H. Waterman, Supt. Ind. Affairs, Wash. Terr., Aug. 31, 1865, in [J. R. Doolittle], *Condition of the Indian Tribes* (1867), *Sen. Rep. No. 156*, 39th Cong., 2nd sess., app., p. 454.
4. Samuel Bowles, *Across the Continent: A Summer's Journey on the Rocky Mountains, the Mormons, and the Pacific States* (Springfield, Mass., and New York, 1865), p. 8.
5. Doolittle, *Condition of the Indian Tribes*, pp. 1–10.
6. See Harry Kelsey, "Background to Sand Creek," *Colo. Mag.*, XLV (Fall 1968), 279–300; Langdon Scully, "The Indian Agent: A Study in Corruption and Avarice," *Am. West*, X (Mar. 1973), 4–9; and David A. Nichols, *Lincoln and the Indians: Civil War Policy and Politics* (Columbia, Mo., 1978), chaps. 2, 6.
7. John Q. Smith, "Rep." (Oct. 30, 1876), *House Exec. Doc. No. 1, Pt. 5*, 44th Cong., 2nd sess., p. 388.
8. George P. Sanger, ed., *The Statutes at Large . . .* (Boston, 1871), XVI, 566.
9. *Nation*, X (June 16, 1870), 375.
10. E. S. Parker, "Rep., Com. Ind. Affairs" (Dec. 23, 1869), in *House Exec. Doc. No. 1, Pt. 3*, 41st Cong., 2nd sess., p. 448. Francis Paul Prucha, *American Indian Policy in Crisis: Christian Reformers and the Indian, 1865–1900* (Norman, Okla., 1976), pp. 63–71, provides a good discussion of the move to end the treaty system.
11. First Inaugural Address, Mar. 4, 1869, in Richardson, *Messages and Papers*, VII, 8.
12. Exec. Order, June 3, 1869, in *ibid.*, VII, 23–24; and J. D. Cox, "Rep., Secy. Interior" (Nov. 15, 1869), in *House Exec. Doc. No. 1, Pt. 3*, 41st Cong., 2nd sess., pp. x–xi.
13. First Ann. Message, Dec. 6, 1869, in Richardson, *Messages and Papers*, VII, 38–39. Also see C. Delano, "Rep., Secy. Interior" (Oct. 31, 1873), in *House Exec. Doc. No. 1, Pt. 5*, 43rd Cong., 1st sess., pp. iii–iv.
14. George Ward Nichols, "The Indian: What We Should Do with Him," *Harper's M.*, XL (Apr. 1870), 739. The division of responsibility between military and civilian suggested here was advocated in "Report of Indian

Peace Commissioners" (Jan. 14, 1868), *House Exec. Doc. No. 97*, 40th Cong., 2nd sess., pp. 20–21.

15. See Robert M. Utley, *Frontier Regulars: The United States Army and the Indian, 1866–1890* (New York, 1973), esp. chaps. 2 and 4; and Donald J. D'Elia, "The Argument over Civilian or Military Indian Control, 1865–1880," *Historian*, XXIV (Feb. 1962), 207–25.

16. [George E. Pond], "The New Indian Hostilities," *Nation*, IV (Jan. 17, 1867), 52.

17. Richard Irving Dodge, *The Plains of the Great West and Their Inhabitants* (New York, 1959 [1877]), p. 437.

18. Sherman to Philip G. Sheridan, Mar. 5, 1870, quoted in Richard N. Ellis, *General Pope and U.S. Indian Policy* (Albuquerque, N.M., 1970), p. 239.

19. John G. Nicolay, "The Sioux War," *Continental Monthly*, III (Feb. 1863), 204.

20. W. W. Ryer, *Islands as Indian Reservations* (San Francisco, n.d.[1876?]), pp. 3–4, 6. John E. Baur, "The Senator's Happy Thought," *Am. West*, X (Jan. 1973), 34–39, 62–63, discusses Nevada Senator James G. Fair's 1886 proposal that warlike Apaches be colonized on Santa Catalina—a proposal connected to speculation in real estate on the island.

21. "Report of J. W. Powell and G. W. Ingalls" (Dec. 18, 1873), in *House Exec. Doc. No. 1, Pt. 5*, 43rd Cong., 1st sess., p. 431.

22. Samuel Bowles, *Our New West. Records of Travel between The Mississippi River and the Pacific Ocean* (Hartford, Conn., 1869), pp. 156–58.

23. [R. J. Hinton], "Our Indian Policy," *Nation* II (Jan. 25, 1866), 103.

24. N. G. Taylor, Commissioner of Indian Affairs, July 12, 1867, in "Indian Hostilities" (July 13, 1867), *Sen. Exec. Doc. No. 13*, 40th Cong., 1st sess., p. 5.

25. "Report of Indian Peace Commissioners" (1868), pp. 17–20.

26. [Francis A. Walker], "The Indian Problem," *Nation*, X (June 16, 1870), 389.

27. Francis A. Walker, "The Indian Question," *NAR*, CXVI (Apr. 1873), 337, 348–51, 358. These ideas also appear in Walker, "Rep., Com. Ind. Affairs" (Nov. 1, 1872), in *House Exec. Doc. No. 1, Pt. 5*, 42nd Cong., 3rd sess., pp. 392–93, 396.

28. Walker, "Indian Question," pp. 359–60, 364–74.

29. See George M. Fredrickson, *The Inner Civil War: Northern Intellectuals and the Crisis of the Union* (New York, 1965), pp. 202–5; and Barbara Miller Solomon, *Ancestors and Immigrants: A Changing New England Tradition* (Cambridge, Mass., 1956), pp. 69–80.

30. Francis A. Walker, "Indian Citizenship," *International Rev.*, I (May 1874), 312–13, 322–26.

31. J. D. C. Atkins, "Rep., Com. Ind. Affairs," (Oct. 5, 1885), in *House Exec. Doc. No. 1, Pt. 5*, 49th Cong., 1st sess., pp. 8–12.

32. *Nation*, XXVII (Sept. 26, 1878), 186.

33. Stanley Clark, "Ponca Publicity," *MVHR*, XXIX (Mar. 1943), 495–516.

34. Rutherford B. Hayes, entry for Dec. 8, 1880, in T. Harry Williams, ed., *Hayes: The Diary of a President, 1875–1881* (New York, 1964), p. 301.

35. William Justin Harsha, "Law for the Indians," *NAR*, CXXXIV (Mar. 1882), 277.

36. President Rutherford B. Hayes, Special Message, Feb. 1, 1881, in Richardson, *Messages and Papers*, VII, 633.

37. Other Indian rights groups that were formed in this period: Indian Rights Association (Philadelphia, 1882); National Indian Defense Association (Washington, D.C., 1885; a solitary voice against allotment and in favor of retaining tribal organization); and, beginning in 1883, annual conferences of "Friends of the Indian" at Lake Mohonk to coordinate the activities of the different societies.

38. Inshtatheamba (Bright Eyes), Intro. to Zylyff [Thomas Henry Tibbles], *The Ponca Chiefs. An Indian's Attempt to Appeal from the Tomahawk to the Courts* (Boston, 2nd ed., 1880), p. vii.

39. Joseph Cook, *Frontier Savages, White and Red* (Philadelphia, 1885), pp. 11, 8.

40. "If I can do one-hundredth part for the Indians as Mrs. Stowe did for the Negro, I will be thankful," Helen Hunt Jackson wrote to William Hayes Ward, Jan. 1, 1884. (Quoted in Andrew F. Rolle, Intro. to Helen Hunt Jackson, *A Century of Dishonor: The Early Crusade for Indian Reform* [New York, 1965], p. xxii.)

41. Jackson to an anonymous friend, Jan. 17, 1880, quoted in "Mrs. Helen Jackson ('H. H.')," *Century*, XXXI (Dec. 1885), 254. See Ruth Odell, *Helen Hunt Jackson (H. H.)* (New York, 1939), esp. pp. 153–69; and Jackson, "The Wards of the United States Government," *Scribner's* XIX (Mar. 1880), 781–82.

42. Helen Jackson (H. H.), *A Century of Dishonor: A Sketch of the United States Government's Dealings with Some of the Indian Tribes* (New York, 1881), p. 341. (Subsequent references will be to this edition.)

43. *Ibid.*, pp. 29–30, 337.

44. *Ibid.*, p. 340. Jackson believed citizenship and allotment to be ultimate, not immediate, goals. She represented a wing of the reform movement that was suspicious of sweeping policies conceived in the nation's own best interests—concentration, the subdivision of the tribal lands, etc.—and stood firmly on the principle of the inviolability of past treaties. The Boston Indian Citizenship Committee, in which Jackson was active, shared this viewpoint on most matters. The dilemma was basic: how to honor past commitments and yet provide for a positive approach in the future.

45. *Ibid.*, p. 10.

46. [J. D. Cox], "A Century of Dishonor," *Nation*, XXXII (Mar. 3, 1881), 152.

47. Theodore Roosevelt, *The Winning of the West*, 4 vols. (New York, 1889–96), I, 331–35. Roosevelt was also referring to George Manypenny.

48. Sarah Newlin, "Indian Treaties and National Honor," *New Princeton Rev.*, II (Sept. 1886), 223–33; S. A. Galpin, "Some Administrative Difficulties of the Indian Problem," *New Englander and Yale Rev.*, XLVI (Apr. 1887), 305–18; and Herbert Welsh, "The Indian Question Past and Present," *New Eng. Mag.*, N.S. III (Oct., 1890), esp. 263–66.

49. William Hobart Hare, *Reminiscences. An Address* (Philadelphia, 1888), pp. 18–19.

Chapter Eleven: A New Order of Things

1. *The Indian Problem: Speech of Hon. J. H. Hibbetts, of Chetopa, in the House of Representatives of the State of Kansas, February 22, 1877* (Topeka, Kan., 1877), p. 36.

2. Carl Schurz, "Present Aspects of the Indian Problem," *NAR*, CXXXIII

(July 1881), 6. Schurz's influential report of Nov. 15, 1879, in *House Exec. Doc. No. 1, Pt. 5*, 46th Cong. 2nd sess., pp. 5–13, was cited by President Hayes and recommended to Congress's attention. (Third Ann. Message, Dec. 1, 1879, in James D. Richardson, *A Compilation of the Messages and Papers of the Presidents, 1789–1902*, 10 vols. [Washington, D.C., 1903], VII, 576.)

3. Georgiana C. Nammack, *Fraud, Politics, and the Dispossession of the Indians: The Iroquois Land Frontier in the Colonial Period* (Norman, Okla., 1969), pp. x, xvi, chap. 6.

4. Henry Knox, 1789, quoted in Walter H. Mohr, *Federal Indian Relations, 1774–1788* (Philadelphia, 1933), p. 171.

5. William Justin Harsha, "Law for the Indians," *NAR*, CXXXIV (Mar. 1882), 292.

6. E. A. Hayt, Jan. 24, 1879, in "Lands to Indians in Severalty" (Mar. 3, 1879), *House Rep. No. 165*, 45th Cong., 3rd sess., p. 2.

7. Joseph E. Brown, Jan. 24, 1881, *Cong. Record*, 46th Cong., 3rd sess., p. 879.

8. *Second Annual Address to the Public of The Lake Mohonk Conference, Held at Lake Mohonk, N.Y., September, 1884 . . .* (Philadelphia, 1884), pp. 6, 26.

9. Views of the Minority, "Lands in Severalty to Indians" (May 28, 1880), *House Rep. No. 1576*, 46th Cong. 2nd sess., p. 10.

10. Herbert Spencer (1873), quoted in Robert C. Bannister, *Social Darwinism: Science and Myth in Anglo-American Social Thought* (Philadelphia, 1979), p. 49.

11. Lewis Henry Morgan, June 1859, Kansas Territory, in *The Indian Journals, 1859–62*, edited by Leslie A. White (Ann Arbor, Mich., 1959), p. 38.

12. Lewis H. Morgan, "The Hue-and-Cry against the Indians," *Nation*, XXIII (July 20, 1876), 41.

13. Lewis H. Morgan, "Factory System for Indian Reservations," *Nation*, XXIII (July 27, 1876), 58–59.

14. Morgan, "Hue-and-Cry against the Indians," 41; and Morgan to President Rutherford B. Hayes, Aug. 6, 1877, in Bernhard J. Stern, *Lewis Henry Morgan: Social Evolutionist* (Chicago, 1931), pp. 56–57.

15. Morgan, "Factory System for Indian Reservations," p. 58.

16. Morgan to Hayes, Aug. 6, 1877, in Stern, *Lewis Henry Morgan*, p. 58; and Morgan, "The Indian Question," *Nation*, XXVII (Nov. 28, 1878), 332–33. Much of the plan Morgan proposed in the 1870s had first been worked up and sent to President Lincoln in 1862. See Carl Resek, *Lewis Henry Morgan: American Scholar* (Chicago, 1960), pp. 144–45.

17. H. V. R., "A Plea for the Indian," *Catholic World*, XLII (Mar. 1886), 850–51.

18. Francis Paul Prucha, "Indian Policy Reform and American Protestantism, 1880–1900," in Ray Allen Billington, ed., *People of the Plains and Mountains: Essays in the History of the West Dedicated to Everett Dick* (Westport, Conn., 1973), pp. 120–45.

19. J. W. Powell, "Sketch of Lewis H. Morgan, President of The American Association for the Advancement of Science," *Pop. Science Monthly*, XVIII (Nov. 1880), 119.

20. Joseph Henry, *Daily Journal: 1872*, p. 121 (entry for July 3, 1872), Smithsonian Institution Archives, Washington, D.C.

21. W J McGee, "The Foundation of Science," *Forum*, XXVII (Apr. 1894), 173–74.

22. J. W. Powell to Carl Schurz, Secretary of the Interior, Nov. 1, 1878, in "Surveys of the Territories: Letters from the Acting President of the National Academy of Sciences Transmitting a Report on the Survey of the Territories" (Dec. 3, 1878), *House Misc. Doc. No. 5*, 45th Cong., 3rd sess., pp. 26–27.

23. *Ibid.*

24. J. W. Powell to John T. Morgan (Jan. 1881) and Jan. 24, 1881, in *Cong. Record*, 46th Cong., 3rd sess., pp. 911–12.

25. Powell to Schurz, Nov. 1, 1878, "Survey of the Territories" (1878), p. 26.

26. Powell to Morgan (Jan. 1881), *Cong. Record*, 46th Cong., 3rd sess., p. 911.

27. J. W. Powell, "The Three Methods of Evolution," *Bulletin, Phil. Soc. Washington*, VI (1884), quoted in William Culp Darrah, *Powell of the Colorado* (Princeton, N.J., 1951), p. 357.

28. Leslie A. White, *Pioneers in American Anthropology: The Bandelier-Morgan Letters, 1873–1881*, 2 vols. (Albuquerque, N.M., 1940), I, 174, 241; II, 199.

29. *Transactions, Anthro. Soc. Washington*, I (Washington, D.C., 1882), 39-46, for Lester Ward's "Politico-Social Functions," Otis T. Mason's "The Savage Mind in the Presence of Civilization," and Powell's comments on both.

30. Fletcher was chiefly responsible for the passage of the Omaha Allotment Act of 1882, and wrote an extended treatise, *Indian Education and Civilization* (1888), *Sen. Exec. Doc. No. 95*, 48th Cong., 2nd sess., which underlined the "national need" for "more schools and better equipped schools" (p. 173).

31. Philip C. Garrett, "Indian Citizenship," *Proceedings of the Fourth Annual Lake Mohonk Conference* (1886), reprinted in Francis Paul Prucha, ed., *Americanizing the American Indians: Writings by the "Friends of the Indian" 1880–1900* (Cambridge, Mass., 1973), p. 59.

32. F. W. Blackmar, "Indian Education," *Annals, Am. Academy Pol. and Soc. Sc.*, II (May 1892), 85. Blackmar taught sociology at the University of Kansas.

33. Schurz, "Present Aspects of the Indian Problem," p. 10.

34. George F. Hoar and Henry L. Dawes, Jan. 24, 1881, *Cong. Record*, 46th Cong., 3rd sess., p. 875–88.

35. Jan. 25, 1881, *Cong. Record*, 46th Cong., 3rd sess., pp. 904–6.

36. Jan. 24, 1881, *ibid.*, p. 877.

37. *Fourth Ann. Rep., Ind. Rights Assn., 1886* (Philadelphia, 1887), p. 9.

38. Jan. 20, 1881, *Cong. Record*, 46th Cong., 3rd sess., p. 783.

39. Feb. 25, 1886, *Cong. Record*, 49th Cong., 1st sess., pp. 1762–63.

40. *Ibid.*

41. Jan. 24, 1881, *Cong. Record*, 46th Cong., 3rd sess., pp. 879–81. Brown, it should be pointed out, supported allotment as the best means of ending special treatment for the Indians. See Frederick B. Hoxie, "The End of the Savage: Indian Policy in the United States Senate, 1880–1900," *Chronicles of Okla.*, LV (Summer 1977), 163.

42. *The Statutes at Large* (Washington, D.C., 1887), XXIV, 388–91.

43. [Henry S. Pancoast], *Indian Land in Severalty, as Provided for by the Coke Bill* (Philadelphia, 1884), pp. 4–7.

44. Francis E. Leupp, *The Indian and His Problem* (New York, 1910), p. vii.

Chapter Twelve: A Matter of Administration

1. *Fourth Ann. Rep., Ind. Rights Assn., 1886* (Philadelphia, 1887), p. 11.
2. "Our Indian Problem and How We Are Solving It," *Rev. of Reviews* (New York), V (June 1892), 551.
3. H. L. Dawes, "Have We Failed with the Indian?" *Atlantic Monthly*, LXXXIV (Aug. 1899), 280.
4. Orville H. Platt, "Problems in the Indian Territory," *NAR*, CLX (Feb. 1895), 200.
5. See David M. Holford, "The Subversion of the Indian Land Allotment System, 1887–1934," *Ind. Historian*, VIII (Spring 1975), 11–21; and [Felix S. Cohen; updated by Frank B. Horne and Margaret F. Hurley], *Federal Indian Law* (Washington, D.C., 1958), pp. 117–25, 245–56.
6. See Frederick E. Hoxie, "The End of the Savage: Indian Policy in the United States Senate, 1880–1900," *Chronicles of Okla.*, LV (Summer 1977), esp. 169–78.
7. D. S. Otis, *The Dawes Act and the Allotment of Indian Lands*, edited by Francis Paul Prucha (Norman, Okla., new ed., 1973 [1934]), pp. 118–21.
8. Frances Campbell Sparhawk, "The Indian's Yoke," *NAR*, CLXXXII (Jan. 1906), 50.
9. George Bird Grinnell, "Tenure of Land among the Indians," *Am. Anthro.*, N.S. IX (Jan.-Mar. 1907), 6–8.
10. Hamlin Garland, "The Red Man's Present Needs," *NAR*, CLXXIV (Apr. 1902), 479.
11. Daniel F. Littlefield, Jr., and Lonnie E. Underhill, "Renaming the American Indian: 1890–1913," *Am. Studies*, XII (Fall 1971), 38.
12. Garland, "Red Man's Present Needs," pp. 479, 481.
13. Second Ann. Message, Dec. 3, 1894, in James D. Richardson, *A Compilation of the Messages and Papers of the Presidents, 1789–1902*, 10 vols. (Washington, D.C., 1903), IX, 544.
14. Grinnell, "Tenure of Land," p. 9.
15. George Bird Grinnell, *The Indians of To-day* (New York, 1911 [1900]), p. 149.
16. "Proceedings of the Anthropological Society of Washington," *Am. Anthro.*, N.S. IX (July-Sept. 1907), 573.
17. [Francis E. Leupp], "Our 'New Policy' with the Red Brother," *Nation*, LXXIX (Sept. 15, 1904), 211.
18. Garland, "Red Man's Present Needs," pp. 486–87.
19. Grinnell, "Tenure of Land," p. 11.
20. Leupp, "Our 'New Policy' with the Red Brother," p. 212.
21. Hermann Hagedorn, *Roosevelt in the Bad Lands* (Boston, 1921), p. 355.
22. See John F. Reiger, *American Sportsmen and the Origins of Conservation* (New York, 1975).
23. See Laurence M. Hauptman, "Governor Theodore Roosevelt and the Indians of New York State," *Proc., Am. Phil. Soc.*, CXIX (Feb. 1975), 1–7; William T. Hagan, "Civil Service Commissioner Theodore Roosevelt and the Indian Rights Association," *Pac. Hist. Rev.*, XLIV (May 1975), 187–200; and George Sinkler, *The Racial Attitudes of American Presidents from Abraham Lincoln to Theodore Roosevelt* (Garden City, N.Y., 1971), pp. 334–36.
24. *Report of Hon. Theodore Roosevelt Made to the United States Civil Service*

Commission, upon a Visit to Certain Indian Reservations and Indian Schools in South Dakota, Nebraska, and Kansas [Oct. 5, 1892] (Philadelphia, 1893), pp. 13–15.

25. Leupp virtually echoed Roosevelt in his "Outlines of an Indian Policy," Outlook, LXXIX (Apr. 15, 1905), 950, and his Report, Sept. 30, 1905, in Ann. Reps., Dept. Interior, 1905: Ind. Affairs, Pt. I (Washington, D.C., 1906), p. 7.

26. William A. Jones, Report, Oct. 15, 1901, in Ann. Reps., Dept. Interior, 1901: Ind. Affairs, Pt. I (Washington, D.C., 1902), pp. 4–7; and "A New Indian Policy," World's Work, III (Mar. 1902), p. 1840.

27. Report of Hon. Theodore Roosevelt, p. 13.

28. Francis E. Leupp, "The Story of Four Strenuous Years," Outlook, XCII (June 5 1909), 328–29.

29. Roosevelt to Secretary of the Interior Ethan Allen Hitchcock, July 22, 1903, in Elting E. Morison, ed., The Letters of Theodore Roosevelt, 8 vols. (Cambridge, Mass., 1951–54), III, 523.

30. T. J. Morgan, "Rep., Com. Ind. Affairs" (Oct. 1, 1891), in House Exec. Doc. No. 1, Pt. 5, 52nd Cong., 1st sess., p. 6.

31. F. E. Leupp, "The Training and Education of the Indian," Ind. Craftsman, I (May 1909), 6.

32. H. B. Peairs, "United States Indian Schools," Red Man, VI (June 1914), 415–17.

33. See Carlisle's Red Man: M. Friedman, "How Education Is Solving the Indian Problem; Some Practical Results," IV (Feb. 1912), 233; IV (Mar. 1912), 282–83, for statistical breakdowns on the post-Carlisle careers of 532 graduates and 4,151 other ex-students; "Facts about Carlisle Indian School," IV (May 1912), 434; and Charles E. Dagnett, "Returned Students," VI (June 1914), 421–25.

34. Francis E. Leupp, In Red Man's Land: A Study of the American Indian (New York, 1914), p. 77.

35. Francis E. Leupp, Rep., Com. Ind. Affairs, 1908 (Washington, D.C., 1908), p. 16, a line he repeated in The Indian and His Problem (New York, 1910), p. 145.

36. Leupp, "Training and Education of the Indian," p. 3.

37. Leupp, "Story of Four Strenuous Years," p. 330.

38. Leupp, Rep. (1908), p. 19.

39. R. H. Pratt, Indian Schools: An Exposure. Address before the Ladies Missionary Societies of the Calvary M. E. Church, Washington, D.C., April 6 (Washington, D.C., ca. 1915), pp. 13, 19.

40. Leupp, The Indian and His Problem, p. 135, echoing his Rep., Com. Ind. Affairs, 1907 (Washington, D.C., 1907), p. 21.

41. "A Meeting of Indian Educators," Outlook, LXXI (July 19, 1902), 713.

42. Leupp, "Training and Education of the Indian," p. 7. Also, see his "Outlines of an Indian Policy," p. 947; The Indian and His Problem, pp. 46, 118; and In Red Man's Land, pp. 74–75.

43. Leupp, Report (1905), p. 8.

44. Elaine Goodale Eastman, "The Education of Indians," Arena, XXIV (Oct. 1900), 413–14.

45. [M. Friedman], "The Record of Four Years," Ind. Craftsman, I (Apr. 1909), 3.

46. Francis E. Leupp, Report, Sept. 30, 1906, in Ann. Reps., Dept. Interior, 1906: Indian Affairs (Washington, D.C., 1906), p. 29.

47. Leupp, *The Indian and His Problem*, 48–49; and "Outlines of an Indian Policy," pp. 948–49. See Necah Furman, "Seedtime for Indian Reform: An Evaluation of the Administration of Commissioner Francis Ellington Leupp," *Red River Valley Hist. Rev.*, II (Winter 1975), 495–517.

48. Sparhawk, "Indian's Yoke," p. 51.

49. Frank Wood, "The Evils of the Reservation System," *Outlook*, LXXV (Sept. 19, 1903), 166.

50. Lyman Abbott, "Our Indian Problem," *NAR*, CLXVII (Dec. 1898), 726, 728.

51. Cato Sells, "A Declaration of Policy" (Apr. 17, 1917), in *Rep., Com. Ind. Affairs, 1917* (Washington, D.C., 1917), pp. 3–5.

52. Cato Sells, *Some Phases of Indian Administration* (Chilocco, Okla., n.d. [1921]), pp. 27–28.

53. Charles H. Burke, *Rep., Com. Ind. Affairs, 1921* (Washington, D.C., 1921), p. 25.

54. Mary Antonio Johnston, *Federal Relations with the Great Sioux Indians of South Dakota, 1887–1933: With Particular Reference to Land Policy Under the Dawes Act* (Washington, D.C., 1948), pp. 21–22.

55. Ross R. Cotroneo and Jack Dozier, "A Time of Disintegration: The Coeur d'Alene and the Dawes Act," *Western Hist. Q.*, V (Oct. 1974), 417.

56. Burke, *Rep.* (1921), p. 26.

57. Leupp, *Rep.* (1906), pp. 27–30.

58. Edgar B. Merritt, "The American Indian: His Progress and Some of His Needs," *Red Man*, IV (Dec. 1911), 148, an address delivered at the Mohonk Conf., Oct. 18, 1911.

59. Sells, *Some Phases of Indian Administration* p. 28.

60. Joseph W. Latimer, "Bureaucracy à la Mode," *Independent*, CXII (Feb. 2, 1924), 75.

61. *Brief Statement of the Aims, Work, and Achievements of the Indian Rights Association* (Philadelphia, 1886), p. 4.

62. *Williamsport Grit*, reprinted in *Red Man*, VI (Oct. 1913), 62.

63. Latimer, "Bureaucracy à la Mode," p. 75.

64. Robert G. Valentine, *Rep., Com. Ind. Affairs, 1911* (Washington, D.C., 1911), p. 23.

65. Thomas J. Morgan, "Supp. Rep. on Ind. Education" (Dec. 1, 1889), in *House Exec. Doc. No. 1, Pt. 5*, 51st Cong., 1st sess., pp. 101–2.

66. "A Ritual of Citizenship," *Outlook*, CXIII (May 24, 1916), 161–62. The script for the ritual is reprinted in Vine Deloria, Jr., ed., *Of Utmost Good Faith* (New York, Bantam, 1972), pp. 142–43; and a press account of the ceremony at Standing Rock, Fort Yates, N.D., in Frank Fiske, *The Taming of the Sioux* (Bismarck, N.D., 1917), pp. 180–81.

67. Red Fox St. James (Skiuhushu), quoted in "A Red-letter Day for Red Americans," *Lit. Digest*, LXXVIII (Sept. 29, 1923), 40. Not all Indians were enthusiastic soldiers. See David L. Wood, "Gosiute-Shoshone Draft Resistance, 1917–18," *Utah Hist. Q.*, XLIX (Spring, 1981), 173–88.

68. Red Fox Skiuhushu, letter to the *Seattle Post-Intelligencer*, reprinted in "If the Red Man Can Fight, Why Can't He Vote?" *Lit. Digest*, LIX (Dec. 21, 1918), 36–37.

69. Cato Sells, "The 'First Americans' as Loyal Citizens," *Am. Rev. of Reviews*, LVII (May 1918), 523. Sells made the same point in his official reports for 1918–20.

70. Edna Dean Proctor, "Citizenship for the Red Man," *The Complete Poetical Works of Edna Dean Proctor* (Boston, 1925), p. 141.
71. *United States v. Nice* (1916), quoted in Michael T. Smith, "The History of Indian Citizenship," *Great Plains Jour.*, X (Fall 1970), 33.
72. Henry L. Dawes, Mar. 26, 1884, *Cong. Record*, 48th Cong., 1st sess., p. 1177.
73. Henry M. Teller, Jan. 20, 1881, *Cong. Record*, 46th Cong., 3rd sess., p. 780.

Chapter Thirteen: We Have Come to the Day of Audit

1. [Francis Parkman], "James Fenimore Cooper," *NAR*, LXXIV (Jan. 1852), 151.
2. Francis Parkman, "Preface to the Edition of 1892," *The Oregon Trail: Sketches of Prairie and Rocky-Mountain Life* (Boston, 1910 ed.), pp. ix–xi.
3. Department of the Interior, Census Office, *Report on Indians Taxed and Indians Not Taxed in the United States (Except Alaska) at the Eleventh Census: 1890* (1894), *House Misc. Doc. No. 340, Pt. 15*, 52nd Cong., 1st sess., pp. 5, 57.
4. Henry W. Longfellow, "The Revenge of Rain-in-the-Face," *Youth's Companion*, L (Mar. 1, 1877), 68.
5. James McLaughlin to S. C. Armstrong, Nov. 9, 1885, quoted in Louis Pfaller, "'Enemies in '76, Friends in '85'—Sitting Bull and Buffalo Bill," *Prologue*, I (Fall 1969), 27.
6. *Chadron* (Neb.) *Democrat*, Jan. 1, 1891, reprinted in Don Huls, comp., *The Winter of 1890 (What Happened at Wounded Knee)* (Chadron, Neb., 1974), p. 34.
7. Henry Davenport Northrup, *Indian Horrors; or Massacres by the Red Man. Being a Thrilling Narrative of Bloody Wars with Merciless and Revengeful Savages* . . . (N.p. [Oakland, Calif.?], 1891), p. 580.
8. John G. Neihardt, *Black Elk Speaks: Being the Life Story of a Holy Man of the Oglala Sioux* (New York, 1932), p. 276. Bernard Barber's influential "Acculturation and Messianic Movements," *Am. Sociolog. Rev.*, VI (Oct. 1941), 663–69, argued that the millenarian movements among the Indians calling for a "reversion to the aboriginal state" were the products of deprivation. Since they projected success in the near future, even at a specified time, they were invariably short-lived, and the ghost dance was no exception. However, a provocative and persuasive rebuttal has been fashioned by Alice B. Kehoe, who maintains that the ghost dance, far from ending at Wounded Knee, simply assumed a less activistic character and remained a vital religious movement which thrives to this day. ("The Ghost Dance Religion in Saskatchewan, Canada," *Plains Anthro.*, XIII [1968], 296–304.)
9. Theodore Roosevelt, *An Autobiography* (New York, 1913), p. 94.
10. Superintendent of the Census, 1890, quoted in Frederick J. Turner, "The Significance of the Frontier in American History," *Ann. Rep., Am. Hist. Assn.*, *1893* (Washington, D.C., 1894), 199.
11. See Ray Allen Billington, *Frederick Jackson Turner: Historian, Scholar, Teacher* (New York, 1973), pp. 124–31; and Don Russell, *The Lives and Legends of Buffalo Bill* (Norman, Okla., 1960), p. 363.
12. C. H. Engle, "A Brief Sketch of Chief Simon Pokagon's Life," in Chief Pokagon, *O-Gi-Maw-Kwe Mit-I-Gwa-Ki (Queen of the Woods)* (Hartford, Mich., 1899), pp. 21, 23.

13. *Chicago Inter Ocean*, Mar. 16, 1899, in *ibid.*, App., pp. 232–33.
14. *Chicago Inter Ocean*, Jan. 29, 1899, in *ibid.*, App., p. 242.
15. B. O. Flower, "An Interesting Representative of a Vanishing Race," *Arena*, XVI (July 1896), 243–44.
16. *Chicago Inter Ocean*, Jan. 29, 1899, in Pokagon, *O-Gi-Maw-Kwe*, App., p. 242.
17. Simon Pokagon, "The Future of the Red Man," *Forum*, XXIII (Aug. 1897), 707–8.
18. Albert Shaw, "The Trans-Mississippians and Their Fair at Omaha," *Century*, LVI (Oct. 1898), 848.
19. R. H. Pratt, *The Indian Industrial School, Carlisle, Pennsylvania* (Carlisle, 1979 [1908]), p. 40. See Robert Bigart and Clarence Woodcock, "The Trans-Mississippi Exposition and the Flathead Delegation," *Montana*, XXIV (Autumn 1979), 14–23.
20. George Bird Grinnell, *The Indians of To-day* (New York, 1911 [1900]), p. 6.
21. Mary Alice Harriman, "The Congress of American Aborigines at the Omaha Exposition," *Overland Monthly*, XXXIII (June 1899), 506.
22. James Mooney, "The Indian Congress at Omaha," *Am. Anthro.*, N.S. I (Jan. 1899), 127.
23. Charles M. Harvey, "The Last Race Rally of Indians," *World's Work*, VIII (May 1904), 4803.
24. Anna Blake Mezquida, "The Door of Yesterday," *Overland Monthly*, LXVI (July 1915), 3–4, 11.
25. Charles Howard Walker, "The Great Exposition at Omaha," *Century*, LV (Feb. 1898), 521.
26. Harriman, "Congress of American Aborigines," pp. 512, 508. See Frederick E. Hoxie, "Red Man's Burden," *Antioch Rev.*, XXXVII (Summer 1979), 326–42, for an interpretation of the Indian exhibits in 1876, 1893, 1904, and 1915.
27. This account of Ishi's discovery is based on A. F. Kessler, "How We Found Ishi," *Pac. Historian*, XII (Summer 1968), 22–29. See A. L. Kroeber, "Ishi, the Last Aborigine," *World's Work*, XXIV (July 1912), 304–8; and Theodora Kroeber, *Ishi in Two Worlds: A Biography of the Last Wild Indian in North America* (Berkeley, Calif., 1961).
28. E. S. Curtis, "Vanishing Indian Types: The Tribes of the Northwest Plains," *Scribner's*, XXXIX (June 1906), 671.
29. Edward S. Curtis, *The North American Indian: Being a Series of Volumes Picturing and Describing the Indians of the United States and Alaska*, edited by Frederick Webb Hodge, 20 vols. and 20 folio supplements (New York, 1907–30), Supp. I, Index page.
30. Ella Higginson, "The Vanishing Race," *Red Man*, VIII (Feb. 1916), 189.
31. W J McGee, Review, *Am. Anthro.*, XII (July–Sept. 1910), 449.
32. Zane Grey, *The Vanishing American* (New York, 1925), pp. 294, 308. It is worth noting that in the original version of his novel serialized in *Ladies Home Journal* Grey defied convention by having Nophaie survive and, a respectable Christian convert, win Marian's undying love. Thus Marian's closing speech was actually Nophaie's as he remarked on the fate of his people. Because popular taste was offended, Grey changed the ending to the novel.

33. Adv., *Motion Picture News*, XXXI (May 16, 1925).

34. Jack Spears, "The Indian on the Screen," *Films in Rev.*, X (Jan. 1959), 22.

35. Richard Koszarski, "Lost Films from the National Film Collection," *Film Q.*, XXIII (Winter 1969–70), 33. See Tom Shales, "The Vanishing American," in Shales, *et al.*, *The American Film Heritage: Impressions from the American Film Institute Archives* (Washington, D.C., 1972), p. 52–55.

36. Joseph K. Dixon, *The Vanishing Race: The Last Great Indian Council* (Garden City, N.Y., 1913), p. 38.

37. Herbert Adams Gibbons, *John Wanamaker*, 2 vols. (New York, 1926), I, 35–36. For Rodman Wanamaker, see John H. Appel, *The Business Biography of John Wanamaker, Founder and Builder: America's Merchant Pioneer from 1861 to 1922; with Glimpses of Rodman Wanamaker and Thomas B. Wanamaker* (New York, 1930), pp. xiii–xiv, 114–15, 440–53.

38. Wanamaker—Originator, *Wanamaker Primer on the North American Indian: Hiawatha, Produced in Life* (N.p., 1909), pp. 36, 38–46; "The Song of Hiawatha," pp. 2–3.

39. Dixon, *Vanishing Race*, p. v.

40. *Ibid.*, pp. 3–6, 35.

41. *Ibid.*, pp. 212, 215, 220.

42. James McLaughlin to Monte W. McConkey, Oct. 1913, quoted in Louis L. Pfaller, "James McLaughlin and the Rodman Wanamaker Expedition of 1913," *N.D. Hist.*, XLIV (Spring 1977), 10.

43. Manfred E. Keune, "An Immodest Proposal: A Memorial to the North American Indian," *Jour. Am. Culture*, I (Winter 1978), 766–86.

44. "The Wanamaker Expedition," *Outlook*, CIV (July 26, 1913), 642–43. See "Wanamaker Party Now with Pueblos," *New York Times*, June 29, 1913, p. 11.

45. Thomas Crawford to Montgomery C. Meigs, Oct. 31, 1853, in Robert L. Gale, *Thomas Crawford: American Sculptor* (Pittsburgh, 1964), p. 111.

46. Henry T. Tuckerman, *Book of the Artists: American Artist Life* (New York, 1966 [1870]), p. 310.

47. Royal Cortissoz, *American Artists* (New York, 1923), p. 71.

48. Selene Ayer Armstrong, "Solon H. Borglum: Sculptor of American Life: An Artist Who Knows the Value of 'Our Incomparable Materials,'" *Craftsman*, XII (July 1907), 389.

49. E. Waldo Long, "Dallin, Sculptor of Indians," *World's Work*, LIV (Sept. 1927), 563.

50. M. Friedman, "Dallin's Statue, 'The Appeal to the Great Spirit,'" *Red Man*, IV (Sept. 1911), 26.

51. Adolph A. Weinman to R. W. Norton, May 3, 1947, quoted in Patricia Janis Broder, *Bronzes of the American West* (New York, 1974), p. 193.

52. Juliet James, *Palaces and Courts of the Expedition: A Handbook of the Architecture, Sculpture and Mural Paintings with Special Reference to the Symbolism* (San Francisco, 1915), pp. 112, 114.

53. Dean Krakel, *End of the Trail: The Odyssey of a Statue* (Norman, Okla., 1973), pp. 4, 11.

54. John T. Grant, "The End of the Trail," in *California Poets: An Anthology of 244 Contemporaries*, edited by the House of Henry Harrison (New York, 1932), p. 254. Also, see Stanton Elliot, "The End of the Trail," *Overland*

Monthly, LXVI (July 1915), 1; Elizabeth Crighton, "The End of the Trail," *Overland Monthly*, LXVI (Dec. 1915), 534; and untitled, in J. L. Hill, *The Passing of the Indian and the Buffalo* (Long Beach, Calif., n.d. [1915?]), p. 20.

55. J. Walker McSpadden, *Famous Sculptors of America* (Freeport, N.Y., 1968 [1924]), p. 281.

56. Oliver H. Smith, Feb. 19, 1828, *Register of Debates in Cong.*, 20th Cong., 1st sess., p. 1543.

57. McSpadden, *Famous Sculptors*, pp. 280–82. See James Earle Fraser, "A Dakota Boyhood," *Am. Heritage*, XX (Dec. 1968), 86. After the exposition closed, Fraser's statue was moved first to Marina Park, then to Visalia in the San Joaquin Valley, where the soft stucco continued to erode with the years until it was moved again, in 1968, to a sheltered haven at the Western Heritage Center in Oklahoma City.

58. Lawrence W. White, "The Indian No Longer a Vanishing Race," *Red Man*, IX (Oct. 1916), 39–48. The quotation from Commissioner Cato Sells originally appeared in his "Save the Indian Babies," *Red Man*, VIII (Mar. 1916), 222, a strong assertion of the proposition that "no race was ever created for utter extinction."

Chapter Fourteen: Now or Never Is the Time

1. First Ann. Message, Dec. 3, 1901, in James D. Richardson, *A Compilation of the Messages and Papers of the Presidents, 1789–1902*, 10 vols. (Washington, D.C., 1903), X, 433. See Roderick Nash, *Wilderness and the American Mind* (New Haven, 1967), which is especially good on the tensions between the preservationist and wise-use philosophies.

2. James Mooney, "The Indian Congress at Omaha," *Am. Anthro.*, N.S. I (Jan. 1899), 126.

3. See Hugh Honour, *The European Vision of America* (Cleveland, 1975), esp. chap. 6; and William C. Sturtevant, "First Visual Images of Native America," in Fred Chiappelli, ed., *First Images of America: The Impact of the New World on the Old*, 2 vols. (Berkeley, Calif., 1976), I, 417–54.

4. Rep., William Clark and Lewis Cass, Feb. 4, 1829, in *House Doc. No. 117*, 20th Cong., 2nd sess., pp. 23–24.

5. George Catlin, *Letters and Notes on the Manners, Customs, and Condition of the North American Indians*, 2 vols. (New York, 1841), I, 258–64.

6. William T. Hornaday, "The Extermination of the American Bison, with a Sketch of Its Discovery and Life History," *Rep., U.S. Nat. Museum, 1887* (Washington, D.C., 1889), pp. 521–25.

7. Theodore Roosevelt, "Big Game Disappearing in the West," *Forum*, XV (Aug. 1893), 768.

8. Richard Irving Dodge, *The Plains of the Great West and Their Inhabitants* (New York, 1959 [1877]), p. 132.

9. Hamlin Russell, "The Story of the Buffalo," *Harper's M.*, LXXXVI (Apr. 1893), 798.

10. Harry Ellard, "The Passing of the Buffalo," *Ranch Tales of the Rockies* (Canon City, Colo., 1899), p. 97.

11. J. Walker McSpadden, *Famous Sculptors of America* (Freeport, N.Y., 1968 [1924]), pp. 282–83.

12. George Bird Grinnell, "The Last of the Buffalo," *Scribner's*, XII (Sept. 1892), 267, 286.

13. George Bird Grinnell, *The Story of the Indian* (New York, 1895), p. 163.

14. Henry R. Schoolcraft, *Personal Memoirs of a Residence of Thirty Years with the Indian Tribes on the American Frontiers* (Philadelphia, 1851), p. vi.

15. Lewis H. Morgan, *The American Beaver and His Works* (Philadelphia, 1868), p. 283.

16. See John R. Ross, "Man over Nature: Origins of the Conservation Movement," *Am. Studies*, XVI (Spring 1975), 49–63; and Whitney R. Cross, "W J McGee and the Idea of Conservation," *Historian*, XV (Spring 1953), 148–62. McGee's philosophy is expressed in "The Conservation of Natural Resources," *Proc.*, *M.V.H.A.*, III (1909–10), 376.

17. Walter McClintock, *The Old North Trail; or, Life, Legends and Religion of the Blackfeet Indians* (London, 1910), chap. 1.

18. George Bird Grinnell, "The North American Indian of To-day," *Cosmopolitan*, XXVI (Mar. 1899), 541, 537.

19. George Bird Grinnell, *Blackfoot Lodge Tales: The Story of a Prairie People* (New York, 1892), p. xiv.

20. George Bird Grinnell, "Portraits of Indian Types," *Scribner's*, XXXVII (Mar. 1905), 270.

21. *Ibid.*, p. 267. Regarding this, see Grinnell's "The Wild Indian" and its companion piece, "The Indian on the Reservation," *Atlantic Monthly*, LXXXIII (Jan., Feb. 1899).

22. Lewis Henry Morgan, *Ancient Society; or, Researches in the Lines of Human Progress from Savagery through Barbarism to Civilization*, edited by Eleanor Burke Leacock (Cleveland, 1963 [1877]), Preface.

23. "Address of Professor Daniel Wilson," *Proc.*, *A.A.A.S.*, *Twenty-sixth Meeting, held at Nashville, Tenn., August, 1877* (Salem, Mass., 1878), pp. 333–34.

24. J. W. Powell, "The Categories," *Am. Anthro.*, N.S. III (July–Sept. 1901), 404–30. For examples of his commitment to field work, see "On Limitations to the Use of Some Anthropologic Data," *First Ann. Rep., Bur. Ethn., 1879–80* (Washington, D.C., 1881), p. 86; and "Indian Linguistic Families of America North of Mexico," *Seventh Ann. Rep., Bur. Ethn., 1885–86* (Washington, D.C., 1891), p. 26.

25. "Address of Professor Daniel Wilson" (1877), pp. 333–34. See George W. Stocking, Jr., "Franz Boas and the Founding of the American Anthropological Association," *Am. Anthro.*, LXII (Feb. 1960), 1–17; and Hamilton Cravens, "The Abandonment of Evolutionary Social Theory in America: The Impact of Academic Professionalization upon American Sociological Theory, 1890–1920," *Am. Studies*, XII (Feb. 1971), esp. 5–9.

26. For a helpful guide to Boas's chronology—a chronology that is at times surprisingly tangled—see Ronald P. Rohner, comp. and ed., *The Ethnography of Franz Boas: Letters and Diaries of Franz Boas Written on the North-west Coast from 1886 to 1931* (Chicago, 1969), pp. 309–13.

27. B.A.A.S., *Fourth Rep. of the Committee . . . appointed for the purpose of investigating and publishing reports on the physical characters, languages, and industrial and social condition of the North-Western Tribes of the Dominion of Canada* (London, 1888), pp. 2–3.

28. Franz Boas, "Ethnological Problems in Canada," *Congrès International des Américanistes: XVe Session tenue à Quebec en 1906* (Quebec, 1906), p. 152.

29. Franz Boas, "Ethnological Problems in Canada," *Jour. Royal Anthro. Instit.*, XL (1910), 536 (which is also summarized in *Rep., Seventy-ninth Meeting,*

B.A.A.S., *Winnipeg: 1909* [London, 1919], p. 621). For the milieu in which Boas was working, see Jacob W. Gruber, "Ethnographic Salvage and the Shaping of Anthropology," *Am. Anthro.*, LXXII (Dec. 1970), 1289–99; and Douglas Cole, "The Origins of Canadian Anthropology, 1850–1910," *Jour. Can. Studies*, VIII (Feb. 1973), esp. 40–44.

30. "Humanity, What Is It?: An Interview with Claude Lévi-Strauss" (1960), *Kroeber Anthro. Soc. Papers* No. 35 (1966), 41, 43–44.

31. E. Sapir, "An Anthropological Survey of Canada," *Science*, XXXIV (Dec. 8, 1911), 793.

32. Horatio Hale to Franz Boas, July 12, 1889, quoted in Jacob W. Gruber, "Horatio Hale and the Development of American Anthropology," *Proc., Am. Phil. Soc.*, CXI (Feb. 1967), 30.

33. Clark Wissler, *Indian Cavalcade; or, Life on the Old-Time Indian Reservations* (New York, 1938), pp. 5–6.

34. Robert H. Lowie, *Robert H. Lowie, Ethnologist: A Personal Record* (Berkeley, Calif., 1959), pp. 12, 90, 106–7.

35. Boas's phrase appeared in his obituary for Rudolf Virchow (1902) and was meant as high praise (quoted in Clyde Kluckhohn and Olaf Prufer, "Influences During the Formative Years," in Walter Goldschmidt, ed., *The Anthropology of Franz Boas: Essays on the Centennial of His Birth, Am. Anthro. Assn. Memoir No. 89* [Oct. 1959], 23).

36. See Helen Codere, "The Understanding of the Kwakiutl," in *ibid.*, pp. 61–65; Marian W. Smith, "Boas' 'Natural History' Approach to Field Method," in *ibid.*, pp. 52, 54–56; and George W. Stocking, Jr., "From Physics to Ethnology: Franz Boas' Arctic Expedition as a Problem in the Historiography of the Behavioral Sciences," *Jour. Hist. Behavioral Sciences*, I (Jan. 1965), 57, 64.

37. "The Boas Anniversary," *Am. Anthro.*, N.S. IX (July-Sept. 1907), 647.

38. Marvin Harris, *The Rise of Anthropological Theory: A History of Theories of Culture* (New York, 1968), p. 286. See Leslie A. White, *The Ethnography and Ethnology of Franz Boas*, Bulletin of the Texas Memorial Museum No. 6 (Apr. 1963), pp. 35, 53–56, 59; and Murray Wax, "The Limitations of Boas' Anthropology," *Am. Anthro.*, LVIII (Feb. 1956), 63–74.

39. Franz Boas, "The Limitations of the Comparative Method of Anthropology" (1896), in his *Race, Language and Culture* (New York, 1940), pp. 276–77, 280.

40. Henry W. Henshaw, "Popular Fallacies Respecting the Indians," *Am. Anthro.*, N.S. VII (Jan.-Mar. 1905), 110.

41. Frederick Webb Hodge, ed., *Handbook of American Indians North of Mexico*, B.A.E. Bulletin 30, 2 vols. (Washington, D.C., 1907–10), II, 282–87: H. W. H., "Popular Fallacies" and J. M., "Population."

42. J. W. Powell, "Rep.," *Seventh Ann. Rep., Bur. Ethn., 1885–86* (Washington, D.C., 1891), pp. xxxiii–xxxvi.

43. See J. W. Powell's reports in the *Ann. Rep., Bur. Ethn.: Tenth* (1893), pp. xviii–xx; *Eleventh* (1894), pp. xxvii–xxix; *Twelfth* (1894), pp. xxx–xxxi; *Thirteenth* (1896), pp. xxxii–xxxiii.

44. George Grant MacCurdy, "Anthropology at the New York Meeting," *Am. Anthro.*, N.S. IX (Jan.-Mar. 1907), 183.

45. F. W. Hodge, "Rep.," *Thirty-first Ann. Rep., B.A.E., 1909–1910* (Washington, D.C., 1916), pp. 9–10.

46. W. H. Holmes, "Rep.," *Twenty-ninth Ann. Rep., B.A.E., 1907–1908* (Washington, D.C., 1916), p. 13.

47. Mooney, "Population," p. 287. Mooney broke his estimate down as follows: United States, 846,000; British America, 220,000; Alaska, 72,000; and Greenland, 10,000. For the accepted figures previously, see Dept. of the Interior, Census Office, *Report on Indians Taxed and Indians Not Taxed in the United States (Except Alaska) at the Eleventh Census: 1890* (1894), *House Misc. Doc. No. 340, Pt. 15*, 52nd Cong., 1st sess., p. 57; and J. W. Powell, "Are Our Indians Becoming Extinct?" *Forum*, XV (May 1893), 345, 349, which opts for an estimate between 500,000 and 750,000.

48. James Mooney, "The Passing of the Delaware Nation," *Proc., M.V.H.A.*, III (1909–10), 329–30.

49. James Mooney, "The Passing of the Indian," *Proc. of the Second Pan American Scientific Congress*, Sec. I: *Anthropology* (Washington, D.C., 1917), pp. 174–79.

50. James Mooney, *The Aboriginal Population of America North of Mexico*, Smithsonian Misc. Coll., Vol. 80, No. 7 (Feb. 6, 1928), pp. 1–2 (Preface by John R. Swanton), 33. See Douglas H. Ubelaker, "The Sources and Methodology for Mooney's Estimates of North American Indian Populations," in William M. Denevan, ed., *The Native Population of the Americas in 1492* (Madison, Wisc., 1976), chap. 8.

51. "James Mooney," *Am. Anthro.*, XXIV (Apr.-June, 1922), 210.

52. James Mooney, "The End of the Natchez," *Am. Anthro.* N.S. I (July 1899), 510.

53. A. L. Kroeber, "Native American Population," *Am. Anthro.*, XXXVI (Jan.-Mar. 1934), 1, accepted Mooney's figures with one modification: as a student of California cultures, he thought that Mooney's estimate of 260,000 natives in California was too high and substituted a figure of 133,000, thereby cutting the total aboriginal population of North America down to 1,025,950. Subsequently, Kroeber had second thoughts and concluded that "Mooney's figures are probably mostly too high rather than too low, so far as they are in error." It was his impression that Mooney's total of 1,150,000 "will ultimately shrink to around 900,000, possibly somewhat farther." Nevertheless, he still made Mooney's work the foundation of his own population study. (*Cultural and Natural Areas of Native North America*, University of California Publications in American Archaeology and Ethnology, vol. 38 [1939], 132, 134.)

54. "Telling History by Photographs: Records of Our North American Indians Being Preserved by Pictures," *Craftsman*, IX (Mar. 1906), 846.

Chapter Fifteen: There Will Be No "Later" for the Indian

1. [Edwart Everett], "On the State of the Indians," *NAR*, XVI (Jan. 1823), 39–40.

2. First Ann. Message, Dec. 3, 1901, in James D. Richardson, *A Compilation of the Messages and Papers of the Presidents, 1789–1902*, 10 vols. (Washington, D.C., 1903), X, 450. Roosevelt was quoting Merrill Gates, a leading reformer.

3. See David A. Nichols, *Lincoln and the Indians: Civil War Policy and Politics* (Columbia, Mo., 1978), chaps. 3–5.

4. C. J. Hillyer, *Atlantic and Pacific Railroad and the Indian Territory* (Wash-

ington, D.C., n.d. [1871]), pp. 32–35, 55. See H. Craig Miner, *The Corporation and the Indian: Tribal Sovereignty and Industrial Civilization in Indian Territory, 1865–1907* (Columbia, Mo., 1976), for railroad involvement in the erosion of tribal sovereignty in Indian Territory.

5. Theodora R. Jenness, "The Indian Territory," *Atlantic Monthly*, XLIII (Apr. 1879), 448.

6. Henry Gannett, "Survey and Subdivision of Indian Territory," *Nat. Geographic*, VII (Mar. 1896), 113.

7. W. J. Watts, *Cherokee Citizenship; and A Brief History of Internal Affairs in the Cherokee Nation, with Records and Acts of National Council from 1871 to Date* (Muldrow, I.T., 1895), pp. 128–29, 145.

8. Henry King, "The Indian Country," *Century*, XXX (Aug. 1885), 600. See Commissioner to the Five Civilized Tribes, comp., *Laws, Decisions, and Regulations Affecting the Work of the Commissioner to the Five Civilized Tribes, 1893 to 1906* . . . (Washington, D.C., 1906), pt. 1, for legislation bearing on the work of the Dawes Commission, and for the commission's mandate, Grover Cleveland's Fourth Annual Message, Dec. 7, 1896, in Richardson, *Messages and Papers*, IX, 735–36.

9. Thomas F. Millard, "The Passing of the American Indian," *Forum*, XXXIV (Jan. 1903), 466.

10. Charles M. Harvey, "The Red Man's Last Roll-call," *Atlantic Monthly*, XCVII (Mar. 1906), 323.

11. Baxter Taylor, "The Newest American State," *Taylor-Trotwood Mag.*, VI (Feb. 1908), 500.

12. Jenness, "Indian Territory," p. 449. By an act of Congress passed Aug. 9, 1888, whites were prohibited from acquiring a share in tribal property through intermarriage, but the Five Civilized Tribes were exempted. When the final rolls were drawn up for the Five Nations, of approximately 28,000 Cherokees enrolled over 21,000 were mixed bloods. (Daniel F. Littlefield, Jr., and Lonnie E. Underhill, "Renaming the American Indian: 1890–1913," *Am. Studies*, XII [Fall 1971], 34.)

13. J. W. Powell, "From Savagery to Barbarism," *Transactions, Anthro. Soc. Washington*, III (1885), 194.

14. Thomas J. Mays, "The Future of the American Indian," *Pop. Sc. Monthly*, XXXIII (May 1888), 104–8.

15. See Franz Boas, "The Half-Blood Indian: An Anthropometric Study," *Pop. Sc. Monthly*, XLV (Oct. 1894), 761–66 (reprinted in Boas's *Race, Language and Culture* [New York, 1966 (1940)], pp. 138–48, along with another, "Modern Populations of America" [1917], which states Boas's conclusions even more strongly in light of the 1910 census data [pp. 20–21]); Albert Ernest Jenks, *Indian-White Amalgamation: An Anthropometric Study* (Minneapolis, 1916), a case study of more than 300 Ojibwas on the White Earth Reservation, Minn.; and "Full-blood Indians Going Fast, He Says," *New York Times*, Apr. 1, 1923, p. 2E, reporting an address by Alex Hrdlicka of the Smithsonian.

16. Department of Commerce, Bureau of the Census, *Indian Population in the United States and Alaska, 1910* (Washington, D.C., 1915), pp. 159, 31, 35, 157. Also see tables 12–22, 25–26, 29–33, 53–58.

17. Francis E. Leupp, *The Indian and His Problem* (New York, 1910), pp. 343–44.

18. "President Roosevelt's Desire," *Am. Ind.*, II (Feb. 1928), 4.

19. John Snyder, "Prejudice Against the Negro," *Forum*, VIII (Oct. 1889), 223.

20. Robert Watson Winston, "Should the Color Line Go?" *Current Hist.*, XVIII (Sept. 1923), 947.

21. NAACP, *Thirty Years of Lynching in the United States, 1889–1918* (New York, 1919), pp. 7–8.

22. John Roach Straton, "Will Education Solve the Race Problem?" *NAR* CLXX (June 1900), 794, 800–801.

23. See George M. Fredrickson, *The Black Image in the White Mind: The Debate on Afro-American Character and Destiny, 1817–1914* (New York, 1971), chap. 8; and John S. Haller, Jr., *Outcasts from Evolution: Scientific Attitudes of Racial Inferiority, 1859–1900* (Urbana, Ill., 1971), esp. pp. 138–43 and chap. 7.

24. James Parton, "Antipathy to the Negro," *NAR*, CXXVII (Nov.-Dec. 1878), 488–90.

25. George Allen Mebane, "The Negro Vindicated," *Arena*, XXIV (Nov. 1900), 458.

26. Walter L. Williams, "United States Indian Policy and the Debate over Philippine Annexation: Implications for the Origins of American Imperialism," *Jour. of Am. Hist.*, LXVI (Mar. 1980), 810–31.

27. S. D. McConnell, "Are Our Hands Clean?" *Outlook*, LXI (Jan. 28, 1899), 217.

28. John T. Bramhall, "The Red, Black and Yellow," *Overland Monthly*, N.S. 2, XXXVII (Feb. 1901), 725.

29. Charles E. Woodruff, "The Normal Malay and the Criminal Responsibility of Insane Malays," *Am. Medicine* (1905), reprinted in *Jour. U.S. Cav. Assn.*, XVI (Jan. 1906), 499–502, 515, 517.

30. John Higham, *Strangers in the Land: Patterns of American Nativism, 1860–1925* (New York, Atheneum, 1970 [1955]), pp. 136–44; and Barbara Miller Solomon, *Ancestors and Immigrants: A Changing New England Tradition* (Cambridge, Mass., 1956), chap. 4.

31. Robert DeC. Ward, "Our Immigration Laws from the Viewpoint of National Eugenics," *Nat. Geographic*, XXIII (Jan. 1912), 41, 39.

32. Madison Grant, Introduction to Lothrop Stoddard, *The Rising Tide of Color Against White World Supremacy* (New York, 1920), pp. xxxii.

33. Leupp, *The Indian and His Problem*, p. 360.

34. *Sister to the Sioux: The Memoirs of Elaine Goodale Eastman, 1885–91*, edited by Kay Graber (Lincoln, Neb., 1978), pp. 169, 172.

35. Albert K. Kirwan, *Revolt of the Rednecks: Mississippi Politics, 1876–1925* (Lexington, Ky., 1951), pp. 146–47.

36. Ella Wheeler Wilcox, "Custer," *Custer and Other Poems* (Chicago, 1896), p. 129. The captivity narratives have been extensively analyzed; especially pertinent is David T. Haberly, "Women and Indians: *The Last of the Mohicans* and the Captivity Tradition," *Am. Q.*, XXVIII (Fall 1976), 431–43.

37. See Louise K. Barnett, *The Ignoble Savage: American Literary Racism, 1790–1890* (Westport, Conn., 1975), pp. 119–21, 127; and William J. Scheick, *The Half-Blood: A Cultural Symbol in 19th-Century American Fiction* (Lexington, Ky., 1979), pp. 85–87.

38. Benjamin Franklin to Peter Collinson, May 9, 1753, in John Bigelow,

ed., *The Works of Benjamin Franklin*, 12 vols. (New York, 1904), II, 411.

39. Alfred I. Hallowell, "American Indians, White and Black: The Phenomenon of Transculturalization," *Current Anthro.*, IV (Dec. 1963), 519–31.

40. The Pocahontas legend is based on historical fact. Smith first told the story in full detail in 1624; it is conveniently reprinted in David Freeman Hawke, ed., *Captain John Smith's History of Virginia: A Selection* (Indianapolis, 1970), pp. 35–37. Smith's credibility was assailed and his story rejected in the late nineteenth century, but historians today are more willing to accept the tale at face value.

41. See Rayna Green, "The Pocahontas Perplex: The Image of Indian Women in American Culture," *Mass. Rev.*, XVI (Fall 1975), 698–714.

42. Reginald Horsman, *Expansion and American Indian Policy, 1783–1812* (East Lansing, Mich., 1967), pp. 108–9. The Virginia bill as well as a similar proposal brought before Congress in 1824 are discussed in an older study only recently published, James Hugo Johnston's *Race Relations in Virginia and Miscegenation in the South, 1776–1860* (Amherst, Mass., 1970), pp. 269–70.

43. See Lewis O. Saum, *The Fur Trader and the Indian* (Seattle, 1965), pp. 84–87; three essays by Sylvia Van Kirk, "Women and the Fur Trade," *Beaver*, Outfit 303 (Winter 1972), 4–21. "'The Custom of the Country': An Examination of Fur Trade Marriage Practices," in Lewis H. Thomas, ed., *Essays on Western History in Honour of Lewis Gwynne Thomas* (Edmonton, Alta., 1976), pp. 47–68, and "'Women in Between': Indian Women in Fur Trade Society in Western Canada," Canadian Historical Association, *Historical Papers/Communications Historiques*, 1977, pp. 31–46, which makes the important point that the red woman could be seen as a cultural intermediary just as much as her white partner; two essays by John E. Foster, "The Origins of the Mixed Bloods in the Canadian West," in Thomas, ed., *Essays on Western History*, pp. 69–81, and "The Home Guard Cree and the Hudson's Bay Company: The First Hundred Years," in D. A. Muise, ed., *Approaches to Native History in Canada: Papers of a Conference Held at the National Museum of Man, October, 1975* (Ottawa, 1977), pp. 49–64; John C. Ewers, "Mothers of the Mixed Bloods," in *Indian Life on the Upper Missouri* (Norman, Okla., 1968), pp. 57–67; and Harry H. Anderson, "Fur Traders as Fathers: The Origins of the Mixed-Blooded Community among the Rosebud Sioux," *S.D. Hist.*, III (Summer 1973), 233–70.

44. See William T. Hagan, "Squaw Men on the Kiowa, Comanche, and Apache Reservation: Advance Agents of Civilization or Disturbers of the Peace?" in John G. Clark, ed., *The Frontier Challenge: Responses to the Trans-Mississippi West* (Lawrence, Kan., 1971), pp. 171–202.

45. *Memoirs of a White Crow Indian (Thomas H. Leforge)*, as told by Thomas B. Marquis (New York, 1928), p. 171.

46. Anne McDonnell, ed., "Letter to a Brother: Granville Stuart to James Stuart, April, 1873," *Montana*, III (Summer 1953), 4–5, 7.

47. Albert Keiser, *The Indian in American Literature* (New York, 1933), chap. 5.

48. Alexander Ross, *The Red River Settlement* (1856), quoted in Saum, *Fur Trader and Indian*, p. 236.

49. "Removal of Indians" (Feb. 24, 1830), *House Rep. No. 227*, 21st Cong., 1st sess., p. 23.

50. Lewis Henry Morgan, *The Indian Journals, 1859–62*, edited by Leslie A. White (Ann Arbor, Mich., 1959), p. 94 (entry for June 1860).

51. T. R. Garth, "The Intelligence of Indians," *Science*, LVI (Dec. 1, 1922), 635–36.

52. Otis T. Mason, "The Savage Mind in the Presence of Civilization" (abstract), *Transactions, Anthro. Soc. Washington*, I (1882), 45.

53. Thomas C. Moffett, *The American Indian on the New Trail: The Red Man of the United States and the Christian Gospel* (New York, 1914), p. 274.

54. Andrew Draper (1889), quoted in Ronald M. Johnson, "Schooling the Savage: Andrew S. Draper and Indian Education," *Phylon*, XXXV (Mar. 1974), 79.

55. Elaine Goodale Eastman, *Pratt: The Red Man's Moses* (Norman, Okla., 1935), p. 193.

56. Luther Standing Bear, edited by E. A. Brininstool, *My People the Sioux* (London, 1928), chap. 19.

57. Luther Standing Bear, *Land of the Spotted Eagle* (Boston, 1933), p. 251.

58. Norman B. Wood, *Lives of Famous Indian Chiefs* (Aurora, Ill., 1906), p. 670.

59. Leon Summit, "Carlos Montezuma, Apache M.D.," *Westerners Brand Book* (Chicago), XXIII (Jan. 1967), 81–83; 85–88.

60. Ohiyesa (Charles A. Eastman), *Indian Boyhood* (Boston, 1902), pp. 288, 3.

61. Charles A. Eastman (Ohiyesa), *From the Deep Woods to Civilization: Chapters in the Autobiography of an Indian* (Boston, 1916), p. 59.

62. Donald L. Parman, "J. C. Morgan: Navajo Apostle of Assimilation," *Prologue*, IV (Summer 1972), 83–98.

63. Hazel W. Hertzberg, *The Search for an American Indian Identity: Modern Pan-Indian Movements* (Syracuse, N.Y., 1971), p. 80.

64. *Commercial* (Bangor, Me.), Oct. 13, 1911, reprinted in *Red Man*, IV (Nov. 1911), 123–27.

65. Memorial, Society of American Indians, to the President of the United States, Dec. 10, 1914, in Arthur C. Parker, "The Awakened American Indian," *Red Man*, VII (Jan. 1915), 165.

66. Montezuma, quoted in Hertzberg, *Search for an American Indian Identity*, p. 86.

67. See the following stories in *Am. Ind.*: Frank C. Sherman, "The Indians Made an Enviable Record During World War," II (Jan. 1928), 12; O'Hara Smith, "Chief 'Lo' Was with the 'Lost Battalion' in France," I (Nov. 1926), 9.

68. "Definition of 'Negro Freedman,'" *Am. Ind.*, I (Mar. 1927), 8; and A. L. Beckett, "Tribes Met at Okmulgee in 1870 to Frame Indian State," *Am. Ind.*, III (Jan. 1929), 2.

69. *Indian Population in the United States and Alaska, 1910*, p. 38.

70. Iktomi Licala, *America Needs Indians!* (Denver, 1937), pp. 137–38.

71. "Carlisle Not a 'Mixed School,'" *Am. Ind.*, I (Mar. 1927).

72. Chief Buffalo Child Long Lance, *Long Lance* (New York, 1928), p. 41.

73. Indian Council Fire of Chicago, quoted in Eastman, *Pratt*, p. 202.

74. "A New Indian Policy," *Am. Ind.*, IV (Jan. 1930), 4.

75. "Copy of Letter to Charles Curtis [Jan. 17, 1931]," *Am. Ind.*, V (Dec. 1930–Jan. 1931), 4.

76. Evon Z. Vogt, "The Acculturation of American Indians," *Annals, Am. Academy Pol. and Soc. Sc.*, CCCXI (May 1957), 137, 144.

77. William R. Draper, "The Last of the Red Race," *Cosmopolitan*, XXXII (Jan. 1902), 244–46.

Chapter Sixteen: To Each Age Its Own Indian

1. Chas. H. Burke, *Rep., Com. Ind. Affairs, 1921* (Washington, D.C., 1921), p. 25.
2. Mary Austin, "Our Indian Problem: The Folly of the Officials," *Forum*, LXXI (Mar. 1924), 287.
3. Erna Fergusson, "Crusade from Santa Fé," *NAR*, CCXLII (Winter 1936–37), 376.
4. See Randolph C. Downes, "A Crusade for Indian Reform, 1922–1934," *MVHR*, XXXII (Dec. 1945), 331–54; Margaret Garretson Szasz, "Indian Reform in a Decade of Prosperity," *Montana*, XX (Winter 1970), 16–27; Helen Marie Bannan, "Reformers and the 'Indian Problem,' 1878–1887 and 1922–1934" (unpub. Ph.D. diss., Syracuse University, 1976); and Michael Morgan Dorcy, "Friends of the American Indian, 1922–1934: Patterns of Patronage and Philanthropy" (unpub. Ph.D. diss., University of Pennsylvania, 1978).
5. "'Minority Rights' at Home," *New York Times*, Jan. 4, 1923, p. 18.
6. Herbert Welsh, "Caring for the Pueblos," *New York Times*, Jan. 7, 1923, Sec. 8, p. 6.
7. Fergusson, "Crusade from Santa Fé," p. 379. See New Mexico Association on Indian Affairs and Indian Welfare Committee, General Federation of Women's Clubs, *Shall the Pueblo Indians of New Mexico Be Destroyed?: A Critical Analysis of Senate Bill 3855 . . .* (N.p., n.d. [1922]).
8. See Stephen J. Junitz, "The Social Philosophy of John Collier," *Ethnohistory*, XVIII (1971), 213–29; and Kenneth R. Philp, *John Collier's Crusade for Indian Reform, 1920–1954* (Tucson, 1977).
9. John Collier, "The Pueblos' Last Stand," *Sunset*, L (Feb. 1923), 21.
10. D. H. Lawrence to Bessie Freeman, Oct. 30, 1922, in Harry T. Moore, ed., *The Collected Letters of D. H. Lawrence*, 2 vols. (New York, 1962), II, 727.
11. "A Square Deal for the Pueblos," *Outlook*, CXXXIII (Feb. 7, 1923), 249.
12. Charles F. Lummis, "The Indian Who Is Not Poor,' *Scribner's*, XII (Sept. 1892), 361–72.
13. "New Struggle Ahead of Congress on Disposal of Indian Lands," *New York Times*, Jan. 21, 1923, Sec. 8, p. 4. See Richard H. Frost, "The Romantic Inflation of Pueblo Culture," *Am. West*, XVII (Jan.-Feb. 1980), 4–9, 56–60.
14. John Collier, "Plundering the Pueblo Indians," *Sunset*, L (Jan. 1923), 25, 56.
15. "New Struggle Ahead of Congress on Disposal of Indian Lands," p. 4.
16. "Square Deal Sought for Pueblos," *New York Times*, Jan. 28, 1923, Sec. 7, p. 12. See Kenneth Philp, "Albert B. Fall and the Protest from the Pueblos, 1921–23," *Ariz. and the West*, XII (Autumn 1970), 237–54.
17. Collier, "Plundering the Pueblo Indians," pp. 21, 25.
18. "Deny Pueblos Suffer," *New York Times*, Feb. 16, 1923, p. 4.
19. "Pueblo Indians" (Feb. 27, 1923), *House Rep. No. 1730*, 67th Cong., 4th sess., pp. 8–9.
20. Collier, "Plundering the Pueblo Indians," p. 23.
21. Editorial, *New Republic*, XXXIII (Nov. 29, 1922), 2.
22. "Justice for the Pueblo Indians," *New York World*, reprinted in *Science*, N.S. LVI (Dec. 8, 1922), 665.

23. *Ind. Truth*, I (Nov. 1924), 2.

24. Letter from John Collier, Dec. 22, 1924, in *Ind. Truth*, II (Jan. 1925), 3. Besides the split between the Indian Rights Association and Collier's American Indian Defense Association, Collier's organization had a falling-out with the Eastern Association on Indian Affairs. The two eventually made up and in 1937 merged as the Association on American Indian Affairs.

25. O[swald] G[arrison] V[illard], "For the Indian's Sake," *Nation*, CXVII (Dec. 26, 1923), 734–35.

26. John Collier, "The Red Slaves of Oklahoma," *Sunset*, LII (Mar. 1924), 96.

27. G. E. E. Lindquist, *The Red Man in the United States: An Intimate Study of the Social, Economic, and Religious Life of the American Indian* (New York, 1923), p. 69.

28. Francis E. Leupp, *In Red Man's Land: A Study of the American Indian* (New York, 1914), p. 95. See "Extracts from Personal Letters by the Commissioner: 1. Indian Dances," *Ind. Craftsman*, I (June 1909), 4.

29. See John Collier, "Persecuting the Pueblos," *Sunset*, LIII (July 1924), 50, 92, and Hugh A. Studdert Kennedy, "The Indian and Religious Freedom," *Independent*, CXVI (Mar. 6, 1926), 267–68, for hostile summaries of the commissioner's circulars.

30. Secretary Work, letter to the council of the San Ildefonso Pueblo, *Ind. Truth*, I (Mar. 1924), 4.

31. Leo Crane, quoted by Kate Leah Cotharin, "Setting a Bad Example," *Independent*, CXVI (May 1, 1926), 532.

32. Editorial, *Survey*, LI (Dec. 1, 1923), 277.

33. Hubert Work, *Ann. Rep., Secy. Interior, 1924* (Washington, D.C., 1924), p. 2.

34. Witter Bynner, "Truth About Indians," *Forum*, LXXI (May 1924), 689.

35. D. H. Lawrence, "Certain Americans and an Englishman," *New York Times*, Dec. 24, 1922, Sec. 4, p. 9.

36. Austin, "Folly of the Officials," p. 286.

37. Collier, "Pueblos' Last Stand," p. 19.

38. See F. H. Matthews, "The Revolt against Americanism: Cultural Pluralism and Cultural Relativism as an Ideology of Liberation," *Can. Rev. Am. Studies*, I (Spring 1970), 4–31; and Richard Weiss, "Ethnicity and Reform: Minorities and the Ambience of the Depression Years," *Jour. of Am. Hist.*, LXVI (Dec. 1979), 571–78.

39. Franz Boas, "Ethnological Problems in Canada," *Jour. Royal Anthro. Instit.*, XL (1910), 536. This essay is reprinted in Boas's *Race, Language and Culture* (New York, 1940), pp. 331–43, along with others bearing on the matter: "The Aims of Ethnology" (1888), esp. pp. 631–38; "The Limitations of the Comparative Method of Anthropology" (1896), pp. 270–80; "The Methods of Ethnology" (1920), pp. 281–89; "Evolution or Diffusion?" (1924), pp. 290–94; and "The Aims of Anthropological Research" (1932), esp. pp. 251–54.

40. Franz Boas, "Human Faculty as Determined by Race," *Proc., A.A.A.S., Forty-third Meeting Held at Brooklyn, N.Y., Aug., 1894* (Salem, Mass., 1895), pp. 301–2, 324–27.

41. Leslie Spier, "Some Central Elements in the Legacy," in Walter

Goldschmidt, ed., *The Anthropology of Franz Boas: Essays on the Centennial of His Birth*, Am. Anthro. Assn. Memoir No. 89 (Oct. 1959), p. 147.

42. Franz Boas, *The Mind of Primitive Man* (New York, 1938), pp. 125, 118. See George W. Stocking, Jr., "Franz Boas and the Cultural Concept in Historical Perspective," *Am. Anthro.* LXVIII (Aug. 1966), 867–82.

43. Franz Boas, letter diary entry for Dec. 23, 1883, quoted in George W. Stocking, Jr., "From Physics to Ethnology: Franz Boas' Arctic Expedition as a Problem in the Historiography of the Behavioral Sciences": *Jour. Hist. Behavioral Sciences*, I (Jan. 1965), 61.

44. H. F. C. Ten Kate, "Frank Hamilton Cushing," *Am. Anthro.*, N.S. II (Oct.-Dec. 1900), 769. See also the contributions, especially Alice C. Fletcher's, to "In Memoriam: Frank Hamilton Cushing," *Am. Anthro.*, N.S. II (Apr.-June 1900), 354–80.

45. Cushing's most popular work was a three-part series in *Century* (1882–83) titled "My Adventures in Zuñi." See Jesse Green, ed., *Zuñi: Selected Writings of Frank Hamilton Cushing* (Lincoln, Neb., 1979).

46. Ten Kate, "Frank Hamilton Cushing," p. 769.

47. Stanley Vestal, "The Wooden Indian," *Am. Mercury*, XIII (Jan. 1928), 84.

48. Frederick Monsen, "The Primitive Folk of the Desert: Splendid Physical Development that Yet Shows Many of the Characteristics of an Earlier Race than Our Own," *Craftsman* XII (May 1907), 177.

49. Robert H. Lowie, *Robert H. Lowie, Ethnologist: A Personal Record* (Berkeley, Calif., 1959), pp. 73, 68.

50. Frank B. Linderman, *American: The Life Story of a Great Indian* (New York, 1930), p. 311 (Plenty Coups, Crow). Also, Linderman, *Red Mother* (New York, 1932), p. 10 (Pretty Shield, Crow); Peter Nabokov, *Two Leggings: The Making of a Crow Warrier*, based on a field manuscript prepared by William Wildschut for the Museum of the American Indian, Heye Foundation [1919–23] (New York, 1967), p. 197; John G. Neihardt, *Black Elk Speaks: Being the Life Story of a Holy Man of the Oglala Sioux* (New York, 1932), pp. 9, 217–18; and Stanley Vestal, *Warpath: The True Story of the Fighting Sioux Told in a Biography of Chief White Bull* (New York, Popular Library, ca. 1973 [1934]), pp. 217–18.

51. Louis Akin, "Hopi Indians—Gentle Folk: A People without Need of Courts, Jails or Asylums," *Craftsman*, X (June 1906), 314–29.

52. Paul Monnet, "The Land of the Hopis," *Overland Monthly*, N.S. LXV (Mar. 1915), 211.

53. J. H. Eaton, "Description of the True State and Character of the New Mexican Tribes," in Henry R. Schoolcraft, *Information Respecting the History, Condition and Prospects of the Indian Tribes of the United States*, 6 vols. (Philadelphia, 1851–57), IV, 216.

54. S. C. Armstrong, *The Navajos. A Crisis in the History of an Indian Tribe* (Philadelphia, 1883), p. 2.

55. Oscar H. Lipps, *The Navajos* (Cedar Rapids, Iowa, 1909), p. 96.

56. James Mooney, "The Passing of the Indian," *Proc. of The Second Pan American Scientific Congress*, Sec. I: *Anthropology* (Washington, D.C., 1917), p. 179.

57. Department of Commerce, Bureau of the Census, *Indian Population in the United States and Alaska, 1910* (Washington, D.C., 1915), pp. 31, 40.

58. *New York Post*, reprinted in Therese O. Deming, *Edwin Willard Deming*, edited by Henry Collins Walsh (New York, 1925), p. 43.

59. Rose Henderson, "A Painter of Pueblo Indians," *El Palacio*, X (Apr. 15, 1921), 4.

60. Laura M. Bickerstaff, *Pioneer Artists of Taos* (Denver, 1955), p. 86.

61. Warwick Ford, "Immortalizing a Disappearing Race," *Arts & Decoration*, XVII (May 1922), 13, 70.

62. Ernest L. Blumenschein, quoted in *El Palacio*, VIII (July 1920), 239.

63. Ruth Benedict, *Patterns of Culture* (Boston, 1934), p. 57.

64. Fergusson, "Crusade from Santa Fé," p. 377.

65. D. H. Lawrence, "America, Listen to Your Own," *New Republic*, XXV (Dec. 15, 1920), 70.

66. Walter Lippmann, "Apropos of Mr. Lawrence: The Crude Barbarian and the Noble Savage," *ibid.*, pp. 70–71.

67. "Mrs. Austin Protests," *New Republic*, XXV (Jan. 5, 1921), 170.

68. Blanche C. Grant, *Taos Today* (Taos, N.M., 1925), p. 16.

69. Ernest Hemingway, *The Torrents of Spring: A Romantic Novel in Honor of the Passing of a Great Race* (1926), in *The Hemingway Reader*, selected by Charles Poore (New York, 1953), chap. 12.

70. "A White Man's Holiday," *New York Times*, Mar. 15, 1929, p. 24.

71. Carl Van Vechten, *Nigger Heaven* (New York, 1926), p. 246.

72. Mary Austin, *The Land of Journey's Ending* (New York, 1924), p. 443.

73. Elizabeth Barbara Canaday, "Earth's Breast," *Forum*, LXXII (Aug. 1924), 258.

74. Advs. in *Rev. of Reviews*, LXXIX (May 1929), 149, and (Apr. 1929), 101.

75. Charles F. Lummis, *The Land of Poco Tiempo* (New York, 1893).

76. D. Maitland Bushby, ed., *The Golden Stallion: An Anthology of Poems Concerning the Southwest and Written by Representative Southwestern Poets* (Dallas, 1930), p. ix.

77. Alice Corbin Henderson, comp., *The Turquoise Trail: An Anthology of New Mexico Poetry* (Boston, 1928), p. vii.

78. Bessie R. Ferguson, "Across the Desert to Moencapi," *Overland Monthly*, N.S. LXVI (Oct. 1915), 287.

79. D. H. Lawrence to E. H. Brewster, Nov. 16, 1921, and to Mabel Dodge Luhan, Nov. 5, 1921, in Moore, ed., *Collected Letters*, II, 6–7, 671.

80. D. H. Lawrence, *Mornings in Mexico* (New York, 1927), p. 108.

81. D. H. Lawrence, "Indians and an Englishman," *Dial*, LXXIV (Feb. 1923), 148. Especially interesting is Lawrence's poem "The Red Wolf" in Henderson, comp., *Turquoise Trail*, pp. 77–81. The best attempt to put Lawrence's concern with the Indian into the context of his whole literary development is L. D. Clark, "D. H. Lawrence and the American Indian," *D. H. Lawrence Rev.*, IX (Fall 1976), 305–72.

82. Lawrence, "Indians and an Englishman," p. 152.

83. D. H. Lawrence to Mabel Dodge Luhan, Nov. 8, 1923, in Moore, ed., *Collected Letters*, II, 760.

84. D. H. Lawrence, *Studies in Classic American Literature* (New York, 1923), p. 33.

85. D. H. Lawrence to Willard Johnson, ca. Aug. 1924, in Moore, ed., *Collected Letters*, II, 804.

86. Lawrence, "Indians and an Englishman," p. 144.
87. Lawrence, *Mornings in Mexico*, p. 120; and, for his escapism, his letter to Catherine Carswell from Taos, Sept. 29, 1922, in Moore, ed., *Collected Letters*, II, 723.
88. Oliver La Farge, *Laughing Boy* (Boston, 1929), p. 257.
89. Oliver La Farge, *Raw Material* (Boston, 1945), p. 177.
90. John Collier, *From Every Zenith: A Memoir* (Denver, 1963), pp. 115, 124–26.
91. John Collier, "Our Indian Policy," *Sunset*, L (Mar. 1923), 13, 93.
92. Editorial headnote to John Collier, "Navajos," *Survey*, LI (Jan 1, 1924), 333.

Chapter Seventeen: To Plow Up the Indian Soul

1. Flora Warren Seymour, "'Let My People Go,'" *Outlook*, CXLI (Nov. 18, 1925), 441, 444.
2. "General Scott Said," in Francis Fisher Kane, "East and West: The Atlantic City Conference on the American Indian," *Survey*, LXI (Jan. 15, 1929), 474.
3. John Collier, "Are We Making Red Slaves?" *Survey*, LVII (Jan. 1, 1927), 454–55.
4. John Collier, "The Vanquished Indian," *Nation*, CXXVI (Jan. 11, 1928), 38–41.
5. John Collier, "Senators and Indians," *Survey*, LXI (Jan. 1, 1929), 425.
6. John Collier, "Hammering at the Prison Door," *Survey*, LX (July 1, 1928), 403.
7. John Collier, "Navajos," *Survey*, LI (Jan. 1, 1924), 338. See Kenneth R. Philp, *John Collier's Crusade for Indian Reform, 1920–1954* (Tucson, 1977), chap. 4.
8. Lewis Meriam, *et al.*, *The Problem of Indian Administration: Report of a Survey Made at the Request of Honorable Hubert Work, Secretary of the Interior, and Submitted to Him, February 21, 1928* (Baltimore, 1928), pp. 7, 32.
9. *Ibid.*, pp. 41, 36, 21–22.
10. *Ibid.*, pp. 86–88, 51, 112.
11. Kane, "East and West," p. 472.
12. Collier, "Hammering at the Prison Door," p. 389.
13. Collier, "Senators and Indians," pp. 425, 428.
14. "The Red Man's Burden," *Nation*, CXXVIII (Feb. 20, 1929), 219.
15. "A New Deal for the Indian," *Rev. of Reviews*, LXXIX (June 1929), 76.
16. "A 'Weaning' Program for Indians," *Lit. Digest*, CI (Apr. 20, 1929), 14.
17. Ray Lyman Wilbur, *Ann. Rep., Secy. Interior, 1929* (Washington, D.C., 1929), pp. 14–15.
18. John Collier, "Helping the Indian," *Forum*, LXXXII (Oct. 1929), LII.
19. Mary Ross, "The New Indian Administration," *Survey*, LXIV (June 15, 1930), 268.
20. "Condition of Indians in the United States: Speech of Hon. William H. King . . . Delivered in the Senate February 8, 1933" (Mar. 3, 1933), *Sen. Doc. No. 214*, 72nd Cong., 2nd sess., p. 3.
21. John Collier, "The Indian Bureau's Record," *Nation*, CXXXV (Oct. 5, 1932), 303.

22. *Cong. Record*, 72nd Cong., 1st sess. (Mar. 10, 1932), pp. 5677–81.

23. Ray Lyman Wilbur, *Ann. Rep., Secy. Interior, 1932* (Washington, D.C., 1932), p. 20.

24. Charles J. Rhoads and J. Henry Scattergood, *Ann. Rep., Com. Ind. Affairs, 1931* (Washington, D.C., 1931), p. 4.

25. Charles J. Rhoads and J. Henry Scattergood, *Ann. Rep., Com. Ind. Affairs, 1932* (Washington, D.C., 1932), p. 4.

26. Ray Lyman Wilbur, *Ann. Rep., Secy. Interior, 1930* (Washington, D.C., 1930), p. 5.

27. Ray Lyman Wilbur, *Ann. Rep., Secy. Interior, 1931* (Washington, D.C., 1931), pp. 9–10. See Wilbur and William Atherton Du Puy, *Conservation in the Department of the Interior* (Washington, D.C., 1931), esp. pp. 112, 125, 135; and *The Memoirs of Ray Lyman Wilbur, 1875–1949*, edited by Edgar Eugene Robinson and Paul Carroll Edwards (Stanford, Calif., 1960), chap. 27.

28. Collier, "Indian Bureau's Record," p. 304. In *From Every Zenith: A Memoir and Some Essays on Life and Thought* (Denver, 1963), Collier discussed the Wilbur-Rhoads administration under the title "False Dawn." See Kenneth Philp, "Herbert Hoover's New Era: A False Dawn for the American Indian, 1929–1932," *Rocky Mountain Soc. Sc. Jour.*, IX (Apr. 1972), 53–60, and *John Collier's Crusade for Indian Reform*, chap. 5.

29. Petition to Roosevelt (Jan. 28, 1933), in [King], "Condition of Indians," p. 26.

30. Oliver La Farge, *As Long as the Grass Shall Grow* (New York, 1940), p. 70.

31. Donald Young, *American Minority Peoples: A Study in Racial and Cultural Conflicts in the United States* (New York, 1932), p. 460.

32. John Collier, "Does the Government Welcome the Indian Arts?" *Am. Mag. of Art*, XXVII (Sept. 1934): Anniv. Supp., Proc., Twenty-fifth Ann. Convention of the Am. Fed. of Arts, Washington, D.C., May 14–16, 1934, p. 11. See Richard Weiss, "Ethnicity and Reform: Minorities and the Ambience of the Depression Years," *Jour. of Am. Hist.*, LXVI (Dec. 1979), 566–85.

33. See Harold L. Ickes, *The New Democracy* (New York, 1934), esp. chaps. 1–2; and his *Ann. Rep., Secy. Interior*, 1940 (Washington, D.C., 1940), XVIII.

34. Sen. Charles S. Thomas, quoted in J. Leonard Bates, "Fulfilling American Democracy: The Conservation Movement, 1907 to 1921," *MVHR*, XLIV (June 1957), 43.

35. Nathanael West, *A Cool Million and The Dream Life of Balso Snell* (New York, Avon, 1965), p. 86.

36. Ernest Thompson Seton and Julia M. Seton, comps., *The Gospel of the Redman: A Way of Life* (Santa Fe, N.M., 1966 [1936], pp. 105, 107–8. For Seton's influence on Collier, see Collier's *From Every Zenith*, p. 159.

37. Franklin D. Roosevelt, quoted in William E. Leuchtenburg, *Franklin D. Roosevelt and the New Deal, 1932–1940* (New York, 1963), p. 4.

38. Oliver La Farge, "Revolution with Reservations," *New Republic*, LXXXIV (Oct. 9, 1935), 233–34.

39. Collier, *From Every Zenith*, pp. 172–73.

40. [King], "Condition of Indians," p. 39.

41. William H. King, Apr. 11, 1932, *Cong. Record*, 72nd Cong., 1st sess., pp. 7938, 7935.

42. John Collier, "America's Treatment of Her Indians," *Current Hist.*, XVIII (Aug. 1923), 777–78.

43. John Collier, "A Lift for the Forgotten Red Man, Too," *New York Times Mag.*, May 6, 1934, pp. 10–11.

44. See John Collier, "Indian Family Camps Do Conservation Work," *New York Times*, Aug. 27, 1933, Sec. 9, p. 12; Donald L. Parman, "The Indian and the Civilian Conservation Corps," *Pac. Hist. Rev.*, XL (Feb. 1971), 39–56; and Roger Bromert, "The Sioux and the Indian-CCC," *S.D. Hist.*, VIII (Fall 1978), 340–56.

45. John Collier, "Rep., Com. Ind. Affairs," *Ann. Rep., Secy. Interior, 1933* (Washington, D.C., 1933), pp. 100, 69–70.

46. "Indians Suffering in S. Dakota," *New York Times*, Oct. 8, 1933, Sec. 4, p. 6.

47. Robert Gessner, *Massacre: A Survey of Today's American Indian* (New York, 1931), p. v.

48. *H.R. 7902* (Feb. 12, 1934), 73rd Cong., 2nd sess., pp. 1–2, 5–8, 14, 16–17, 25.

49. John Collier, "The Purpose and Operation of the Wheeler-Howard Indian Rights Bill (S.2755; H.R. 7902)" (mimeographed memorandum 81642, Feb. 19, 1934), pp. 17, 8.

50. Sen. Henry F. Ashurst, Ariz., June 12, 1934, *Cong. Record*, 73rd Cong., 2nd sess., p. 11130.

51. See Kenneth R. Philp, "John Collier and the Controversy over the Wheeler-Howard Bill," in Jane F. Smith and Robert M. Kvasnicka, eds., *Indian-White Relations: A Persistent Paradox* (Washington, D.C., 1976), pp. 171–200 (chap. 7 of *John Collier's Crusade for Indian Reform*); and Graham D. Taylor, *The New Deal and American Indian Tribalism: The Administration of the Indian Reorganization Act, 1934–45* (Lincoln, Neb., 1980), chap. 2.

52. *Cong. Record*, 73rd Cong., 2nd sess., p. 11733.

53. Ray W. Jimerson to Alfred F. Beiter, Apr. 12, 1934, in *ibid.*, p. 11228.

54. Joseph Bruner, Ind. Nat. Confederacy, to Beiter, Mar. 12, 1934, in *ibid.*, pp. 11228–29.

55. William W. Hastings, Okla., May 22, 1934, in *ibid.*, p. 9267.

56. John Collier to James A. Frear, June 15, 1934, in *Ibid.*, p. 11743.

57. William Hughes, "Indians on a New Trail," *Catholic World*, CXXXIX (July 1934), 461.

58. Edgar Howard, June 16, 1934, *Cong. Record*, 73rd Cong., 2nd sess., p. 12164. For Wheeler's reservations, see *ibid.*, p. 11124; and for Howard's stronger advocacy of the original bill, *ibid.*, p. 7807.

59. Franklin D. Roosevelt to Burton K. Wheeler and Edgar Howard, Apr. 28, 1934, in *ibid.*, p. 7807.

60. *Ibid.*

61. Edgar Howard, June 15, 1934, *Cong. Record*, 73rd Cong., 2nd sess., p. 11727.

62. Clarence C. Dill and Burton K. Wheeler, June 12, 1934, in *ibid.*, pp. 11134–35.

63. Howard, June 15, 1934, in *ibid.*, p. 11726. Howard was not simply engaging in hyperbole; the statistics for Indian land loss under allotment in severalty were as appalling as he said. A recent study of the Coeur d'Alene shows that they were in possession of 400,000 acres when their reservation

was opened to allotment in 1908; by 1933 they had lost all but 62,400 acres, and 45,120 of these were being leased to white men. See Ross R. Cotroneo and Jack Dozier, "A Time of Disintegration: The Coeur d'Alene and the Dawes Act," *Western Hist. Q.*, V (Oct. 1974), 418.

64. Howard, June 15, 1934, *Cong. Record*, 73rd Cong., 2nd sess., pp. 11727, 11729.

65. Roy Ayers, in *ibid.*, pp. 12001–4, 12161–65.

66. *The Statutes at Large* (Washington, D.C., 1934), XLVIII, pt. 1, 984–88.

67. John Collier, "Office of Ind. Affairs," *Ann. Rep., Secy. Interior, 1935* (Washington, D.C., 1935), p. 115.

68. *Fifty-First and Fifty-Second Ann. Reps., Ind. Rights Assn.* (Philadelphia, 1935), p. 13.

69. [Herbert Welsh], *The Indian Problem* (Philadelphia, 1886), pp. 3, 6.

70. Ayers, June 16, 1934, *Cong. Record*, 73rd Cong., 2nd sess., p. 12164.

71. Collier, "Office of Ind. Affairs" (1935), p. 116.

72. John Collier, Feb. 6, 1935, quoted in *Cong. Record*, 74th Cong., 1st sess., p. 4874. The figures quoted in this paragraph derive from the only rigorous statistical breakdown of the voting on the Reorganization Act and its various provisions, Lawrence C. Kelly, "The Indian Reorganization Act: The Dream and the Reality," *Pac. Hist. Rev.*, XLIV (Aug. 1975), 301–15. See Theodore H. Haas, *Ten Years of Tribal Government Under I.R.A.* (Washington, D.C., 1947), pp. 13–34, and Taylor, *New Deal and American Indian Tribalism*, pp. 32–36, for variant data.

73. W. David Baird, "Commentary," in Smith and Kvasnicka, eds., *Indian-White Relations*, p. 216.

74. Elaine Goodale Eastman, "Collier Indian Plan Held Backward Step," *New York Times*, June 3, 1934, Sec. 4, p. 5.

75. *Ind. Truth*, May 1934, quoted in *Cong. Record*, 73rd Cong., 2nd sess., p. 11736.

76. Petition to Roosevelt by the American Indian Federation, Dec. 21, 1934, in *Cong. Record*, 74th Cong., 1st sess., p. 4874.

77. Collier, "Office of Ind. Affairs" (1935), p. 116.

78. "Affirmation of Sovereignty of the Indigenous Peoples of the Western Hemisphere" (July 1978), *Akwesasne Notes*, X (Summer 1978), 15.

79. Wilbur, *Memoirs*, p. 491.

80. Frank Ernest Hill, "A New Pattern of Life for the Indian," *New York Times Mag.*, July 14, 1935, p. 10.

81. John Collier, "Office of Ind. Affairs," *Ann. Rep., Secy. Interior, 1939* (Washington, D.C., 1939), pp. 24–26.

82. Hill, "New Pattern of Life," p. 10.

Chapter Eighteen: It Is Only Well Begun

1. John Collier, "Policies and Problems in the United States," in C. T. Loram and T. F. McIlwraith, eds., *The North American Indian Today: University of Toronto–Yale University Seminar Conference* [1939] (Toronto, 1943), p. 151.

2. John Collier, "United States Indian Administration as a Laboratory of Ethnic Relations," *Soc. Research* XII (Sept. 1945), 303.

3. John Collier, *The Indians of the Americas* (New York, 1947), p. 17. See Kenneth R. Philp, "John Collier and the Indians of the Americas: The Dream and the Reality," *Prologue*, XI (Spring 1979), 4-21.

4. Lyndon B. Johnson, "The Forgotten American" (Mar. 6, 1968), *Ind. Record*, Mar. 1968, p. 13; and Stewart L. Udall, "Udall Hails LBJ's 'Bold Action Charter,'" *ibid.*, pp. 20–21.

5. John Collier, "Office of Ind. Affairs," *Ann. Rep., Secy. Interior, 1934* (Washington, D.C., 1934), p. 84.

6. See Margaret Szasz, *Education and the American Indian: The Road to Self-Determination, 1928–1973* (Albuquerque, N.M., 1974), about half of which concerns Indian education under Ryan and Beatty.

7. Willard W. Beatty, "Twenty Years of Indian Education," in David A. Baerreis, ed., *The Indian in Modern American: A Symposium Held at The State Historical Society of Madison* [*sic*] (Madison, Wisc., 1956), pp. 42, 45. See Margaret C. Szasz, "Federal Boarding Schools and the Indian Child: 1920–1960," *S.D. Hist.*, VII (Fall 1977), 371–84.

8. Beatty, "Twenty Years," pp. 26–27, 49.

9. *H.R. 7902* (Feb. 12, 1934), 73rd Cong., 2nd sess., p. 24.

10. Collier, "Policies and Problems in the United States," p. 143.

11. J. L. Morris, "Religious Liberty: Right of Navajos to Worship as They Wish Defended," *New York Times*, June 16, 1935, Sec. 4, p. 9.

12. John Collier, *From Every Zenith: A Memoir and Some Essays on Life and Thought* (Denver, 1963), pp. 256–57.

13. Ernest L. Schusky, *The Right to Be Indian* (N.p., 1965), pp. 55–57, 84–86. The Indian Civil Rights Act (1968), intended as a response to the abuse of individual rights by tribal governments, was found to have potentially far-reaching ramifications for the concept of tribal sovereignty, suggesting how complex the religious question confronted by Collier in the 1930s actually was.

14. Frank Ernest Hill, "A New Pattern of Life for the Indian," *New York Times Mag.*, July 14, 1935, p. 22.

15. John Collier, "Office of Ind. Affairs," *Ann. Rep., Secy. Interior,* 1940 (Washington, D.C. 1940), p. 360.

16. "Indian Arts and Crafts" (May 13, 1935), *Sen. Rep. No. 900*, 74th Cong., 1st sess., pp. 3, 5–12.

17. Mary Austin, "Indian Arts for Indians," *Survey*, LX (July 1, 1928), 381. And see Henrietta K. Burton, *The Re-establishment of the Indians in Their Pueblo Life through the Revival of Their Traditional Crafts: A Study in Home Extension Education* (New York, 1936).

18. William A. Brophy and Sophie D. Aberle, comps., *The Indian, America's Unfinished Business: Report of the Commission on the Rights, Liberties, and Responsibilities of the American Indian* (Norman, Okla., 1966), pp. 99–101.

19. Collier, "Indian Administration as a Laboratory," p. 275.

20. "Anthropologists and the Federal Indian Program," *Science*, LXXXI (Feb. 15, 1935), 170–71.

21. Collier, *From Every Zenith*, pp. 171, 216–17. See Jay B. Nash, Oliver La Farge, and W. Carson Ryan, *The New Day for the Indians: A Survey of the Working of the Indian Reorganization Act of 1934* (New York, 1938), pp. 4–6, and Graham D. Taylor, "Anthropologists, Reformers, and the Indian New Deal," *Prologue*, VII (Fall 1975), 156–57.

22. Collier, *From Every Zenith*, p. 216.

23. Melville J. Herskovits, "The Significance of the Study of Acculturation for Anthropology," *Am. Anthro.*, XXXIX (Apr.-June 1937), 259.

24. Margaret Mead to Ruth Benedict, July 21, 1930, in Mead, *An Anthropologist at Work: Writings of Ruth Benedict* (Boston, 1959), p. 313.

25. Harold E. Fey and D'Arcy McNickle, *Indians and Other Americans: Two Ways of Life Meet* (New York, Perennial, rev. ed. 1970 [1959]), p. 118.

26. Scudder Mekeel, "An Appraisal of the Indian Reorganization Act," *Am. Anthro.*, XLVI (Apr.-June 1944), 217.

27. John Collier, "Collier Replies to Mekeel," *Am. Anthro.*, XLVI (July-Sept. 1944), 424. See Graham D. Taylor, *The New Deal and American Indian Tribalism: The Administration of the Indian Reorganization Act, 1934–45* (Lincoln, Neb., 1980), chap. 4.

28. Oliver La Farge, ed., *The Changing Indian* (Norman, Okla., 1942), p. X.

29. Collier, *From Every Zenith*, p. 222.

30. See Laura Thompson and Alice Joseph, *The Hopi Way* (Chicago, 1947 [1944]); Gordon MacGregor, *Warriors without Weapons: A Study of the Society and Personality Development of the Pine Ridge Sioux* (Chicago, 1946); and Clyde Kluckhohn and Dorothea Leighton, *The Navaho* (Garden City, N.Y., Anchor, rev. ed. 1962 [1946]).

31. Collier, *From Every Zentih*, pp. 218, 225.

32. Clyde Kluckhohn, "Covert Culture and Administrative Problems," *Am. Anthro.*, XLV (Apr.-June 1943), 213–27.

33. Laura Thompson, *Culture in Crisis: A Study of the Hopi Indians* (New York, 1973 [1950]), p. xvii.

34. John Collier, Foreword to Thompson and Joseph, *Hopi Way*, p. 8. See Lawrence C. Kelly, "Anthropology and Anthropologists in the Indian New Deal," *Jour. Hist. Behavioral Sciences*, XVI (Jan. 1980), 6–24.

35. Felix S. Cohen, "The Erosion of Indian Rights, 1950–1953: A Case Study in Bureaucracy," *Yale Law Jour.*, LXII (Feb. 1953), 371n.

36. Harold L. Ickes, Foreword to Felix S. Cohen, *Handbook of Federal Indian Law* (Washington, D.C., 1942), pp. v–vi; and Cohen, Author's Acknowledgments, *ibid.*, p. xviii.

37. Elmer F. Bennett, Preface to [Felix S. Cohen; updated by Frank B. Horne and Margaret F. Hurley], *Federal Indian Law* (Washington, D.C., 1958), p. 1.

38. Collier, *From Every Zenith*, p. 185. See "Office of Ind. Affairs," *Ann. Rep., Secy. Interior, 1938* (Wasington, D.C., 1938), p. 210.

39. See Donald L. Parman, *The Navajos and the New Deal* (New Haven, 1976), pp. 56–57, *passim*; *The Navajo Indian Problem: An Inquiry Sponsored by the Phelps–Stokes Fund* (New York, 1939), pp. 7–8; Collier, "Office of Ind. Affairs" (1940), pp. 370–71; and Harold E. Fey, *Indian Rights and American Justice* (Chicago, 1955), p. 18.

40. Collier, *From Every Zenith*, pp. 251–52.

41. George A. Boyce, *When Navajos Had Too Many Sheep: The 1940's* (San Francisco, 1974), p. 172.

42. "Wrecking a Nation," *Ind. Truth*, XIII (May 1936), 2.

43. "The Navajos," *Ind. Truth*, XIV (Oct. 1937), 3.

44. John Collier, "Our Mingling Worlds," *El Crepusculo* (Taos, N.M.), Oct. 1, 1959.

45. Iktomi Licala, *America Needs Indians!* (Denver, 1937), p. 172.

46. Collier, "Indian Administration as a Laboratory," p. 289.

47. Collier, *From Every Zenith*, p. 243.

48. Graham D. Taylor, "The Tribal Alternative to Bureaucracy: The Indian's New Deal, 1933–1945," *Jour. of the West*, XIII (Jan. 1974), 135–40, and *New Deal and American Indian Tribalism*, esp. chaps. 5, 7.

49. Ruth Roessel, ed., *Navajo Studies at Navajo Community College* (Many Farms, Ariz., 1971), p. 37.

50. D. H. Lawrence to Mabel Dodge Luhan, Nov. 8, 1923, in Harry T. Moore, ed., *The Collected Letters of D. H. Lawrence*, 2 vols. (New York, 1962), II, 761.

51. "Land Acquisition," *Ind. Truth*, XIV (Oct. 1937), 4.

52. John Collier, "Office of Ind. Affairs," *Ann. Rep., Secy. Interior, 1941* (Washington, D.C., 1941), p. 450.

53. See Lawrence C. Kelly, "The Indian Reorganization Act: The Dream and the Reality," *Pac. Hist. Rev.*, XLIV (Aug. 1975), 306–8.

54. John Collier, "Letter to General Eisenhower," *Nation*, CLXXVI (Jan. 10, 1953), 29–30; "Back to Dishonor?" and *From Every Zenith*, pp. 301–3, 373–74. See Clayton R. Koppes, "From New Deal to Termination: Liberalism and Indian Policy, 1933–1953," *Pac. Hist. Rev.*, XLVI (Nov. 1977), 543–66.

55. Harold L. Ickes, "The Indian Loses Again," *New Republic*, CXXV (Sept. 24, 1951), 16.

56. John Collier, "The Red Slaves of Oklahoma," *Sunset*, LII (Mar. 1924), 94–95.

57. House Concurrent Resolution No. 108, 83rd Cong., 1st sess. (Aug. 1, 1953), reprinted in Boyce, *When Navajos Had Too Many Sheep*, pp. 265–66.

58. Felix Cohen, "Indian Wardship: The Twilight of a Myth" (1953), in Lucy Kramer Cohen, ed., *The Legal Conscience: Selected Papers of Felix S. Cohen* (New Haven, 1960), pp. 332–33.

59. Felix Cohen, "Field Theory and Judicial Logic" (1950), in *ibid.*, p. 150.

60. [Harold E. Fey], "Churches Oppose U.M.T.," *Christ. Cent.*, LXXII (Mar. 16, 1955), 327.

61. George E. Simpson and J. Milton Yinger, eds., "American Indians and American Life" issue of *Annals, Am. Academy Pol. and Soc. Sc.*, CCCXI (May 1957), vii.

62. Joseph P. Garry, president, NCAI, quoted in "The American Indian Now," *University of Chicago Round Table* No. 828 (Feb. 21, 1954), p. 2.

63. John C. Rainer, *et al.*, letter, *Harper's*, CCXIII (July 1956), 8.

64. Watkins and D'Ewart, quoted in Boyce, *When Navajos Had Too Many Sheep*, pp. 234–35.

65. Myer quoted in Cohen, "Erosion of Indian Rights," p. 358.

66. John Collier, "Indian Takeaway: Betrayal of a Trust," *Nation*, CLXXIX (Oct. 2, 1954), 291. Also see Oliver La Farge, "The New Administration: Indian Affairs in the Balance," *Am. Ind.*, VI (Summer 1953), 3–7.

67. John Provinse, *et al.*, "The American Indian in Transition," *Am. Anthro.*, LVI (June 1954), 388–89.

68. Sol Tax, in *University of Chicago Round Table*, p. 8.

69. Edward H. Spicer, letter, *Am. Anthro.*, LVI (Oct. 1954), 890.

70. Collier, "Letter to General Eisenhower," p. 30.

71. Robert A. Manners, "Pluralism and the American Indian," *America Indigena* (1962), reprinted in Deward E. Walker, Jr., ed., *The Emergent Native Americans: A Reader in Culture Contact* (Boston, 1971), pp. 126, 129.

72. Johnson, "Forgotten American," p. 2.
73. Richard M. Nixon, "A New Era for the American Indians" (July 8, 1970), *Ind. Record*, Aug. 1970, p. 2. For John F. Kennedy's commitment to New Deal principles, see Collier, *From Every Zenith*, pp. 225–26.
74. Fey, *Indian Rights and American Justice*, p. 13.
75. Fey and McNickle, *Indians and Other Americans*, p. 141.
76. "Indian Education: A National Tragedy and Challenge" (1969), reprinted in Alvin M. Josephy, Jr., ed., *Red Power: The American Indians' Fight for Freedom* (New York, 1972), pp. 156–62.
77. Angie Debo, letter, *Harper's*, CCXII (May 1956), 6.
78. Vine Deloria, Jr., *Behind the Trail of Broken Treaties: An Indian Declaration of Independence* (New York, 1974), p. 205.
79. Maury Maverick, Jan. 31, 1936, *Cong. Record*, 74th Cong., 2nd sess., p. 1302.

Epilogue

1. John Collier, Introduction to Oliver La Farge, ed., *The Changing Indian* (Norman, Okla., 1942), 10.
2. See, for example, John Collier, "The Red Atlantis," *Survey*, XLIX (Oct. 1, 1922), 16, 20, 63, and "The Pueblos' Last Stand," *Sunset*, L (Feb., 1923), 21; Alice Corbin Henderson, "The Death of the Pueblos," *New Republic*, XXXIII (Nov. 29, 1922), 11; and "The Last First Americans," *Nation*, CXV (Nov. 29, 1922), 570.
3. "A Red-Letter Day for Red Americans," *Lit. Digest*, LXXVIII (Sept. 29, 1923), 36.
4. "The Red Man's Burden," *New Republic*, LII (Oct. 19, 1927), 226.
5. John Collier, "The Vanquished Indian," *Nation*, CXXVI (Jan. 11, 1928), 39; and Robert Gessner, *Massacre: A Survey of Today's American Indian* (New York, 1931), Chaps. 8, 16.
6. Sen. William H. King, Apr. 11, 1932, *Cong. Record*, 72 Cong., 1 sess., 7939; and "Condition of Indians in the United States: Speech of Hon. William H. King . . . Delivered in the Senate February 8, 1933" (Mar. 3, 1933), *Sen. Doc. No. 214*, 72 Cong., 2 sess., 35.
7. John Collier, "Rep., Com. Ind. Affairs," *Ann. Rep., Secy. Interior, 1933* (Washington, D.C., 1933), 111.
8. "Indian Population Up," *N.Y. Times*, Dec. 20, 1933, 12; also, "A New Deal for the American Indian," *Lit. Digest*, CXVII (Apr. 7, 1934), 20.
9. John Collier, "Office of Ind. Affairs," *Ann. Rep., Secy. Interior, 1934* (Washington, D.C., 1934), 121–2.
10. John Collier, "Office of Ind. Affairs," *Ann. Rep., Secy. Interior, 1935* (Washington, D.C., 1935), 156.
11. John Collier, "Office of Ind. Affairs," *Ann. Rep., Secy. Interior, 1936* (Washington, D.C., 1936), 207.
12. John Collier, "Office of Ind. Affairs," *Ann. Rep., Secy. Interior, 1937* (Washington, D.C., 1937), 248.
13. John Collier, "Office of Ind. Affairs," *Ann. Rep., Secy. Interior, 1938* (Washington, D.C., 1938), 258, 209.
14. *Ibid.*, 258.
15. John Collier, "Office of Ind. Affairs," *Ann. Rep., Secy. Interior, 1939* (Washington, D.C., 1939), 65–8.

16. John Collier, "Office of Ind. Affairs," *Ann. Rep., Secy. Interior, 1940* (Washington, D.C., 1940), 360.

17. Clark Wissler, "The Rebirth of the 'Vanishing American,'" *Nat. Hist.,* XXXIV (Sept., 1934), 422–3, 430. When Wissler began to tabulate the data for certain northern plains groups, he got a different picture. In "Population Changes among the Northern Plains Indians," *Yale University Publications in Anthropology, No. 1* (New Haven, 1936), 3–20, he determined that Blackfoot numbers "increased rapidly" between 1809–71, that the Assiniboines reached their maximum about 1838, and the Western Cree about 1860. This contradicted the idea of a sizable decline after 1780. Wissler's data did confirm the notion that there was a general decline in plains Indian population in Canada and the United States after the tribes were confined to reserves and reservations, but stabilization followed by the mid-1890s, and after 1920 growth began. Also see Wissler, "Changes in Population Profiles among the Northern Plains Indians," *Anthro. Papers, Am. Mus. Nat. Hist.,* XXXVI, Pt. 1 (1936); and "American Indians Show Birth Gains," *N.Y. Times,* May 2, 1936, 6, reporting an address by Wissler to the American Association of Physical Anthropologists.

18. "'Vanishing American' No Longer Vanishing," *Lit. Digest,* CXVIII (Sept. 15, 1934), 17.

19. "Red Men Thrive," *New York Times,* May 4, 1936, 18.

20. Collier, "Office of Ind. Affairs" (1940), 360.

21. H. L. Shapiro, "The Mixed-Blood Indian," in La Farge, ed., *Changing Indian,* 19–27.

22. Iktomi Licala, *America Needs Indians!* (Denver, 1937), 176–7.

23. Dr. James R. Shaw, quoted in O. K. Armstrong, "Set the Indians Free," *Westerners Brand Book* (Chicago), XIV (Apr., 1957), 10.

24. Ben H. Bagdikian, *In the Midst of Plenty: A New Report on the Poor in America* (New York, 1964), 108. For the improved but still grim picture of Indian health since 1960, see William A. Brophy and Sophie D. Aberle, comps., *The Indian, America's Unfinished Business: Report of the Commission on the Rights, Liberties, and Responsibilities of the American Indian* (Norman, Okla., 1966), 159–65, 227; *The Indian Health Program of the U.S. Public Health Service* (Washington, D.C., 1972), 28–9, 32–3; and *American Indian Policy Review Commission: Final Report . . . May 17, 1977* (Washington, D.C., 1977), 371–86 (1970–71 comparative figures showed Indian life expectancy at 65 years, the national average at 71; and Indian infant deaths at 23.8 per 1,000, with the national average at 19.2).

25. Oliver La Farge, "The Enduring Indian," *Sc. Am.,* CII (Feb. 1960), 37.

26. "Return of the Red Man," *Life,* LXIII (Dec. 1, 1967), cover.

27. Clyde Warrior, quoted in Stan Steiner, *The New Indians* (New York, 1968), 68.

28. Felix S. Cohen, "To Secure These Rights: The Report of the President's Committee on Civil Rights" (1948), in Lucy Kramer Cohen, ed., *The Legal Conscience: Selected Papers of Felix S. Cohen* (New Haven, 1960), 465–6.

29. See, for example, Sidney M. Willhelm, "Black Man, Red Man and White America: The Constitutional Approach to Genocide," *Catalyst* No. 4 (Spring, 1969), 1–62; David R. Wrone and Russell S. Nelson, Jr., eds., *Who's the Savage?: A Documentary History of The Mistreatment of the Native North Americans* (Greenwich, Conn., 1973); and Richard Drinnon, *Facing West: The Metaphysics of Indian-Hating and Empire-Building* (New York, 1980).

30. *Cherokee Examiner* No. 2 (ca. 1968), 10.

31. *American Indian Policy Review Commission: Final Report* (1977), 1–46, 82, 621–4.

32. Al Logan Slagle, "The American Indian Policy Review Commission: Repercussions and Aftermath," in *New Directions in Federal Indian Policy: A Review of the American Indian Policy Review Commission* (Los Angeles, 1979), 115–32.

33. "Affirmation of the Sovereignty of the Indigenous Peoples of the Western Hemisphere" (July, 1978), *Akwesasne Notes*, X (Summer, 1978), 16.

34. See William T. Hagan, "Tribalism Rejuvenated: The Native American since the Era of Termination," *Western Hist. Q.*, XII (Jan., 1981), 8–16.

INDEX